P9-AEY-881

The Economics of School Choice

**A National Bureau
of Economic Research
Conference Report**

The Economics of
School Choice

Edited by **Caroline M. Hoxby**

The University of Chicago Press

Chicago and London

CAROLINE M. HOXBY is professor of economics at Harvard University and a research associate of the National Bureau of Economic Research.

The University of Chicago Press, Chicago 60637
The University of Chicago Press, Ltd., London
© 2003 by the National Bureau of Economic Research
All rights reserved. Published 2003
Printed in the United States of America
12 11 10 09 08 07 06 05 04 03   1 2 3 4 5
ISBN: 0-226-35533-0 (cloth)

Library of Congress Cataloging-in-Publication Data

The economics of school choice / edited by Caroline M. Hoxby.
     p.   cm. — (A National Bureau of Economic Research conference report)
     Includes bibliographical references and index.
     ISBN 0-226-35533-0 (cloth : alk. paper)
     1. School choice—Economic aspects—United States.
    2. Educational vouchers—United States.   I. Hoxby, Caroline Minter.
    II. National Bureau of Economic Research.   III. Series.

LB1027.9 .E27 2003
379.1′11—dc21

2002032045

Since this volume is a record of conference proceedings, it has been exempted from the rules governing critical review of manuscripts by the Board of Directors of the National Bureau (resolution adopted 8 June 1948, as revised 21 November 1949 and 20 April 1968).

Contents

Acknowledgments

The idea for this book grew out of a series of conferences held by the National Bureau of Economic Research (NBER) that were related to the topics of school finance and public economics. A great debt is owed to Martin Feldstein and James Poterba for suggesting and supporting these conferences, which Caroline Hoxby organized. At these conferences, it became clear that the topic drawing the most interest was school choice. A critical mass of NBER researchers were working on school choice, although they came from a variety of fields (public economics, labor economics, macroeconomics, and industrial organization). Researchers' approaches initially differed a good deal with their backgrounds, but by 2001, it was clear that the group as a whole had developed joint approaches and joint insights. It was at this point that we were able to envision this book and the conference in Islamorada, Florida, where it was presented.

The authors wish especially to acknowledge the contribution of Martin Feldstein, who recognized that the economics of school choice had "come of age" and whose support was invaluable. They next wish to thank the fellow researchers who offered critical comments on the book at the Florida conference: Joseph Altonji, John Chubb, Chester Finn, Jane Hannaway, Thomas Kane, Michael Kremer, Helen Ladd, Charles Manski, Richard Murnane, Derek Neal, and Ananth Sheshadri. The discussion at the Florida conference and at previous conferences were also enriched by the comments of Roland Benabou, William Evans, Martin Feldstein, Robert Inman, John Kain, James Poterba, Robert Schwab, and William Testa. Two anonymous reviewers gave us pointed and wise comments that helped us make crucial last revisions. Indeed, all of the authors wish to acknowledge that a great share of the insights and an even greater share of the clarity in their chapters would not be there without the persistent, targeted questions of others interested in school choice—policy makers, legislators, fellow researchers, philanthropists, and the audiences we face when presenting research publicly. They often provide us with the best method of saying or showing something. For help with data, the authors are very grateful to numerous staff members at the Children's Scholarship Fund, the Texas Schools Microdata Project, the Arizona Department of Education, the Florida Department of Education, the Michigan Department of Education, the Wisconsin Department of Public Instruction, and the National Center for Education Statistics.

Many people helped transform the manuscript into a book. At the NBER, Helena Fitz-Patrick in publications kept the manuscript on the rails, and we thank her for her care and persistence. Carl Beck and Amy Tretheway in the NBER's conference department managed the Florida conference; we are grateful for their smooth organization of us, the papers, and the discussants' comments. At the University of Chicago Press, John Tryneski and Rodney Powell guided us skillfully through the review process, displaying insight into what the book should look like. Amanda DeWees at Graphic Composition, Inc., was a scrupulous and thoughtful copy editor, and Nitsuh Abebe has taken care over the book's reception. The issue of school choice is a timely one, and the authors are grateful for the efficiency of all these people, who have made every effort to make the book a reality in real time.

Finally, the authors would like to thank their families, whose support is so essential.

Preface
School Choice in the Wake of the Supreme Court Decision on Vouchers

June 28, 2002, turned out to be an exciting day for people who, like the authors of this book, are seriously interested in school choice. The twenty-eighth was the day the Supreme Court of the United States issued its pro-voucher decision in *Zelman* v. *Simmons-Harris,* the Cleveland voucher case.

At least one contributor to this volume was greatly surprised to find that the day was exciting. For a long time, I have thought that the church-state issue in school choice debates was a red herring. Although the church-state question is an important constitutional question, most commentators greatly exaggerate its *practical* importance for school choice. Specifically, most commentators observe that many private school students currently attend a school with religious affiliation, and they forecast that a full-scale voucher program would lead a great many more students to attend religious schools. This forecast is simply incorrect. All of the evidence we have on urban parents' preferences suggests that their desire to send their children to religious schools has been declining steadily for at least forty years. Thus, in urban areas where school choice could be an active force, very few voucher recipients would choose a religious private school if a full-blown voucher program were in effect.

The tendency of current voucher recipients to attend religiously affiliated schools is an artifact of the tiny scale and uncertain prospects of the voucher experiments we have observed so far in cities like Cleveland, New York, Dayton, and Washington, D.C. Educational entrepreneurs will not start up private schools when the number of voucher recipients is constrained to remain tiny and the voucher program is in danger of being shut down. Therefore, the private schools that take voucher students do *not* reflect the preferences of voucher parents; they reflect the preferences of much earlier generations of urban parents who set up the parochial schools that linger today. Think of the mostly black voucher students in the four programs mentioned above. Hardly any of them are Catholics, yet the modal school they attend is affiliated with the Roman Catholic church. Their parents do not choose Catholic schools in the hope that their children will convert. They choose Catholic schools because the schools exist and seem to work. Under a full-blown, permanent voucher program, private schools would arise that more closely match their preferences. The evidence we have suggests that these private schools would be nonreligious. Indeed, in Milwaukee (the only city with a large, stable voucher program), nearly all of the private schools that have been created to enroll voucher students are nonreligious. Religious private schools are essential only for voucher *experiments;* a full-blown voucher program could easily avoid using them at all.

In short, if school choice ever becomes a major force in American education, it will almost certainly be a largely nonreligious educational force. The church-state issue would gradually disappear as school choice grew— simply because school choice is ultimately about parents' preferences, and the vast majority of parents prefer nonreligious schools.

This is why I thought that the church-state issue was a red herring. I *still* think that it is a red herring. This is why I did not expect the Supreme Court's opinion in *Zelman* v. *Simmons-Harris* to be exciting. But it was.

One reason the *Zelman* decision was exciting is that it opened the way for a wide variety of new school choice programs. Any researcher of school choice will tell you that the principal problem for research is the scarcity of new and different school choice programs. The Court's majority opinion set a standard that, boiled down to its essence, says that a school choice program is constitutional if its *design* does not induce parents to choose religious private schools. That is, so long as the design is neutral, the parents who use it may disproportionately favor (or disfavor) religious schools. The Court's standard is one that most proposed school choice programs already meet or could easily meet. Thus, we should expect that many school choice proposals that were stalled by the church-state issue will now emerge from the back rooms of legislatures and philanthropies. Indeed, to my knowledge, many states' school choice proposals have already been revivified.

Not only will the enactment of new programs greatly improve our understanding of school choice, the debates that take place in the enactment process will be productive also, even when no enactment actually occurs. This is because debates on school choice are more productive when an actual program is at stake. At that time, policy makers are wrestling with details, and they suddenly become more interested in research that shows the effect of different designs. Moreover, policy makers barrage researchers with profusion of *targeted* questions about school choice. These targeted questions are "a shot in the arm" for research. Instead of setting their research agendas by *guessing* what school choice programs might be considered, researchers let real proposals (with real political viability) set their agendas.

In short, the first reason the *Zelman* decision matters is that it ushers in an era in which our understanding of school choice is likely to improve rapidly.

The second reason I found the *Zelman* decision exciting is more subtle, but very important. When I read the Court's opinions, both majority and minority, I was struck by the degree to which the justices cared about the *details* of the Cleveland school choice program and the *environment* in which it operated. The justices might have focused narrowly on the church-state question, but they did not. They considered the *amount* of the vouchers; they considered the *other school choice programs* operating in Cleveland (especially charter and magnet schools); they recognized that a parent who was able to pick and choose among suburban districts *was* exercising some school choice; they realized that educational entrepreneurs would switch from operating a private school to a charter school to a magnet school, depending on the incentives. The justices considered the much higher level of per-pupil spending in the Cleveland Public Schools than in the voucher or charter schools. The justices described the record of failure of the Cleveland Public Schools, in spite of previous reform efforts and infusions of cash from the state. Simply put, the justices, after devoting serious thought and energy to the problem of school choice, started to think a lot like researchers who have devoted serious thought and energy to the problem of school choice.

I do not mean to suggest that Supreme Court justices should ideally behave like researchers, but that the justices' opinions were an enormous validation and encouragement of the sort of research contained in this book. Indeed, I have no doubt that the justices would now be eager and incisive questioners at the conference that generated this book, if somehow it could be repeated and involve them as freely operating participants. The justices realized that school choice is not an isolated issue; it is a phenomenon that has a context (such as spending and achievement in districts like Cleveland), that already has a place in American education (such as the tradition of choosing a school by choosing a residence, a practice exercised by most middle-income Americans), and in which the details matter.

The justices who wrote minority opinions generally took the position that school choice must be wrong if the details mattered. One might crudely paraphrase their thought as: "If school choice *could* go wrong with some details, it should never be permitted." This minority response does not surprise me; it is a common initial reaction to the realization that the effects of a school choice program will depend on its structure. However, I have witnessed this initial response wear off again and again with researchers of school choice, as they become more expert. Veteran researchers of school choice come to *appreciate* the fact that details matter; it means that a school choice plan can be designed to attain a state's or city's goals. One size need not fit all. The capacity of school choice to flexibly accommodate a variety of educational and social goals is what often persuades skeptical researchers to keep working on school choice, even if they initially took up the issue in order to conduct a study that they thought would be simple, thorough, and damning.

I must close my description of June 28, 2002, not with the Supreme Court or researchers, but with the affected families. The point that seemed crucial to the Cleveland families who stood on the steps of the Supreme Court was whether they would be able to remove their children from a system that was obviously failing its students. To many poor parents, *this* is the issue of justice that is at stake. They feel that the conventional public school system—in which affluent families exercise school choice through traditional means, but in which poor families cannot choose because they cannot afford a different residence or private school tuition—is a discriminatory system. They believe that school choice programs are a matter of equal educational opportunity. Contrary to the preconceptions of many affluent Americans, the Cleveland families were not obsessed with getting more money for their schools or getting their children into elite suburban districts. They believed that they were denied the opportunity to protect their children from a parlous educational environment, *given* the money available and the city in which they lived.

The Cleveland parents might have limited sympathy with this book. They do not believe that their right to choose should depend on whether someone can demonstrate (empirically or theoretically) that school choice has positive effects. They point out that no such requirement is made of the traditional forms of school choice exercised by more affluent parents.

I readily admit that the authors of this book do attempt to show how school choice affects students; in taking up this task, they may appear to support the view that the right to school choice *should* depend on whether it has positive effects on everyone. I hope, however, that the evidence in the book is taken simply as evidence, and that thoughtful readers consider the Cleveland parents' view seriously. Any question of justice that seems so obvious to the families at the heart of the school choice debate deserves consideration.

Introduction

Caroline M. Hoxby

I recall attending a conference on education in Washington, D.C. in 1994 that was attended by leading policymakers and expert researchers. At that time, the topic of school choice occupied only a small share of the discussion, and I was the only economist presenting research related to choice. In fact, although economist Milton Friedman is generally credited with spurring modern interest in school choice,[1] economists were contributing relatively little to the school choice debate at the time. The two practical choice proposals that were best known were authored by, respectively, a sociologist, Christopher Jencks, and two legal scholars, John Coons and Stephen Sugarman.[2] A few programs with choice features had recently been enacted (vouchers in Milwaukee, Minnesota's open enrollment plan, intradistrict choice in Cambridge, and so on), but these programs had been initiated by politicians and courts with at least as much of an eye to politics (especially racial politics) as to school improvement. Moreover, *analysis* of school choice was largely out of the hands of economists. If a policymaker asked for research on choice, he was likely to be referred to work by a political scientist—for instance, John Witte's comparison of Milwaukee's voucher students to Milwaukee public school students (see, e.g., Witte 1990), studies of the short-lived Alum Rock choice program authored by

Caroline M. Hoxby is professor of economics at Harvard University and a research associate of the National Bureau of Economic Research.
1. See Friedman (1955). Friedman also discusses school choice in Friedman and Friedman (1980).
2. Jencks's proposal may be found in a variety of writings, including Jencks (1970). For the work of John E. Coons and Stephen Sugarman, see Coons and Sugarman (1971). Also see Coons and Sugarman (1978).

RAND researchers (none of whom was an economist),[3] or legal scholarship on church-state issues.

In the years since 1994, the economic analysis of school choice has burgeoned. As economists have worked on choice, their areas of ignorance and confusion have narrowed enormously, and their discussion has become much more coherent. Perhaps this will be a surprise to the outside observer, who assumes that economists always disagree. However, the rapid growth in economists' understanding of school choice should really be no surprise. At its core, school choice relies on very basic economic theory about the effects of competition. Moreover, the tools needed for analyzing the more complex aspects of choice were at hand in 1994. They had been built for related economic problems and could be applied readily to school choice.

It would be optimistic to suggest that economists fully understand school choice and agree about all its intricacies. Nevertheless, there is now a consensus about what we know (and do not know) and about the sorts of evidence and analysis that we need in order to resolve uncertainties. This volume is a testament to the rapid growth of that consensus and to the richness of the economic analysis of school choice. Not only do the authors represent a good share of the economists who have written on choice, but each chapter was subjected to expert critique by other economists and authorities who work on the topic: Joseph Altonji, John Chubb, Chester Finn, Jane Hannaway, Thomas Kane, Helen Ladd, Charles Manski, Richard Murnane, Derek Neal, and Ananth Seshadri. The authors are very grateful for their comments and wish to acknowledge how they have shaped the book.

Why the *Economics* of School Choice?

What does it mean to perform an economic analysis of school choice? It does *not* mean that the authors in this volume are interested only in the financial aspects of school choice. The authors are deeply interested in (and analyze) many nonfinancial aspects of choice, including student achievement, parental satisfaction, school segregation, mainstreaming of disabled children, and parents' choice of where to live. What it does mean is that the authors rely on methods that were originally developed for the purpose of economic analysis. (In fact, when I refer to "economists," I refer to people who practice such methods—thereby including some people who are not card-carrying economists.)

Perhaps this statement will leave readers still in doubt. Why, they will ask, should we think that economists are naturals when it comes to school choice? After all, learning the institutional details of elementary and sec-

3. Alum Rock was the only school district in the United States willing to volunteer for the Office of Economic Opportunity's study of school choice (later managed by the National Institute of Education). No private schools were involved in the study, and schools were guaranteed that no money or jobs would be lost. The RAND reports were published as RAND (1978–81).

ondary schools is not part of the typical economist's training, and anyone who wants to make important contributions on school choice had better know what actually goes on in schools. There are also legal issues associated with school choice, and economists are generally not experts in school law. Economists *do* have some learning to do when they take up the topic. Nevertheless, economists are naturals in several other, arguably much more important, ways.

An Unabashed Apologia for *The Economics of School Choice*

I would argue that there is a simple reason why economists have made and will continue to make so much progress on school choice: tools. In a typical discussion of school choice, a variety of questions arise. Answering these questions generally requires the use of some analytic tools that are not necessarily complicated but that do require practice if they are to be used effectively. I will elaborate on these tools below. For now, all we need to know is that, when the school choice problem fell into the laps of policy analysts, economists were unusually well equipped to start answering the questions that arose. As a consequence, economists quickly got immersed in practical tasks, unraveling questions about choice and refining economic methods so that they could be applied to schools.

In contrast, many other commentators on education found that they could not make much headway against the questions that arose in a typical debate on choice. Discussions often ended with the participants more confused than they were initially. As a result, many commentators abandoned the idea of trying to find analytic answers to questions about choice and decided instead that it was essentially a matter of principle. Unfortunately, when commentators view school choice purely as a matter of principle, their positions (of support or opposition) tend to become hardened. Consensus is unlikely to grow.

Let us consider some of the tools—or, more properly, areas of familiarity—that economists bring to the analysis of school choice. This exercise is not merely a justification of economic analysis. It is the way to see where the confusions arise in school choice debates, and how it is that research (like that contained in this volume) clarifies them.

Market Structure Makes the Difference

If school choice makes a difference (good or bad), it will be because it changes the *structure* of the market for K-12 education. When one says that school choice affects market structure, one means that it affects basic constraints that schools and students face. For instance, choice makes it easier for students to be mobile among schools, and choice often makes a school's revenue directly dependent on its attracting students.

There are two reasons why it is important that an analyst of school choice be comfortable with markets. First, we need to understand how market structure affects how market participants (schools and students) behave and how, in turn, their behavior affects outcomes (achievement, school productivity, and so on). This relationship is often summarized in a phrase familiar to every economist: "structure, conduct, performance." Understanding this relationship is important because we *can* usually describe how a school choice program affects market structure. If an analyst is good at reducing a program to its effects on market structure and knows how to predict the results of that structure, he can make significant progress.

People who are not able to reduce a school choice plan to its effects on market structure tend to get distracted by its superficial details—the transportation plan, the school buildings currently in use, and so on. They do not distinguish between local idiosyncrasies and phenomena that are systemically affected by the choice program, and therefore their analysis gets bogged down.

The second reason why it is important that an analyst of school choice be comfortable with markets is that he must, at a minimum, be *open* to the idea that market forces matter—that is, that people may alter their behavior in response to the pressures and incentives that the market generates. Economists are open to this idea. Although economists may not share the same prior beliefs about the *degree* to which people respond to market forces, they do share the belief that the degree of response ought to be measured. Many noneconomists in the educational sector *assume* that market forces do not affect educators or students. Sometimes this assumption is a matter of principle: It is ignoble to describe market forces in education, let alone measure them. In other cases, this assumption stems from a belief that only for-profit firms respond to market forces. Economists have a long acquaintance with governments, individuals, and nonprofit organizations responding to market forces, and therefore they do not dismiss the task of measuring their responses.

It Helps to Call a Spade a Spade

In some localities, the idea of school choice is more popular with the public than it is with interest groups in the education sector. As a result, one often sees programs that include "choice" in their title but that contain few elements that are recognizable as choice. Even more confusingly, many Americans have grown accustomed to the idea that traditional public schools are wholly *public* (in the sense of being equally open to all people) when, in fact, the traditional system contains some strong market elements. Discrepancies between the nomenclature and the reality confuse many would-be analysts of school choice.

Because economists focus on how school choice programs affect market structure, they do not get hung up on the names of programs. They know that when no money follows a student, they should expect different outcomes than when money does follow a student. They know that a program in which schools are not allowed to contract or expand, to enter or exit, is different from one in which the suppliers of schooling are elastic. They know to look at the constraints that a school faces, rather than whether it is called "public," "private," "charter," "community," "magnet," or something else. In short, economists eliminate myriad sources of confusion by knowing how to extract the market structure from the description of a school system (whether or not its name includes the word "choice").

One Cannot Avoid the Interdependence of School Choice and School Finance, so One Might as Well Enjoy It

Every school choice program contains provisions about money. For instance, voucher amounts must be set in some fashion and must be funded by some stream of revenue. Charter schools receive a per-student fee that must be related in some fashion to local per-pupil spending.

Thus, school choice inevitably intersects with school finance, which is the study of (a) how school districts spend and raise property taxes and other sources of revenue, (b) how state and federal aid affects school districts' revenues and expenditures, and (c) the relationship between property tax rates and property tax revenue. This intersection is dreaded by many education policymakers, whose eyes glaze over at the thought of learning more about taxes than they need to know in order to avoid being audited. As a result, financing is sometimes only an afterthought (and often a poorly designed afterthought) in school choice plans.

In contrast, economists are not only not repelled by the school finance issues implicit in school choice; they are actively drawn to the intersection between school choice and school finance. The intersection interests economists because school choice makes it possible to fund students at an *individual* level and to fund schools *flexibly*. That is, choice expands the set of financial instruments that are available to fulfill the goals of school finance. Nowhere has economic analysis been more productive than at the intersection of school finance and school choice.

School Choice Is More Interesting to People Who Are Puzzled by the Inefficacy of School Inputs

The man on the street thinks that it is obvious that a school with more resources—higher per-pupil spending or smaller classes, say—will produce higher achievement. In fact, an examination of school data shows that this is far from obvious. There are literally thousands of economic studies that attempt to estimate "education production functions"—that is, the relationship between school inputs and outputs (student achievement). For at least the past thirty years, since the 1966 publication of the influential Coleman Report,[4] these attempts have focused on the question of whether there is *any* relationship at all. The measured productivity of school inputs is so low, even by the most optimistic estimates, that it would greatly shock the man on the street. For instance, the *most optimistic* widely accepted estimates of the effect of class size reduction suggest that lowering class size by 10 percent (approximately two students) for all the years that a student is in elementary school raises his or her achievement by 0.17 of a standard deviation.[5] Because the man on the street is ignorant of such facts, he remains unpuzzled. In contrast, economists are impatient to solve the puzzle of why money does not matter more in schools.

The lack of market forces in education is one of the most promising potential explanations of the puzzle that has yet been put forward. After all, market pressures are generally credited with stimulating firms to be productive. Thus, it is natural that economists are interested in the productivity consequences of choice: They know that there is a puzzle to solved, and they know that market pressures are a potential solution that is worth understanding.

You Cannot Predict the Effects of School Choice on Student Sorting Without the Tools of General Equilibrium

The most complicated effects of choice are on student sorting—how students will allocate themselves among schools when allowed to choose schools more freely. In popular parlance, such issues are described as "cream-skimming" or segregation, even though these are only two forms of student sorting that could arise. Debates about choice often run aground on such issues, because opponents and proponents find themselves getting confused about how choice would affect student sorting. Even if debaters do not admit to being confused, they find it hard to explain the logic behind their assertions that a certain type of cream-skimming or segregation will occur.

It is natural that confusion occurs. In fact, it is impossible to predict the effects of choice on student sorting without

- knowing numerous parameters about households and schools, such as how a child's achievement is affected by his peers and what the efficient scale is for producing education with various types of children, such as disabled, limited English proficient, or gifted students;

---

4. The report that is generally known as the Coleman Report is Coleman et al. (1966).

5. The estimates described come from Alan Krueger (1999). Other modern, credible research finds no effect of class size reduction: See Hoxby (2000) and the review by Eric Hanushek (1996).

- having an accurate characterization of *current* student sorting, which is very strong in most metropolitan areas;
- having tools for finding equilibria in which students will be allocated to schools in a stable way. This is a general equilibrium problem that requires simultaneously solving for three equilibria: equilibrium in the market for schooling, equilibrium in the market for housing, and equilibrium in the labor market (solving for the income distribution). In practice, a combination of closed-form proofs, simulations, and computable general equilibrium techniques are required.

It goes without saying that the typical commentators on school choice lack all of these requirements for understanding student sorting. Moreover, they often do not realize that they lack them, and thus do not even try to acquire what they need in order to answer questions about student sorting.

Economists attempt to fulfill the first of these requirements by making a variety of assumptions about the parameters and obtaining a corresponding variety of predictions about student sorting. Empirical economists can supply some of the information for the second requirement, although the other information remains obscure because schools do not keep much data on their students' backgrounds. Economic theorists are girded with the general equilibrium tools listed in the third requirement, although these tools are often seriously strained by the complexities of the student sorting problem.

It would be optimistic to say that economists will soon be able to predict the student sorting consequences of any proposed school choice plan. Our theoretical machinery is too crude to incorporate the actual complexity of households, schools, and housing markets, especially because the information fed into the machinery falls far short of what is needed. Nevertheless, compared to the typical commentator on school choice, economists have made significant strides on the student sorting problem: They grasp the structure of the problem, they understand what information they need in order to proceed, and they have some idea of how *various* the plausible outcomes are. Economists can at least maintain a proper sense of humility about predicting how school choice will affect student sorting.

School Choice Will Affect Labor Markets for Educators

In a discussion of school choice, it is common to hear one of the following protests: "Teachers in my district cannot be paid that way. It is not in their contract"; "Teachers cannot be paid that much: A lot of the budget has to be spent on other staff"; "Voters in my area will not support teacher salaries that are that high"; "Administrators in my district do not get to make that kind of hiring (firing) decision. Their decisions are constrained by the union"; or "Good teachers in my area leave the profession quickly.

They say that there is no appreciation of their skills (room for advancement)." Such protests often bring a discussion of school choice to a halt, as participants shake their heads over the labor market for educators.

All such protests are excessively rigid when school choice is the issue. The market for educators is an upstream market (a provider of inputs) for the market for schooling. Anything that fundamentally changes the structure of the market for schooling, as school choice can, can deeply affect the way its upstream markets function. Indeed, the typical protests *reflect* the structure of the current market for schooling; they are not preconditions to which it is subject. For example, the salaries that parents are willing to pay reflect their satisfaction with schools, and choice generally gives schools stronger incentives to satisfy parents.

Analyzing how a change in market structure affects upstream markets is a classic problem in economics. Thus, not only are economists not stymied by protests like those listed above; they can borrow experience from other sectors in which upstream labor markets changed in response to downstream market structure. Such experience is not derived exclusively from for-profit industries. Much recent experience comes from industries that include not-for-profit and government providers, like health care.

In fact, analysis of how choice would change the market for teachers is already in progress: Hanushek and Rivkin present some results in their chapter, and I have published a study focusing exclusively on how choice has affected the teaching profession (see Hoxby 2002).

Evidence on School Choice Requires the Latest Methods in Nonexperimental Empirical Analysis

As a rule, it is impossible to conduct controlled, double-blind experiments on schoolchildren, primarily because it is considered unethical to experiment on them. That is, if the policy under consideration is considered likely to be beneficial, then it is considered unethical to allow some children to experience the policy while forbidding it to others. Furthermore, controlled, double-blind experiments are impractical in many cases. It would be impossible, for instance, to let some families exercise school choice and forbid other families to exercise it but to keep them blind about the group to which they had been assigned (or even to keep schools ignorant of the families' group assignments). In addition, if we were to allow only some families to exercise school choice (keeping others in the control group), we could not observe some of the effects of a full-blown school choice program. For instance, the labor market for educators might not change much if educators could easily avoid being in a choice school (by working at a control school).

The lack of a laboratory-like experimental setting is nothing new to economists, given that they cannot experiment on workers, the unemployed, trainees, or any number of other people affected by economic policies. Particularly over the last thirty years, economists have worked intensely to develop statistical techniques for analyzing policies in nonexperimental settings. Empirical economists now have methods for exploiting policy enactments ("policy experiments") and accidental policy changes ("natural experiments"). These methods work because they extract from the real world those events that most closely mimic the controlled setting of a laboratory experiment. Economists are acutely aware of problems like selection (the families who use a school choice program may be different from those who do not), policy endogeneity (school choice policies may be enacted in response to problems that continue to affect students after enactment), and the inadequacies of partial equilibrium analysis (the effect of a choice plan in which only a fraction of students can participate may differ from the effect of one in which all students can participate).

Given the rapid improvement in these techniques during the 1980s and early 1990s, the school choice debate could not have arisen at a better time for empirical economists. Put another way, it is a quirk of timing that has made economists (and others using their methods) the best empirical analysts of school choice: When the need for analysis arose, they were simply the most experienced users of the right tools for the job.

It Is Important to Know Which Students Are Likely to Be Affected by School Choice

The current make-up of private schools is a source of considerable confusion in school choice debates. Children who currently attend private schools belong to several diverse groups: central city children who attend inexpensive schools that are charitably subsidized by a religious denomination (such as the Roman Catholic church) to which most of the children do not belong; suburban children who attend private schools that are affiliated with their own religious group; disabled children who attend private schools that cater to their special needs; and children of affluent parents who attend college preparatory schools. The first two groups account for approximately 85 percent of private school students in the United States.

There are two things to note about all of these students. First, they are *by definition* not constrained to attend the public school to which they would otherwise be assigned. Second, they are unusual. Central city private school students are unusual because they are children who have had the good fortune to land one of the highly rationed places in a subsidized nonpublic school. Places in such schools are not rationed on tuition (that is, such schools would be glad to offer more school places if the marginal students could pay tuition equal to the per-pupil costs). Instead, such schools maintain low tuition in order to remain accessible to poor families, and they distribute their limited places on relatively arbitrary bases, such as "first come, first served." The second group of students is unusual because they come from families who place so much weight on religious education that they are willing to make considerable financial sacrifices for it. Not only do they pay tuition on top of paying taxes for public schools that their children do not use, but their private schools also spend only about half of what their public schools spend (and their children consequently experience fewer amenities). The third group—disabled students—is obviously unusual, and the fourth group (which makes up only about 1 percent of American K-12 enrollment) is unusual because the vast majority of affluent parents simply live in an affluent area and send their children to a school that is public but nevertheless caters almost exclusively to people like them.

Many commentators, when attempting to envision a world with school choice, turn to the current private school sector for illumination, and they predict that children like those described above will be the children who are most affected by choice.

Economists, in contrast, understand that what choice programs do is *relax constraints* on students' mobility among schools. Therefore, the students who will be most affected by choice are those for whom the current constraints are most binding. None of the students described above fit into this category, since they have already overcome the constraints that would be relaxed by school choice. (This is not to say that they would be unaffected by choice, since school choice could change the availability of private schools.) Economists, therefore, focus on students who are currently constrained to attend a school that unconstrained families avoid. Economists also focus on students who live in an area that can support multiple schools (since allowing a rural student to choose a school that is far away is not a meaningful relaxation of constraints). Thus, the students who are most likely to be affected by choice are *urban* students who (a) are either sufficiently poor or sufficiently discriminated against that their parents are constrained to live where the schools are unappealing, and (b) are too poor to pay tuition equal to some private school's per-pupil costs.

School Choice Is All about School *Supply*

The school choice debate is also plagued by confusion about the *supply* of schools of choice. A common misapprehension is that, under school choice, students would have to be allocated among each existing school's current number of places. Another common misapprehension is that, under a voucher program that allowed religious private schools to accept vouchers, approximately 85 percent of private school enrollment would be in religious schools because that is the current composition of private schools. Such misapprehensions stem from the belief that the supply of schooling is inelastic.

Economists realize that such an assumption is extreme and very unlikely to be true. In every sector, there are factors that determine supply, and economists know that understanding such factors is the key to predicting supply accurately. Economists focus on factors that would determine what the supply of schools would look like under choice: the cost of school inputs, economies of scale, and the features on which parents are willing to spend their vouchers.

For example, it is useful to know how much it costs to build new schools and how much it costs to refurbish current schools so that they can be used for reorganized or new schools. Those who believe that the supply of schools is inelastic apparently believe that such costs are prohibitively high. They are not, as is demonstrated by the ability of school management companies that now routinely build new schools and renovate current schools for their use (Edison Schools, Advantage Schools, etc.). Moreover, many school inputs are in elastic supply and can be purchased at a price that can be readily established: classroom equipment, school accounting software, computers, and so on. There are numerous economic studies of how the quantity and quality of teachers responds to salaries and benefits, and we can use estimates from such studies.

If we wish to understand what the supply of schools would look like under choice, it is also useful to know the preferences of the parents who are most bound by the constraints that a school choice program would relax. For instance, unless constrained parents have a great taste for religious education, it is unlikely that the supply of choice schools would end up being dominated by schools with religious affiliation. In short, current private school parents have unusual tastes, so their preferences tell us little about the preferences of future choice parents. Economists realize that it is more useful to examine the stated preferences, from the National Household Education Survey or opinion surveys, of parents who are likely to be constrained. Such survey evidence is imperfect, but it is a better guide to future supply than are the preferences of current private school parents.

It Is the *Threat* of Competition That Matters

Part of understanding markets is understanding that the schools' conduct and performance will depend on the availability of alternative schools, not on whether the parents actually use the alternatives. That is, it is the threat of competition that matters, not whether the threat results in (a) the incumbent school's improving so much that parents do not want to use the alternative school or (b) parents' leaving the incumbent school for a better alternative.

There are two important implications of realizing that it is the threat of competition that matters. First, if we observe a public school that loses many students to choice schools (voucher, charter, and private schools), we should realize that the school faces competition *and* is responding poorly to it. A similar school that loses few students to choice schools is not necessary facing less competition: It may just be responding better. Therefore, cross-sectional comparison of schools that do and do not lose students to choice schools is not good evidence about the effects of competition. What one needs to do, in order to obtain evidence on competition, is find schools that are and are not subjected to the threat of competition. Economists understand the distinction (between the threat of competition and actual loss of students) and can design an empirical study of the threat of competition.

Second, once we recognize that it is the *threat* of competition that matters, we see that students who do not attend choice schools may benefit from competition just as much as students who do. Indeed, if we want to know whether choice matters, then students at seriously threatened incumbent schools are not a good control group for students at choice schools.

Insights from the Chapters That Follow

Each of the chapters in this volume takes up a different aspect of school choice and is the culmination of a research agenda. As a result, reading each chapter is like opening a door into a body of research. The authors themselves are the best guides to their particular areas, and the authors are certainly best at presenting their own results. Therefore, I will not attempt to summarize their chapters here but will use this opportunity to draw attention to insights and features of each chapter that I found to be particularly striking.

Eric A. Hanushek and Steven G. Rivkin, in "Does Public School Competition Affect Teacher Quality?" explore the hypothesis that choice will force schools to employ teachers of a more consistent, high quality. The study is central to the question of how choice (the structure of the downstream market for education) will affect teaching (the key upstream market). Ordinarily, teacher quality is very difficult to measure. For instance, in a related study, I had to use the selectivity of a teacher's college and whether a teacher had a subject-area degree as proxies for quality. Hanushek and Rivkin, however, are able to measure a teacher's quality by his or her systematic effect on student achievement. Their clever empirical strategy requires very detailed and complete data, which they have obtained for the entire state of Texas.

Hanushek and Rivkin exploit variation in the most common, traditional form of public school choice: parents' choosing among schools by choosing where to live. Two interesting insights arise in relation to this strategy. First, the evidence suggests that, although both choice *among schools* (within a district) and choice *among districts* are meaningful, they are not the same. When parents choose a district, there are financial implications of their choice because districts are financially autonomous and depend on local property values. When parents choose a school within a district, their choice does not have the same implications. Second, the Texas data clearly show that choice is more meaningful for metropolitan students than for rural students.

David N. Figlio and Marianne E. Page's chapter, "Can School Choice and School Accountability Successfully Coexist?" examines Florida's voucher system, in which students are offered vouchers if they attend a school that consistently fails to meet Florida's achievement standards. Proposals for similar programs (in which choice is limited to students who would otherwise attend failing schools) enjoy considerable political popularity.

Figlio and Page's study exposes a fundamental difference between such choice programs and more conventional programs in which eligibility is based mainly on students' own characteristics (not his school's failure). Conventional choice programs rely on the idea that parents are inclined to choose better schools for their children when they can. Thus, conventional programs attempt to make escape easier for parents who are currently *constrained* (by their incomes, job locations, or other factors) to choose a bad school. Conventional programs often include provisions that increase the information available to parents, in the form of school report cards and so on. Nevertheless, choice plans usually depend on parents to filter and judge the information they receive about schools, and parents are the main source of discipline for underperforming schools.

In contrast, the Florida program relies on the idea that the state is better than parents at determining whether a school is underperforming. In the Florida program, a school's being attractive to parents is no guarantee against state sanctions, nor is a school's being unattractive to parents a guarantee of vouchers. Figlio and Page demonstrate empirically that the Florida system, regardless of whether it depends on achievement levels or value-added measures of achievement, does not give vouchers to many students who are currently constrained and does give vouchers to many students who are currently unconstrained. A deep inconsistency in the Florida program is that its success depends on parents' using the vouchers wisely, even though its structure implies that parents are poor judges of schools compared to the state.

In short, Figlio and Page's paper should make us think carefully about the fundamental claims on which choice programs are justified. Their paper is a wake-up call for people who ignore differences between Florida-style and conventional choice programs.

Julie Berry Cullen and Steven G. Rivkin study the ticklish intersection between school choice and special education in their chapter, "The Role of Special Education in School Choice." The authors bring to light several important questions about school choice and special education. Can a choice program ensure that all (or most) schools have the resources to fulfill a student's individual education plan (IEP)? If the answer is no, then special education students may have limited choice in practice, either because schools will attempt to exclude them or because they themselves will stay away from schools that do not have adequate resources. Also, would other students attempt to avoid special education students in a system with greater choice?

Using data from the Texas public school system, the authors conclude that there is little evidence that regular education students attempt to avoid special education students. However, the data do suggest that special education students are disproportionately likely to make use of opportunities to choose among public schools. Moreover, special education students already use private school vouchers in a number of states. Thus, one of the key things that we learn from Cullen and Rivkin is that choice does not merely generate unique risks for special education students; it also presents them with unique opportunities.

The authors' results lead them to ask, "In a system of school choice, who should decide what a student's IEP is?" Cullen and Rivkin show that special education families value school choice because it allows them to seek not only sympathetic environments for their children, but also the IEP that they feel is appropriate. This is the positive side of IEP seeking. Cullen and Rivkin also suggest that some IEP seeking may be less positive: A family may switch schools until it finds an administrator whom it can bully into writing an inappropriate IEP for its child. Moreover, Cullen and Rivkin inform us that, empirically, it appears that schools already over- or under-classify students in response to financial incentives to do so. Gaming of the system can be exacerbated by a poorly designed choice program. For instance, the authors describe Minnesota's open enrollment plan, in which receiving schools were inclined to overclassify students because the sending schools were responsible for paying the costs of the IEP. Designers of choice plans will come away from the Cullen and Rivkin chapter with many ideas about how to (and how not to) design the special education provision of their programs.

Paul E. Peterson, William G. Howell, Patrick J. Wolf, and David E. Campbell compare the outcomes of students who are randomly given and not given vouchers in "School Vouchers: Results from Randomized Experiments." The randomization occurs when applicants for vouchers put their names into lotteries, because the number of available vouchers is fewer than the number of applicants. The randomized design has features that are obviously desirable. In particular, it is extremely plausible that the randomly selected "treatment" and "control" groups of students have similar unobserved characteristics. Because we cannot check students' unobserved characteristics, it is valuable to have a design that guarantees similarity to the maximum extent possible.

Readers will naturally want to focus on Peterson et al.'s comparison of the standardized test achievement of voucher and control students. In this chapter, the authors describe these results for several voucher programs, all of which target poor children. Readers should be encouraged, however, to look further than the achievement results, because Peterson et al.'s data are rich on other dimensions. We can derive what anthropologists call a "thick description" of the entire voucher experience.

For instance, we learn that younger children adjust more readily to voucher schools and consequently improve their achievement more quickly after the choice opportunity is made available to them. Older children are more likely to complain about tough new discipline or academic demands, at least in the immediate aftermath of the transition. (As we might expect, the parents of older children do not always share their children's dissatisfaction.)

A large share of the students in Peterson et al.'s data are black, owing to the location and eligibility criteria of the programs that they study. Thus, the results for white students are less precise than they are for black students, and we should be circumspect about interpreting differences between the black students' and white students' results. Nevertheless, the data suggest that black students benefit more from vouchers, perhaps because black families are more constrained without choice (they are poorer or have more limited housing choices) or because black students suffer from more discrimination in public schools than in voucher schools. These results are intriguing and suggest leads for unraveling the puzzle of America's significant black-white achievement gap.

Even with a randomized design, some empirical problems arise in Peterson's study, and he shares his solutions to them. For instance, are the families who apply for the vouchers very different from nonapplicants? The randomized design does not have a natural way of comparing applicants to nonapplicants. Peterson et al. solve this problem with additional data, which they gathered through representative surveys of local families. Another tricky question is what to do about families who win vouchers but do not use them. After all, the randomization is only over voucher receipt, not voucher use. Instrumenting for voucher use with voucher receipt allows Peterson et al. to recover an unbiased estimate of the effect of voucher use— that is, the effect of voucher use uncontaminated by biases that might creep in if a certain type of families were more likely to leave the voucher unused.

The inclusion of Peterson et al.'s study in this volume deserves special comment, not because Peterson is a political scientist (which is unimportant, given that he uses modern econometrics), but because economists' initial response to a study like this one is nearly always, "Why are such studies needed at all?" Economists reason that if parents use the vouchers (when they could easily continue to use the public schools or return to the public schools), then it is obvious that "treatment" parents are more satisfied than they would otherwise have been. Is not it obvious that their children are doing better, in some parentally defined sense if not in terms of standardized tests? That is, economists tend to take a revealed preference view: They are as unwilling to believe that families will choose their less-preferred school (when another is freely available) as they are to believe that families will shop at their less-preferred grocery store. In addition, economists wonder how to use the study's results: They are disinclined to extrapolate from *some* voucher schools to *all* potential voucher schools—just as they would be disinclined to say that all grocery stores are preferred to A&P just because certain grocery stores are preferred to A&P in some localities. Finally, economists are loath to believe that families can be made worse off when they are given an option that they did not have before, except when their default public school deteriorates because other families were given the option to leave it too. (The possibility of such deterioration is the reason why economists are interested in how choice affects student sorting and school finance.) Since Peterson et al. examine voucher programs that are tiny relative to the public school systems from which they draw students, it is very unlikely that the families' default public schools could deteriorate significantly because of the voucher program. Thus, economists reason, families cannot be made worse off in the situations that Peterson et al. study.

Given economists' initial reactions to studies like Peterson et al.'s, why do they return again and again to such studies, and where do such studies belong in the economic analysis of choice? The answer is that Peterson et al.'s study helps us to learn about *fundamental* parameters that are necessary for predicting the response to school choice. For instance, commentators on education sometimes doubt whether parents—especially central city, poor parents—take achievement into account at all when they judge a school. Commentators often suggest that poor parents are drawn to schools mainly on the basis of ethnic concerns (they like ethnocentric curricula regardless of the effect on achievement), laziness (they choose whatever school minimizes their effort), or superficial attributes (they like attractive uniforms). Not only does Peterson et al.'s study allow us to estimate how much parents seek achievement when they make school choices, but the study also gives us a relatively rich picture of the families whose behavior will be important in a choice environment.

A final note on Peterson et al.'s analysis is in order. It is not subject to the criticism, mentioned above, that students at incumbent schools are invalid control students because their schools may be affected by the threat of competition, even if they do not exercise choice. The voucher programs that Peterson et al. study enroll just a few percent of local students, and they are *privately funded* (so the public schools do not lose any money when they lose a student). Thus, the incumbent schools attended by the control students are unlikely be significantly changed by the voucher programs.

Thomas J. Nechyba, in "Introducing School Choice into Multidistrict Public School Systems," demonstrates how important it is to model the *current* school system realistically before attempting to predict the effects of school choice. Nechyba manages to reduce the complexity of the current system to its essentials, without losing any of those essentials. In his model, people simultaneously choose their public school district and residence and whether to send their children to private schools. Voters of each school district choose the level at which their schools will be funded, with the tax base being the property they actually own. In short, he manages to incorporate a housing market, private schools, and political economy in a tractable model. He uses data from actual school districts to bound the parameters for his model.

Nechyba emphasizes that the current system pressures families to live in school districts with other families who have similar demand for housing (in other words, similar incomes). This force is responsible for much of the inequality in school spending that we see in the current system. Vouchers sever the link between housing and schooling, and thereby reduce the incentive for families to segregate themselves on the basis of income. For instance, well-off couples who currently leave the central city for the suburbs as soon as they have school-aged children would be more likely to remain under a voucher program. Nechyba demonstrates that, because vouchers induce greater *income integration,* they do not raise the inequality of schools' resources much, if at all. He demonstrates how incorrect a commentator's predictions will be if he (the commentator) characterizes the current system as an idealized system in which all public schools are equal and no areas are segregated on the basis of income.

In a series of studies, Raquel Fernández and Richard Rogerson have examined how school finance affects the growth and distribution of income in a nation. Each of their studies has wrestled with the same fundamental problem. The market for investments in human capital is flawed because little children do not borrow against their future earnings to finance the investment in education that would be optimal for them. (Little children cannot borrow for several reasons. They are not competent to sign contracts that would bind them for life to a schedule of repayments; their parents cannot sign such contracts on their behalf; families know little about a child's abilities and about the future labor market; and human capital is not collateral that could be repossessed by a lender if the borrower were to default on his education loan.)

The flawed market for human capital investments generates investments that are systematically inadequate for certain groups, especially poor families who are unable to provide internal (family) financing of education. Such inoptimal investment translates into slow growth for a country and unnecessary intergenerational transmission of economic status. Fernández and Rogerson first remind us of how well current school finance systems remedy the market flaws. They treat pure local finance as their benchmark, but they also discuss some popular state aid systems. They go on to examine three different types of vouchers that would be straightforward to enact: lump-sum vouchers (every student gets the same voucher), means-tested vouchers (every student with less than a certain income gets a voucher), and power-equalizing vouchers (every student with less than a certain income gets a voucher that rises as his family's income falls and as the share of his family's income that is devoted to schooling rises).

Using a calibrated theoretical model, Fernández and Rogerson demonstrate that the vouchers, especially the power-equalizing vouchers, generate large increases in a nation's income and well-being. One key insight is that vouchers, because they are specific to individual students (rather than entire districts), generate more optimal investments in education than any version of current school finance (which operates at the district level) could generate.

Dennis Epple and Richard Romano, in "Neighborhood Schools, Choice, and the Distribution of Educational Benefits," study intradistrict choice. The distinctive feature of intradistrict choice is that there is no channel by which a school gains per-pupil spending when it attracts a student (or loses per-pupil spending when it loses a student). Intradistrict choice plans are used in some large cities (for instance, Chicago). Some states, if they were to adopt public school choice plans, would effectively adopt intradistrict plans: Hawaii has one school district for the entire state; California is approximately one district for financial purposes; and a few other states (such as New Mexico) allow very little variation in per-pupil spending among their districts.

Epple and Romano compare *intra*district choice to typical neighborhood schools, in which each student attends his assigned local school. They demonstrate that there is an important trade-off between intradistrict choice and neighborhood schools, so long as every student benefits from being with students of higher ability (a crucial assumption). The trade-off is as follows: Intradistrict choice encourages segregation of students on the basis of ability, compared to neighborhood schools, but discourages segregation of students on the basis of income, compared to neighborhood schools.

Another insight to take away from Epple and Romano's chapter is that the effects of intradistrict choice depend very much on whether surrounding districts use intradistrict choice too (or retain neighborhood schools) and whether surrounding districts are close substitutes for the district with intradistrict choice. For instance, if one district in the midst of many others unilaterally enacts intradistrict choice, then well-off families who prefer to send their child to an income-segregated neighborhood school will move out of the district with intradistrict choice. The systematic departure of such families will drive down per-pupil spending in the district with intradistrict choice.

In "School Choice and School Productivity: Could School Choice Be a Tide That Lifts All Boats?" I begin by reviewing some facts that suggest that American schools could be substantially more productive. (The productivity of schools is measured by dividing a standardized measure of students' achievement by per-pupil spending.) In the last thirty years, the productivity of American schools has fallen by between 45 and 75 percent, depending on how one controls for changes in the sociodemographic composition of the population and for the increased cost of hiring well-educated female workers. Therefore, even if choice could make American schools recoup only one-third or one-half of the productivity that they have recently lost, then the productivity effect might easily swamp other effects of choice. For instance, suppose that choice, through a channel like student sorting, has negative effects on some students' peer groups. What we know about the scale of peer effects suggests that regaining half of the lost productivity would easily outweigh such negative effects.

In the chapter, I examine how three recent choice reforms affected the productivity of *incumbent public schools*. The three reforms (Milwaukee vouchers, Michigan charter schools, and Arizona charter schools) were selected because the number of eligible students and the fees associated with them were large enough that incumbent public schools might begin to feel threatened. I show that, as one would expect, the schools that lost students under choice were schools that were underperforming when the choice programs were enacted. In fact, it appears that charter schools, which have some discretion about where they will locate, picked locations at which they would have access to a population of dissatisfied families.

I find that incumbent schools reacted surprisingly quickly and positively to the threat of competition. For instance, public schools in Milwaukee, which began to be seriously threatened only in 1998–99, rose remarkably in their test scores in first two years they were threatened (with no relative increase in spending), compared to similar, but unthreatened, public schools elsewhere in Wisconsin. School superintendents sometimes claim that they have a backlog of changes that need to be made, and that a serious competitive threat allows them to make several changes at once. Because the quick, large reactions may reflect such backlogs, the chapter also reviews evidence of long-term productivity reactions to the availability of traditional forms of choice (choosing a public school by choosing a residence and sending a child to a regular private school).

Looking Forward

In the coming years, we can look forward to further advances in the economic analysis of school choice. Empirical evidence will grow in proportion to the enactment of reforms, and—fortunately for research—the number and variety of charter school, voucher, and public school choice programs are continually increasing. It would be particularly helpful, from the research point of view, to have one state or one large metropolitan area enact a choice plan that is both stable and relatively universal. Arizona's charter school program is the nearest approximation to this that we currently have, and it has been in place only since 1994. So far, we have had to rely on traditional forms of choice in order to get evidence on the long-term, general equilibrium effects of choice, such as the effects on the market for teachers, student sorting, residential segregation, school finance, and the housing market.

There is a great deal of variation in the financial arrangements of the experimental choice plans enacted over the past several years, but much of the variation is not useful for empirical research. Many of the experimental plans have financial arrangements that are obviously unsuitable for full-scale choice, and we can learn only a limited amount from them. The future is brighter: The happy merger between research on school choice and school finance is already leading to more thoughtful construction of the financial side of choice plans. As the plans get refined, it will be easier for researchers to learn about how choice changes the school finance environment.

We can learn from foreign school choice programs, as well as American ones, but on this front, I am obliged to raise warning flags as well as hopes. Empirical evidence may be helpful if it comes from a foreign country that has similar school finance, market orientation, and culture to those of the United States, but very few countries fulfill one of these criteria, and no foreign country fulfills all the criteria. (Canada is the closest by far.) Some research on foreign school choice assumes that the results will translate readily to the United States. This is naïve. School choice plans are layered on top of America's current system of public and private schools, which is an outlier in the world. American schools are more locally controlled, more reliant on local funding, and more entwined with the housing market (because of property tax revenue and Americans' greater residential mobility) than any other schools in the world. Inequality and disability exist everywhere, but America has a unique legal history regarding school desegregation and special education. In short, many of the questions that arise in a typical American debate on school choice are peculiar to the United States.

More importantly, school choice is fundamentally a market-based reform, and Americans have very different experience with markets than most people in the world. By world standards, Americans are confident consumers who negotiate markets well but take dictation poorly from social planners, even when the social planners are benevolent. In France, for instance, an educational elite chooses the curriculum for the entire nation and determines which students will be able to attend academic high schools and college. This system may work well for the French, but Americans have consistently resisted letting an elite group decide how their children should be educated and which children deserve further education. That is, Americans appear to like making choices about their children's education. Also, the American labor market is less regulated than other countries'. Typical

American teachers are not only familiar with jobs in which pay and promotions are market-oriented (unless they have a strange lack of acquaintances among the nonunion, private-sector workers who make up most of the workforce), but they would probably be shocked to learn that most foreign teachers are on *nationwide* contracts and are *assigned* to a school by a national ministry. American teachers are already more market oriented than their foreign counterparts and probably value their ability to change their pay or working conditions by moving to a new district. In many other countries, government provision of services and elite decisions about education are not only more common, but they enjoy far stronger social support. It is poor inference to assume that, because foreign families or teachers react in a certain way to a choice program, Americans will necessarily react similarly. We will learn the most from research on foreign school choice when we take the trouble to articulate and quantify the differences in institutions and typical economic behavior.

I can return to a more optimistic tone with theoretical economic analysis of school choice. On this front, there is little that constrains research from continuing at a good rate of progress, except for the energy of researchers. As a theory problem, school choice sits neatly at the intersection of several fields: labor economics (because investment in education is a human capital problem), public economics (because schools must be financed), and industrial organization (because schools must compete with one another under choice). In addition, analysis of school choice draws upon general equilibrium and overlapping generations models most often used by macroeconomists. We have not yet come close to exhausting *existing* tools' capacity for analyzing school choice. However, nearly every existing tool was initially designed for another purpose than the analysis of school choice, and thus each tool must be modified to fit American educational institutions. Also, analysts find themselves having to learn economics outside their "home" field. In short, although progress is very likely, it must proceed at a somewhat measured pace.

Theory is likely to advance, especially along the lines of *optimal design* of choice programs. In the first years of analysis, economists were (not surprisingly) absorbed in analyzing existing choice plans or proposals. Such analysis led to greater understanding of the issues, but the natural consequence of such understanding was that economists began to envision programs that dealt better with choice problems than existing programs do. Design of more optimal programs is a productive agenda, and recent papers (including the one by Fernández and Rogerson in this volume) illustrate its usefulness. We are just beginning to explore the potential of school choice to solve long-standing problems in school finance, racial and income segregation, and special education. We will continue to learn about the risks of school choice and its capacity to make schools more effective and to match students better to schools.

References

Coleman, James S., Ernest Q. Campbell, Carol J. Hobson, James McPartland, Alexander M. Mood, Frederic D. Weinfeld, and Robert L. York. 1966. *Equality of educational opportunity* (Coleman report). Washington, D.C.: U.S. Government Printing Office for the National Center of Educational Statistics.

Coons, John E., and Stephen D. Sugarman. 1971. *Family choice in education: A model state system for vouchers.* Berkeley, Calif.: University of California, Institute of Governmental Studies.

———. 1978. *Education by choice: The case for family control.* Berkeley: University of California Press.

Friedman, Milton. 1955. The role of government in education. In *Economics and the public interest*, ed. Robert A. Solo, 123–44. New Brunswick, N.J.: Rutgers University Press.

Friedman, Milton, and Rose Friedman. 1980. *Free to choose.* New York: Harcourt Brace Jovanovich.

Hanushek, Eric. 1996. Measuring investment in education. *Journal of Economic Perspectives* 10:9–30.

Hoxby, Caroline. 2000. The effects of class size on student achievement: New evidence from population variation. *Quarterly Journal of Economics* 115 (4): 1239–85.

———. 2002. Would school choice change the teaching profession? *Journal of Human Resources* 38 (4): 846–91.

Jencks, Christopher. 1970. Education vouchers: Giving parents money to pay for schooling. *New Republic* 163 (1): 19–21.

Krueger, Alan. 1999. Experimental estimates of education production functions. *Quarterly Journal of Economics* 114:497–532.

RAND Corporation. Various years. *A study of alternatives in American education.* Santa Monica, Calif.: RAND Corporation.

Witte, John F., and William H. Clune, ed. 1990. Choice and control in American education: An analytical overview. In *Choice and control in American education*, 11–47. New York: Falmer.

1

Does Public School Competition Affect Teacher Quality?

Eric A. Hanushek and Steven G. Rivkin

Vouchers, charter schools, and other forms of choice have been promoted as a way to improve public schooling, but the justification for that position is largely based on theoretical ideas. Until quite recently there was little evidence on public school responsiveness to competition from private schools, other public school districts, or charter schools, and empirical research remains quite thin. Under most conceivable scenarios of expanded choice, even with private school vouchers, the public school system will still remain the primary supplier of schooling. Therefore, it is important to know what might happen to quality and outcomes in the remaining public schools. This research is designed to provide insights about that from an analysis of how public schools respond to competition from other public schools.

The empirical analysis has two major components. First, estimates of average school quality differences in metropolitan areas across Texas are compared to the amount of public school competition in each. At least for the largest metropolitan areas, the degree of competition is positively related to performance of the public schools. Second, the narrower impact of metropolitan area competition on teacher quality is investigated. Because teacher quality has been identified as one of the most important determinants of student outcomes, it is logical to believe that the effects of competition on

Eric A. Hanushek is the Paul and Jean Hanna Senior Fellow at the Hoover Institution of Stanford University and a research associate of the National Bureau of Economic Research. Steven G. Rivkin is professor of economics at Amherst College and a research associate of the National Bureau of Economic Research.

This research has been supported by grants from the Smith Richardson Foundation and the Packard Humanities Institute. The authors would like to thank Joe Altonji, Patrick Bayer, Caroline Hoxby, and participants at the NBER Conference on the Economics of School Choice for their many helpful comments.

hiring, retention, monitoring, and other personnel practices would be one of the most important aspects of any force toward improving public school quality. The results, although far from conclusive, suggest that competition raises teacher quality and improves the overall quality of education.

Prior to the analysis of Texas public schools we briefly consider the various margins of competition for public schools. Although many simply assume that expanded availability of alternatives will lead to higher public school quality, the institutional structure of public schools raises some questions about the strength of any response.

1.1 The Margins of Competition

Competition for public schools may emanate from a variety of sources. Neighborhood selection places families in particular public school districts and specific school catchment areas within districts. Families also choose whether to opt out of the public schools and send their children to parochial or other private school alternatives.[1] Although these choices have operated for a long time, recent policy innovations have expanded competition within the public school sector. The ability to attend school in neighboring districts, charter schools, and private schools with public funding enhances choice and potentially imposes additional competitive pressures on public schools.

Most of the attention to private schools has concentrated on student performance in Catholic schools.[2] The literature on Catholic school performance is summarized in Neal (1998) and Grogger and Neal (2000). The evidence has generally indicated that Catholic schools on average outperform public schools.[3] This superiority seems clearest in urban settings, where disadvantaged students face fewer options than others.

Our main interest, however, centers on the reactions of public schools to the private sector. In an important article about the impact of private schools on schools in the public sector, Hoxby (1994) demonstrates that

1. Magnet schools have also existed for a long time. However, their small numbers, targeted curricula, and frequent use of entrance examinations limit the extent to which they provide competition for other public schools. Moreover, because they are often introduced to meet school desegregation objectives, choice is frequently limited by racial quotas (Armor 1995).

2. Currently, almost 90 percent of all students attend public elementary and secondary schools. This percentage has been stable for some time, although the exact character of the alternative private schooling has changed. The percentage of private school students in Catholic schools has declined, whereas other religious based schooling has increased to offset this decline. Nonetheless, adequate data on non-Catholic schools have not been readily available.

3. As has been recognized since some of the earliest work on the topic (Coleman, Hoffer, and Kilgore 1982), it is difficult to separate performance of the private schools from pure selection phenomena. A variety of alternative approaches have dealt with the selection problem, and a rough summary of the results of those efforts is that there remains a small advantage from attending Catholic schools. Grogger and Neal (2000) suggest, however, that there is no advantage to attending private elite schools—a surprising result given the high average tuitions.

public schools in areas that have larger concentrations of Catholic schools perform better than those facing less private competition. This analysis provides the first consistent evidence suggesting that public schools react to outside competition.

The most important element of competition comes from other public schools. Specifically, households can choose the specific jurisdiction and school district, à la Tiebout (1956), by their choice of residential location. Although adjustment is costly, these choices permit individuals to seek high-quality schools if they wish. Residential location decisions are of course complicated, involving job locations, availability of various kinds of housing, school costs and quality, and availability of other governmental services. Nonetheless, given choice opportunities plus voting responses, this model suggests pressure on schools and districts to alter their behavior; competitive alternatives that lead families to choose other schools would yield downward pressure on housing prices and perhaps even an enrollment decline.

The ensuing public pressures might be expected to lead administrators and teachers to respond. For example, job performance may affect a super-intendent's ability to move to another district or a principal's autonomy or ability to remain in a school. Better performance by teachers may make the school more attractive to other high-quality teachers, thereby improving working conditions.

Offsetting forces may, nonetheless, mute any competitive pressures. The current structure of many school systems including tenure for teachers and administrators likely lessens the impact of competitive forces. Institution-ally, district survival is virtually guaranteed under plausible changes in the competitive environment.

The empirical analysis of Borland and Howsen (1992) and its extension and refinement in Hoxby (2000) investigate public school responses to Tiebout forces using the concentration of students in school districts within metropolitan areas as a measure of competition. Borland and Howsen find that metropolitan areas with less public school competition have lower school quality. Noting, however, that the existing distribution of families across districts reflects endogenous reactions to school quality, Hoxby pursues alternative strategies to identify the causal impact of concentrations. She finds that consideration of endogeneity increases the estimated impact of competition on the performance of schools. Our analysis builds on these specifications of public school competition.

The general consideration of Tiebout competition, however, leaves many questions open. For example, it is not obvious how to define the "competi-tive market." Although the district is the fundamental operating and decision-making unit in most states, districts themselves can be very large and heterogeneous. This heterogeneity could lead to competition, and re-sponses, that are more local in nature—say, at the school rather than the district level. For example, Black (1999) and Weimer and Wolkoff (2001) suggest that school quality differences are capitalized into housing prices at the individual school rather than the district level. This ambiguity motivates our use of alternative measures of the level of competition.

Much recent attention has focused on more radical forms of competition such as vouchers or charter schools. Again, whereas most debate focuses on the performance of these alternatives, our interest is the reaction of public schools to these competitive alternatives. With the exception of Hoxby (chap. 8 in this volume), however, little consideration has been given to the actions of public schools.

1.2   The Importance of Teacher Quality

The difficulty of identifying and measuring school quality constitutes a serious obstacle to learning more about the effects of competition. A substantial body of work on the determinants of student achievement has failed to yield any simple descriptions of the key school and teacher factors. Although class size and other variables may significantly affect outcomes for specific populations and grades, financial measures (spending per pupil and teacher salaries) and real resources (teacher experience and degrees, class size, facilities, and administration) do not appear to capture much of the overall variation in school or teacher quality (Hanushek 1986, 1997).[4]

On the other hand, schools and teachers have been shown to be dramatically different in their effects on students. A variety of researchers have looked at variations among teachers in a fixed effect framework and have found large differences in teacher performance (see, e.g., Hanushek 1971, 1992; Murnane 1975; Armor et al. 1976; Murnane and Phillips 1981). The general approach has been to estimate value added achievement models and to assess whether or not performance gains differ systematically across teachers. It is important to note that value added models control for differences in entering achievement and thus remove a number of potential sources of bias, including differences in past performance and school factors, individual ability, and so forth. In every instance of such estimation, large differences have been found. Of particular significance for the work here, these differences have generally been weakly related to the common measures of teachers and classrooms found in the more traditional econometric estimation.

These analyses have not, however, conclusively identified the impacts of different teachers. Because parents frequently set out to choose not just spe-

4. Although parts of this discussion have generated controversy—largely over the policy conclusions that might be drawn—none of the discussion has suggested that any of these resource measures are good indicators of overall school quality. The focus in the discussion has been whether policy changes in any of these measures could be expected to yield positive effects on student performance. See, for example, the paper by Burtless (1996).

cific schools but also specific teachers within schools, the makeup of individual classrooms may not be random. This possibility is compounded by two other influences. First, teachers and principals also enter into a selection process that matches individual teachers with groupings of children.[5] Second, if the composition of the other children in the classroom is important—that is, if there are important peer group effects on achievement—the gains in an individual classroom will partially reflect the characteristics of the children and not just the teacher assigned to the classroom.[6] These considerations suggest a possibility that classroom outcome differences reflect more than just variations in teacher quality.

A recent paper by Rivkin, Hanushek, and Kain (2001) uses matched panel data for individual students and schools to estimate differences in teacher quality that are not contaminated by other factors. Because that work forms the basis for the investigation here, it is useful to understand the exact nature of it. The authors use a value added model that compares the pattern of school average gains in achievement for three successive cohorts as they progress through grades five and six. The value added model, by conditioning on prior achievement, eliminates unmeasured family and school factors that affect the level of beginning achievement for a grade and permits concentration on just the flow of educational inputs over the specific grade. The analysis then introduces fixed effects for individual schools and for specific grades in each school, allowing for effects of stable student ability and background differences, of overall quality of schools, and of the effectiveness of continuing curricular and programmatic elements for individual grades. This basic modeling provides what is essentially a prediction of achievement growth for individuals based on each one's past performance and specific schooling circumstances. The central consideration, then, is how much changes in teachers affect the observed patterns of student achievement growth within each school.[7]

This analysis shows that cohort differences in school average gains rise significantly as teacher turnover increases. By controlling for other potentially confounding influences, the methodology generates a lower bound estimate of the variance in teacher quality based on within-school differences in test score gains among the cohorts.

The estimation of "pure" teacher quality differences reveals that the variation in teacher quality within schools (i.e., ignoring all variation across

5. Hanushek, Kain, and Rivkin (2001b) show that teachers both leave schools and select new districts based on the achievement and racial composition of the schools.

6. Hanushek et al. (forthcoming) and Hanushek, Kain, and Rivkin (2002) show that peer characteristics related to achievement and race influence individual student achievement.

7. The analysis does not look at the achievement growth in individual classrooms, because that could confound individual student placement in specific classrooms with differences in teacher skills. Therefore, it aggregates students across classrooms in a specific grade, effectively instrumenting with grade to avoid selection effects. Even if we had wished to pursue individual classrooms, however, we could not because of data limitations.

schools) is large in Texas elementary schools. One standard deviation of teacher quality—for example, moving from the median to the 84th percentile of the teacher quality distribution—increases the annual growth of student achievement by at least 0.11 standard deviations, and probably by substantially more. This magnitude implies, for example, that having such an 84th percentile teacher for five years in a row rather than a 50th percentile teacher would be sufficient to eliminate the average performance gap between poor students (those eligible for free or reduced lunch) and nonpoor students.

Evidence on the importance of teacher quality forms the basis for a major segment of the empirical analysis here. Specifically, if the degree of local competition is important, it should be possible to detect its impact on teacher quality by examining performance variation along with the amount of local competition across the state of Texas. In particular, it would be surprising for competition to exert a substantial effect on students without influencing the quality of teaching, and investigating these effects provides information about the mechanism behind any observed impacts of competition.

1.3   Empirical Analysis

We investigate how varying amounts of public school competition in the classic Tiebout sense affect student performance and the hiring of teachers. It is important to note that our efforts are not general. We leave aside many of the issues discussed previously and in the other papers of this volume about possible details and dimensions of competition and concentrate entirely on issues of academic performance across broadly competitive areas. Nonetheless, the importance of this topic for individual labor market outcomes and for the politics of schools justifies the choice.

The empirical work exploits the rich data set on student performance of the University of Texas at Dallas Texas Schools Project. Because Texas is a large and varied state, a wide range of local circumstances is presented. Indeed, there are twenty-seven separate metropolitan statistical areas (MSAs) in Texas. These areas, described in table 1.1, vary considerably in size and ability to mount effective competition across districts. The basic Tiebout model assumes a wide variety of jurisdictional choices such that people can choose among alternative public service provision while retaining flexibility in housing quality and commuting choices. Clearly, the smaller MSAs of Texas offer limited effective choice in all dimensions, so it will be interesting to contrast results across the various areas of the state.

We employ the Texas Schools Project data first to estimate overall quality differences between MSAs and to compare these results with the degree of public school competition. Following that, we investigate whether or not competition raises the quality of teaching.

As suggested by the previous discussions, this analysis is best thought of as a reduced-form investigation. We do not observe the underlying decision-

Table 1.1   **Metropolitan Statistical Areas (MSAs) in Texas**

Metropolitan Area	1997 Population (1000s)	Density (persons per square mile)	Population Change 1990–97 (%)	Number of Districts	Number of Elementary Schools
Houston	3,852	651	15.9	45	699
Dallas	3,127	505	16.8	77	590
Fort Worth-Arlington	1,556	533	14.4	37	311
San Antonio	1,511	454	14.1	25	318
Austin-San Marcos	1,071	253	26.6	29	210
El Paso	702	693	18.6	9	137
McAllen-Edinburg-Mission	511	326	33.2	15	121
Corpus Christi	387	253	10.6	20	96
Beaumont-Port Arthur	375	174	3.8	16	72
Brownsville-Harlingen-San Benito	321	354	23.3	10	81
Killeen-Temple	300	142	17.4	14	63
Galveston-Texas City	243	609	11.8	9	64
Odessa-Midland	243	135	7.9	2	28
Lubbock	231	256	3.6	8	57
Brazoria	225	163	17.6	8	48
Amarillo	208	114	11.0	5	59
Longview-Marshall	208	118	7.5	20	44
Waco	203	195	7.3	18	58
Laredo	183	55	37.5	4	53
Tyler	167	180	10.2	8	40
Wichita Falls	137	89	5.2	9	35
Bryan-College Station	133	227	9.1	2	18
Texarkana	123	82	2.7	13	24
Abilene	121	133	1.5	5	39
San Angelo	103	67	4.3	6	32
Sherman-Denison	102	109	6.9	13	30
Victoria	82	93	10.3	4	21

making by school officials; nor do we have detailed and precise measures of the competition facing individual schools and districts. Instead we use aggregate indicators of potential competition from public schools and concentrate on whether or not there are systematic patterns to student outcomes.

1.3.1   The Texas Database

The data used in this paper come from the data development activity of the UTD Texas Schools Project.[8] Its extensive data on student performance are compiled for all public school students in Texas, allowing us to use the universe of students in the analyses. We use fourth-, fifth-, and sixth-grade

8. The UTD Texas Schools Project has been developed and directed by John Kain. Working with the Texas Education Agency (TEA), this project has combined a number of different data

data for three cohorts of students: fourth-graders in 1993, 1994, and 1995. Each cohort contributes two years of test score gains. Students who switch public schools within the state of Texas can be followed just as those who remain in the same school or district, a characteristic we use in our analysis.

The Texas Assessment of Academic Skills (TAAS), which is administered each spring, is a criterion-referenced test used to evaluate student mastery of grade-specific subject matter. We focus on test results for mathematics, the subject most closely linked with future labor market outcomes. We transform all test results into standardized scores with a mean of zero and variance equal to one. The bottom 1 percent of test scores and the top and bottom 1 percent of test score gains are trimmed from the sample in order to reduce measurement error. Participants in bilingual or special education programs are also excluded from the sample because of the difficulty in measuring school and teacher characteristics for these students.

The empirical analysis considers only students attending public school in one of the twenty-seven MSAs in Texas (identified in table 1.1). A substantial majority of all Texas public school students attend schools in one of these MSAs. Each MSA is defined as a separate education market, and measures of competition are constructed for each. The analysis is restricted to MSAs because of the difficulty of defining school markets for rural communities. Below we discuss potential problems associated with defining education markets in this way.

1.3.2   Competition and School Quality

How will public school competition affect the provision of education? Although Tiebout-type forces would be expected to raise the efficiency of schooling, it is not clear that more competition will necessarily result in higher school quality. If wealth differences or other factors related to school financing lead to more resources in areas with less competition, the efficiency effects of competition could be offset by resource differences. Therefore we consider differences in both school quality and school efficiency across metropolitan areas.

A second important issue is precisely how to define the relevant competition. The importance of district administrators in allocating funds, determining curriculum, hiring teachers, and making a variety of other decisions suggests that much if not most of the effects of competition should operate at the district level. However, anecdotal evidence on school choice provides strong support for the notion that parents actively choose among schools

---

sources to compile an extensive data set on schools, teachers, and students. Demographic information on students and teachers is taken from the Public Education Information Management System (PEIMS), which is TEA's statewide educational database. Test score results are stored in a separate database maintained by TEA and must be merged with the student data on the basis of unique student identifiers. Further descriptions of the database can be found in Rivkin, Hanushek, and Kain (2001).

within urban and large suburban school districts, consistent with the view that principals and teachers exert substantial influence on the quality of education. This anecdotal information is reinforced by the aforementioned research on housing capitalization.

We treat the basis for competition as an empirical question. In the estimation, we conduct parallel analyses where competition is measured on the basis of the concentration of students both in schools and separately in districts.

Although Hoxby (2000) provides the empirical context within which to place this study of school efficiency, the methodology employed here is much closer to the work by Abowd, Kramarz, and Margolis (1999) on interindustry wage differences. Just as interindustry wage differences reflect both worker heterogeneity and industry factors, interschool or district differences in student performance reflect both student heterogeneity and school factors. However, a comparison of wage differences for a worker who switches industries or of achievement differences for a student who switches schools effectively eliminates problems introduced by the heterogeneity of workers or students. In this way the availability of matched panel data facilitates the identification of sector effects.

Equation (1) describes a value added model of learning for student i in grade g in MSA m at time t:

$$(1) \quad \Delta \text{Achievement}_{igmt} = \text{family}_i + \text{family}_{igt} + \text{MSA}_m + \text{error}_{igmt},$$

where the change in achievement in grade g equals test score in grade g minus test score in grade $g - 1$.

The overall strategy concentrates on estimation of metropolitan area fixed effects (MSA_m) for each of the twenty-seven MSAs in Texas. Importantly, this model removes all fixed family, individual, and other influences on learning (family_i) as well as time-varying changes (family_{igt}) in family income, community type (urban or suburban), specific year effects, and the effect of moving prior to the school year (students may or may not move prior to fifth grade).[9]

In this model of student fixed effects in achievement gains, the MSA quality fixed effects are identified by students who switch metropolitan areas. These twenty-seven MSA fixed effects provide an index of average school quality for the set of metropolitan areas. Although most of the variation in school quality likely occurs within an MSA, such variation is ignored because of the focus on competition differences among MSAs.[10] Importantly,

9. The empirical specification with the emphasis on the effects of moving reflects our prior analysis that shows an average decline in learning growth in the year of a move (Hanushek, Kain, and Rivkin 2001a).

10. The choice of individual schools does introduce one complication. The average effects will be weighted by the student choices of schools within metropolitan areas instead of the overall distribution of students across an area. Our econometric estimates assume that any differential selectivity of schools within metropolitan areas (after allowing for individual fixed effects for movers) is uncorrelated with the level of competition.

by removing student fixed effects in achievement gains, this approach effectively eliminates much of the confounding influences of student heterogeneity present in analyses based on cross-sectional data.

Nevertheless, we do not believe that students switch districts at random, and changes in circumstances not captured by the student fixed effects may dictate the characteristics of the destination school as well as affecting student performance. For example, families who experience job loss or divorce may relocate to inferior districts, whereas families who experience economic improvements may tend to relocate to better districts.[11] If the limited number of time-varying covariates does not account for such changes in family circumstances, the estimates of metropolitan area school quality will reflect both true quality differences and differences in family circumstances.

However, even if the rankings of metropolitan area average quality are contaminated, regressions of these rankings on the degree of competition may still provide consistent estimates of competition effects as long as the omitted student and family effects are not related to the degree of competition. The fact that mobility across regions is most importantly linked to job relocations and less to seeking specific schools or other amenities certainly mitigates any problems resulting from nonrandom mobility (Hanushek, Kain, and Rivkin 2001a). On the other hand, other factors, including school resources, that may be correlated with the measures of competition may confound the estimated effects of competition on school quality and, more importantly, on school efficiency. We do include average class size as a proxy for school efficiency. Although average class size captures at least a portion of any difference in resources, there is a good chance that influences of confounding factors remain.[12]

Two other important issues more specific to the study of school competition are the measurement of the degree of competition and the identification of separate public school markets. Following general analyses of market structure, we calculate a Herfindahl index based alternatively on the concentration of students by district and by school across the metropolitan areas.[13] As Hoxby (2000) points out, the Herfindahl index is itself endogenously determined by the location decisions of families. Any movement of families into better districts within a metropolitan area will change the

11. Note that the direction of any bias is ambiguous. Negative or positive shocks that precipitate a move may affect performance prior to the move as much as or even more than performance following a move. The range of responses and the effects over time are discussed in Hanushek, Kain, and Rivkin (2001a).

12. Inter-metropolitan area differences in the price of education quality raise serious doubts about the validity of expenditure variables as measures of real differences in resources. Such differences result from cost-of-living differences, variability in working conditions, and differences in alternative employment opportunities for teachers, as well as other factors.

13. The Herfindahl index is the sum of squared proportions of students (by district or school) for the MSA. A value of one indicates all students in a single location (no competition), whereas values approaching zero show no concentration and thus extensive competition.

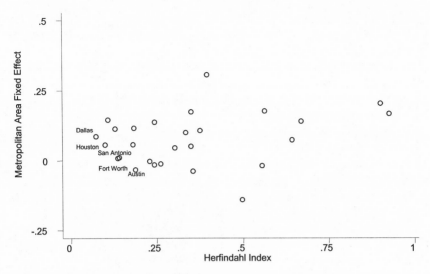

Fig. 1.1   School quality and district concentration

value of the Herfindahl index, raising it if families concentrate in larger districts and lowering it if families move to smaller districts, as would be the case with urban flight. In essence, the Herfindahl index reflects both the initial administrative structure of schools and districts as well as within-metropolitan area variation in school or district quality. Only the former provides a good source of variation, and that is the source of variation Hoxby attempts to isolate with her instrumental variable approach, which deals with the endogeneity of school districts. We do not have available instruments, so the second source of variation may introduce bias of an indeterminate direction.

The identification of the relevant education market (i.e., defining the appropriate set of schools from which parents choose) also presents a difficult task. It is certainly the case that a number of families who work in an MSA choose to live outside the MSA, and thus measuring school competition using the census definitions of MSAs almost certainly introduces some measurement error in the calculation of the Herfindahl index that would tend to bias downward the estimated effects of competition.

Results

Figures 1.1 and 1.2 plot the metropolitan area school quality fixed effects against the Herfindahl index, the measure of competition.[14] The estimates of school quality are obtained from student fixed effect regressions of

14. Average enrollments in fifth and sixth grade for the three years of data are used to construct the Herfindahl index. The district (school) Herfindahl index is the sum of squared proportions of enrollment in each district (school).

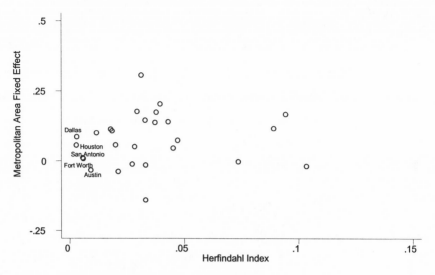

Fig. 1.2   School quality and school concentration

achievement gain on twenty-seven metropolitan area dummy variables and
controls for free lunch eligibility, community type, and whether the student
moved prior to the grade. The five largest metropolitan areas are specifically identified in the figures. Figure 1.1 measures competition by the concentration of students into school districts, whereas figure 1.2 measures
competition by the concentration of students into schools, implicitly permitting competition to occur both within and across districts. The overall
patterns presented in figures 1.1 and 1.2 do not reveal a strong positive relationship between competition at either the district or school level and
school quality. Rather, the scatter of points moves roughly along a horizontal line regardless of whether competition is measured at the school or district level. Not surprisingly, the coefficient on Herfindahl index from a regression of the metropolitan area fixed effect on the Herfindahl index is
small and not significantly different from zero regardless of whether competition is measured at the school or district level (table 1.2).[15] Note that
competition varies far less when measured at the school level, because any
dominance of large districts is ignored.

In contrast to the lack of an overall positive relationship between competition and school quality, the school fixed effects for the five largest metropolitan areas suggest the presence of a positive relationship between
school quality and competition: the ordering of Dallas, Houston, San Antonio, Fort Worth, and Austin according to school quality exactly matches

15. All regressions are weighted by the number of students in each metropolitan area in the
first-stage regressions.

Table 1.2   **Relationship between MSA Average School Quality and Competition, by MSA Size**

	Competition between Districts		Competition between Schools	
	All Areas	By Area Size	All Areas	By Area Size
Herfindahl index	0.11		0.82	
	(1.43)		(1.24)	
Herfindahl index · large MSA[a]		−1.07		−17.3
		(2.76)		(−2.53)
Herfindahl index · (1 − large MSA)		0.09		0.16
		(1.01)		(0.18)
Large MSA		0.11		0.03
		(1.82)		(0.69)
R^2	0.08	0.36	0.06	0.31

Notes: All regressions use the estimated average quality of the MSA schools from equation (1). Observations are weighted by students in the MSAs. *T*-statistics are presented below each coefficient. For competition between districts, Herfindahl index is defined by proportionate shares of students across districts. For competition between schools, Herfindahl index is defined by proportionate shares of students across schools.

[a]Interaction of Herfindahl index and dummy variable for the five largest MSAs (Houston, Dallas, Ft. Worth, San Antonio, and Austin).

the ordering by competition regardless of how competition is measured. This is confirmed by the regression results in table 1.2 that allow for separate slope coefficients for the five largest MSAs. Although there is little or no evidence that competition at the school or district level is significantly related to school quality for the smaller MSAs, the competition effect is positive and significant at the 1 percent level for the five largest metropolitan areas. Because some of the smaller MSAs in Texas actually get quite small and offer far fewer choices of districts (see table 1.1), it would not be surprising if the incentive effects of competition were much weaker in comparison to the effects in the large MSAs. Effective competition may require a minimum range of housing and public service quality (Tiebout 1956).

Regardless of MSA size, however, competition should have its sharpest effects on reducing inefficiencies in resource use and education production. In a coarse effort to isolate competition effects on efficiency, the first-stage regressions underlying figures 1.3 and 1.4 include average class size as a control for resource differences. Not surprisingly, given the strong evidence that class size and other resource differences explain little of the total variation in school quality, the inclusion of class size has little impact on either the observed patterns in the figures or the Herfindahl index coefficients (see table 1.3).

All in all, the figures and regression results suggest that competition improves school quality in larger areas with substantial numbers of school and district choices. However, a sample size of twenty-seven with only five very

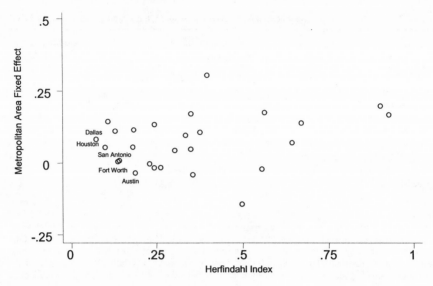

Fig. 1.3   School efficiency and district concentration

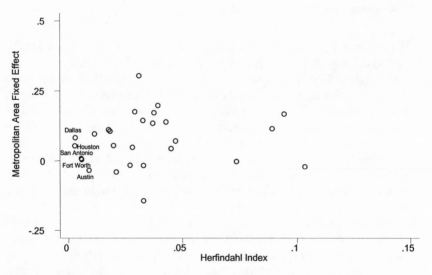

Fig. 1.4   School efficiency and school concentration

large MSAs is quite small, and there may simply not be enough variation to identify more precisely the effect of competition on average school quality and efficiency. Moreover, although the matched panel data remove many of the most obvious sources of bias, the limited number of time-varying characteristics may fail to control for all confounding family and student influences.

Table 1.3   **Relationship between MSA Average School Efficiency and Competition, by MSA Size**

	Competition between Districts		Competition between Schools	
	All Areas	By Area Size	All Areas	By Area Size
Herfindahl index	0.11		0.83	
	(1.44)		(1.26)	
Herfindahl index · large MSA[a]		–1.07		–17.2
		(2.27)		(–2.51)
Herfindahl index · (1 – large MSA)		0.09		0.18
		(1.01)		(0.19)
Large MSA		0.11		0.03
		(1.80)		(0.69)
R^2	0.08	0.36	0.06	0.31

Notes: See notes to table 1.2. School quality is adjusted for resources (class size).
[a]Interaction of Herfindahl index and dummy variable for the five largest MSAs (Houston, Dallas, Ft. Worth, San Antonio, and Austin).

1.3.3   Competition and Teacher Quality

The suggestive results for the effects of competition on overall quality leave uncertainty about the strength of the Tiebout forces. This portion of the empirical analysis investigates a much narrower question with a methodology that likely does a far better job of controlling for confounding influences on student outcomes. Although the quality of teaching is only one of many possible determinants of school quality, evidence in Rivkin, Hanushek, and Kain (2001) strongly suggests that it is the most important factor. Consequently, it would be highly unlikely that competition would exert a strong effect on school quality without affecting the quality of teachers.

At first glance the problem might appear to be quite simple: More competitive areas should lead schools to hire better teachers as measured by teacher education, experience, test scores, and other observable characteristics. However, two issues complicate any simple analysis: (a) evidence overwhelmingly shows that observable characteristics explain little of the variation in teacher quality in terms of student performance (see Hanushek 1986, 1997); and (b) competition could lead schools to raise teacher quality per dollar spent but not the level of quality, and it is quite difficult to account for cross-sectional differences in the price of teacher quality.

Isolating the contributions of teachers to between-school or between-district differences in student performance is inherently very difficult. Given the added difficult task of accurately capturing cross-sectional differences in the price of teacher quality, we do not believe that an analysis of the effect of competition on teacher quality per dollar in salary is likely to produce compelling evidence. We pursue a very different empirical approach focusing on the within-school and -district variations in the quality of teaching, using the methodology developed in Rivkin, Hanushek, and Kain (2001).

In essence, our approach here examines the link between competition and the variance in teacher quality, testing the hypothesis that more competition should lead to less variance in the quality of teaching within schools and districts. Lower variance would result if competition pushes schools to hire the most qualified applicants and to be more aggressive in pushing teachers to perform better and in dismissing teachers who do not teach well. Schools not facing much competition would be free to pursue other considerations in hiring and to avoid potentially unpleasant retention decisions and serious monitoring.

Consider a job search framework in which firms differ in the extent to which they maximize profits (student outcomes such as achievement in the case of schools). Firms facing few competitive pressures in which management cannot capture residual profits would probably not place much emphasis on teacher quality in making personnel decisions. Rather, other aspects of teachers might play a more important role. If these other characteristics are not highly correlated with those related to instructional quality, the variance in instructional quality would be quite large. Firms facing substantial competitive pressures, on the other hand, would probably place much more emphasis on characteristics related to instructional quality. The variation in quality at each firm would be much smaller as management attempted to hire and retain the best staff possible given the level of compensation.

Such factors suggest that quality variation within schools or districts in part reflects administrator commitment to instructional quality. Notice that schools with low salaries and poor working conditions will be likely to attract lower-quality teachers than other schools despite the best attempts of administrators. It is not that variance measures quality; rather, it is the case that the variance in instructional quality should decline the stronger the commitment to such quality.

The linkage between competition and the variance in teacher quality reflects two underlying assumptions. First, improving the quality of teachers is primarily achieved by hiring and retention decisions for teachers. Second, because of the incentives, average quality will not decline while a teaching force with a more homogeneous impact on student performance is selected.

If competition leads schools to concentrate on the hiring and retention of better teachers, the prior arguments suggest that the variance in teacher quality will also decline. However, teacher quality may also be raised by increased effort or an improvement in the skills of teachers through in-service training. Such skill or effort improvements have a more ambiguous effect on the within-school or -district variance in teacher quality, because the effect depends on where attention is focused or is most effective. Holding constant the distribution of teachers in a school, increases in the effort or skill (through training) of teachers initially at the lower end of the skill distribution would unambiguously reduce variance.[16] Moreover, as long as effort and skill are not negatively correlated, policies aimed at increasing effort at the bottom of the effort distribution would generally reduce the variance in teacher quality. On the other hand, if policies to increase effort or to provide effective in-service training were to exert larger impacts at the upper end of the initial skill distribution, the variance could be raised. We believe, based on past research of the inefficacy of teacher development programs and additional education, that there is more support for the teacher selection route than for the effort or development route as a way to increase teacher quality. Nonetheless, we cannot rule out that there is some potential for a lessened effect of competition on the variance in teacher performance to the extent that the latter approaches are employed, are effective, and have a larger impact at the top of the skill distribution.

Although it is possible that schools move to more homogeneous but lower quality with competition, this movement seems very unlikely in a system that also emphasizes accountability, as the Texas system does. Common conceptual models of school behavior, even those based on nonmaximizing approaches, would generally not support a lessened variance with a lower mean from competition.

The within-school variance in teacher quality, measured in terms of the student achievement distribution, is estimated from year-to-year changes in average student test score gains in grades five and six.[17] We hypothesize that teacher turnover should lead to greater variation in student performance differences among cohorts if there is less competition. This would result from the inferior personnel practices of schools facing little competition, which would increase both the variance of the quality of new hires and the variance of the quality of teachers retained following the probationary period. Of course, other factors that contribute to differences across cohorts might be systematically related to teacher turnover and competition, and we take a number of steps to control for such confounding influences.

The methodology and identifying assumptions are described in detail in Rivkin, Hanushek, and Kain (2001) and are only summarized here. Throughout, we look only at within-school variance in teacher quality and ignore any between-school variance. This approach, while giving a lower bound on teacher quality differences, avoids any possible contamination of family selection of schools. In order to sort out teacher quality effects from other things that might be changing within a school, we concentrate on the

16. This impact would be consistent with the focus of many in-service programs on remediation or improving basic teaching skills.

17. We concentrate on grade average achievement largely because the data do not permit us to link students with individual teachers, but also to avoid problems of within-grade sorting of students and teachers.

divergence of patterns of achievement gains across cohorts for each school. The idea behind the estimation is that the pattern of achievement gains across grades and cohorts of students within a school should remain constant (except for random noise) if differences among individual students are taken into account and if none of the characteristics of the school (teachers, principal, curriculum, etc.) change. When teachers change, however, variations in teacher quality will lead to a divergence of achievement patterns over time. We then relate systematic changes in teachers and in other aspects of schools to any changes in the pattern of achievement gains that are observed.

The basic framework regresses the between-cohort variance in school average test score gains on the proportion of teaching positions occupied by new people in successive years. The dependent variable generally analyzed is

(2) $$[(\Delta \overline{A}_{6s}^{c} - \Delta \overline{A}_{5s}^{c}) - (\Delta \overline{A}_{6s}^{c'} - \Delta \overline{A}_{5s}^{c'})]^2.$$

Each term in this expression involves the average growth in achievement (ΔA) for a given grade (five or six) and a given cohort (c or c') in a specific school (s). This measure focuses on the pattern of achievement changes and how it differs across cohorts. The term can be interpreted as the degree that achievement patterns diverge over time: If nothing changes in the grade pattern of achievement across cohorts, this term will be zero.

Intuitively, if teacher quality differences are important, high turnover of teachers should lead to more variation in teacher quality over time; this should show up in lack of persistence of student gains across cohorts.[18] To be precise, if no teachers in a school change and if the effectiveness of teachers is constant across adjacent years, teachers would add nothing to the divergence of achievement patterns across cohorts. On the other hand, if all of the teachers change and if teachers are randomly selected into schools, the divergence of achievement across cohorts would reflect the underlying variance in teacher quality. Our estimation strategy formalizes these notions and shows that there is a precise relationship between achievement changes as in equation (2) and the proportion of teachers who are different between years of observation (given the prior assumptions). In general, if the assumptions are violated, it would imply that we have underestimated the variation in achievement. In looking at the effects of competition, the most likely effect is that any effects of competition will be underestimated.[19]

To control for other influences on the variation in cohort performance,

18. Rivkin, Hanushek, and Kain (2001) show that the magnitude of the coefficient on teacher turnover has a simple interpretation. It equals four times the within-school variance in teacher quality.

19. The exception would be if the teacher development/effort models were dominant and if the cost-effective response of school districts is to emphasize the top of the existing distribution of teachers—something that we believe is unlikely.

the regressions also standardize for the inverse of the number of teachers in the grade,[20] the inverse of student enrollment, and a dummy variable for one of the cohort comparisons. We also restrict the sample to students who remain in the same school for both grades, effectively removing fixed student effects.[21] Some regressions also remove school or even school-by-grade fixed effects, identifying effects on competition by differences in the rate of teacher turnover between the 1993 and 1994 cohorts and the 1994 and 1995 cohorts.

Finally, we aggregate across the teachers and classrooms within each grade of each school. Aggregation overcomes what is possibly the largest form of selection within schools: that which occurs when parents maneuver their children toward specific, previously identified teachers or when principals pursue purposeful classroom placement policies. Looking at overall grade differences, which is equivalent to an instrumental variable estimator based on grade rather than classroom assignment, circumvents this within-grade teacher selection.

The new contribution of this work is the introduction of competition into the analysis in the form of an interaction between the proportion of teachers who are different and the Herfindahl index for the MSA. If competition works to reduce the within-school or within-district variance in teacher quality, the coefficient on the interaction term should be positive. (Because variation over time in the Herfindahl index is not used, the main effect of the index cannot be identified in the fixed effect specifications, so it is not included.)

The fact that districts exert substantial control over teacher hiring suggests that it is the competition between districts that should have the strongest influence on teacher quality. However, there are a number of reasons to believe that the competition should be measured at the school level. First, principals exert a great deal of control over hiring, retention, and monitoring; second, within-district variation in working conditions in the absence of flexible salaries could lead to substantial variation in quality; and, third, on the practical side, the methodology depends on variation in the proportion of new teachers divided by the number of teachers. In districts with many teachers, high values of the denominator overwhelm any variation in teacher turnover, and it may preclude detecting the effects of variations in quality. Nevertheless, for completeness, the empirical analysis measures competition at both the school and district level.

20. The proportion of teachers who are different must be divided by the number of teachers in a school because of the aggregation to grade averages. The total within-school variance in teacher quality includes not only variation across grades but also variation within grades. The variance of grade averages equals the total variance divided by the number of teachers per grade as long as the hiring process is identical for adjacent cohorts and grades.

21. Some specifications (not reported here) include controls for new principals and new superintendents. Each may directly affect the variation in achievement and be correlated with teacher turnover. However, the results are quite insensitive to the inclusion of these variables.

It is important to note that extensive teacher sorting among schools and districts on the basis of teacher quality could make it difficult to disentangle any behavioral effects of additional competition from a reduction in the average metropolitan area within-school variance in teacher quality that followed structurally from reducing teacher concentration in schools or districts. Compare the cases of three equally sized districts and four equally sized districts where teachers are sorted into a perfect quality hierarchy across districts. If teachers are drawn from the same initial distribution in both areas, the additional district will mechanically lead to smaller within-school variance. However, evidence from Rivkin, Hanushek, and Kain (2001) suggests that sorting of teachers on the basis of quality may in fact be quite limited in many areas. Work by Ballou (1996) and Ballou and Podgursky (1997) documents teacher hiring practices in which applicant skill does not play a primary role. Moreover, we have very little information about the nature of the teacher quality pool, but one would expect competitive pressures to change the hiring practices regarding where teachers are drawn from the overall distribution of skills in the labor market.

Nevertheless, the possibility remains that a lower Herfindahl index may be associated with more extensive sorting without inducing a behavioral change. In an effort to address this issue, we divide metropolitan areas up into separate school markets on the basis of student income, under the assumption that an expansion in the number of wealthy districts, while permitting increased teacher sorting, does not effectively increase the number of choices for poor children and vice versa. A finding that income-specific competition measures are more strongly related to the within-school variance in teacher quality than the overall competition measure would support the belief that competition induces a behavioral response.

Results

Tables 1.4 and 1.5 report the main results on the effects on variations in teacher quality of school and district competition, respectively.[22] The focus of attention is the interaction of the proportion of different teachers and the Herfindahl index. The main effect for the within-school variance in teacher quality is the proportion of different teachers divided by the number of teachers, and the interaction term identifies how the variance in teacher quality is affected by different degrees of competition within metropolitan areas. Consistent with expectations, the estimates in table 1.4 using school-level competition are much more precise. No interaction coefficients using district competition are significant even at the 10 percent level.

The school competition results support the hypothesis that competition raises school quality through its effect on teacher personnel practices. All

22. The sample is restricted to schools with at least ten students in a grade, and the results are somewhat sensitive to this assumption.

Table 1.4   Estimated Effect of Math Teacher Turnover on the Squared Difference in School Average Test Score Gains Between Cohorts (absolute value of *t*-statistics in parentheses)

	No Fixed Effects	School Fixed Effects	School-by-Grade Fixed Effects
% math teachers different/# teachers	0.013	0.036	0.039
	(0.85)	(2.58)	(1.46)
% different/# teachers · school	1.35	1.18	2.05
Herfindahl Index	(2.60)	(2.38)	(2.01)
N	1,140	1,140	1,140

Notes: See text and Rivkin, Hanushek, and Kain (2001) for a description of the specification and estimation approach. All regressions control for the inverse of student enrollment and restrict the sample to students remaining in the same school.

Table 1.5   Estimated Effect of Math Teacher Turnover on the Squared Difference in District Average Test Score Gains between Cohorts (absolute value of *t*-statistics in parentheses)

	No Fixed Effects	School Fixed Effects	School-by-Grade Fixed Effects
% math teachers different/# teachers	−0.040	−0.030	0.100
	(1.55)	(1.38)	(1.91)
% different/# teachers · school	0.11	0.06	−0.28
Herfindahl Index	(1.25)	(0.93)	(1.56)
N	832	832	832

Notes: See notes to table 1.4.

interaction terms are positive and significant at the 5 percent level, even in the specification that includes school-by-grade fixed effects. In other words, less competition leads to a larger within-school variance in teacher quality. The magnitude of the interaction coefficients in the fixed effects model suggests that a one standard deviation increase in the degree of competition (a 0.02 point decline in the Herfindahl index) would reduce the within-school variance of teacher quality by roughly 0.09 standard deviations in the teacher quality distribution.

Although this effect size might appear small, it is in fact large relative to that of measured inputs such as class size. Rivkin, Hanushek, and Kain (2001) find that a one standard deviation reduction in class size (roughly three students per class) would lead to an increase in achievement of 0.02 of a standard deviation. In other words, effect sizes for class size reduction are between one-fourth and one-fifth as large as the effect size for competition and teacher quality.

Importantly, a metropolitan area-wide variable may provide a noisy measure of competition for most students and be susceptible to the structural problems described earlier. Although the estimation cannot be easily divided in terms of individual high- and low-income students, it is nevertheless informative to focus on schools serving a large proportion of low-income students and those serving a small proportion. Therefore we divide the sample into schools in which at least 75 percent of students are eligible for a subsidized lunch and those in which fewer than 25 percent are so eligible (the middle category is excluded) and compute two Herfindahl indexes for each metropolitan area.

Table 1.6 reports the results for these two samples of schools. The results suggest that public school competition is much more important for lower-income students, for whom the interaction coefficients are positive and strongly significant. In contrast, the estimates for schools with very few lower-income students are small and statistically insignificant. To the extent that private school alternatives are much more relevant and place much more pressure on schools serving middle- and upper-middle-class students, this result is not altogether surprising, and it is consistent with the belief that the observed effects capture a behavioral response. At the very least, more should be learned about competition effects for lower-income and minority students, because most of the large urban districts in the country serve increasingly lower income populations.

In summary, these results provide support for the notion that competition affects teacher quality. Importantly, the inferences drawn about quality from estimates of effects on within-school variance rest upon the assumption that administrators do not systematically act to ensure the highest quality of teaching possible. Evidence from Ballou and Podgursky (1995) and Ballou (1996) of school hiring decisions not driven primarily by applicant quality supports the view that there is a great deal of slack in the hiring process. Moreover, the small number of teachers released on the ba-

Table 1.6   Estimated Effect of Math Teacher Turnover on the Squared Difference in School Average Test Score Gains between Cohorts, by School Demographics (absolute value of *t*-statistics in parentheses)

	Schools with >75% Eligible for Subsidized Lunch			Schools with <25% Eligible for Subsidized Lunch		
	No Fixed Effects	School Fixed Effects	School-by-Grade Fixed Effects	No Fixed Effects	School Fixed Effects	School-by-Grade Fixed Effects
% math teachers different/	0.006	0.044	0.060	0.110	0.053	0.056
# teachers	(0.23)	(1.61)	(1.15)	(2.90)	(1.55)	(0.94)
% different/# teachers · school	1.15	0.97	1.19	–0.18	–0.08	0.06
Herfindahl Index	(2.50)	(3.71)	(2.11)	(1.07)	(0.55)	(0.21)
N	306	306	306	272	272	272

Notes: See notes to table 1.4.

sis of poor performance and anecdotal evidence of weak efforts by many teachers are consistent with lax monitoring procedures.

On the other hand, the positive coefficient on the interaction term could reflect the fact that schools in more competitive metropolitan areas hire more systematically but not any better than others—that is, that they hire more similar teachers but not ones of higher quality. Because it is not possible to identify the part of the variation in which the decline in variation is concentrated, statistical evidence cannot be brought to bear on this question. However, to the extent that alternative job opportunities tend to thin out or even truncate the right side of the distribution, it is quite likely that the reduction in variance occurs predominantly in the left tail. Moreover, there is little a priori reason to support the hypothesis that competition leads to more systematic but not necessarily any better personnel practices.

1.4 Conclusions

These results provide the first piece of evidence on the mechanisms through which competition may affect school quality; they suggest that more competition tends to increase teacher quality, particularly for schools serving predominantly lower-income students. Given the evidence that teacher quality is an important if not the primary determinant of school quality, a finding that competition was not related to the quality of teaching would have raised doubts about the strength of the link between competition and overall school quality.

Future work in this area should explore specific aspects of the teacher/management relationship such as hiring, tenure, and monitoring, as well as the effects of competition on the use of inputs and other aspects of school operations. Such information will provide a much better understanding of the processes that generate the observed link between competition and school quality. It is also relevant for efforts to improve the existing public schools.

References

Abowd, John M., Francis Kramarz, and David N. Margolis. 1999. High wage workers and high wage firms. *Econometrica* 67 (2): 251–333.

Armor, David J. 1995. *Forced justice: School desegregation and the law.* New York: Oxford University Press.

Armor, David J., Patricia Conry-Oseguera, Millicent Cox, Niceima King, Lorraine McDonnell, Anthony Pascal, Edward Pauly, and Gail Zellman. 1976. *Analysis of the school preferred reading program in selected Los Angeles minority schools.* Santa Monica, Calif.: RAND Corporation.

Ballou, Dale. 1996. Do public schools hire the best applicants? *Quarterly Journal of Economics* 111 (1): 97–133.
Ballou, Dale, and Michael Podgursky. 1995. Recruiting smarter teachers. *Journal of Human Resources* 30 (2): 326–38.
————. 1997. *Teacher pay and teacher quality*. Kalamazoo, Mich.: W. E. Upjohn Institute for Employment Research.
Black, Sandra E. 1999. Do better schools matter? Parental valuation of elementary education. *Quarterly Journal of Economics* 114 (2): 577–99.
Borland, Melvin V., and Roy M. Howsen. 1992. Student academic achievement and the degree of market concentration in education. *Economics of Education Review* 11 (1): 31–39.
Burtless, Gary. 1996. *Does money matter? The effect of school resources on student achievement and adult success*. Washington, D.C.: Brookings Institution.
Coleman, James S., Thomas Hoffer, and Sally Kilgore. 1982. *High school achievement: Public, Catholic, and private schools compared*. N.Y.: Basic Books.
Grogger, Jeffrey, and Derek Neal. 2000. Further evidence on the effects of Catholic secondary schooling. In *Brookings-Wharton papers on urban affairs, 2000*, ed. William G. Gale and Janet Rothenberg Pack, 151–93. Washington, D.C.: Brookings Institution.
Hanushek, Eric A. 1971. Teacher characteristics and gains in student achievement: Estimation using micro data. *American Economic Review* 60 (2): 280–88.
————. 1986. The economics of schooling: Production and efficiency in public schools. *Journal of Economic Literature* 24 (3): 1141–77.
————. 1992. The trade-off between child quantity and quality. *Journal of Political Economy* 100 (1): 84–117.
————. 1997. Assessing the effects of school resources on student performance: An update. *Educational Evaluation and Policy Analysis* 19 (2): 141–64.
Hanushek, Eric A., John F. Kain, Jacob M. Markman, and Steven G. Rivkin. Forthcoming. Does peer ability affect student achievement? *Journal of Applied Econometrics*.
Hanushek, Eric A., John F. Kain, and Steve G. Rivkin. 2001a. Disruption versus Tiebout improvement: The costs and benefits of switching schools. NBER Working Paper no. 8479. Cambridge, Mass.: National Bureau of Economic Research, September.
————. 2001b. Why public schools lose teachers. NBER Working Paper no. 8599. Cambridge, Mass.: National Bureau of Economic Research, November.
————. 2002. New evidence about *Brown v. Board of Education:* The complex effects of school racial composition on achievement. NBER Working Paper no. 8741. Cambridge, Mass.: National Bureau of Economic Research, January.
Hoxby, Caroline Minter. 1994. Do private schools provide competition for public schools? NBER Working Paper no. 4978. Cambridge, Mass.: National Bureau of Economic Research, December.
————. 2000. Does competition among public schools benefit students and taxpayers? *American Economic Review* 90 (5): 1209–38.
Murnane, Richard J. 1975. *Impact of school resources on the learning of inner city children*. Cambridge, Mass.: Ballinger.
Murnane, Richard J., and Barbara Phillips. 1981. What do effective teachers of inner-city children have in common? *Social Science Research* 10 (1): 83–100.
Neal, Derek. 1998. What have we learned about the benefits of private schooling? Federal Reserve Bank of New York *Economic Policy Review* 4 (March): 79–86.
Rivkin, Steven G., Eric A. Hanushek, and John F. Kain. 2001. Teachers, schools,

and academic achievement. NBER Working Paper no. 6691 (revised). Cambridge, Mass.: National Bureau of Economic Research.

Tiebout, Charles M. 1956. A pure theory of local expenditures. *Journal of Political Economy* 64 (October): 416–24.

Weimer, David L., and Michael J. Wolkoff. 2001. School performance and housing values: Using noncontiguous district and incorporation boundaries to identify school effects. *National Tax Journal* 54 (2): 231–53.

Can School Choice and School Accountability Successfully Coexist?

David N. Figlio and Marianne E. Page

2.1 Introduction

Education is currently at the forefront of the nation's political agenda: Everyone, regardless of political persuasion, wants to see an improvement in American schools' performance. Everyone does not support an increase in governments' (federal, state, or local) education budgets, however. In the current climate, in which many state and local governments face financial constraints but many voters are demanding tangible evidence of school improvement, policies that increase school choice through the use of vouchers have become increasingly popular.

Many economists find vouchers appealing because they increase schooling options for families whose choices might otherwise be constrained (by low incomes, job location, residential segregation, etc.). If parents are well informed then vouchers will increase efficiency by increasing families' abilities to sort into optimal schools. At the same time, vouchers are expected to improve average school quality by increasing competition among schools. When a student uses a voucher to attend a private school, the local public school's funding is decreased by the amount of the voucher, and this threat of budget cuts will provide schools with an incentive to improve. The larger the number of voucher-eligible students in a school, the more incentive the school has to improve performance.

Recent voucher proposals have also been justified on the grounds that students should be provided a means of exiting low-quality schools so that they do not experience failure. A voucher program built around this prem-

David N. Figlio is the Walter Matherly Professor of Economics at the University of Florida and a faculty research fellow of the National Bureau of Economic Research. Marianne E. Page is assistant professor of economics at the University of California, Davis.

ise would provide vouchers to all students attending a low-performing school regardless of whether they are economically constrained. Economists are typically less comfortable with this type of program because (a) it suggests that the state is better than parents at assessing school quality, and (b) it is unclear why vouchers would lead to better schooling choices among parents who are not liquidity constrained yet voluntarily select low-quality schools. An advantage of this type of program, however, is that failing schools face the prospect of losing all of their students (not just the economically disadvantaged ones), which presumably provides a strong incentive to improve.

School accountability is an alternative policy that aims to improve school quality without increasing costs. Accountability systems reward and punish schools by allocating funding according to whether the school meets certain performance criteria. When vouchers are targeted toward economically disadvantaged children, the performance measures created by an accountability system provide information that helps parents optimize. Many states have some form of school choice that coexists with a system of grading schools.[1] Currently popular, however, is the idea of integrating school choice and accountability so that students attending schools that the state has identified as failing have the option of moving elsewhere. Florida has recently adopted an integrated accountability/voucher program, and President Bush proposed such an initiative as part of his national accountability-based education plan. Although private school vouchers are excluded from the federal law that eventually passed, the No Child Left Behind Act of 2001 integrates increased public school choice into a national school accountability system.

The purpose of this paper is to identify which students would be eligible for a voucher under different types of voucher programs. We use data from the state of Florida and pay particular attention to the distributional impact of vouchers targeted toward disadvantaged students versus the distributional impact of vouchers targeted toward students attending low-performing schools. Although at first one might expect these two types of targeting schemes to reach approximately the same students, in fact the extent to which this is true will depend on the distribution of children across schools and on the way in which a school's performance is measured. As we will discuss in the next two sections, there are many different ways of evaluating a school's performance. Our results suggest that the performance criteria that may seem most appropriate from an accountability perspective may not do the best job of targeting economically and socially disadvantaged children. In fact, a voucher system that uses value-added measures of performance to determine voucher awards may do little better in achieving this goal than a system that randomly assigns vouchers. Thus, although

---

1. States include Arizona, California, Minnesota, Michigan, and North Carolina.

vouchers and accountability programs have similar goals, economists' justifications for vouchers may be undermined when vouchers are integrated with accountability.

In the remainder of this paper we describe our data and the voucher program in Florida. We then compare the stratification effects of targeting vouchers using family income to the stratification effects of targeting vouchers using school characteristics, including the types of performance measures being adopted in Florida and proposed by President Bush. In the final section, we discuss our results' implications.

2.2   Vouchers and Accountability in Florida

Our eligibility simulations are based on aggregated student-level data provided by the state of Florida's Department of Education for the 1998–1999 and 1999–2000 school years. The data include information on every public school student's race or ethnicity, test scores, free or reduced-price lunch eligibility, and school attended. Florida is one of the only states that has collected detailed enough information for our project to be pursued. An advantage of using these data is that our simulations can speak directly to the one state that currently has an integrated voucher/accountability program. Our findings will be relevant beyond Florida, however. The idea of imbedding a voucher program within an accountability system is attractive to many state legislators and has been proposed by President Bush. Although the magnitude of the effects will differ across states depending on the distribution of students across schools and the degree to which accountability and vouchers are linked, the general patterns should be the same.[2]

2.2.1   Overview of the Florida Program

School accountability in Florida is based on student performance on the Florida Comprehensive Assessment Test (FCAT). Students in Florida are given reading examinations and the Florida Writes! exam in fourth, eighth, and tenth grade, and they are given mathematics examinations in fifth, eighth, and tenth grade. Test scores are then converted into a five- or six-point scale, which is used to assign a letter grade ranging from "A" through "F." In order to attain a "C" grade, at least 60 percent of the school's test-takers must achieve at level two or above (on the five-point scale) in reading

2. The generalizability of our results rests largely on whether low-income and minority students are similarly distributed across schools in other states. We used the 1996–97 *Common Core of Data* to look at how the distribution of students in Florida compared to the distribution of students in California and Texas (since these are two large states). Minorities in California and Texas are more concentrated than in Florida. For example, in California, 75 percent of minorities attend schools that are at least 58 percent minority, in Texas 75 percent of minorities attend schools that are at least 52 percent minority, and in Florida 75 percent of minorities attend schools that are at least 37 percent minority. Similar, although less dramatic, patterns exist with respect to the concentration of poverty.

and math, and at least 50 percent of test-takers must achieve at level three or above (on a six-point scale) on the Florida Writes! examination.[3] If a school misses one or two of these thresholds it receives a grade of "D." If it misses all three of these thresholds it receives a grade of "F." The first assignment of school letter grades occurred in May 1999, and about 8 percent of schools receiving grades[4] earned grades of "A," whereas 13, 51, and 25 percent received grades of "B," "C," and "D," respectively. Just over 3 percent of schools were graded "F."[5]

Letter grades affect schools on both ends of the spectrum: Those who receive an "A" grade, or who increase their letter grades from one year to the next, are eligible to receive an additional $100 per pupil. On the other hand, students attending schools that are rated "F" in two years out of four are eligible for "opportunity scholarships" that can be used to attend private school or nearby public schools with ratings of "C" or higher. Students who choose to transfer may remain in their school of choice until the terminal grade of that school, regardless of whether their initial school improves in subsequent years. Although the Florida plan currently bases school grades, and, thus, voucher eligibility, on aggregate levels of test performance, its architects viewed level test scores as only an interim metric for grading performance. The accountability law requires that by the 2002–03 academic year school grades be based, at least in part, on value added measures of student performance. President Bush's proposal also relied on value added performance measures to determine voucher eligibility. Although the specific nature of value added school assessment is still under deliberation in Florida, it is clear that school grades will soon be based in large measure on features other than levels of aggregate student performance.

Florida's grading system is complicated, but when schools are ranked using these grading criteria, their ordering is very similar to the ordering that emerges if average math performance or average reading performance is used to order schools instead. The correlation between a school's ranking determined using Florida's current criteria and a school's ranking based on average test scores is about 0.95. On the other hand, correlations between school rankings that are based on single-year measures of school performance and the rankings that emerge when within-cohort test score growth (value added) is used instead are close to zero.[6] These low correlations in

3. These levels were determined by the Florida Department of Education, based on expert opinion on how well students satisfied the "Sunshine State Standards" for the appropriate grade.
4. Schools did not receive letter grades if their tested cohorts were sufficiently small.
5. "A" and "B" grades in Florida are based on cross-cohort changes in test scores, as well as differences in attendance, suspension, and test-taking rates.
6. The correlation between a school's position based on its average reading score in a particular year and its rank when ordering is based on within-cohort changes in average reading scores from one year to the next, for example, is only 0.05. Currently, we can only make this comparison using reading test scores because 1999–2000 was the first year that the state tested

turn hint that when vouchers are embedded within an accountability system, the types of students who qualify for vouchers may vary a great deal with the type of performance measure that is used. The purpose of the next section is to determine how important the choice of performance criteria is.

2.3   Who Is Eligible for a Targeted Voucher?

We begin by looking at the socioeconomic composition of the choice-eligible population when voucher eligibility is determined using school-level attributes. Next, we turn our attention toward understanding the ramifications of school-based accountability/voucher systems. In all of the simulations we assume that the amount of the school voucher would remain the same as it currently is in Florida—that is, full payment of tuition and fees by the student's private school of choice. Eligibility is, of course, not affected by this assumption, although take-up rates will strongly depend on the amount of the voucher.

As a point of comparison, the first column of table 2.1 provides information about the demographic characteristics of the student population in Florida. This column tells us that if vouchers were made universally available, then approximately 26 percent of recipients would be black, 18 percent would be Hispanic, and 44 percent would be eligible for a free lunch. We have standardized Florida's test scores, so the average test score for the sample is close to zero.[7]

2.3.1   Voucher Eligibility Based on Socioeconomic Status

Although universal vouchers have been proposed by some policymakers (indeed, California's recent voucher initiative would have made vouchers available to all students), those programs that are actually implemented are likely to be targeted toward specific subsets of the student population. Milwaukee's voucher program is probably the best known, and so our first step

---

in every grade from three through ten. Therefore, although we could construct a student-level test score change in reading from grade four to grade five this year, we have to wait until next year before a similar exercise can be conducted in mathematics, because historically, reading has been tested in fourth grade and mathematics in fifth grade. None of the rankings that emerge using different performance measures are very correlated with school spending at the district level. Using expenditures reported by the Florida Department of Education for 1998–99, we find a correlation between per-pupil district spending and a school's average reading score of –0.14. We estimate the same correlation between per-pupil district spending and a school's average math score. This result is unsurprising given that higher-spending districts tend to be located in urban areas, where costs are higher. Correlations between per-pupil expenditures and any of the value added measures we use in this paper range from 0.01 to 0.06. It should be noted, however, that relative to many states Florida has a flat spending distribution. The 95:5 ratio in spending is only 1.2.

7. The mean is not precisely zero because a small number of eligible test-takers are not part of the accountability system (because of small school size) but were still used to standardize the test for basis of comparison. The decision to include or exclude these test-takers from the standardization makes no difference for the results presented in this paper.

Table 2.1   Characteristics of Voucher-Eligible Students in Various Simulations: Voucher Based on Socioeconomic Status of School or Neighborhood

Characteristics of Voucher-Eligible Students	Universal Voucher (1)	Voucher Given to All Free Lunch Eligibles (2)	Voucher Given to All Free/Reduced Lunch Eligibles (3)	Voucher Based on Socioeconomic Status of Students in School (4)				
				2	5	10	20	44
Voucher coverage (%)	100	44	53	2	5	10	20	44
% black	25.5	34.5	32.7	69.4	68.6	65.2	58.6	41.8
% Hispanic	18.0	21.2	20.8	27.1	26.4	26.7	26.8	24.6
% free lunch eligible	44.2	100.0	82.6	94.5	91.5	87.0	80.6	67.9
% residing in high poverty neighborhood	25.3	41.1	38.1	95.7	93.8	91.0	85.6	55.7
Standardized reading test score, fourth grade (2000)	0.02	−0.69	−0.58	−1.97	−1.75	−1.45	−1.17	−0.72
Standardized math test score, fifth grade (2000)	0.05	−0.64	−0.55	−1.66	−1.52	−1.29	−1.02	−0.64

Notes: Each column represents a different voucher simulation: one in which a voucher is given to all students (column [1]); one in which a voucher is given to all free lunch eligible students, regardless of school performance (column [2]); one in which a voucher is given to all free or reduced price lunch eligible students (column [3]); and five scenarios in which vouchers are given to all students in schools with the 2 percent (column [4]), 5 percent (column [5]), 10 percent (column [6]), 20 percent (column [7]), or 44 percent (column [8]) highest poverty rates (measured as the fraction of students who qualify for a free lunch). Each row represents a different attribute of the students receiving vouchers in each situation.

is to replicate the eligibility criterion used in that program. In Milwaukee, students with family incomes below 175 percent of the poverty line are eligible to receive a voucher. We do not have explicit information on students' income, but we can look at how stratification is affected when vouchers are targeted to students who are eligible for free or reduced-price lunches. The income cutoffs for free and reduced-price lunch eligibility are close to Milwaukee's threshold: The free lunch eligibility cutoff is 130 percent of the poverty line, and the reduced-price lunch threshold is 185 percent of the poverty line.

The second two columns in table 2.1 present the characteristics of students eligible for free (or free and reduced-price) lunches in Florida. If every free lunch–eligible student were to receive a voucher, then 44 percent of the state's student body would be voucher-eligible. If the eligibility threshold were increased to include students eligible for reduced-price lunches, coverage would rise to 53 percent. Free lunch–eligible students are disproportionately minorities (primarily black) and disproportionately reside in low-income neighborhoods.[8] By definition, all of these students have low incomes. In addition, because low-income students in Florida, as in the rest of the country, tend to have lower test scores than high-income students, the average test score of the voucher-eligible population would be around six-tenths of a standard deviation below the state mean.

It is important to remember that in practice no voucher programs have targeted such a high fraction of students. In Milwaukee, for example, roughly half of the students are eligible, but only 15 percent are allowed to participate. Voucher assignment in Milwaukee is determined by lottery. If recipients in Florida were to be randomly selected from the income-eligible population, then although the number of served students would be lower than 44 percent, the distribution of their characteristics would still look much as it does in column (2).

If poverty is highly concentrated, then a disadvantage of targeting vouchers according to family income is that they may not increase competition among very many schools. As in the rest of the country, poverty in Florida is not evenly distributed across schools, but providing vouchers to every free lunch–eligible student could still significantly affect the level of resources available to schools. Fourteen percent of Florida's elementary schools have 75 percent or more students eligible for free lunches, and 44 percent of schools are at least half free lunch eligible. If voucher recipients were drawn at random from the eligible population (as in Milwaukee), then a smaller number of students would ultimately receive a voucher, and competition would be lessened.

An alternative method of delivering vouchers to disadvantaged students

8. We define a low-income neighborhood as a zip code ranking in the top quarter statewide (weighted by school-aged population) of percentage of children in poverty.

is to base voucher eligibility on the poverty status of the school to which they are assigned. The fourth through eighth columns of table 2.1 offer the demographic characteristics of students who would be eligible for vouchers under such a program. In these cases, and all subsequent cases, we assume that vouchers are distributed to everyone in a school, so each affected school would face the prospect of losing its entire student body. We rank schools according to the fraction of their students who qualify for a free lunch, and then we present four scenarios in which increasing numbers of students qualify. In column (4), for example, we show the demographic composition of the voucher-eligible population if the two percent of children attending the poorest schools were made eligible. This column shows that under such a plan, 69 percent of qualifying students would be black, 95 percent would be eligible for a free lunch, and the average test score among those students would be almost two standard deviations below the population mean.

Moving across the next four columns, we see the impact of providing coverage for larger fractions of the student population, who are attending increasingly affluent schools. As children attending schools with lower fractions of poor students become eligible, the recipient population is less likely to be poor and black, and the average recipient's test score increases. When students attending the bottom fifth of schools are eligible, the average reading score of the choice students is a full standard deviation above the average reading score of the students attending the bottom 2 percent of schools. Average math scores are nearly two-thirds of a standard deviation higher. These results confirm that black students are disproportionately located in low-income schools and that test scores and income are negatively correlated, facts that are well established. It is interesting to note that changing the income criteria and allowing more students to qualify has little impact on the fraction of the eligible population that is Hispanic. This suggests that Hispanics are more evenly distributed across school attendance areas than are blacks, although the difference in Hispanic representation between the first and second columns still indicates that they are somewhat concentrated in poor schools.

In the eighth column of table 2.1 we present the characteristics of students who would be choice eligible if the 44 percent of students attending the lowest-income schools were provided with a voucher. We include these results in order to provide a direct comparison with the student-based voucher scheme presented in column (2). This column indicates that, relative to using eligibility criteria that are based on student income levels, school-based eligibility criteria are much less efficient at targeting low-income children, at least when the fraction of students eligible for a voucher is sufficiently high. Whereas all of the children who receive vouchers under the student-based system have low incomes, only 68 percent of the students who receive vouchers under the school-based system have low incomes.

Conversely, the school-based criterion produces a choice-eligible population that has a higher representation of minorities. The higher representation of minorities is exactly what one would expect, given that high-income blacks and Hispanics are more likely to live in poor neighborhoods than high-income whites or Anglos. The average test scores of the targeted students are remarkably similar under both eligibility schemes.

A comparison of columns (2) and (5) is more appropriate if vouchers are randomly assigned to 5 percent of students (from among the income-eligible population). Here we see that student-based assignment would serve significantly fewer minorities and that average test score performance of the recipients would be substantially higher. To the extent that the voucher population is nonrandomly selected from the eligible population (as would be expected if eligible individuals need to apply for vouchers[9]), differences between the two schemes would be more dramatic. Of course, a student-based program that targeted the 5 percent of students with the lowest incomes would undoubtedly produce stratification effects more similar to those presented in the fifth column.

2.3.2   Tying Voucher Eligibility to School Accountability

Voucher programs that are embedded within an accountability system base eligibility on school test performance, rather than on individual or school-level demographic characteristics. This section investigates the characteristics of children who are eligible for school vouchers when eligibility is determined by school performance. We consider several different ways of evaluating schools: Some performance measures are based on test score levels, some are based on test score levels adjusted for demographic characteristics, and some are based on value-added test scores. All of the performance measures we present are based on reading tests. Our results are trivially affected by the use of math scores, or combinations of math and reading scores that emulate Florida's program.[10]

The first type of performance measure that we consider is the school's average test score in a single year. We rank schools according to their average test score on the fourth grade FCAT reading test, and as in table 2.1 we choose eligibility cutoffs according to whether choice is to be made available to 2, 5, 10, or 20 percent of the population. Schools can also be ranked (and vouchers allocated) according to the fraction of students who attain a particular competency level. This performance measure is closer to Florida's current school grading system.

A problem with these two measures is that they may penalize schools that serve disadvantaged communities, since disadvantaged students do not typ-

---

9. The available evidence on voucher experiments such as Milwaukee's suggests that this may be the case.
10. Results based on the other performance measures are available from the authors.

ically perform as well on exams as their more advantaged peers. If the aim of vouchers is to give choice to students attending poorly performing schools, then it may be more appropriate to measure schools' success using test scores that take differences in student composition into account. Therefore, we also consider the ramifications of a system that bases eligibility on the school's average test score after controlling for its demographic and income composition.[11] An alternative to regression-adjusting test scores for the purposes of controlling for student body characteristics is to use value added test scores. Two types of value added constructs are generally considered in policy discussions of accountability systems: measures of value added constructed from changes in test scores from one cohort to the next (within grade changes). As with the regression-adjusted levels method, value added test scores net out school demographics, which may be a more appropriate way of measuring schools' effectiveness. Value added test scores are also popular because they are perceived to reward and punish schools according to improvements or declines in quality over time.[12]

2.3.3   Voucher Eligibility under Different Accountability Systems

The next four tables show how the population of voucher-eligible students varies with the parameters of the accountability system. Each row in tables 2.2–2.5 represents a different method of rating schools, and the columns indicate the size of the program (extending eligibility from 2 percent to 20 percent of the state's student population). Each table presents the results for a different sociodemographic characteristic of the population: Table 2.2 reports the fraction of voucher-eligible students who are free lunch–eligible under each scheme, table 2.3 reports the average standardized reading test score of voucher-eligible students, table 2.4 presents the fraction of voucher-eligible students who are black, and table 2.5 presents the fraction of voucher-eligible students who are Hispanic.

As table 2.2 makes clear, the socioeconomic composition of voucher-eligible students varies dramatically across the different accountability systems. When 2 percent of the population is made voucher eligible, the fraction of eligibles who are also able to receive free lunch ranges from 44 percent to 89 percent, depending on which performance measure is used. As the fraction of the population eligible for vouchers increases, the demographic variation across accountability systems falls somewhat, but even when 20 percent of students are eligible the difference across the systems is

11. An alternative, but very similar, approach involves regression-adjusting the school ranking based on the fraction of the school's student body attaining some particular threshold of achievement.
12. Several authors have pointed out technical challenges associated with using test scores for the purpose of school accountability and with constructing value added measures of school productivity. See, for example, Clotfelter and Ladd (1996), Koretz (1996), Ladd and Walsh (2002), Ladd (2001), and Meyer (1996). Some of these issues are summarized in Ladd and Hansen (1999).

Table 2.2   **Percentage of Voucher-Eligible Students Who Are Free Lunch–Eligible under Different Accountability Scenarios**

Accountability System Basis of School Ranking	% of State's Student Body Eligible for a Voucher			
	2	5	10	20
Average performance on fourth-grade FCAT reading examination	88.6	86.2	80.3	73.8
% of students achieving at least minimum competency on FCAT reading examination	89.1	86.9	82.3	74.4
Average performance on fourth-grade FCAT reading examination, adjusted for racial/ethnic composition and socioeconomic status in school	44.6	49.0	49.8	47.9
% of students achieving at least minimum competency on FCAT reading examination, adjusted for racial/ethnic composition and socioeconomic status in school	48.3	54.5	51.4	49.5
Cross-cohort changes in the average performance on fourth-grade FCAT reading examination	52.4	49.4	51.8	46.4
Cross-cohort changes in the average performance on fourth-grade FCAT reading examination, adjusted for racial/ethnic composition and socioeconomic status in school	55.0	52.0	52.9	50.1
Within-cohort changes in performance on the FCAT reading examination, from fourth grade to fifth grade	60.6	57.1	53.6	49.8
Within-cohort changes in performance on the FCAT reading examination, from fourth grade to fifth grade, adjusted for racial/ethnic composition and socioeconomic status in school	57.7	55.8	50.3	47.0

Notes: The numbers in this table reflect the percentage of voucher-eligible students who would be free lunch–eligible in each of thirty-two different voucher plans. Each row represents a different targeting scheme, and each column represents a different level of voucher coverage.

substantial. The accountability systems based on level test performance provide vouchers to a much more disadvantaged population than do accountability systems based on regression-adjusted test score levels or value added.

The patterns are subtly different when students are stratified by their test performance. These results are shown in table 2.3. As with income status, the average standardized test score of voucher-eligible students increases with the fraction of students eligible to receive a voucher. This is not at all surprising, given that school grades are constructed using test scores. Also comparable to the results shown in table 2.2 is the finding that value added measures systematically produce a voucher-eligible population that has higher test scores. Unlike in table 2.2, however, in this case we observe that the more completely we control for school and student fixed effects, the

Table 2.3   **Average Standardized Reading Test Scores of Voucher-Eligible Students under Different Accountability Scenarios**

Accountability System Basis of School Ranking	% of State's Student Body Eligible for a Voucher			
	2	5	10	20
Average performance on fourth-grade FCAT reading examination	−2.69	−2.21	−1.84	−1.41
% of students achieving at least minimum competency on FCAT reading examination	−2.59	−2.18	−1.80	−1.37
Average performance on fourth-grade FCAT reading examination, adjusted for racial/ethnic composition and socioeconomic status in school	−1.55	−1.36	−1.16	−0.82
% of students achieving at least minimum competency on FCAT reading examination, adjusted for racial/ethnic composition and socioeconomic status in school	−1.61	−1.45	−1.12	−0.84
Cross-cohort changes in the average performance on fourth-grade FCAT reading examination	−0.99	−0.66	−0.65	−0.41
Cross-cohort changes in the average performance on fourth-grade FCAT reading examination, adjusted for racial/ethnic composition and socioeconomic status in school	−1.07	−0.72	−0.69	−0.52
Within-cohort changes in performance on the FCAT reading examination, from fourth grade to fifth grade	−0.31	−0.20	−0.18	−0.11
Within-cohort changes in performance on the FCAT reading examination, from fourth grade to fifth grade, adjusted for racial/ethnic composition and socioeconomic status in school	−0.17	−0.16	−0.07	−0.02

Notes: The numbers in this table reflect the average standardized reading score of voucher-eligible students in each of thirty-two different voucher plans. Each row represents a different targeting scheme, and each column represents a different level of voucher coverage.

higher-performing are the resulting voucher-eligible students. Accountability systems that use each student as his or her own control (the within-cohort models) lead to a group of voucher-eligible students who perform at nearly the same level as the overall population, whereas those that control for only a few background characteristics lead to a group of voucher-eligible students who are substantially higher performing than those controlling for no background characteristics.

Tables 2.4 and 2.5 present the results for race and ethnicity. We find that the patterns in table 2.4, reflecting the percentage of voucher-eligible students who are black, closely mirror the patterns reported in table 2.2. This is unsurprising given the high correlation between race and poverty status. The patterns in table 2.5 are different, however, and do not show a substantial relationship between the construct of the accountability system and the

Table 2.4   **Percentage of Voucher-Eligible Students Who Are African-American under Different Accountability Scenarios**

Accountability System Basis of School Ranking	% of State's Student Body Eligible for a Voucher			
	2	5	10	20
Average performance on fourth-grade FCAT reading examination	71.0	67.6	59.1	51.4
% of students achieving at least minimum competency on FCAT reading examination	74.7	75.2	63.3	53.9
Average performance on fourth-grade FCAT reading examination, adjusted for racial/ethnic composition and socioeconomic status in school	31.1	32.2	31.3	28.1
% of students achieving at least minimum competency on FCAT reading examination, adjusted for racial/ethnic composition and socioeconomic status in school	30.1	34.4	34.0	30.1
Cross-cohort changes in the average performance on fourth-grade FCAT reading examination	28.5	27.3	24.4	24.9
Cross-cohort changes in the average performance on fourth-grade FCAT reading examination, adjusted for racial/ethnic composition and socioeconomic status in school	38.0	34.0	31.4	28.1
Within-cohort changes in performance on the FCAT reading examination, from fourth grade to fifth grade	37.2	33.4	28.0	26.1
Within-cohort changes in performance on the FCAT reading examination, from fourth grade to fifth grade, adjusted for racial/ethnic composition and socioeconomic status in school	38.1	36.3	30.6	26.6

Notes: The numbers in this table reflect the percentage of voucher-eligible students who would be African American in each of thirty-two different voucher plans. Each row represents a different targeting scheme, and each column represents a different level of voucher coverage.

fraction of voucher-eligible students who are Hispanic. This finding is due to the fact that Florida's Hispanic students are considerably more affluent and less concentrated in particular schools than are Florida's black students.

Our finding that value added performance measures lead to a more advantaged voucher-eligible population is intuitive given that school quality and *changes* in school quality are not the same thing. In fact, ceiling effects are likely to produce a negative correlation between test score levels and test score changes: Schools with high average test scores in a particular year cannot experience large test score gains from one year to the next, whereas schools with low average test scores in a particular year have more room to move up. Furthermore, Kane and Staiger (2000) show that value added measures may be noisy signals of test score performance, leading to an ar-

Table 2.5   Percentage of Voucher-Eligible Students Who Are Hispanic under Different
                   Accountability Scenarios

Accountability System Basis of School Ranking	% of State's Student Body Eligible for a Voucher			
	2	5	10	20
Average performance on fourth-grade FCAT reading examination	21.9	26.0	28.7	29.2
% of students achieving at least minimum competency on FCAT reading examination	19.7	19.6	27.1	27.5
Average performance on fourth-grade FCAT reading examination, adjusted for racial/ethnic composition and socioeconomic status in school	14.6	19.6	20.7	18.9
% of students achieving at least minimum competency on FCAT reading examination, adjusted for racial/ethnic composition and socioeconomic status in school	18.5	20.4	18.0	18.9
Cross-cohort changes in the average performance on fourth-grade FCAT reading examination	29.6	26.6	31.7	24.3
Cross-cohort changes in the average performance on fourth-grade FCAT reading examination, adjusted for racial/ethnic composition and socioeconomic status in school	18.9	17.9	20.3	21.7
Within-cohort changes in performance on the FCAT reading examination, from fourth grade to fifth grade	24.3	24.9	28.0	24.4
Within-cohort changes in performance on the FCAT reading examination, from fourth grade to fifth grade, adjusted for racial/ethnic composition and socioeconomic status in school	17.5	17.7	18.8	20.1

Notes: The numbers in this table reflect the percentage of voucher-eligible students who would be Hispanic in each of thirty-two different voucher plans. Each row represents a different targeting scheme, and each column represents a different level of voucher coverage.

bitrary assignment of school grades. We find that the correlation between the 1999–2000 test score change and the 1998–1999 test score change is actually negative (–0.33), suggesting that value added measures are failing to pick up real changes in school quality.[13]

Kane and Staiger (2000) note that the noisiness of value added measures is a more serious problem for small schools because the set of students over

13. Our limited evidence also suggests that parents are able to tell the difference between the information provided by test score levels versus test score changes. Using data from the Gainesville, Florida metropolitan area and following the methodology used by Figlio and Lucas (2000), we find that level scores are more capitalized into housing prices than are value added test scores, even when student demographics are taken into account. Similarly, families in Gainesville request zoning exceptions to send their children to schools with high test score levels at five times the rate of those requesting zoning exceptions to send their children to schools with high value added.

which test scores are aggregated is smaller. Consistent with Kane and Staiger, we find that a one standard deviation reduction in school size is associated with a 0.15 standard deviation increase in the absolute difference between 1999–2000 value added and 1998–1999 value added. Kane and Staiger's findings, together with our own, suggest that although value added test scores may at first blush appear to be reasonable measures of school improvement, their use may actually undermine the goals of school accountability and vouchers.[14]

In summary, we observe considerable differences between the types of students who are eligible for vouchers when voucher eligibility is based on level test scores and the types of students eligible for vouchers when eligibility is based on "purer" measures of school performance. Voucher awards that are based on measures of school performance that do not take background characteristics into account tend to be better at targeting disadvantaged students than are voucher awards based on value added measures. We conclude that, in voucher systems tied to school accountability, there may be a disconnect between the appropriate ways of assessing schools for the purposes of accountability and the desire to provide additional choices to students who are arguably most constrained.[15]

2.4 Implications

Although many states were already considering school voucher programs and accountability systems, President Bush's education proposal has catapulted these school "fixes" into prime time. Even though only the

14. One solution proposed by Kane and Staiger is to use "filtered" test score estimates. Filtered estimates use past relationships between test scores to optimally construct summary performance measures. The summary measure includes weighted averages of current and past test scores in multiple subjects, with the weights varying by school size. We have constructed a crude filter by averaging both math and reading test scores over a two-year period (averaging a total of four test scores) and then ranking schools according to cross-cohort changes in this average. Our results differ very little from those shown in the fourth rows of tables 2.2–2.5. This suggests that although filtered estimates may do a better job of capturing true changes in school performance, using filtered estimates to target vouchers will not necessarily affect which types of individuals end up qualifying. In other words, even if changes in school performance can be measured accurately, using these changes to target vouchers will lead to a substantially different population of voucher eligibles than a system that provides vouchers to students in schools with low performance *levels*.

15. One might argue that sending a child to a low-performing school is evidence of constraint. For instance, high-income families with heavy debt loads may elect to send their children to low-performing schools despite their "observed" ability to select a higher-performing school. Although these families are surely less constrained than low-income households, this should serve as an important caveat to our assertion that the "purer" the accountability system, the least constrained are the households potentially offered vouchers in an embedded system. An alternative story would bias the conclusion in the other direction, however: If unconstrained households resettle in neighborhoods zoned for failing schools to take advantage of school vouchers, as has been predicted theoretically by Nechyba (2000), this could exacerbate the disconnect between the goals of school accountability and the goals of school choice described in the paper.

public school choice portion of the President's proposal became law, the struggle to improve school quality without increasing costs ensures that these programs will be at the top of legislators' agendas for the foreseeable future. It is likely that, as in Florida, new voucher programs will be developed within the context of accountability systems.

At first glance, it might seem appropriate for accountability systems and voucher initiatives to go hand in hand. Both types of plans have been proposed as a way of increasing school efficiency, and the rhetoric surrounding both accountability and voucher discussions has particularly focused on improving educational opportunities for America's most disadvantaged children. Our results suggest that a voucher program embedded within an accountability system could fail to achieve this latter goal, however.

This interpretation of our results depends on one's interpretation of what it means to be disadvantaged. Economists usually promote voucher programs on the grounds that they increase school choice among individuals whose mobility would otherwise be constrained. In these discussions, disadvantage is measured with the usual socioeconomic indicators (income and minority status) because these characteristics are thought to have a strong impact on an individual's ability to move. The measure of disadvantage that is inherent in an integrated voucher/accountability system, however, is whether the individual attends a poorly performing school. Because school test scores are so strongly correlated with the socioeconomic background of the student body, and because much of the difference in outcomes across student types can be attributed to family background, it makes sense to base accountability on measures of performance that net out socioeconomic factors or that measure growth in student test scores, rather than levels of test performance. When vouchers are targeted this way, however, the composition of choice-eligible children is vastly different.

One can make a case that the students most deserving of vouchers are those whose schools are doing the least to educate them, but there are several reasons we believe that such a targeting scheme will be less successful at helping the "truly" disadvantaged. First, because value added measures of school performance are noisy, vouchers allocated in this way may bypass many of the students attending the least effective schools in favor of those attending more effective schools. Second, ranking schools according to their performance net of socioeconomic characteristics necessarily ignores the possibility of peer effects. Although this may be appropriate for determining school performance, it could lead to an inaccurate assessment of which students are being schooled in the worst environments and, thus, who would most benefit from receiving a voucher.

Like most economists, our third argument against basing voucher eligibility on school effectiveness is that such a targeting scheme will be less successful at reaching the students whose schooling choices are constrained. Our results indicate that choice-eligible children are much less likely to come from low-income families when eligibility is determined according to school performance (when effectiveness is measured net of students' family background) than when it is determined using income criteria. If vouchers are provided to students who are already able to choose private schools but have elected not to, then they will accomplish very little.

Of course, important caveats accompany our interpretation of the simulations. Foremost is the obvious point that if Florida's distribution of student types across schools is atypical, then the eligibility differences that we have documented across targeting schemes may not be generalizable. In particular, the eligibility differences will be less dramatic if, in other states, low-income and minority students are more evenly distributed across schools. Our results may understate the stratification differences in states where students are more concentrated by race, ethnicity, and income, however, as they appear to be in California and Texas.[16]

Another important limitation to our study is that we do not have information on students' income level, only on whether they are free- or reduced-price lunch–eligible. Our results might look less dramatic if we were able to see how the entire income distribution of voucher eligibles was affected by the various targeting schemes. Nevertheless, our findings suggest that education policymakers should be very careful about articulating their goals when designing voucher programs that are part of an accountability system. In spite of their seemingly similar aims, it may be very difficult to achieve the goals of an accountability system and a voucher program in an integrated system.

References

Clotfelter, Charles, and Helen Ladd. 1996. Recognizing and rewarding success in public schools. In *Holding schools accountable: Performance-based reform in education*, ed. Helen Ladd, 23–64. Washington, D.C.: Brookings Institution.

Figlio, David, and Maurice Lucas. 2000. What's in a grade? School report cards and house prices. Working Paper no. 8019. Cambridge, Mass.: National Bureau of Economic Research, November.

16. Some evidence of this possibility is present in Florida. Broward and Miami-Dade Counties, two adjacent south Florida counties that have the largest student populations in the state, are starkly different in their concentrations of minorities and low-income students. Whereas Broward County's concentrations are about the same as the state as a whole, Miami-Dade's concentrations are much higher. The correlation between level test performance (in reading) and the one-cohort and two-cohort measures of value added in reading are, respectively, 0.16 and 0.12 in Broward County, and –0.22 and –0.01 in Miami-Dade County. Although this should not be taken as definitive evidence of our point, it corroborates the assertion that the effects we describe in this paper may be larger in places where minorities and low-income students are more concentrated in schools.

Kane, Thomas, and Douglas Staiger. 2000. Improving school accountability measures. Hoover Institution, Stanford University. Working Paper.
Koretz, Daniel. 1996. Using student assessments for educational accountability. In *Improving America's schools: The role of incentives*, 171–95. Washington, D.C.: Commission on Behavioral and Social Sciences and Education, National Research Council, National Academy Press.
Ladd, Helen. 2001. *School-based educational accountability systems: The promise and the pitfalls. National Tax Journal* 54 (2): 385–400.
Ladd, Helen, and Janet Hansen, ed. 1999. *Making money matter: Financing America's schools*. Washington, D.C.: National Academy Press.
Ladd, Helen, and Randall Walsh. 2002. Implementing value-added measures of school effectiveness: Getting the incentives right. *Economics of Education Review* 21 (1): 1–17.
Meyer, Robert. 1996. Value-added indicators of school performance. In *Improving America's schools: The role of incentives*, Commission on Behavioral and Social Sciences and Education, 197–223. Washington, D.C.: National Research Council, National Academy Press.
Nechyba, Thomas. 2000. Mobility, targeting, and private-school vouchers. *American Economic Review* 90:130–46.

The Role of Special Education in School Choice

Julie Berry Cullen and Steven G. Rivkin

3.1 Introduction

There are differing views of the impact of school choice programs on the distribution of student opportunity. Proponents claim that all students, both those who take advantage of choice and those who remain in their neighborhood schools, will benefit as schools improve in response to competitive pressures. Others fear that only the more advantaged and informed students will opt out to better schools, leaving the more disadvantaged students isolated in the worst schools with declining resources.

Among the students who may be left behind are special needs students. Students with disabilities are more costly to educate and may therefore encounter explicit or implicit barriers to attending choice schools. Also, high concentrations of special needs students may be a deterrent to other students deciding on schooling options. These considerations may lead some schools to adopt policies that discourage students with special needs from attending, thereby limiting the choices available to these students. Such concerns about the relative access and participation of students with disabilities overlap with concerns about low-income and minority students, although the degree of legal protection differs.

Julie Berry Cullen is assistant professor of economics at the University of Michigan and a faculty research fellow of the National Bureau of Economic Research. Steven G. Rivkin is professor of economics at Amherst College and a research associate of the National Bureau of Economic Research.

The authors would like to thank Caroline Hoxby, David Monk, Richard Murnane, Ben Scafidi, and participants in the NBER Economics of School Choice Conference for helpful comments and suggestions. The authors would also like to thank John Easton of the Consortium on Chicago School Research and the Chicago School Board for providing access to the Chicago Public Schools data and Brian Jacob for processing the data.

Since 1975, disabled students have been guaranteed a free and appropriate public education (FAPE) by the passage of the Education for all Handicapped Children Act (EHA) and its successor, the Individuals with Disabilities Education Act (IDEA). Prior to the passage of the legislation, a congressional investigation revealed that a majority of disabled students received inadequate educational services and at least one-third of severely disabled students were excluded altogether from public schools (Verstegen 1994). Now, nearly one in every eight students is classified as disabled and one in every five new dollars of per-pupil spending is dedicated to special education (Hanushek and Rivkin 1997). The costs associated with educating the typical disabled student are approximately 2.3 times those for nondisabled students, and this ratio can be as high as 30 for the most severely disabled (Moore et al. 1988; Chambers 1998). In order to support localities in providing the mandated services, the federal government and states provide on average 8 percent and 56 percent of the funding, respectively.

This chapter considers the impact of expanded school choice on the quality of special education services, on the size and composition of the special education sector, and on the distribution of students with disabilities among schools and districts. The crucial role played by the structure of special education funding in the determination of each of these outcomes is highlighted throughout the chapter. The tensions inherent in the development of a finance system that encourages schools to provide special services where appropriate but not to classify students as disabled inappropriately in order to procure additional resources will persist regardless. However, expanding schooling choices has the potential to mitigate these tensions through competitive discipline or to exacerbate them through increased sorting.

Recognizing that special education is essentially a social insurance program helps to clarify the source of the trade-offs between adequacy and incentives. The economic justification for the entitlement to special education is that it provides insurance for families who have a child who turns out to be expensive to educate. Similarly, the justification for federal and state funding to support special education programs is to insure local schools against the high costs of serving student populations that happen to have a high rate of disability.

Just as Medicare and Medicaid may distort the behavior of patients and health care providers, the insurance provided through special education may distort the behavior of parents and educators. The higher the quality of special education relative to regular education, the more likely that parents will aggressively seek to gain admittance to special education, so that program generosity and size will be positively correlated. From the perspective of schools as agents, how well the amount of additional federal and state revenue matches the marginal costs of serving disabled students will determine whether schools have incentives to under- or overclassify students as disabled and to offer too few or too many additional services.[1]

In addition to the potentially perverse incentives for both parents and schools, there may also be adverse selection. Parents with disabled children may seek out schools that provide more generous services. If special education is not fully funded and these choices reduce resources dedicated to other instructional programs, regular education students may flee to other schools that provide fewer services for disabled students. The danger of attracting high-cost students and repelling less expensive nondisabled students can discourage the provision of high-quality services. In an attempt to balance the potential for overclassification and adverse selection against the desire and legal mandate to provide appropriate services for children classified as disabled, state school finance policies have oscillated between case mix systems that reimburse schools and districts based on the actual number and mix of students with disabilities and prospective payment systems in which the amount of funding is decoupled from the actual number and type of disabilities.

The ramifications of expanded school choice in this context will depend upon the structure of school finance and the interpretation of the legal mandate to provide special services. If special needs students are "priced" to cover the total costs of service provision, then increased choice can improve the quality and perhaps the efficiency of special education programs as schools compete for special needs students. If instead they are underpriced, fewer schools may open or participate in any choice program, and schools that do participate may attempt to discourage matriculation of high-cost students, perhaps by providing low-quality programs. This would reduce the gains from competition for students with disabilities, particularly if not all schools are required to provide special education services. Because private schools are currently exempt from federal requirements for students with disabilities and the treatment of charter schools is evolving over time, legal interpretations will play an important role in determining how disabled students fare under nontraditional forms of choice.

The next section describes the issues related to financing the special education component of a school choice program, incorporating existing evidence from traditional public schooling. Section 3.3 then presents and interprets new evidence on the stratification of special needs students across and within public school districts in Texas. The subsequent three sections review the relevant evidence and the unique considerations that arise for

1. Given the ambiguity in determining disability and needed services in many cases as well as the potential for high costs, special education has become the most litigated area in education (Katsiyannis and Maag 1998).

special education under open enrollment, charter schools, and vouchers, respectively. In the section on open enrollment, we provide new evidence from the Chicago public schools. Sections 3.3 through 3.6 demonstrate that variations in the impact of different forms of public- and private-sector choice are likely to be heavily moderated by the generosity of the reimbursement system. The final section summarizes and discusses the most salient policy issues.

3.2   Financing Special Education under School Choice

There are two features of school choice programs that will most directly determine the impact on special education students and programs. The first, and the focus of this section, is how closely the reimbursement for serving disabled students reflects marginal costs. The second is whether or not choice schools are required to serve applicants with special needs. The payment structure will be particularly important for inducing competition when institutions exist that have no legal responsibility to serve disabled students. We first consider these issues in a world in which disability status is given and not affected by family or school behavior, and we then incorporate the complexities introduced by the participation of families and schools in the special education classification process.

3.2.1   Exogenous Disability Status (Innate)

We begin by considering how special education affects the choices of parents and schools when a student's disability status is innate. In this case, student disability is much like any other identifiable characteristic that is correlated with higher educational costs, such as economic disadvantage, and a guiding principle for school finance is to provide enough revenue to insure adequate service provision and access to schooling opportunities. When we incorporate the fact that the classification of students is responsive to fiscal incentives, this imposes the additional requirement that the system be designed to discourage gaming.

Parents are assumed to recognize the multidimensional nature of schools when making housing and schooling choices. For our purposes, the relevant dimensions of schools are regular and special education quality. Both regular and special education quality will be a function of the level of resources, the quality of instruction, and peer characteristics. Parents of special needs children undoubtedly place much greater weight on the quality of special services than do other parents, although most special education children spend much of the day in regular classrooms. How parents and students perceive special education quality will depend on the types of settings in which special needs students are served. More intensive resources may not be highly valued if those resources are accompanied by more isolated placements and reduced contact with nondisabled students.[2] There is very little consensus about what types of interventions are effective for special needs students, so that parent preferences and beliefs about what is effective will play a particularly important role.

The quality of regular education programs is tied to special education through two channels: the budget and classroom dynamics. Depending on the reimbursement rate, the marginal cost of serving disabled students might either exceed, match, or fall short of the additional revenue generated. In the case of traditional public schools, the net local financial burden will lead to some combination of reduced spending on other educational programs and increased taxes. Lankford and Wyckoff (1996) and Cullen (1997) find evidence of nearly one-for-one crowdout of spending on other programs by local excess special education costs in New York and Texas, respectively. For schools that are financed purely based on student enrollment, such as charter schools, such one-for-one crowdout is mechanical. Special education may also enhance or detract from the regular education classroom by affecting the distribution of abilities and behaviors. In cases in which students are mainstreamed, there may be negative spillovers through peer effects or positive spillovers through increased resource intensity in regular classes.[3]

For expanded school choice to improve school quality for disabled students, schools must compete to serve these students. To foster this kind of competition, reimbursement rates should reflect the expected effective net resource and peer costs of serving students with differing disabilities. This form of case-mix reimbursement would ensure that all special needs students have access to a variety of schooling options, that regular education students do not have an incentive to avoid special needs students, and that schools have an incentive to control costs. Importantly, appropriate reimbursement based solely on the more easily measured *financial* costs would leave peer group composition as the only factor discouraging the provision of special education.

One complication that arises in determining the appropriate reimbursement rate in this setting is economies of scale in the provision of services to severely disabled students. In order to minimize costs, the reimbursement rate could incorporate average fixed per capita costs at the efficient size. However, this would lead to the concentration of severely disabled students

2. IDEA explicitly includes the requirement that schools serve students in the most integrated environment possible. Although inclusion has been a long-standing goal of disability rights activists, there is little evidence about the relative benefits of serving disabled students in more and less restrictive environments. Hanushek, Kain, and Rivkin (forthcoming) do not find significant differences in achievement gains by type of setting in Texas public schools.

3. Evidence on the effect of special education programs on regular education quality is mixed. Whereas Cullen (1997) finds that resource crowding-out harms the quality of regular education, Hanushek, Kain, and Rivkin (forthcoming) find that an increase in the share of students classified as disabled is positively related to the quality of regular education.

in a limited number of schools. There is, therefore, a conflict between unrestricted choice and cost minimization.

3.2.2 Endogenous Disability Classification (Subjective)

The above discussion assumes that the presence and type of disability are exogenously determined. Although this is likely to be true for severely disabled students, Singer et al. (1989) find that there is substantial variation in the functional status of students classified with mild disabilities across districts. Despite the procedural safeguards, the classification of students who exhibit academic or behavioral difficulties is far from an objective process. Both family and school pressures and preferences will affect whether and how students are classified and served.

There is evidence that where districts draw the line between able and disabled varies directly with the amount of state revenue generated by disabled students.[4] The dominant mechanism that states use to distribute special education aid to districts is essentially a case-mix system under which special education students are weighted more heavily than general education students within the basic school finance formula.[5] The weights are often specific to the type of disability, the type of instructional setting, and/or the grade level to account for heterogeneity in costs. Under this type of reimbursement, districts have an incentive to shift students from regular to special education and to classify students in the most highly reimbursed categories in order to maximize revenue. The dramatic growth over the past decades in the percentage of students classified as disabled has been widely attributed to the direct link between disability rolls and revenues.

Under a case-mix reimbursement system that applies different weights based on student needs, any expansion of school choice may not only foster active competition but may also affect the efforts of families and schools to seek inappropriate classifications. The greater ease with which families are able to switch schools may exacerbate the rates of inappropriate classifications and unnecessary provision of services because of the increased likelihood that parent and school interests are aligned in attempting to acquire greater resources. However, to the extent that overclassification results from school incentives to misclassify children in a way that provides no or even a negative educational benefit, school choice can provide another means of disciplining schools in addition to legal action or the undertaking of a more costly residential move.

---

4. Using variation in state aid according to district wealth and year under such a formula in Texas, Cullen (forthcoming) finds that student disability rates rise 1.4 percent with every 10 percent increase in the amount of additional revenue generated by disabled students. She finds that the specific categories to which disabled students are assigned also respond to changes in relative formula weights.
5. See Parrish et al. (1997) for a thorough discussion of the various mechanisms states use to distribute special education aid.

An alternative solution to overclassification is the adoption of a prospective payment system that prices all students in the same way. In fact, many states have responded to growing special education populations by switching to systems that allocate special education aid based only on overall enrollment and the expected rate of disability.[6] While eliminating the over-classification incentives associated with case-mix systems, prospective payment provides strong incentives for schools to discourage attendance by students with disabilities and to provide low-cost, low-quality special education services. It is important to recognize that incentives to provide special education services were first implemented as a remedy to widespread underprovision. A strong accountability system could provide a partial counterbalance to ensure that students receive adequate services. In practice, the extent to which an active market develops for disabled students can signal policymakers about the adequacy of any finance structure.

3.2.3   Interpreting Enrollment Patterns

In our empirical analyses of traditional choice in Texas and open enrollment in Chicago in the next sections, we explore patterns in the stratification of students by disability status across schools and districts. Evidence that special education students exhibit different school attendance patterns may reflect avoidance behavior on the part of nondisabled students or reluctance of some schools or districts to provide adequate services. These factors contribute to the involuntary segregation of disabled students. Alternatively, students with disabilities may concentrate in particular schools or districts because of preferences for specific programs known to provide higher quality services. This would be considered voluntary segregation. In order to determine whether the patterns are consistent with equal opportunities for disabled students, we attempt when possible to distinguish between voluntary and involuntary segregation.

At first glance it is tempting to conclude that involuntary segregation is problematic but voluntary segregation is desirable. However, involuntary segregation caused by high fixed costs of serving some disabilities clearly reflects the trade-off between the advantages of expanded choice and the reality of economies of scale. Moreover, a decision by some special education students to avoid nondisabled students may conflict with integration goals.

3.3   Traditional Public School Choice: Evidence from Texas

The previous section covered what is currently known about the interplay between special and regular education programs under traditional public school choice. In this section, we rely on data from the Texas public schools

---

6. A case study of such a reform in Vermont (Kane and Johnson 1993) does in fact find that disability rates fell noticeably (by 17 percent) by three years after the change.

to provide new evidence on how the choices of special needs and regular education students affect stratification by disability. It is important not to generalize the Texas results to all traditional public school districts, because other school systems differ along a number of dimensions. Perhaps most important, the state of Texas has a fairly generous case-mix reimbursement system that is unlikely to discourage districts from classifying students as disabled or providing quality services in most cases.

The analysis follows one cohort of students from third to seventh grade.[7] We first describe the distribution of special education students and other demographic groups into schools and districts in third grade and how the distribution evolves as students progress through school. Next we provide a detailed description of the interrelationship between transitions into and out of special education and mobility that underlies changes in the overall distributions. Finally, we examine whether special and general education students tend to systematically move to schools with higher or lower proportions of students classified as disabled. We do not attempt to identify the causal impact of either peer characteristics or other aspects of special education on school choice. Rather, we use enrollment and mobility patterns to provide indirect evidence on the strength of "race to the bottom" pressures in the provision of special education and of "push" factors for students without disabilities.

3.3.1   Data

This analysis is based on a unique matched panel data set of school operations constructed by the University of Texas at Dallas Texas Schools Project, directed by John Kain. Our cohort includes the universe of students who began the third grade in 1993. The data report race and ethnicity, eligibility for a subsidized lunch, and a unique identifier (ID) for each student. Students who switch public schools within the state of Texas can be followed just as students who remain in the same school or district. The cohort contains over 200,000 students in over 3,000 public schools. The substantial numbers of students who change schools and change special education status provide a detailed picture of the association between mobility and special education. The student IDs link the student records with a separate special education module. These data contain information on disability type and instructional setting. A much more detailed discussion of the data can be found in Hanushek, Kain, and Rivkin (forthcoming).

3.3.2   Distribution of Special Needs Students
across Schools and Districts

Figures 3.1 and 3.2 describe the distribution of students across schools and districts using analogues of Lorenz curves. Schools (figure 3.1) or dis-

---

7. It is important to note that third grade is not the first year in which students can receive special education, and active sorting by disability may have taken place before then. Unfortunately, we are unable to explore the trends for earlier grades.

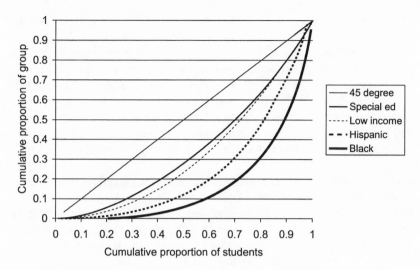

Fig. 3.1   **Third-grade school segregation curves**

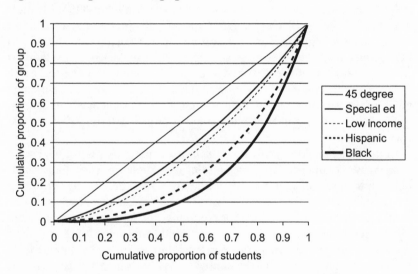

Fig. 3.2   **Third-grade district segregation curves**

tricts (figure 3.2) are ordered according to the proportion of students in a specific category (e.g., special education). The cumulative proportion of all third-grade special education students in Texas public schools is plotted against the cumulative proportion of all students. The diagonal line represents complete integration, meaning that each school has the population share of special education students. The more unevenly that disabled students are distributed across schools, the farther the curve will fall below the

45 degree line, so that curves farther from the line indicate greater segregation.[8]

The district segregation curves are derived from data aggregated to the district level. Just as school segregation curves ignore the allocation of students among classrooms, these curves ignore the allocation of students across schools within districts. Comparisons of the school and district segregation curves reveal how much of any existing concentration occurs within versus across districts. We focus the discussion on the curves shown in the figures, but we also report the corresponding Gini coefficients in table 3A.1.[9]

In order to gain a better sense of the degree of segregation of special education students, the first two figures also present segregation curves for Black, Hispanic, and free lunch–eligible students. Figure 3.1 shows that despite a substantial degree of sorting according to special education program participation at the school level, there is much more segregation by other demographic characteristics, particularly race. Whereas nearly one-third of special needs students are educated in schools with below-median shares of special needs students, less than one-tenth of Black students attend schools with below-median Black shares.[10] Not only do the district segregation curves in figure 3.2 preserve the same ordering by student characteristics as the school curves, but they largely preserve the distances between them as well. Although all of the district curves do lie closer to the 45 degree line than the school curves, aggregation to the district level does not eliminate much of the variation on any dimension. Clearly the extent of segregation by income, ethnicity, and disability status is largely determined at the district level.

In the case of income and ethnicity, housing patterns determine district enrollment, but differences in special education program participation cannot be attributed solely to the distribution of disabilities among communities. Unlike the case of race, schools and districts must actively classify students as disabled, so the differences among districts also emanate from differences in the ways districts implement state guidelines. Of course, families may respond to district policies in their choice of districts, making it extremely difficult to separate the contributions of residential location and district policies.

---

8. When curves cross there is no simple segregation ranking because crossing implies that different parts of the distribution are more or less unequal. See Allison (1978) for a discussion of this issue.

9. These summary measures are equal to the ratio of the area between the 45 degree line and the segregation curve to 1/2 (the area under the 45 degree line). The Gini coefficient varies from 0 (no segregation) to 1 (complete segregation).

10. To simplify the discussion, percentiles of schools (and districts) are described where the percentiles are determined by student enrollment or are from the student perspective. For example, what we describe as schools with below-median disability shares are schools that have disability shares below that faced by the median student.

Figures 3.3, 3.4, and 3.5 begin to disentangle the contributions of the underlying distribution of disabilities and district classification practices. Figures 3.3 and 3.4 are based on school- and district-level data, respectively. Figure 3.5 is based on school catchment area data, so that elementary schools are grouped by the junior high school that students most often attend. Each figure consists of four graphs that show results first for students

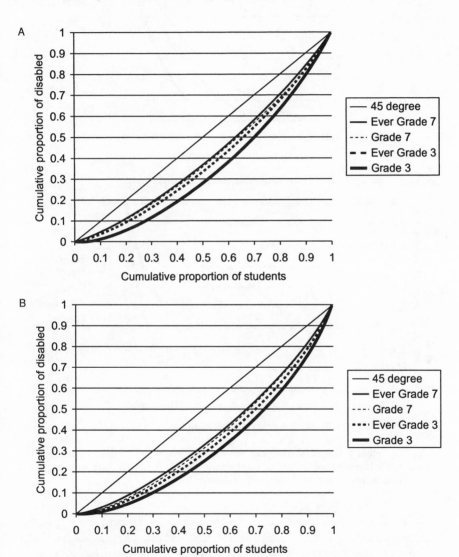

Fig. 3.3   *A,* Special education school segregation curves; *B,* learning disabled school segregation curves; *C,* emotionally disturbed school segregation curves; *D,* physically disabled school segregation curves

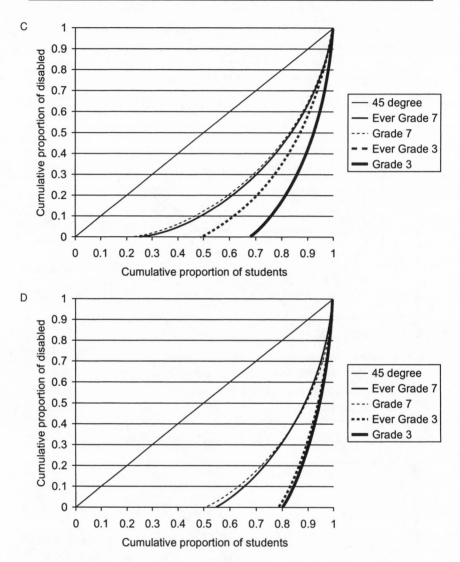

Fig. 3.3   (cont.) *A,* **Special education school segregation curves;** *B,* **learning disabled school segregation curves;** *C,* **emotionally disturbed school segregation curves;** *D,* **physically disabled school segregation curves**

classified with any disability and then separately for students with specific learning disabilities, emotional disturbances, and physical disabilities. Each graph presents four distribution curves. Two of the curves are based on concurrent disability classification status, with one for students served in special education in third grade and one for students served in special education in seventh grade. The other two show the distribution of students in

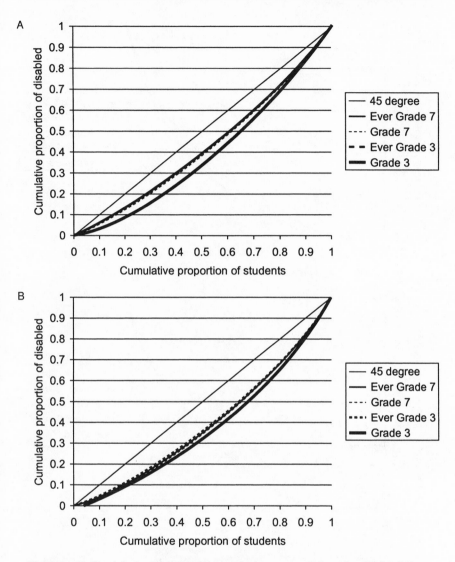

Fig. 3.4   *A,* **Special education district segregation curves;** *B,* **learning disabled district segregation curves;** *C,* **emotionally disturbed district segregation curves;** *D,* **physically disabled district segregation curves**

these two grades on the basis of whether they were ever classified as disabled between third and seventh grade, inclusive.

Focusing on the curves based on concurrent status, changes in the distribution of special needs students across grades provides a sense of whether special needs program sizes are becoming more disparate as students progress through school. Changes across grades will be driven by several fac-

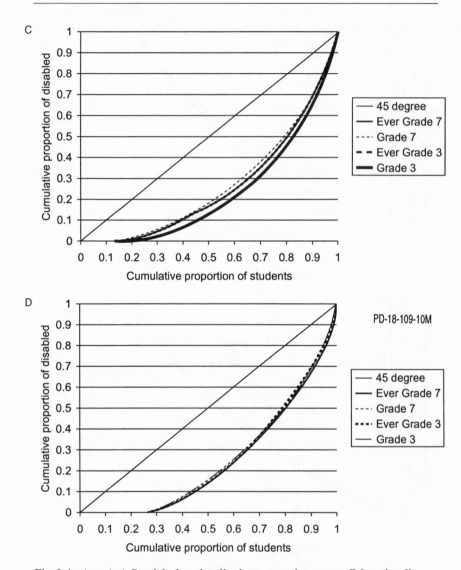

Fig. 3.4 (cont.) *A*, Special education district segregation curves; *B*, learning disabled district segregation curves; *C*, emotionally disturbed district segregation curves; *D*, physically disabled district segregation curves

tors. First, special education status may change without a school or district transfer. Although some disabilities may be treated by effective interventions, others may develop over time. In addition, the aggressiveness and timing of district and school labeling and interventions may also vary because of the beliefs of school leaders, community pressures, or changes in financial incentives. Second, a change in classification may occur following

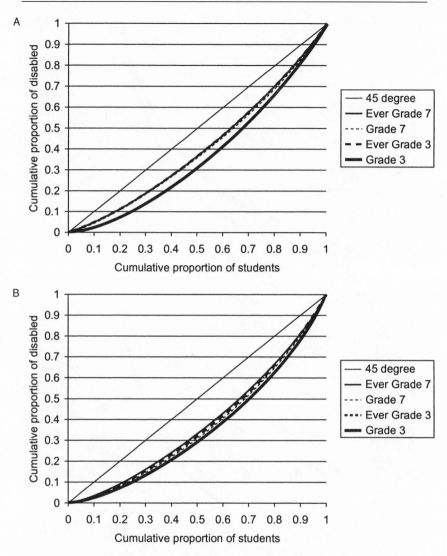

Fig. 3.5 *A,* **Special education catchment area curves;** *B,* **learning disabled catchment area curves;** *C,* **emotionally disturbed catchment area curves;** *D,* **physically disabled catchment area curves**

a school or district transfer. There is likely to be variation in classification procedures across schools and districts. In addition, parents may switch schools either in order to obtain a label or to escape a previous classification and obtain a fresh start.

In contrast, classification of students based on their entire special education histories isolates changes in the distribution of special needs students between third and seventh grades that arise strictly due to school changes.

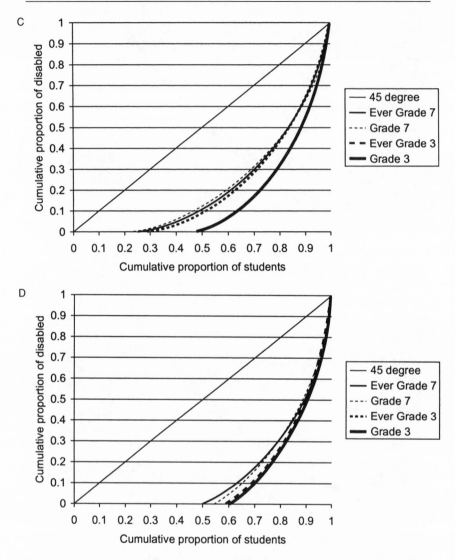

Fig. 3.5   (cont.) *A*, Special education catchment area curves; *B*, learning disabled catchment area curves; *C*, emotionally disturbed catchment area curves; *D*, physically disabled catchment area curves

Consequently, differences between the curves based on concurrent status and those based on special education classification throughout the period are driven by differences in classification rates for specific grades and schools.

Although the segregation curves in figures 3.3 and 3.4 reveal some heterogeneity by disability type, there are strong similarities, particularly at the district level. In fact, the four district curves lie virtually on top of one another regardless of disability type, suggesting that specific districts are not magnets to special education students (at least following third grade) and that families do not tend to relocate en masse to avoid large special education programs. In addition, there is little evidence of much variation in classification timing among districts, because the district distributions do not appear to become more equal as students age.

The school-level diagrams, on the other hand, display much more heterogeneity across disabilities and greater changes in segregation over time. In particular, physically disabled students become significantly less concentrated between grades three and seven. However, the school catchment area level diagram in figure 3.5 shows that this results almost entirely from the consolidation of students into more heterogeneous junior high schools rather than because of active school or district transfers.

There is a trend toward less segregation as students age for emotionally disturbed students as well, but the mechanism appears to be different in this case. Here the third-grade distribution of those ever classified is over two-thirds of the way toward both seventh-grade distributions, suggesting that differences in school classification behavior in the third grade account for a portion of the variation in the fraction of students classified as emotionally disturbed. An alternative explanation is that students differ systematically in the grade at which they manifest symptoms of the disability, and the two explanations cannot be distinguished from one another. The pattern for students with learning disabilities and all disabled students is similar to that for students with emotional disabilities, but the changes across grades are smaller.

Overall these figures provide no evidence of increasing segregation as students age. Although families may segregate prior to the third grade, one would still expect to find movements during these grades if responses to special education programs played an important role in the typical family's location decision. Note that the slight convergence occurs at the same time that classification rates for lower-income students diverge from those of students not eligible for subsidized lunch (see table 3A.3). However, both income groups experience similar percent changes in classification rates, and the reported segregation curves are invariant to equiproportional changes throughout the initial distribution.

3.3.3 Student Mobility

We provide further evidence on how choices correlate with special education program size by analyzing movement in and out of special education and across schools and districts. Table 3.1 reports annual special education transition rates by disability type and student mobility based on annual observations of students in the 1993 cohort pooled across grades three through seven. Students are divided among four categories: not classified as disabled in either year; classified in both years; not in special education in

Table 3.1   **Annual Mobility Rates by Special Education Transition for Grades Three through Seven, by Disability Type**

| | Special Education Transition (%) | | | | |
	Not Classified Either Year	Classified in Both Years	Enters Special Education	Exits Special Education	Number Classified as Disabled
Learning disabled					89,915
Same school	85.4	82.5	81.6	68.7	
Within district	7.9	9.6	10.7	8.5	
Between district	6.0	6.7	6.4	19.6	
Total	99.3	98.8	98.7	96.8	
Distribution of special education transitions	90.2	8.5	0.8	0.4	
Emotionally disturbed					9,269
Same school	85.4	69.3	65.2	63.4	
Within district	7.9	17.8	20.7	15.4	
Between district	6.0	9.9	10.0	18.1	
Total	99.3	97.0	95.9	96.9	
Distribution of special education transitions	98.9	0.9	0.1	0.1	
Physically disabled					3,027
Same school	85.4	82.9	73.4	72.3	
Within district	7.9	10.9	12.7	8.9	
Between district	6.0	5.6	12.7	15.8	
Total	99.3	99.4	98.8	97.0	
Distribution of special education transitions	99.7	0.3	0.0	0.0	
All disabilities					172,919
Same school	85.4	79.6	77.2	77.0	
Within district	7.9	11.0	12.4	8.5	
Between district	6.0	7.8	8.6	12.6	
Total	99.3	98.4	98.2	98.1	
Distribution of special education transitions	82.8	13.5	2.1	1.6	

Note: Column totals do not total 100 percent because of rounding and a small number of students who change schools more than once in a year.

the first year but classified in the following year; and in special education in the first year but exiting from the program prior to or during the following year. Within each of these categories, students are divided further on the basis of school transfer patterns: "Same school" refers to students who either remain at the same campus or transition from middle to junior high school along with their class; "Within district" refers to students who switch to a new school in the same district; and "Between district" refers to students who change districts. A small number of students who either change disability types or who move multiple times are excluded from consideration, as are students who exit the Texas public schools entirely.

A number of similarities appear across disabilities in the pattern of transitions. First, students not classified as disabled are less likely to move than students classified in one or both years; the gap is greatest for the emotionally disturbed. Second, a substantial proportion of students remaining in special education switch schools within districts. For the emotionally disturbed and physically disabled, roughly twice as many students transfer within as transfer between districts, whereas for the learning disabled the differential is approximately 50 percent. With the exception of the physically disabled, a similar pattern holds for those entering special education. On the other hand, those who exit special education exhibit by far the highest mobility rates, and they are much more likely to move to new districts than to find a new school in the same district. Less than 70 percent of emotionally disturbed and learning disabled students who exit special education remain in the same school, and almost 20 percent switch districts. A similar although slightly muted pattern emerges for the physically disabled. Note that the lower mobility rate for all students who exit special education reflects the lower mobility of those previously classified as speech impaired, a disability category that constitutes a large share of those who exit special education between grades three and seven. These students are not very different from their peers that do not have special needs because the impairment is short-lived and readily treated with proper therapy.

Overall, the table suggests that students with disabilities move around more than others, and those who move do tend to change their classification status more often. The greater mobility of those classified as disabled may result partly from income and other family factors that affect both mobility and disability rates. For example, mobility rates are much higher for lower-income students eligible for a subsidized lunch regardless of special education status, and these students are also more likely to have special needs. However, table 3.2 shows that the same broad conclusions hold when subsidized and nonsubsidized student populations are analyzed separately. It remains possible that the higher rates of change in special education status can be attributed to movers systematically experiencing greater changes in personal conditions. On the other hand, it seems more plausible that mobility facilitates the change, particularly for those exiting special education. This more detailed analysis of individual student mobility is consistent with marginal students' relocating to either obtain or shed the special education label.

Tables 3.3 and 3.4 provide information on changes in peer disability rates by the above transitions.[11] There is no evidence that students who are in regular education in consecutive years move to schools or districts with smaller

11. We also examine differences in the lagged growth in percentage special education by transition type. Similar to the case for levels, there is little or no evidence that non–special education students tend to switch schools following unusually large increases in the percentage classified as disabled (see table 3A.4).

Table 3.2   **Annual Mobility Rates by Special Education Transition for Grades Three through Seven, by Family Income**

	Special Education Transition (%)			
	Not Classified Either Year	Classified in Both Years	Enters Special Education	Exits Special Education
Eligible for subsidized lunch				
Same school	81.8	76.6	74.0	70.8
Within district	9.9	12.6	14.3	11.1
Between district	7.1	8.6	9.4	15.3
Total	98.8	97.8	97.7	97.2
Distribution of special education transitions	79.7	16.2	2.5	1.5
Not eligible				
Same school	90.2	86.9	85.0	85.5
Within district	5.2	7.0	7.8	5.0
Between district	4.4	5.6	6.4	8.9
Total	99.8	99.5	99.2	99.4
Distribution of special education transitions	87.4	1.6	1.5	9.5

Table 3.3   **Change in Percent Classified as Disabled, by Special Education Transition, Mobility, and Disability Type**

	Special Education Transition (%)			
	Not Classified Either Year	Classified in Both Years	Enters Special Education	Exits Special Education
Learning disabled				
Same school	0.5	0.4	2.0	−0.4
Within district	0.4	1.1	2.2	−1.2
Between district	0.4	0.5	1.9	−1.8
All	0.5	0.4	1.9	−0.6
Emotionally disturbed				
Same school	0.1	−0.3	0.6	−1.5
Within district	0.0	1.5	4.3	−2.2
Between district	0.1	−2.8	13.5	−1.8
All	0.1	−0.1	2.9	−1.6
Physically disabled				
Same school	0.0	−0.4	0.2	−0.3
Within district	0.0	0.4	3.4	−3.0
Between district	0.0	1.0	0.2	−6.2
All	0.0	−0.2	0.6	−1.5
All disabilities				
Same school	0.1	0.1	1.9	−0.8
Within district	0.0	1.2	3.0	−1.9
Between district	−0.3	−0.8	2.7	−1.8
All	0.1	0.0	2.0	−0.9

Table 3.4   Change in Proportion Classified as Disabled, by Special Education
                   Transition, Mobility, and Family Income

	Special Education Transition (%)			
	Not Classified Either Year	Classified in Both Years	Enters Special Education	Exits Special Education
Eligible for subsidized lunch				
Same school	0.3	0.2	2.2	−0.9
Within district	0.3	1.4	3.1	−2.1
Between district	−0.1	−0.8	2.9	−2.1
Not eligible				
Same school	0.0	0.0	1.2	−0.7
Within district	−0.6	0.2	2.6	−1.3
Between district	−0.6	−0.8	1.9	−1.1

special education programs; nor is there a systematic pattern for students who remain in special education in both years. However, table 3.3 shows that entrants to special education tend to experience increases in the proportion of schoolmates classified as disabled, and those exiting special education tend to experience declines. Entrants and exiters who move experience significantly larger changes than those who remain in the same school, with the exception of entrants classified as learning disabled.[12] Note that the estimates of changes in peer composition for emotionally disturbed and physically disabled students are noisy and are greatly affected by the minority of students who move to separate special education schools.

Table 3.4 reports differences in changes in peer disability rates by student income. Not surprisingly, the largest increases occur among those eligible for a subsidized lunch whose classification rates rise much more rapidly in absolute terms. For both groups, movers tend to experience the largest changes.

There are at least two hypotheses that are consistent with the results for movers who exit or enter special education: Families may be attempting to find a more preferred classification system and special education program, or students who move to schools with larger special education populations may be more likely to be classified because the new schools utilize more liberal classification criteria. The pattern we observe confounds deliberate

12. Tests of the hypothesis that the average change in proportion special education for entrants who move is equal to the change for entrants who do not move show that this hypothesis is rejected for all of the disability types at the 0.01 level. A test for those who exit special education leads to a rejection of the equality hypothesis for the learning disabled and all categories combined at the 0.01 level, for the physically disabled at the 0.10 level, but not for the emotionally disturbed at any conventional level. Note that the latter two disabilities had only a small number of students who exited.

family efforts and any incidental effects of school regime, although it is certainly consistent with the notion that school classification procedures affect family choices.

3.3.4   Lessons

The results from both the segregation and mobility analyses suggest that fears about regular education students self-segregating from disabled students are not confirmed by actual enrollment patterns in the state of Texas. Those who appear to be most responsive to special education when making schooling decisions are marginal students who are on the border between classification as disabled or nondisabled. We find that these students move to schools with programs that are systematically larger or smaller than their initial schools.

There are several caveats restricting the generalizability of these results to other settings. First, we analyze changes in sorting between third and seventh grade rather than trying to explain initial sorting. The impact of any decisions that are made based on special education programs is therefore understated. Second, as we have emphasized, both student and school responses are dependent on the pricing regime. In Texas, special education students generate additional marginal revenue for their school district. Cullen (forthcoming) calculates that there is likely to be a net financial gain from serving mildly disabled students for most districts during the time period of our analysis. Third, because of the small size of many rural districts in Texas, over 80 percent of districts participate in some type of cooperative arrangement for providing certain types of special education services. Finally, the preponderance of neighborhood schools implies that families must undertake costly residential moves in order to change public schools, and a system that expands choice at the current residence may lead to greater responsiveness to special education considerations. For these reasons, the incentives for regular education students to avoid special needs students and for special needs students to shop across programs may be weaker than in other states or under nontraditional choice systems.

3.4   Open Enrollment

The pressures that affect whether schools compete for special needs students under traditional public school choice are magnified under open enrollment within or across school districts. Not only is financial responsibility for excess costs more difficult to assign, but officials may also have more scope for counseling students either in or out of their schools. Moreover, with a greater number of schooling options, it may simply become more costly to guarantee special needs students FAPE at any given school.

This section provides evidence on two quite different open enrollment systems, those of the state of Minnesota and the city of Chicago. Whereas

Minnesota permits movement across districts, the Chicago program limits students to movement across schools within the district. In addition, receiving districts receive ample reimbursements for special education services in Minnesota, whereas there appears to be only a weak link between the size and composition of special education programs and revenue allocated from the district for Chicago schools. Not surprisingly, the manifestation of open enrollment in Minnesota appears to have led to more active participation of and competition for special education students.

3.4.1 Evidence from Minnesota

Most of the existing evidence on open enrollment comes from Minnesota, which was the first state to introduce this type of choice legislation in 1990. In Minnesota, students can apply to transfer to any other district in the state. Districts can only refuse to accept transfer students on the basis of capacity constraints. State per-pupil revenue follows all students who choose to travel, and any excess costs for services provided to special needs students are billed back to the district of residence. This type of financial arrangement greatly reduces any potential resistance to accepting transfer students with special needs. At the same time, it increases incentives to try to keep special needs students, because home districts largely lose control of costs if these students choose to travel. Parent and school responses are conditioned, therefore, by what should be a relatively competitive special education environment.

It appears that special needs students are in fact taking advantage of choice at rates similar to other students. Over the first four years of the program, special education participation rates doubled, rising from 5 percent to 10 percent of transfers between 1990–91 and 1993–94 (Lange, Ysseldyke, and Delaney 1995). In making their transfer decisions, parents of disabled students are sensitive to special education program characteristics. Based on interviews with parents, Ysseldyke, Lange, and Gorney (1994) find that parents of children with disabilities most often report that they opted to transfer in order to better meet their children's special needs.[13] Moreover, they find that 4 percent of parents with disabled children report transferring to obtain special education labels, whereas 3 percent transfer to shed labels. Parents of children with behavioral disorders are often simply looking for a new start.

Despite the fact that disabled students actively participate in open en-

---

13. In their analysis of school districts with particularly high gains or losses of disabled students, Lange, Ysseldyke, and Delane (1995) provide insight into the program characteristics valued by families. Parents do not seem to perceive higher special education quality as synonymous with lower pupil-staff ratios. Disabled children are more likely to transfer to schools with larger special education caseloads per teacher. However, districts that gain special education students demonstrate better home-school communication practices and a higher commitment to spending on special services.

rollment, there is some evidence that the choices of schools for nondisabled students lead to increased involuntary segregation. Jimerson (1998) analyzes trends in special education populations before and after open enrollment was introduced. She finds a steady decrease in the fraction classified as disabled in districts that are primarily receiving districts, compared to a much more erratic pattern for sending districts.

The variation in school districts' experiences with special education and open enrollment highlights other potential hazards. Lange, Ysseldyke, and Delaney (1995) find that districts that gain special education students largely respond by absorbing students into existing programs and increasing class size, thereby bearing few additional costs. Districts that lose disabled students, however, are not able to proportionately cut back on special education staff because of the requirement to maintain minimum services for the remaining students.[14] Further, these home districts face escalating costs when any additional services are provided to transfer students due to the lack of incentives for the district of attendance to control costs under the bill-back policy. Finally, districts find it very difficult to plan for low incidence populations because of the uncertainty in enrollment.

3.4.2   Evidence from Chicago

We provide additional evidence on special education participation rates and stratification from the open enrollment program within the Chicago public school (CPS) district. The origin of the policy dates back to court-ordered desegregation in 1980. Currently, each high school student is assigned to a default school based on residence and attendance area zones. Students can then apply to any one of the more than sixty high schools, which include magnet schools and career academies as well as more traditional high schools. Most schools that are oversubscribed use a lottery to admit students, although the most selective magnet schools rely on test scores.

Our analysis is based on the cohort of students enrolled in eighth grade in a CPS school in the spring of 1995.[15] Of the 31,485 students in this cohort, only 81.0 percent enter a CPS high school in the following year. Four-fifths of this attrition can be attributed to students who leave the CPS after eighth grade. The majority of these students either switch to the private sector or move outside of Chicago. Special education students leave at similar overall rates as nondisabled students, but they are somewhat less likely to leave

---

14. Jimerson (1997) finds that special education expenditures per special needs student increased in districts with high student loss rates compared to districts with high gain rates. This may be consistent with the tendency of the more severely disabled to remain behind or with increased costs because of the bill-back policy, as she notes, and would also be consistent with decreased economies of scale.

15. See Cullen, Jacob, and Levitt (2000) for a more detailed description of the policy and of the data.

to attend a Chicago private school (28.7 percent vs. 35.9 percent). The remaining attrition is due to student retention. Whereas only 2.0 percent of regular education students repeat eighth grade, 17.4 percent of special needs students do. Due to the dramatic difference in rates at which special needs and other students are held back, the fraction served in special education in eighth grade falls from 14.9 percent in the full eighth-grade sample to 13.0 percent in the subsample that enters a CPS high school the following year.

We identify sixty-one high schools that serve regular populations. There are a variety of other schools and institutions that serve special populations of secondary students, such as juvenile delinquents and other troubled youths. Although only 1.2 percent of nondisabled students in our cohorts entering ninth grade attend one of these alternative schools, a disproportionate share (5.9 percent) of special needs students attend alternative schools that serve only special needs students. The students placed in these more isolated settings tend to have relatively severe disabilities. For example, most physically disabled students (69.6 percent) are assigned to special schools, compared to a negligible share (1.8 percent) of learning disabled students. The specialized instruction appropriate to students with severe disabilities places some limits on the range of integrated choices that is available to these students.

For the more than 24,000 students who attend one of the regular CPS schools, we consider the impact that open enrollment has on the ninth-grade concentration of students who were served in special education in eighth grade. To do this, we compare the actual distribution to that which would prevail under the counterfactual where all students attend their assigned high school. Figure 3.6 shows that stratification by disability based on residential choices is relatively weak, but the degree of stratification is increased by choice. Very little of this increase can be explained by the three selective magnet schools that use test scores in admissions.

Table 3.5 shows that different patterns of participation in open enrollment underlie this shift toward greater segregation of disabled students. Whereas nondisabled students opt out of their assigned schools 52 percent of the time, special education students opt out only 36 percent of the time.[16] Only one in ten special needs students who opt out attends a school that is ranked in the top fifth in terms of average achievement, compared to one in three of other travelers. Surprisingly, both the least severely and most severely disabled

16. Controlling for individual and family demographic characteristics as well as residential tract fixed effects explains only 20 percent of the difference between the rates at which special needs students and other students participate. Interestingly, when we control for eighth-grade math and reading test scores (most special education students take the exams), the participation patterns of special needs students and equally low-achieving students are not significantly different from one another. Although difficult to interpret because there may be systematic differences in observable characteristics across the groups, this could be evidence that there are not specific barriers to special needs students over and above those for other low achievers.

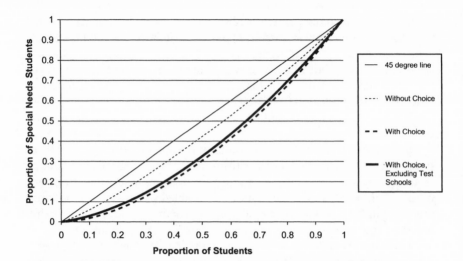

Fig. 3.6 Distribution of special needs students across high schools within the Chicago public school district

Notes: The sample is the full sample of 24,404 students who attended a CPS school for eighth grade in the spring of 1995 and attended a (nonspecial) CPS high school in the fall of the following year, as described in the text. Special education status is based on classification in eighth grade, and the distributions are based on ninth-grade school assignments and enrollments. The counterfactual with no choice calculates special education fractions given the schools to which students are assigned (Gini = 0.112). The distribution labeled "with choice" is based on actual attendance patterns (Gini = 0.269). We also show the distribution given actual attendance patterns but excluding the three selective magnet schools that use achievement tests to determine admissions (Gini = 0.237).

Table 3.5   Opting Out of the Assigned Chicago Public School by Disability Type

		% Opting Out of Assigned School To:			
	% of Students	Any Other High School	Career Academy	High-Achieving School	Other High School
Not in special education in eighth grade	88.0	51.5	14.5	16.5	20.5
In special education in eighth grade	12.0	35.8	8.2	4.0	23.6
Learning disabled	9.0	33.8	8.0	2.7	23.1
Emotionally/behavariorally disturbed	1.3	28.2	7.0	0.3	20.9
Speech/language impaired	0.8	52.3	12.8	12.8	26.7
All other disabilities	0.9	52.3	7.4	14.8	30.1

Notes: The results are based on the cohort of students who entered a Chicago public high school in the fall of 1995 and who attended eighth grade in the prior year. We exclude students who attended special schools, such as centers for juvenile delinquents and schools that only serve disabled students, as described in the text. The total number of students in the sample is 24,404. High-achieving schools are the schools in the highest fifth in terms of average eighth-grade test scores among the entering ninth-grade class. "Other" schools are high schools that are neither career academies nor high-achieving.

students are more likely to opt out than moderately disabled students, although the severely disabled students in this sample are a select group. Students who opt out tend to choose schools with smaller disability caseloads regardless of disability status. Both disabled and nondisabled travelers were initially assigned to schools with average disability rates of approximately 16 percent.[17] By traveling, disabled students attend programs with caseloads that are 2.3 percentage points lower, and nondisabled students lower their exposure to disabled students by 5.7 percentage points on average.

The evidence from Chicago presents a mixed picture for special education students. On one hand, disabled students are actively participating in open enrollment, with more than one in three students with disabilities opting to attend an alternative high school. On the other hand, these students are participating at significantly lower rates and attending schools with lower average achievement than students not classified as disabled.

The financial incentives schools face within CPS are difficult to identify. The district has a policy of distributing more funds to small schools and schools with more students who qualify for special programs, such as disabled students. However, observable student program participation rates and other student and school characteristics explain relatively little of the variation in per-pupil expenditures across schools.[18] It appears that the tie between special education program size and funding is weak.

3.5 Charter Schools

Charter schools are becoming increasingly prevalent, with over 2,300 schools in operation in thirty-four states and the District of Columbia in the beginning of fiscal year 2002 (Center for Education Reform 2002). In order to offer innovative alternatives to traditional public schools, charter schools are granted waivers from many state and local regulations. However, like any other public school, they must be in compliance with federal civil rights legislation (Heubert 1997).[19] These federal regulations may have a profound influence on instruction and operation, yet most states have not articulated how they are to be implemented in the charter school context (Fiore and Cashman 1998). Not surprisingly, charter school applicants and operators tend to have very little knowledge of what constitutes discrimination, of the procedures involved in providing FAPE, and of how the services are funded (McKinney 1996; Powell et al. 1997; Urhan and Stewart 1994).

17. This disability share is higher than the average in the full sample because a school's fraction of disabled is based on the status of students who actually attend, and no students are assigned to certain magnet and vocational schools, so these schools are excluded.

18. A regression of per-pupil special education expenditures on the share of enrollment within each detailed disability category has an adjusted R-squared of 0.32, suggesting that the reimbursement is not very strongly correlated with caseload characteristics.

19. Charter schools that are independent local education agencies (LEAs) have full procedural and financial responsibility for implementing special education programs, whereas those attached to LEAs negotiate with the sponsoring agency.

The regulations that accompany students with disabilities potentially conflict with the type of flexibility that characterizes charter schools.[20] Rhim and McLaughlin (2000) quote one state charter school director as saying, "The biggest challenge is that special education law and ideology is based on the thought that all schools need to be all things to all people, . . . but we have allowed charters to focus their program and not be all things to all people" (22). Legally, charter schools must ensure students with disabilities equal consideration for admission, although interpretation of the law varies by state. Some states require schools to accept all students who wish to attend and to use a lottery if a school is oversubscribed.[21] Others permit schools to use selection criteria, such as test scores, that are consistent with the school's purpose. The possibility for charter schools to "cream-skim" the best students has fueled concerns about charter schools serving as elite academies (Szabo and Gerber 1996; Fuller and Elmore 1996).

Once students are enrolled, charter schools must also abide by federal laws regarding special education provision, including the requirements to identify students with special needs and to provide appropriate services. Although charter schools are often not required to hire certified regular teachers, they must provide special education services using certified teachers. Table 3.6 summarizes these and other current state charter school provisions that most affect the degree to which serving a disabled student is an encumbrance to a charter school relative to serving a nondisabled student.

There has also been widespread concern about the budgetary impact of special education on charter schools. These schools tend to be small, and per-pupil funding is often below costs (Bierlein and Fulton 1996). Although IDEA requires states to distribute funds to charter schools in the same way as to other schools, local resources are typically negotiated. Compared to traditional schools and school districts, charter schools have a limited ability to absorb unexpected costs associated with high disability rates or low incidence disabilities, in part because they do not have the same access to general operating funds and cooperative arrangements that can help to smooth costs (Buechler 1996). Independent charter schools are especially vulnerable because, by default, they bear the costs of severely disabled students who require expensive placements. To mitigate the potential destabilizing impact of special education, many states have implemented schemes that transfer some or all of the expenditure risk to traditional local education agencies.[22]

20. Ahearn (1999) and Rhim and McLaughlin (2000) provide thorough discussions of the tension between the special education and charter school environments.
21. In order to receive federal funds, charter schools must use a lottery to determine admission.
22. For example, Massachusetts requires districts of residence to cover the costs of any residential placements. Minnesota charters are independent LEAs, but they are able to bill back any excess special education costs to the district of residence. Also, some charter schools in Colorado use prospective payment, whereby charter schools pay home districts a fixed fee per

Table 3.6   State Charter School Provisions Relevant to Special Education

State	No.	Legal Autonomy	Automatic Waiver	Enrollment Preferences	Special Education Funding	Teacher Certification
Alaska	17	No	No	Not permitted	Matches district's special education revenue (constant across disabilities)	Required
Arizona	352	Yes	Yes	Not permitted	No additional funding for low-cost disabilities/weighting system to fund higher-cost students	Not required
Arkansas	0	No	No	Not addressed	Negotiated with school district	Required
California	239	Yes	Yes	Not permitted	Negotiated with school district	Required
Colorado	65	No	No	Not permitted	Negotiated with school district	Required (but often waived)
Connecticut	16	No	No	Not permitted	District of residence pays actual costs if charter school provides service/otherwise negotiated	50% must have regular certification
Delaware	5	Yes	Yes	Can screen on interest or ability	Based on students' disabilities	Exceptions may be made
District of Columbia	31	Varies	Yes	Can screen on area of focus	Based on students' disabilities	Not required
Florida	111	Yes	No	Not permitted	Based on students' disabilities	Not required
Georgia	32	No	Yes	Not permitted	Based on students' disabilities and same as any school in the district	Specified in charter
Hawaii	2	No	Yes	Not applicable	Based on students' disabilities and same as any school	Required
Idaho	8	No	Yes	Not applicable	Uses Idaho code to calculate funding based on support units	Required
Illinois	19	Yes	Yes	Not permitted	District of residence pays actual costs if charter school provides service/otherwise negotiated	Not required
Kansas	15	No	No	Specified in charter	Based on students' disabilities and same as any in the district	May grant waivers

(*continued*)

Table 3.6 (continued)

State	No.	Legal Autonomy	Automatic Waiver	Enrollment Preferences	Special Education Funding	Teacher Certification
Louisiana	17	Varies	Yes	May screen on area interest	Matches school district's special education revenue	25% may be non-certified
Massachusetts	39	Varies	No	Not permitted	Matches school district's special education revenue	Not always required
Michigan	173	Yes	No	Not permitted	Based on students' disabilities	Required
Minnesota	59	Yes	Yes	Not permitted	Based on actual cost	Required
Mississippi	1	No	Yes	Not permitted	Not addressed	Required
Missouri	18	Yes	Yes	Can limit based on age/grade	Proportionate share of state and federal special education funds follows students	Up to 20% may be noncertified
Nevada	5	No	No	Not permitted	Not available	70% must be licensed
New Hampshire	0	Yes	Yes	May screen on aptitude if related to mission		
New Jersey	48	Yes	No	Can use reasonable criteria	District special education funding follows students	50% must be certified
New Mexico	3	No	No	Not permitted	Based on students' disabilities and same as any school in the district	Required
New York	5	Yes	Yes	Not permitted	Not available	30% may be noncertified
North Carolina	75	Yes	Yes	Not permitted	Matches districts' special education revenue (not based on specific disability)	Up to 50% may be uncertified
Ohio	48	Yes	Yes	Can limit enrollment to at-risk students	Special needs funding follows students	Alternative certification is available

Oklahoma	0	No	No	Not permitted	Not available	Specified in charter
Oregon	4	Varies	Yes	Not permitted	Not available	50% must be licensed
Pennsylvania	47	Varies	Yes	Can screen based on area of focus or other reasonable criteria	Special needs funding follows students (not based on specific disability); can apply for transitional state grants if a student has a budgetary impact	Up to 25% may be uncertified
Rhode Island	2	No	No	May use academic standards[a]	Matches district's special education revenue	Required
South Carolina	8	Varies	Yes	Not permitted	Based on students' disabilities	Up to 25% may be uncertified
Texas	167	Varies	Yes	No enrollment preferences	Based on students' disabilities	Not required
Utah	3	No	No	Not permitted	Not available	May have alternative certification
Virginia	0	No	No	Not permitted	Treated as public school with fees negotiated	Required
Wisconsin	55	Yes	Yes	Can use at-risk criteria	No additional funding for low-cost students/weighting system to provide funds for high-cost disabilities	Special licenses available
Wyoming	0	No	No	Cannot be based only on ability	Negotiated with sponsor district	Required

Notes: The source for this information is the Center for Education Reform's charter school legislation profiles [http:www.edreform.com/charter_schools/laws]. The second column shows the number of charter schools in operation as of spring 2000. The third column indicates whether charters are legally autonomous. The fourth column indicates whether charters receive an automatic waiver from most state education laws, regulations, and policies. The remaining columns describe policies related to enrollment decisions, funding, and teacher certification. The special education funding facts shown combine information from the Center for Education Reform and *Venturesome Capital: State Charter School Finance Systems* (U.S. Department of Education 2000).

[a]The combined fraction of special needs, LEP, and free lunch must equal the fraction in the district.

Despite the administrative and financial burdens of providing special education, the evidence on whether special education students have equal access to charter schools in practice is encouraging.[23] Whereas early studies found that disabled students were participating at rates far below other students (e.g., McKinney 1996), the most recent National Charter School Study (U.S. Department of Education 1999) reports that the gap has closed as more charter schools have opened. In the states studied, 8 percent of charter school enrollment is classified as disabled, compared to 11 percent in traditional public schools. There is substantial heterogeneity across charter schools, with start-ups being less likely to serve special needs students and some schools specifically targeting them. There is also heterogeneity across disability type, with more severely disabled students choosing to remain in traditional public schools.

Part of the remaining discrepancy between caseloads at charter and traditional schools can be explained by differences in classification policies. Finn, Manno, and Bierlein (1996) and Vanourek et al. (1997) discover that a large proportion of students who would have been served in special education in their former school are not in the chosen charter school. Consistent with this, some parents report choosing charter schools to escape the stigma of labels and to take advantage of effective mainstreaming options (Vanourek et al. 1997).

Finally, there is no direct evidence of which we are aware that shows how special education programs affect the decisions of regular education students to attend a charter school. Indirect evidence through charter school location decisions is mixed.[24]

3.6   Private Schools and Vouchers

Private schools have a dual relationship with special education. On the one hand, public school administrators regularly contract with private schools to educate students with severe disabilities who cannot be adequately served in public schools. A number of private schools have been established specifically to accommodate low-incidence, severely disabled populations. On the other hand, most other private schools have admis-

---

pupil or per disabled student to cover any excess special education costs (McLaughlin, Henderson, and Ullah 1996). *Venturesome Capital: State Charter School Finance Systems* (U.S. Department of Education 2000) provides an overview of how closely each state's system matches the costs of providing special education in charter schools.

23. See Fiore, Warren, and Cashman (1999) for a recent review of the existing empirical evidence pertaining to special education and charter schools.

24. Glomm, Harris, and Lo (2001) uncover a positive correlation between the number of charter schools in an area and the level of per-pupil special education expenditure in Michigan school districts. For Texas, Grosskopf, Hayes, and Taylor (2000) find an insignificant relationship between the proportion of students in special education and the number of charter schools.

sions requirements, only half offer remedial reading and math, and very few offer special education services (McLaughlin and Broughman 1997).

Fox (1999) argues that the fact that a market has evolved to educate severely disabled students implies that special needs students will not be left behind in a voucher system. However, students served in private special education settings are not representative of the typical student with special needs. Not only do these severely disabled students make up a negligible share of the disabled population, but the intensive equipment and services involved necessitate that students with similar disabilities be pooled in separate instructional or residential settings.[25] For other disabled students, this type of pooling would be in direct conflict with the philosophy of IDEA that requires students to be served in the least restrictive environment possible. When a student with disabilities attends a private school that serves a general student population, it is unclear how market pressures and federal regulations interact, because it is public and not private schools that are responsible for guaranteeing FAPE.

The precise obligations of public schools for students with disabilities who voluntarily enroll in private schools have not been fully established. Whereas the full costs of educating disabled students *assigned* to private school settings are paid from federal, state, and local funds, those who *choose* to opt out of the public sector are not protected to the same degree. IDEA (1990) requires public schools to ensure that these students have "equitable" access to special education services, so public schools cannot categorically deny private school students services (Linden 1995). However, schools have discretion in deciding which private students will be served, which services will be provided, and where those services will be provided (Osborne 1999).[26] The 1997 amendments to IDEA offered a quantitative minimum standard by requiring local school districts to expend at least a proportionate share of federal IDEA funds on services for private school students.

Given the stark contrast between public and private schools' roles, only carefully designed voucher programs will lead to expanded choice options for disabled students. If private schools are not required to serve students with disabilities, they are unlikely to admit special needs students unless the schools receive full compensation for all financial and external costs of providing special education services. More generally, theoretical models predict that vouchers will lead to increased segregation by ability if the vouch-

25. Students served in private settings make up 1.8 percent of the special education population, and average contracted tuitions for day and residential placements are $22,000 and $66,000, respectively (Fox 1999).

26. Although private school students are not entitled to any given services, the amendments require public school districts to identify and evaluate all resident students with disabilities who attend private schools. A recent legal debate has centered on whether public schools can provide special education services on site at parochial schools without violating the Constitution. See Katsiyannis and Maag (1998) for a detailed discussion.

ers do not vary to compensate for undesirable student characteristics (Epple and Romano 2000; Bearse, Glomm, and Ravikumar 2000). On the other hand, the requirement that all participating schools serve disabled students would likely limit the number of schools willing to accept vouchers if compensation is inadequate.

Existing evidence does suggest that there are barriers to the participation of special education students in voucher programs. Based on interviews with 200 administrators in urban areas across the United States, Kapel, Faison, and Gallagher (1995) find that private schools would be likely to reject many special education students. Two-thirds of the schools in their sample use testing for academic ability in admissions and most would exclude students who lack academic readiness or have emotional or behavioral problems. A few schools reported that they would categorically exclude disabled students. Results from early voucher experiments support these qualitative findings. Peterson, Myers, and Howell (1999) report that only 8 percent of the students enrolled in the Horizon Scholarship Program in Texas were learning disabled, compared to 16 percent in the public school district. Only 1.5 percent of participants were physically disabled, compared to 4.5 percent of nonparticipants. Peterson, Howell, and Greene (1999) find similar patterns of underenrollment in the Cleveland Scholarship program. Parents of disabled students who chose to remain in the public sector were more likely to report that programs were available to address their special needs, testimony that echoes parents' sentiments from national public opinion polls comparing public and private schools (Sconyers 1996).

Although the above programs do not specifically target disabled students, Florida introduced a plan that does in 2000.[27] Through the Opportunity Scholarships program, general education students are able to obtain vouchers to attend private schools as long as they are currently attending a local school that is failing. In contrast, special needs students can access McKay Scholarships if their parents are dissatisfied with their public school for any reason. The vouchers are funded at the minimum of the private school tuition or the sending district's per-pupil special education revenue under the state school finance formula. Participating private schools must agree to accept the state scholarship funds as full tuition and fees. Nearly 1,000 disabled students took advantage of this program in the first year, and the number is expected to increase to more than 7,000 (about 1.6 percent of disabled students) once the program is fully phased in. At this time it is too early to judge the program's impact.

Although the limited number of voucher programs has generally not

27. See [http:/www.opportunityschools.org] for more details on the Florida voucher program.

been providing opportunities that are equally attractive or accessible to special education students, this does not mean that private schools cannot provide viable alternatives to public special education. Particularly if school participation in voucher programs were contingent on full compliance with IDEA, many private schools would probably participate if disabilities were priced correctly. Legal responsibilities for private schools are likely to expand for states that embrace public funding of private schooling.

3.7 Conclusion

The additional costs, real or perceived peer influences, concerns about overclassification, and the potential for discrimination and segregation of the disabled combine to make special education the most litigious area and one of the most politicized areas of education in the United States. However, amidst the concerns about costs and potential negative peer spillovers, it is important not to lose sight of the fact that government-financed special education insures that disabled children receive appropriate interventions without imposing severe financial burdens on families. There is also strong evidence that the interventions significantly raise achievement for students classified as disabled (Hanushek, Kain, and Rivkin forthcoming).

As with any type of insurance, there is tension between cost containment and the provision of high-quality services, and expanded choice does not fundamentally alter the key issues. Whether more choice will lead to less involuntary segregation of students with disabilities, fewer inappropriate classifications as disabled, and more efficient and higher-quality special education programs depends in large part on the ability of policymakers to match actual costs of service provision with the funds provided. Any deviations from optimal pricing will be manifested in over- or underprovision and other undesirable outcomes.

One potential nonfinancial solution is the designation of a central agency that does not have a budgetary interest in how students are labeled to assess students and design individual education programs. However, such a solution is probably not practical in the context of special education. Unless all students can be screened for mild disabilities, as they are for hearing impairments, someone has to start the referral process. The need for flexibility in designing treatments and the lack of simple screening instruments necessitate that teachers and other personnel involved in the day-to-day schooling operations play an active role in referring students for special services. Moreover, a great deal of uncertainty remains about the success of particular types of interventions and the appropriateness of special services for a range of marginal students. Perhaps one of the greatest benefits of increasing schooling options for special education students will come through learning about the types of programs that make the most difference.

Appendix

Table 3A.1   **Gini Coefficient Corresponding to Segregation Curves for Figures 3.1 and 3.2**

	Third-Grade Peer Characteristic			
Aggregation Level	% Special Education	% Low Income	% Hispanic	% Black
School	0.32	0.36	0.52	0.67
Catchment area	0.27	0.33	0.50	0.64
District	0.23	0.28	0.45	0.55

Table 3A.2   **Gini Coefficients Corresponding to Segregation Curves for Figures 3.3, 3.4, and 3.5**

	Third-Grade Peer Characteristic		Seventh-Grade Peer Characteristic	
	% Disabled	% Ever Disabled	% Disabled	% Ever Disabled
Learning disabled				
School level	0.36	0.30	0.27	0.25
Catchment area	0.30	0.26	0.27	0.25
District level	0.25	0.22	0.23	0.22
Emotionally disturbed				
School level	0.80	0.67	0.55	0.57
Catchment area	0.69	0.58	0.55	0.57
District level	0.54	0.49	0.46	0.48
Physically disabled				
School level	0.87	0.86	0.71	0.71
Catchment area	0.75	0.73	0.70	0.71
District level	0.51	0.51	0.51	0.52
All disabilities				
School level	0.32	0.23	0.21	0.19
Catchment area	0.27	0.19	0.21	0.19
District level	0.23	0.16	0.16	0.16

Table 3A.3   Special Education Transition Rates by Grade, Disability, and Family Income

	Entering Grade							
	Not Eligible for Subsidized Lunch (%)				Eligible for Subsidized Lunch (%)			
	4	5	6	7	4	5	6	7
Learning disabled								
Not classified in either year	93.6	93.6	93.4	93.3	88.8	88.2	87.5	87.0
Classified in both years	4.9	5.6	6.0	6.0	8.5	10.2	11.6	12.0
Enters special education	1.2	0.5	0.3	0.3	2.3	1.2	0.5	0.4
Exits special education	0.3	0.3	0.4	0.5	0.4	0.4	0.5	0.6
Emotionally disturbed								
Not classified in either year	99.4	99.4	99.3	99.2	98.8	98.7	98.5	98.2
Classified in both years	0.4	0.5	0.6	0.7	0.9	1.1	1.3	1.4
Enters special education	0.1	0.1	0.1	0.1	0.3	0.1	0.1	0.1
Exits special education	0.0	0.0	0.0	0.1	0.0	0.0	0.1	0.2
Physically disabled								
Not classified in either year	99.0	98.9	98.9	98.7	99.1	99.1	99.0	98.8
Classified in both years	0.8	0.9	1.0	1.1	0.7	0.8	0.9	1.0
Enters special education	0.2	0.1	0.1	0.1	0.1	0.1	0.1	0.1
Exits special education	0.0	0.0	0.0	0.1	0.0	0.0	0.0	0.1
All disabilities								
Not classified in either year	85.6	86.8	87.7	88.6	80.1	79.4	79.2	79.5
Classified in both years	9.2	10.2	9.8	9.5	13.6	16.5	17.7	17.5
Enters special education	2.8	1.4	1.1	0.8	4.6	2.8	1.8	1.3
Exits special education	2.3	1.6	1.4	1.2	1.7	1.3	1.4	1.6

Table 3A.4   Change in School Percent Classified as Disabled in Prior Year, by Special Education Transition, Mobility, and Disability Type

	Special Education Transition (%)			
	Not Classified Either Year	Classified in Both Years	Enters Special Education	Exits Special Education
Special education				
Same school	0.3	0.2	0.6	−0.1
Within district	0.2	0.0	0.3	−0.3
Between district	0.3	0.1	0.5	0.0
All	0.3	0.2	0.5	−0.1

References

Ahearn, E. 1999. *Charter schools and special education: A report on state policies.* Alexandria, Va.: National Association of State Directors of Special Education.

Allison, P. 1978. Measures of inequality. *American Sociological Review* 43 (6): 865–80.

Bearse, P., G. Glomm, and B. Ravikumar. 2000. On the political economy of means-tested education vouchers. *European Economic Review* 44:904–51.

Bierlein, L., and M. Fulton. 1996. *Emerging issues in charter school financing.* Denver, Colo.: Education Commission of the States.

Buechler, M. 1996. *Charter schools: Legislation and results after four years.* Bloomington, Ind.: Indiana Education Policy Center, School of Education, Indiana University.

Center for Education Reform. 2002. Charter school highlights and statistics. Available at [http://www.edreform.com/pubs/chglance.htm]. 1 June 2002.

Chambers, J. 1998. The patterns of expenditures on students with disabilities: A methodological and empirical analysis. In *Funding special education,* ed. T. Parrish, J. Chambers, and C. Guarino, 89–123. Thousand Oaks, Calif.: Corwin Press.

Cullen, J. 1997. The incidence and incentives of special education policies. Ph.D. diss., Massachusetts Institute of Technology.

———. Forthcoming. The impact of fiscal incentives on student disability rates. *Journal of Public Economics.*

Cullen, J., B. Jacob, and S. Levitt. 2000. The impact of school choice on student outcomes: An analysis of the Chicago public schools. NBER Working Paper no. 7888. Cambridge, Mass.: National Bureau of Economic Research.

Epple, D., and R. Romano. 2000. Educational vouchers and cream-skimming. Carnegie-Mellon University, Department of Economics; University of Florida, Department of Economics. Unpublished manuscript.

Finn, C., B. Manno, and L. Bierlein. 1996. *Charter schools in action: What have we learned?* Washington, D.C.: Hudson Institute.

Fiore, T., and E. Cashman. 1998. *Review of charter school legislation provisions related to students with disabilities.* Washington, D.C.: Department of Education.

Fiore, T., S. Warren, and E. Cashman. 1999. *Charter schools and students with disabilities: Review of existing data.* Research Triangle Park, N.C.: Research Triangle Institution.

Fox, J. 1999. Sending public school students to private schools. *Policy Review* 93: 25–29.

Fuller, B., and R. Elmore. 1996. *Who chooses? Who loses? Cultures, institutions, and the unequal effects of school choice.* New York: Teachers College Press.

Glomm, G., D. Harris, and T. Lo. 2001. Charter school location. Indiana University, Department of Economics; Economic Policy Institute; e-progress, Inc. Unpublished manuscript.

Grosskopf, S., K. Hayes, and L. Taylor. 2000. Competition and efficiency: The impact of charter schools on public school performance. Oregon State University, Department of Economics; Southern Methodist University, Department of Economics; Federal Reserve Bank of Dallas. Unpublished manuscript.

Hanushek, E., J. Kain, and S. Rivkin. Forthcoming. Does special education raise academic achievement for students with disabilities? *Review of Economics and Statistics.*

Hanushek, E., and S. Rivkin. 1997. Understanding the twentieth-century growth in U.S. school spending. *Journal of Human Resources* 32 (1): 35–68.

Heubert, J. 1997. School without rules? Charter schools, federal disability law, and the paradoxes of deregulation. *Harvard Civil Rights-Civil Liberties Law Review* 32:301–53.

Jimerson, L. 1997. Effects of school choice in rural districts: The Minnesota experience. Ph.D. diss., University of Vermont, Burlington.

———. 1998. The students "left behind": School choice and social stratification in non-urban districts. Paper presented at the American Educational Research Association Annual Meeting. 13–17 April, San Diego, California.

Kane, D., and P. Johnson. 1993. *Vermont's Act 230: A new response to meeting the demands of diversity.* Montpelier, Vt.: Vermont Department of Education.

Kapel, D., C. Faison, and J. Gallagher. 1995. School choice: Education's trickle down theory for urban students attending private schools? Rowan College of New Jersey, College of Education. Unpublished manuscript.

Katsiyannis, A., and J. Maag. 1998. Serving children with disabilities in private and parochial schools: Issues and recommendations. *Remedial and Special Education* 19 (5): 285–90.

Lange, C., J. Ysseldyke, and T. Delaney. 1995. *Open enrollment's impact on school districts when students with disabilities transfer schools.* Enrollment Options for Students with Disabilities Project Research Report no. 14. Minneapolis, Minn.: University of Minnesota.

Lankford, H., and J. Wyckoff. 1996. The allocation of resources to special education and regular instruction. *Holding schools accountable: Performance-based reform in education,* ed. Helen Ladd, 221–57. Washington, D.C.: Brookings Institution.

Linden, M. 1995. Special education services and parochial schools: Constitutional constraints and other policy considerations. *Journal of Law and Education* 24 (3): 345–75.

McKinney, J. 1996. Charter schools: A new barrier for children with disabilities. *Education Leadership* 54 (2): 22–25.

McLaughlin, D., and S. Broughman. 1997. *Private schools in the United States: A statistical profile, 1993–94.* Washington, D.C.: National Center for Education Statistics Survey Report.

McLaughlin, M., K. Henderson, and H. Ullah. 1996. *Charter schools and students with disabilities.* Alexandria, Va.: Center for Policy Research on the Impact of General and Special Education Reform.

Moore, M., E. Strang, M. Schwartz, and M. Braddock. 1988. *Patterns in special education service delivery and cost.* Washington, D.C.: Decision Resources Group.

Osborne, A. 1999. IDEA '97: Providing special education services to students voluntarily enrolled in private schools. *Journal of Special Education* 33 (4): 224–31.

Parrish, T., F. O'Reilly, I. Duenas, and J. Wolman. 1997. *State special education finance systems, 1994–95.* Palo Alto, Calif.: American Institutes for Research.

Peterson, P., W. Howell, and J. Greene. 1999. An evaluation of the Cleveland voucher program after two years. Cambridge, Mass.: Program on Education Policy and Governance.

Peterson, P., D. Myers, and W. Howell. 1999. An evaluation of the Horizon scholarship program in the Edgewood independent school district, San Antonio, Texas: The first year. Cambridge, Mass.: The Program on Education Policy and Governance.

Powell, J., J. Blackorby, J. Marsh, K. Finnegan, and L. Anderson. 1997. *Evaluation of charter school effectiveness.* Menlo Park, Calif.: SRI International.

Rhim, L., and M. McLaughlin. 2000. *Charter schools and special education: Balancing disparate visions.* Washington, D.C.: U.S. Department of Education, Office of Special Education Programs.

Sconyers, N. 1996. What parents want: A report on parents' opinions about public schools. Johns Hopkins University, Center on Families, Communities, Schools, and Children's Learning.

Singer, J., J. Palfrey, J. Butler, and D. Walker. 1989. Variation in special education classification across school districts: How does where you live affect what you are labeled? *American Educational Research Journal* 26:261–81.

Szabo, J., and M. Gerber. 1996. Special education and the charter school movement. *Special Education Leadership Review* 3:135–48.

Urhan, S., and D. Stewart. 1994. *Minnesota charter schools: A research report.* Minneapolis, Minn.: House Research Department.

U.S. Department of Education (DOE). 1999. *The state of charter schools: Third-year report.* Washington, D.C.: Office of Educational Research and Improvement.

———. 2000. *Venturesome capital: State charter school finance systems.* Washington, D.C.: Office of Educational Research and Improvement.

Vanourek, G., B. Manno, C. Finn, and L. Bierlein. 1997. *The educational impact of charter schools, final report, part V.* Washington, D.C.: Hudson Institute.

Verstegen, D. 1994. Fiscal provisions of the Individuals with Disabilities Education Act: Historical overview. Center for Special Education Finance Policy Paper no. 2. Palo Alto, Calif.: American Institutes for Research.

Ysseldyke, J., C. Lange, and D. Gorney. 1994. Parents of students with disabilities and open enrollment: Characteristics and reasons for transfer. *Exceptional Children* 60 (4): 359–72.

4

School Vouchers
Results from Randomized
Experiments

Paul E. Peterson, William G. Howell, Patrick J. Wolf, and David E. Campbell

In the past decade much has been learned about the way in which school vouchers affect low-income families and their children. Ten years ago, the empirical information available about this widely debated question came primarily from a flawed public school choice intervention attempted in Alum Rock, California during the 1960s (Bridge and Blackman 1978; El-

Paul E. Peterson is the Henry Lee Shattuck Professor of Government and director of the Program on Education Policy and Governance at Harvard University. William G. Howell is assistant professor of government at Harvard University. Patrick J. Wolf is assistant professor of public policy at Georgetown University. David E. Campbell is assistant professor of political science at Notre Dame University.

The authors wish to thank the principals, teachers, and staff at the private schools in Dayton, Washington, and New York City who assisted in the administration of tests and questionnaires. We also wish to thank the SCSF, PACE, and WSF for cooperating fully with these evaluations. Kristin Kearns Jordan, Tom Carroll, and other members of the SCSF staff assisted with data collection in New York City. John Blakeslee, Leslie Curry, Douglas Dewey, Laura Elliot, Heather Hamilton, Tracey Johnson, John McCardell, and Patrick Purtill of the Washington Scholarship Fund provided similar cooperation. T. J. Wallace and Mary Lynn Naughton, staff members of Parents Advancing Choice in Education, provided valuable assistance with the Dayton evaluation. Chester E. Finn, Bruno Manno, Gregg Vanourek, and Marci Kanstoroom of the Fordham Foundation, Edward P. St. John of Indiana University, and Thomas Lasley of the University of Dayton provided valuable suggestions throughout various stages of the research design and data collection. We wish to thank especially David Myers of Mathematical Policy Research, a principal investigator of the evaluation of the New York School Choice Scholarship Program; his work on the New York evaluation has influenced in many important ways the design of the Washington and Dayton evaluations. We thank William McCready, Robin Bebel, Kirk Miller, and other members of the staff of the Public Opinion Laboratory at Northern Illinois University for their assistance with data collection, data processing, conduct of the lottery, and preparation of baseline and year-one follow-up data. We are particularly grateful to Tina Elacqua, Matthew Charles, and Brian Harrigan for their key roles in coordinating data collection efforts.

We received helpful advice from Paul Hill, Christopher Jencks, Derek Neal, Donald Rock, and Donald Rubin. Daniel Mayer and Julia Chou were instrumental in preparing the New York City survey and test score data and executing many of the analyses reported in the paper.

more 1990). In the early and mid-1990s, however, new voucher programs sprouted across the country in such cities as Milwaukee, Cleveland, Indianapolis, and San Antonio. Initially, the evaluations of these innovations were limited by the quality of the data or the research procedures employed. Often, planning for the evaluation began after the experiment was under way, which made it impossible to gather baseline data or to ensure the formation of an appropriate control group. As a result, the quality of the data collected was not as high as researchers normally would prefer.[1]

Despite their limitations, these early evaluations provided program operators and evaluation teams with opportunities to learn the problems and pitfalls accompanying the study of school vouchers. Subsequent evaluations of voucher programs in New York, Washington, D.C., and Dayton, Ohio have been designed in such a way as to allow for the collection of higher-quality information about student test score outcomes and parental assessments of public and private schools. Because vouchers in these cities were awarded by lot, program evaluations could be designed as randomized field trials. Prior to conducting the lotteries, the evaluation team collected baseline data on student test scores and family background characteristics. One, two, and three years later, the evaluation team again tested the students and asked parents about their children's school experiences.[2] In the absence of response biases that are conditional on treatment status, any statistically significant differences between students offered a voucher and those not offered a voucher may be attributed to the intervention, because average student initial abilities and family backgrounds are similar between

Additional research assistance was provided by Rachel Deyette, Jennifer Hill, and Martin West; Antonio Wendland, Tom Polseno, Shelley Weiner, Lilia Halpern, and Micki Morris provided staff assistance.

These evaluations have been supported by grants from the following foundations: Achelis Foundation, Bodman Foundation, Lynde and Harry Bradley Foundation, William Donner Foundation, Thomas B. Fordham Foundation, Milton and Rose D. Friedman Foundation, John M. Olin Foundation, David and Lucile Packard Foundation, Smith-Richardson Foundation, Spencer Foundation, and Walton Family Foundation. The methodology, analyses of data, reported findings, and interpretations of findings are the sole responsibility of the authors of this report and are not subject to the approval of SCSF, WSF, PACE, or of any foundation providing support for this research.

1. Disparate findings have emerged from these studies. For example, one analysis of the Milwaukee choice experiment found test score gains in reading and math, particularly after students had been enrolled for three or more years, whereas another study found gains only in math, and a third found gains in neither subject. See Greene, Peterson, and Du (1998); Rouse (1997); and Witte (1997). On the Cleveland program, see Greene, Howell, and Peterson (1998) and Metcalf et al. (1998). Greene, Peterson, and Du (1998) report results from analyses of experimental data; the other studies are based upon analyses of nonexperimental data.

2. Results from the Dayton evaluation after one year are reported in Howell and Peterson (2000). Second-year results for Dayton are described in West, Peterson, and Campbell (2001). First-year results for Washington are reported in Wolf, Howell, and Peterson (2000). Second-year results for Washington are reported in Wolf, Peterson, and West (2001). First-year results from the New York City evaluation are reported in Peterson et al. (1999). Second-year results from New York City are described in David Myers et al. (2000). All of the occasional papers mentioned in this note are available at [http://data.fas.harvard.edu/pepg/].

the two groups. Students and families who were evaluated entered private school in grades two through five in New York City and grades two through eight in Washington, D.C. and Dayton (and other parts of Montgomery County, Ohio).[3] This chapter reports programmatic impacts on student test scores, parents' satisfaction with their child's school, and parent reports of the characteristics of the schools the child attended.

4.1   The Three Voucher Programs

The design of the three voucher programs was similar in key respects, thereby allowing the evaluation team to combine results from the separate evaluations of these programs. All were privately funded; all were targeted at students from low-income families, most of whom lived within the central city; and all provided partial vouchers, which the family was expected to supplement from other resources. All students included in the evaluation had previously been attending public schools. The programs, however, did differ in size, timing, and certain administrative details. In this section we describe the main characteristics of the School Choice Scholarships Foundation program in New York City, the Washington Scholarship Fund program in Washington, D.C., and the Parents Advancing Choice in Education program in the Dayton metropolitan area.

4.1.1   The School Choice Scholarships Foundation
Program in New York City

In February 1997, the School Choice Scholarships Foundation (SCSF) announced that it would provide 1,300 scholarships worth up to $1,400 annually for at least three years to children from low-income families then attending public schools. The scholarship could be applied toward the cost of attending a private school, either religious or secular. After announcing the program, SCSF received initial applications from over 20,000 students between February and late April 1997.

To be eligible for a scholarship, children had to be entering grades one through five, live in New York City, attend a public school at the time of application, and come from families with incomes low enough to qualify for the U.S. government's free or reduced school lunch program. To ascertain eligibility, students and an adult member of their family were asked to attend verification sessions during which family income and the child's public school attendance were documented.

Subsequent to the lottery, SCSF assisted families in identifying possible private schools their children might attend. By the end of the first year,

---

3. Baseline data from the D.C. and Dayton evaluations are reported in Peterson et al. (1998). Baseline data for New York City are reported in Peterson et al. (1997). Both of these reports are available at [http://data.fas.harvard.edu/pepg/].

about 82 percent of the students participating in the evaluation were using a scholarship; 79 percent of the participating students used the voucher for two full years, and 70 percent for three full years.[4]

4.1.2   The Parents Advancing Choice in Education Program in Dayton, Ohio

In the spring of 1998, Parents Advancing Choice in Education (PACE), a privately funded nonprofit corporation, offered low-income families within the Dayton metropolitan area an opportunity to win a scholarship to help defray the costs of attending the school of their choice. Eligible applicants participated in a lottery in which winners were offered a scholarship that could be used at participating private and public schools in Dayton and in other parts of Montgomery County, Ohio. Students entering kindergarten through twelfth grade qualified. For the 1998–99 school year, PACE offered scholarships to 515 students who were in public schools and 250 students who were already enrolled in private schools.

The program was announced in January 1998. Based on census data and administrative records, program operators estimated that approximately 32,000 students met the program's income and eligibility requirements. The PACE program accepted preliminary applications from over 3,000 students, of whom 1,500 attended sessions where administrators verified their eligibility for a scholarship, students took the Iowa Test of Basic Skills (ITBS), and parents completed questionnaires. These verification sessions were held in February, March, and April 1998. The lottery was then conducted on 29 April 1998.

During the first year of the program, the PACE scholarships covered 50 percent of tuition at a private school, up to a maximum award of $1,200. Support was guaranteed for eligible students for at least four years; in addition, the program expects to support students through the completion of high school, provided funds remain available. Scholarship amounts were augmented beginning in 1999 as a result of additional funds available to PACE and support for the program by the Children's Scholarship Fund, a nationwide school choice scholarship program.

Among the public school students offered a scholarship, 78 percent of the students participating in the evaluation attended a private school in the program's first year, and 60 percent were in private schools after two years.

4.1.3   The Washington Scholarship Fund Program in Washington, D.C.

The Washington Scholarship Fund (WSF), a privately funded school voucher program, was originally established in 1993. At that time, a limited number of scholarships, which could be used at a private school of the fam-

---

4. For a description of the kinds of private schools voucher students attended, see Howell et al. (2002).

ily's choice, were offered to students from low-income families. By the fall of 1997, WSF was serving approximately 460 children at 72 private schools. The WSF then received a large infusion of new funds from two philanthropists, and a major expansion of the program was announced in October 1997. Both general news announcements and paid advertising were used to publicize the enlarged school choice scholarship program. The WSF announced that, in the event that applications exceeded scholarship resources, winners would be chosen by lottery. The program expanded further in 1999 with support from the Children's Scholarship Fund.

To qualify, applicants had to reside in Washington, D.C. and be entering grades K-8 in the fall of 1998. The WSF awarded parents with incomes at or below the poverty line vouchers that equaled 60 percent of tuition or $1,700, whichever was less. Families with incomes above the poverty line received smaller scholarships. The maximum amount of tuition support for high school students was $2,200. The WSF has said that it will attempt to continue tuition support to the children in its program for at least three years and, if funds are available, until they complete high school. No family with income above 2.7 times the poverty line was eligible for support.

Over 7,500 telephone applications to the program were received between October 1997 and March 1998; in response to invitations sent by WSF, over 3,000 applicants attended verification and testing sessions. The lottery selecting scholarship winners was held in April 1998. The WSF awarded over 1,000 new scholarships that year, with 811 going to students not previously in a private school.

Provided they gained admission, scholarship students could attend any private school in the Washington area. During the 1998–99 school year, students participating in the evaluation attended seventy-two different private schools. Of those students offered scholarships who participated in the evaluation, 68 percent attended a private school in the first year of the program. Take-up rates declined to 47 percent in the second year and to just 29 percent at the end of the third year.

4.2   Evaluation Procedures

The evaluation procedures used in all three evaluations conform to those used in randomized field trials. The evaluation team collected baseline data prior to the lottery, administered the lottery, and then collected follow-up information one and two years later. This section details the steps taken to collect the relevant information.

4.2.1   Baseline Data Collection

During the eligibility verification sessions attended by voucher applicants, students in first grade and higher took the Iowa Test of Basic Skills (ITBS) in reading and mathematics. The sessions took place during the months of February, March, and April, immediately prior to the voucher lottery, and generally lasted about two hours. The sessions were held in private-school classrooms, where schoolteachers and administrators served as proctors under the overall supervision of the evaluation team and program sponsors. The producer of the ITBS graded the tests.[5] Students in grades four through eight also completed a short questionnaire about their school experiences.

While children were being tested, adults accompanying them filled out surveys that asked about their satisfaction with their children's schools, their involvement in their children's education, and their demographic characteristics. Parents completed these questionnaires in rooms separate from those used for testing. Administrators explained that individual responses to the questionnaire would be held in strict confidence. Respondents had considerable time to complete their surveys, and administrators were available to answer questions about the meaning of particular items. Extensive information from these surveys has been reported elsewhere.[6]

Over 5,000 public-school students participated in baseline testing in New York City. After vouchers were awarded, 960 families were selected at random from those who did not win the lottery to comprise a control group of approximately 960 families.[7]

In Dayton, 1,440 students were tested at baseline, and 1,232 parent questionnaires were completed. Of the 1,440 students, 803 were not at the time attending a private school; of the 1,232 parent questionnaires, 690 were completed by parents of students who were not attending a private school. Follow-up testing information is reported only for families whose children attended public schools at the time of application.

In Washington, D.C., 2,023 students were tested at baseline; 1,928 parent surveys asking questions about each child were completed; 938 student surveys were completed. Of the 2,023 students tested, 1,582 were not attending a private school at the time of application for a scholarship; of the 1,928 parent questionnaires, 1,446 were completed by parents whose children were not then attending a private school. Follow-up testing and survey information was obtained only from families with children then in public schools.

4.2.2   The Lottery

The evaluation team conducted the lotteries in May 1997 in New York City and April 1998 in Dayton and D.C. Program operators notified lottery

5. The assessment used in this study is Form M of the Iowa Tests of Basic Skills, Copyright (c) 1996 by The University of Iowa, published by The Riverside Publishing Company, 425 Spring Lake Drive, Itasca, Illinois 60143-2079. All rights reserved.
6. See Howell et al. (2002). Prior reports include Peterson et al. (1999); Myers et al. (2000); Howell and Peterson (2000); West, Peterson, and Campbell (2001); Wolf, Howell, and Peterson (2000); Wolf, Peterson, and West (2001). All reports available at [http://data.fas.harvard.edu/pepg/].
7. Exact procedures for the formation of the control group are described in Hill, Rubin, and Thomas (1998).

winners shortly thereafter. If a family was selected, all children in that family entering eligible grades were offered a scholarship. Separate lotteries were held in Dayton and D.C. for students then in public and private schools, ensuring random assignment to test and control groups of those families participating in the evaluation.

In New York City, Mathematica Policy Research (MPR) administered the lottery; SCSF announced the winners. The SCSF decided in advance to allocate 85 percent of the scholarships to applicants from public schools whose average test scores were less than the citywide median. Consequently, applicants from these schools, who represented about 70 percent of all applicants, were assigned a higher probability of winning a scholarship. In the information reported in the tables, results have been adjusted by weighting cases differentially so that they can be generalized to all eligible applicants who would have come to the verification sessions had they been invited, regardless of whether or not they attended a low-performing school.

Because vouchers were allocated by a lottery conducted by the evaluation team, those offered scholarships should not be expected to differ significantly from members of the control group (those who did not win a scholarship). For all three cities, baseline data confirm this expectation. For instance, in D.C., the baseline test scores of those entering grades two through eight who were offered a voucher averaged 29.6 national percentile points in reading and 23.3 in mathematics; those not offered the scholarship scored, on average, 30.6 national percentile points in reading and 23.1 points in math. As in D.C., the demographic characteristics of those offered vouchers in Dayton and New York did not differ significantly from the characteristics of those who were not offered a voucher.[8]

4.2.3 Collection of Follow-Up Information

The annual collection of follow-up information commenced in New York City in the spring of 1998 and in Dayton and D.C. in the spring of 1999. Data collection procedures were similar across cities.

In New York City, testing and questionnaire administration procedures replicated those followed at baseline. Adult members of the family completed surveys that asked a wide range of questions about the educational experiences of their oldest child within the age range eligible for a scholarship. Students completed the ITBS and short questionnaires. Both the voucher students and students in the control group were tested in locations other than the school they were then attending.

The SCSF conditioned the renewal of scholarships on participation in the evaluation. Also, non–scholarship winners selected to become members of the control group were compensated for their expenses and told that they could automatically reapply for a new lottery if they participated in these

---

8. For a more extended discussion on these matters, see the initial reports for each city cited in notes 2 and 3.

follow-up sessions. Detailed response rate information for the follow-up survey and testing sessions is reported in appendix A.

In Washington, D.C. and Dayton, the evaluation team began collecting follow-up information between late February and late April of 1999. As in New York, the procedures used to obtain follow-up data were essentially the same as those used to collect baseline data. Students again took the ITBS in mathematics and reading. Caretakers accompanying the children completed surveys that asked a wide range of questions about the educational experiences of the children. Students in grades four through eight also completed a questionnaire that asked about their experiences at school. Testing and questionnaire administration procedures were similar to those that had been followed at baseline.[9] The Dayton evaluation was concluded after two years; in D.C., however, a third-year follow-up collection of testing and survey information was conducted in 2001.

To obtain a high participation rate in the follow-up data collection effort, those who had declined the offer of a voucher and members of the control group were compensated for their expenses. They were also told in Washington, D.C. that if they participated in the follow-up sessions, they would be included in a new lottery. In Dayton, a second lottery was promised as a reward for participating in the first follow-up session. In the second year, however, Dayton families were only given financial rewards for participation.

Because test score results from the second and third years of the evaluation differ significantly between African American students and those from other ethnic backgrounds, the ethnic composition of the students participating in the evaluation is particularly salient. Forty-two percent of the students participating in the second year of the evaluation in New York City were African Americans. In Dayton and D.C., 74 percent and 95 percent were African American, respectively. Hispanic students participating in the second year of the evaluation constituted 51 percent of the total in New York City, 2 percent in Dayton, and 4 percent in Washington, D.C. Finally, 5 percent of the students participating in the evaluation in New York City were white. In Dayton and D.C., 24 percent and 1 percent were white, respectively. The remaining students came from a variety of other ethnic backgrounds.

4.3   Data Analysis and Reporting Procedures

The evaluation takes advantage of the fact that a lottery was used to award scholarships. As a result, it is possible to compare two groups of stu-

---

9. Difficulties were encountered in the administration of the first-year follow-up test at the initial pilot session in Washington, D.C. Test booklets were not available at the testing site for scholarship students in grades three through eight. Copies of the test arrived eventually, but the amount of time available for testing may have been foreshortened. Significant effects on reading scores are not apparent, but significant effects on math performance are evident, probably because the math test was the last to be administered. Statistical adjustments in the test score analysis take into account the special circumstances of the pilot session.

dents that were similar, on average, except that members of the control group were not offered a scholarship. Any statistically significant differences between the two groups may be attributed to the school experience, not the child's initial ability or family background, which were essentially the same at baseline. One possible threat to the validity of this causal inference would be differential response patterns to follow-up testing by members of the treatment and control groups based on conditions that developed after they were tested at baseline.[10] We discuss that possibility in appendix A (see also Howell et al. 2002; Howell and Peterson 2002).

This paper provides data that help answer two questions. The first is what the impact on educational outcomes was of an *offer* of a voucher to low-income families residing within a large central city. This is the intention-to-treat or ITT effect of the voucher. The ITT effect compares educational outcomes of those who were offered a voucher to the outcomes of those who were not offered a voucher. To compute program impacts on children's test scores, we estimated a statistical model that took into account students' treatment or control group status as well as baseline reading and math test scores. Baseline test scores were included to (a) adjust for minor baseline differences between the treatment and control groups on the achievement tests, and (b) to increase the precision of the estimated impacts.

Generalization from these results has the important disadvantage of assuming that usage rates of scholarships are fixed. Depending upon the size of the scholarship, the time the scholarship is offered, and the marketing of the program as a whole, however, usage rates might be highly variable. Consequently, we report ITT results for test scores in appendix B. In the text of this chapter we report answers to a second question: What was the impact on educational experiences, parental satisfaction, and test score performances of students from low-income families residing within a large central city one, two, and three years after switching from a public to a private school? This is the treatment-on-the-treated or TOT effect of the voucher. The answer to this question requires a comparison between those students who were offered vouchers and switched from a public to a private school with public-school students who would have switched to a private school had they been offered a voucher. To compute the program's impact on those who used a scholarship to attend a private school, we estimated two-stage least squares models. The instrument is the voucher lottery, which is highly correlated with attendance at a private school, but because it is randomly determined, is obviously uncorrelated with the error term in the second-stage equation. As a result, the model yields an unbiased estimate of the effects of switching to a private school.[11]

The paper reports the TOT impact on students school experiences, parental satisfaction, and test score performance of a switch from a public

---

10. We are indebted to Derek Neal for calling this interesting contingency to our attention.

11. This procedure is discussed in Angrist, Imbens, and Rubin (1996). The procedure, widely used by statisticians to correct for selection effects, was used to estimate the effects of actual class size reduction in Tennessee; see Krueger (1999).

to a private school for one, two, and three years. Second- and third-year results compare those in private schools for two or three years with comparable members of the control group that were not in private school for two
and three years, respectively.

4.4 Test Score Findings

We compare the performance of public and private school students on
the ITBS in reading and mathematics, as well as their combined performance in both subject areas. Scores range between 0 and 100 National Percentile Ranking (NPR) points, with the national median located at the 50th
percentile. The results reported below represent the first student achievement information from randomized field trials on the effects of school
vouchers. However, they do not so much break new ground as build upon a
body of research that has explored the differences between schooling for
low-income minorities in the public and private sectors.

4.4.1 Prior Research

Studies of attainment levels and test performance of students in public
and private schools usually find that low-income and African American
students attending private schools outperform their public school peers.
According to a recent analysis of 12,000 students in the National Longitudinal Survey of Youth, for instance, even when adjustments are made for
family background, students from all racial and ethnic groups are more
likely to go to college if they attended a Catholic school; however, the effects
are the greatest among urban minorities (Neal 1997). This study's findings
are consistent with others' (Evans and Schwab 1993; Figlio and Stone
1999). After reviewing the literature on school effects on learning, University of Wisconsin Professor John Witte (1996) concludes that the
empirical literature "indicate[s] a substantial private school advantage in
terms of completing high school and enrolling in college, both very important events in predicting future income and well-being. Moreover, . . . the
effects were most pronounced for students with achievement test scores in
the bottom half of the distribution" (167).

Even the most careful of studies, however, can take into account only observed family background characteristics. They cannot be sure that they
have controlled for an intangible factor—the willingness of parents to pay
for their child's tuition, and all that this implies about the importance they
place on education. As a result, it remains unclear whether the findings from
these studies describe actual differences between public and private schools
or simply differences in the kinds of students and families attending them.[12]

12. Major studies finding positive educational benefits from attending private schools include Coleman, Hoffer, and Kilgore (1982) and Chubb and Moe (1997). Critiques of these
studies have been prepared by Goldberger and Cain (1982) and Wilms (1985).

The best solution to the self-selection problem is the random assignment of students to test and control groups. Until recently, evaluations of voucher programs have not utilized a random-assignment research design and therefore have not overcome the possible selection problems. Privately funded programs in Indianapolis, San Antonio, and Milwaukee admitted students on a first-come, first-served basis. In the state-funded program in Cleveland, although scholarship winners were initially selected by means of a lottery, eventually all applicants were offered a scholarship, thereby precluding the conduct of a randomized experiment. The public Milwaukee program did award vouchers by a lottery, but data collection was incomplete.[13]

As a consequence, the findings presented here on New York, D.C., and Dayton provide a unique opportunity to examine the effects of school vouchers on students from low-income families who live in central cities. In contrast to prior studies, random assignment was conducted by the evaluation team, follow-up test-score information was obtained from about one-half to four-fifths of the students who participated in the lottery, and baseline data provided information that allowed the analysts to adjust for non-response.

4.4.2   Impacts of Private-School Attendance on Test Scores

In interpreting the findings reported below, emphasis is placed on the estimated effects of attending a private school on combined test scores for all three cities, taken together. Because of minor fluctuations in data collection, average estimates from more than one city provide a better indication of programmatic effects than do the results from any one city. Also, when student performance is estimated on the basis of one-hour testing sessions, combined test score performance of students on the reading and math tests is a better indicator of student achievement than either test separately. Theoretically, the more test items used to evaluate performance, the more likely it is that one will estimate performance accurately. Empirically, performances on the two tests are highly correlated with one another (r equals about 0.7). In addition, results from the two tests, when combined together, were found to be more stable across time and from place to place, indicating that combining results from the two tests reduces what is probably idiosyncratic variations in observations of student performance.[14]

As can be seen in table 4.1, the impact of private school attendance on student test score performance differed for African Americans and members of other ethnic groups. One observes no significant differences between the test score performance of non–African American students switching from a public to a private school and the performance of their peers in the control group, after one, two, or three years. Nor were significant differ-

13. Results from these evaluations are reported in Peterson and Hassel (1998).
14. This procedure was also employed in Krueger (1999).

Table 4.1   The Impact in Three Cities of Switching to a Private School on Test
                   Score Performance

Test Score Performance	Year One (Percentiles)	Year Two (Percentiles)	Year Three (Percentiles)
African Americans			
Overall	3.9*	6.3***	6.6**
	(2.0)	(2.5)	(2.8)
Math	6.1***	6.1**	4.2*
	(2.4)	(3.1)	(2.2)
Reading	2.1	5.9**	4.2
	(2.4)	(2.9)	(3.5)
All other ethnic groups			
Overall	–1.6	–1.4	–3.5
	(2.4)	(2.9)	(2.7)
Math	–2.5	–2.6	–2.7
	(3.1)	(3.9)	(3.3)
Reading	–0.7	–0.2	–4.2
	(2.5)	(3.0)	(2.9)

Notes: Figures represent the average impact of switching to a private school on test score performance scores in New York, D.C., and Dayton. Averages are based upon effects observed in
the three cities weighted by the inverse of the variance of the point estimates. Standard errors
reported in parentheses. For African Americans, the unweighted average effects after one year
are 2.7 overall, 4.8 in math, and 0.6 in reading; after two years, the unweighted average effect
sizes are 6.6 overall, 6.5 in math, and 6.8 in reading. All models control for baseline test scores
and lottery indicators. Impacts expressed in national percentile rankings.
***Significant at the 1 percent level, two-tailed test.
**Significant at the 5 percent level.
*Significant at the 10 percent level.

ences observed in these students' reading and math tests, considered separately.

The effects of switching to a private school on African American students
differed markedly from the effects on students from other ethnic backgrounds. In the three cities, taken together, African American students who
switched from public to private schools scored, after one year, 3.9 NPR
points higher on the combined math and reading tests, and, after two and
three years, 6.3 percentile and 6.6 points higher, respectively, than the
African American students in the control group. Again, these are the average results for the three cities combined, weighting each city estimate in inverse proportion to its respective variance.

The findings for each city are reported in tables 4.2, 4.3, and 4.4. The
largest differences after three years were observed in New York City. In this
city, African American students attending private schools for three years
scored 9.2 percentile points higher on the two tests combined than did students in the control group. In D.C., however, no significant differences were
observed after three years, despite the fact that large two-year effects were

Table 4.2 **Impact in New York of Switching to a Private School on Test Score Performance**

Test Score Performance	Year One (Percentiles)	N	Year Two (Percentiles)	N	Year Three (Percentiles)	N
African Americans						
Overall	5.4***	622	4.4**	497	9.2***	519
	(1.5)		(2.0)		(2.4)	
Math	6.9***	622	4.1*	497	11.8***	519
	(1.8)		(2.5)		(2.9)	
Reading	4.0**	622	4.5**	497	6.7**	519
	(1.8)		(2.3)		(2.9)	
All other ethnic groups						
Overall	−2.2	812	−1.5	699	−3.5	729
	(1.8)		(2.2)		(2.4)	
Math	−3.2	812	−3.2	699	−2.5	729
	(2.3)		(2.9)		(2.9)	
Reading	−1.2	812	0.2	699	−4.4*	729
	(1.9)		(2.3)		(2.6)	

Notes: Weighted two-stage least squares regressions performed; treatment status used as instrument. Standard errors reported in parentheses. All models control for baseline test scores and lottery indicators. Impacts expressed in terms of national percentile rankings.
***Significant at the 1 percent level, two-tailed test.
**Significant at the 5 percent level.
*Significant at the 10 percent level.

Table 4.3 **Impact in Dayton of Switching to a Private School on Test Score Performance**

Test Score Performance	Year One (Percentiles)	N	Year Two (Percentiles)	N
African Americans				
Overall	3.3	296	6.5*	273
	(3.5)		(3.7)	
Math	0.4	296	5.3	273
	(4.0)		(4.3)	
Reading	6.1	296	7.6*	273
	(4.2)		(4.2)	
All other ethnic groups				
Overall	1.0	108	−0.2	96
	(6.4)		(9.0)	
Math	−0.8	108	0.0	96
	(7.5)		(10.7)	
Reading	2.8	108	−0.4	96
	(7.1)		(9.9)	

Notes: Weighted two-stage least squares regressions performed; treatment status used as instrument. All models control for baseline test scores. Impacts expressed in terms of national percentile rankings. Standard errors reported in parentheses.
*Significant at the 10 percent level.

Table 4.4   Impact in D.C. of Switching to a Private School on Test Score Performance

Test Score Performance	Year One (Percentiles)	N	Year Two (Percentiles)	N	Year Three (Percentiles)	N
African Americans						
Overall	−0.9	891	9.2***	668	−1.9	656
	(2.8)		(2.9)		(4.4)	
Math	7.3**	891	10.4***	668	0.9	656
	(3.3)		(3.4)		(1.9)	
Reading	−9.0**	891	8.0***	668	−4.6	656
	(3.7)		(3.4)		(5.4)	
All other ethnic groups						
Overall	7.4	39	−0.1	42	−1.8	31
	(8.7)		(9.8)		(13.3)	
Math	8.5	39	7.3	42	−9.5	31
	(10.7)		(13.4)		(15.4)	
Reading	6.3	39	−7.6	42	5.9	31
	(12.7)		(10.1)		(18.7)	

Notes: Weighted two-stage least squares regressions performed; treatment status used as instrument. Standard errors reported in parentheses. All models control for baseline test scores; in year one, models also control for initial testing session. Impacts expressed in terms of national percentile rankings.
***Significant at the 1 percent level, two-tailed test.
**Significant at the 5 percent level.

observed. In Dayton, the difference in combined test score performance was 6.5 percentile points after two years, the total duration of the evaluation.

The trend over time also varies from one city to the next. As can be seen in table 4.2, in New York City, substantial test score differences between African American students in private and public schools appear at the end of the first year (5.4 percentile points) and attenuate slightly in the second year (4.4 points) but increase to 9.2 percentile points in year three. In this city, test score gains appeared to grow over time.

In Dayton, there was a steady upward trend in the combined test score performance of African Americans between years one and two. Table 4.3 shows that African American students who switched from public to private schools performed 3.3 percentile points higher on the combined test in year one and 6.5 percentile points higher in year two. Once again, a model of accumulated gains could account for the findings.

The most uncertain results for African Americans come from Washington, D.C. As can be seen in table 4.4, no significant differences were observed in year one, a large impact was observed after two years, but no impact was observed at the end of year three. Three factors could account for such disparate findings. First, because only 29 percent of the students in the evaluation continued to use the voucher after three years (as compared to 70 percent in New York City), third-year estimations are quite imprecise. Second, the voucher experiment in D.C. was contaminated by the inauguration of a charter-school initiative that gave families more choices than

Table 4.5   Size of the Effects of Switching to a Private School on African
                   Americans' Overall Test Score Performances (standard deviations)

Test Score Performance	Year One	Year Two	Year Three
Overall	0.18	0.28	0.30
Math	0.28	0.28	0.18
Reading	0.08	0.23	0.16

Note: Figures represent the unweighted average impact of switching to a private school on test scores in New York, D.C., and Dayton expressed in standard deviations.

those available in New York City; indeed, 17 percent of the treatment group and 24 percent of the control group in D.C. attended charter schools in the third year of the evaluation. Finally, the differences in the third-year results might be attributed to the more established private sector in New York City than in Washington, D.C. Catholic schools, the major provider of private education in the two cities, are better endowed and historically more rooted in the northern port city, whose Catholic, immigrant population dates back to the early nineteenth century.[15]

4.4.3   Interpreting the Magnitude of the Test Score Effects

Overall, the effects of attending a private school on student test scores are moderately large. As can be seen in table 4.5, black students who switched to private schools scored, after one year, 0.18 standard deviations higher than the students in the control group. After two and three years, the size of the effect grew to 0.28 and 0.30 standard deviations, respectively, more than a quarter of the difference in test score performances between blacks and whites nationwide (Jencks and Phillips 1999). Continuing evaluations of voucher programs may provide information on whether or not these gains can be consolidated and extended.

Another way of assessing the magnitude of these effects is to compare them to those observed in an evaluation of a class size reduction intervention conducted in Tennessee, the only other major education reform to be subjected to evaluation by means of a randomized field trial. The effects on African Americans of attendance at a private school shown here are comparable to the estimated effect of a seven-student reduction in class size. According to a recent reanalysis of data from Tennessee, the class size effect for African Americans after two years was, on average, between 7 and 8 percentile points (Krueger and Whitmore 2000).

It is also of interest to compare the size of the effects of the voucher intervention with the size of the effects reported in a RAND study entitled *Improving School Achievement,* released in August 2000 (Flanagan, Kawata, and Williamson 2000, 59). Identifying the most successful states, Texas and North Carolina, which have introduced rigorous accountability systems

---

15. For a fuller discussion, see Howell et al. (2002, chaps. 2, 6).

that involve statewide testing, the study finds what it says are "remarkable" one-year gains in math scores in these states of "as much as 0.06 to 0.07 standard deviation[s] per year"—or 0.18 to 0.21 over three years. The three-year effects of the school voucher intervention on black students observed here are somewhat larger.

4.4.4   Cost-Benefit Analysis

What are these test score gains for African Americans likely to mean in terms of future economic benefits? Richard Murname and his colleagues have calculated the effects of math achievement on future earnings (Murname et al. 2000). According to one estimate, a 0.30 standard deviation increase in average math achievement, if sustained, will yield a 5 percent gain in earnings seven to ten years after the student finishes high school. If an African American student in the control group was expected to earn about $30,000 a year in his late twenties, a comparable student who had switched from public to private school would be expected to earn an additional $1,500 per year.

This suggests that investments in vouchers might yield a moderate rate of return for African American families. Why, then, don't families make this investment on their own? If a control group family had simply absorbed the cost of the voucher (on average, about $1,200), even a rough calculation of the rate of return suggests that it would be an attractive investment, provided that families can borrow moneys at conventional rates. Credit constraints are a possible explanation for the decision not to utilize a private school on the part of control group families. Private lenders may be reluctant to make long-term loans at conventional lending rates to low-income borrowers, who may be high credit risks. If families can borrow the money only at rates charged to high-risk users of bank cards, then the rate of return on an investment in private schooling, although probably still positive, would be considerably less attractive—unless a family perceives nonpecuniary benefits of a private education.

Clearly, though, the lower the initial costs, the more attractive an investment in private schooling becomes. When a voucher reduces the amount that needs to be borrowed from around $2,400 a year (a rough estimate of the average cost of private school tuition, fees, books, and uniforms in these cities) to half that amount, families may decide that the benefits of an investment in private schooling now outweigh the costs. Perhaps this explains why a small voucher induced many low-income families to make the additional investment, even when members of a similarly situated control group (who did not receive the voucher offer) were less likely to do so.[16]

---

16. A careful analysis of this question would require a fuller examination of the probable economic benefits of test score gains, the cost of private schooling, and the interest rates faced by various classes of potential borrowers.

4.4.5   Additional Methodological Considerations

This section addresses two methodological considerations. The first involves the status of background control variables. In table 4.6 we report second- and third-year results for African Americans from statistical models that control not only for initial test scores (as do the analyses in the previous tables) but also for mother's education, mother's employment status, family size, and whether or not the family received welfare benefits. The estimated impacts on the test scores of African Americans of switching from a public to a private school in the three cities remain almost exactly the same: 6.4 percentile points in the second year and (though not shown) 6.7 percentile points in the third. Minor differences are observed when impacts within each individual city are estimated. For instance, when we estimate effects in New York City in the second year without controlling for family background characteristics, the impact is 4.3 NPR points; when family background controls are added, the impact is 4.5 NPR points. In Dayton, Ohio, when controls are introduced, the point estimate drops from 6.5 to 5.9 NPR points. In Washington, D.C., the estimated impact after two years remains 9.2 NPR points.

The second methodological consideration concerns the possibility that African Americans posted significant effects because they received a more uniform treatment. If the black students who used vouchers were dispro-

Table 4.6   **Estimated Effects after Two Years of Switching from a Public to a Private School on African Americans' Combined Test Scores, With and Without Controls for Family Background Characteristics**

	Private School Impact, Original Results	Private School Impact, Controlling for Family Background
Three-city average impact	6.3***	6.4**
	(2.5)	(2.5)
New York City	4.4**	4.5**
	(2.0)	(2.0)
Dayton, Ohio	6.5*	5.9
	(3.7)	(3.8)
Washington, D.C.	9.2***	9.2***
	(2.9)	(2.8)

Notes: P-values reported in parentheses. Weighted two-stage least squares regressions performed; treatment status used as instrument. All models control for baseline test scores, mother's education, employment status, whether or not the family receives welfare, and family size (missing case values for demographic variables estimated by imputation); New York model also includes lottery indicators. Impacts expressed in terms of national percentile rankings. Average three-city impact is based on effects observed in the three cities weighted by the inverse of the standard errors of the point estimates.

***Significant at the 1 percent level.
**Significant at the 5 percent level.
*Significant at the 10 percent level.

portionately concentrated in a small number of good private schools, or their peers in the control group concentrated disproportionately in a few bad public schools, the error term in the estimation of private school effects would be smaller for African Americans than for other students. This would increase the probability that one would observe significant impacts on African American test scores, but not on those of other ethnic groups.

For two reasons, however, we doubt this explanation has much traction. First, the size of the standard errors is not all that differentiates the effects for African Americans and members of the other ethnic groups. For Latinos in New York and whites in Dayton, the point estimates consistently hover around zero, whereas for African Americans in both cities the point estimates are quite large. Second, when surveying the private school attendance patterns of students from different ethnic groups, one finds little evidence that treatment effects were more uniform for some groups than others. African Americans, for the most part, did not attend a relatively smaller number of public or private schools than did members of other ethnic groups.[17]

4.5 Parent Satisfaction

Most studies have found that families who use vouchers to attend an area private school are much more satisfied with their schooling than are families who remain in public schools.[18] The results presented in table 4.7 confirm these earlier findings. A significantly higher proportion of private school parents were "very satisfied" with the following aspects of their schools: school safety, teaching, parental involvement, class size, school

17. Since information about the distribution of students among schools is available from the first year of the Dayton evaluation, we were able to estimate the extent to which African Americans and non–African Americans were subject to uniform treatment simply by dividing the number of students in a category by the number of schools they attended. On the whole, we found fairly low uniformity of treatment and not much difference between racial groups. For both African American and non–African American students receiving treatment, the degree of concentration among schools was, on average, just three students. Among students in the control group, the degree of concentration was 3 students per school for African Americans and 1.3 students for non–African Americans. According to this estimation, then, some difference in the degree of concentration between African American and non–African American students is evident, but the difference is not large.

One may also estimate the degree of uniformity of treatment by examining the percentage of students in the three schools serving the largest number of students. When one estimates in this way, one again finds some difference between treatment and control groups. However, in this case it is the non–African Americans who appear the most concentrated. A total of 37 percent of the African American treatment students enrolled in just three schools, as compared to 15 percent of the African American members of the control group. For non–African Americans, these figures were 56 percent and 16 percent, respectively. According to this estimate, the nonblack members of the Dayton experiment experienced a more uniform dose of treatment than did the black students in the study.

18. A summary of findings from earlier studies is available in Peterson (1998, 18). Schneider et al. (1998) finds higher levels of parental satisfaction within New York City public schools when parents are given a choice of school.

Table 4.7   **Parent Satisfaction with School, Two Years After Beginning of Voucher Programs (% "very satisfied")**

Parent Satisfaction Category	Switched to Private School (1)	Public School Control Group (2)	Year Two Programmatic Impact (3)
What taught in school	44	15	29***
Ability to observe religious traditions	37	8	29***
School safety	44	16	27***
Teacher skills	43	17	26***
Teacher-parent relations	43	18	25***
Student respect for teachers	40	16	24***
Academic quality	38	15	23***
Teaching values	36	14	23***
Discipline	35	14	22***
Staff teamwork	34	13	21***
Class size	32	12	20***
Clarity of school goals	34	14	20***
Parental involvement	30	15	15**
Location	40	33	7

Notes: These figures represent the average results for New York City, Dayton, and D.C. Observations from each city are weighted by the inverse of their variance. Column (1) presents those who were offered a scholarship and subsequently used it to attend a private school. Column (2) presents those in the control group who would have used a scholarship had they been offered one. Column (3) presents estimated impact of participation in the program, using a two-stage least squares model.
***Significant at the 1 percent level.
**Significant at the 5 percent level.

facility, student respect for teachers, teacher communication with parents with respect to their child's progress, extent to which child can observe religious traditions, parental support for the school, discipline, clarity of school goals, staff teamwork, academic quality, the sports program, and what is taught in school. Thirty-eight percent of private school parents were very satisfied with the academic quality of the school after two years, as contrasted with just 15 percent of the control group. Similarly, 44 percent of the private school parents expressed the highest satisfaction with "what's taught in school," compared with 15 percent of the control group.

To see whether satisfaction levels are the result of a Hawthorne effect, the propensity of individuals to welcome change for its own sake, an index of satisfaction was constructed from the items reported above. The positive impact on satisfaction levels in the three cities, as measured by this index, was 0.97 standard deviations in the first year, 0.89 in the second, and 0.85 in the third year.[19] In other words, although overall satisfaction levels attenu-

19. Procedures for constructing the index as well as additional information on satisfaction levels are reported in Howell et al. (2002, chap. 7).

ated slightly from the first to the second and third years of the evaluation, Hawthorne effects appear minimal.

4.6 Other Voucher Impacts

Although test score performance and parental satisfaction are the outcomes of greatest interest to most observers, parental surveys provided additional information about the impacts of voucher opportunities on selected characteristics of the schools attended by students. Significant differences were identified in the school facilities available to students, school size, class size, school climate, homework assignment practices, and school communication with families.

4.6.1 School Facilities

Public school expenditures eclipse private school expenditures. Nationwide, the average private school expenditures per pupil in 1993–94 were estimated at $3,116, considerably less than the $6,653 spent, on average, on public school pupils (Coulson 1999, 277). In part, this disparity is due to the wider array of services that public schools provide their students. Nonetheless, even when adjustments are made for the kinds of services rendered, public schools in New York City, Dayton, and D.C. spend roughly twice as much as private schools.

Per-pupil expenditures for both Catholic and public schools were available for schools in three boroughs of New York City.[20] In comparing expenditures, the amount spent by New York public schools for all items that did not clearly have a private school counterpart was deducted. Among other things, deductions were taken for all monies spent on transportation, special education, school lunch, other ancillary services, and the cost of financing the far-flung bureaucracy that runs the citywide, boroughwide, and districtwide operations of the New York City public schools.

All these deductions from public school expenditures amounted to no less than 40 percent of the cost of running the New York City public schools. However, even after all these and other deductions were taken, public schools were still spending over $5,000 per pupil each year, more than twice the $2,400 spent on similar services in New York City's Catholic schools.

In Washington, D.C., the median tuition at the private schools attended by the scholarship students included in the evaluation was $3,113 in the year 1998–99.[21] The average is substantially higher than the median because of the high tuition charged by a few independent schools, such as Sidwell

20. Estimates are based on information about Catholic schools in Manhattan, the Bronx, and Brooklyn from an unpublished memorandum submitted to the Program on Education Policy and Governance from the New York archdiocese in August 1999. Public school expenditure by school for the city of New York is available on the Board of Education website.
21. Private school tuition rates were estimated in part from information provided in Coerper and Mersereau (1998). For schools not listed in this volume, information was obtained in

Table 4.8   **Size and Quality of School Facilities, One Year After Beginning of Voucher Programs (%)**

Parental Reports	Switched to Private School (1)	Public School Control Group (2)	Programmatic Impact (3)
Average school size	278	450	–172***
Average class size	20	23	–3***
Percentage satisfied with school facilities	28	9	19***
Percentage with the following resources:			
Special programs for non-English speakers	43	71	–28***
Nurses' office	75	94	–19***
Special programs for learning disabled	67	81	–14***
Cafeteria	86	96	–10***
Child counselor	77	85	–8***
Library	92	96	–5**
Gym	88	88	0
Special programs for advanced learners	59	58	1
Arts program	82	81	1
Computer lab	86	84	2
Music program	88	84	4
After-school program	91	86	6**
Individual tutors	70	54	16***

Notes: See notes to table 4.7.

Friends, which charged the Clintons over $15,000 per year for their daughter's tuition. Assuming that the ratio of tuition to total educational expenditure in Washington, D.C. is the same as in the three boroughs in New York City discussed previously, private educational expenditures, on average, totaled roughly $4,000. Again, considering only those services and programs that both public and private schools cover, adjusted per-pupil expenditures in Washington public schools reached $8,185, as estimated from data for the 1995–96 school year.[22]

Much the same patterns emerge in Dayton. In 1998–99, students in the Dayton voucher program paid, on average, $2,600 in tuition, whereas the Dayton public school system spend an adjusted average of $5,528 per pupil.

Parental reports help explain these expenditure data. According to the parental surveys, private schools were less likely to have a library, a nurse's office, a cafeteria, child counselors, and special programs for non–English speakers and students with learning problems (see table 4.8). The greatest difference was for programs for non-English-speaking students. Forty-

telephone conversations with school staff. Some schools have a range of tuition charges, depending on the number of students from the family attending the school and other factors. The tuition used for this calculation is the maximum charged by the school. The tuition also includes all fees, except for the registration fee, which is ordinarily treated as partial payment toward tuition. Figures are weighted proportionate to the number of students in the evaluation attending a particular school. Public school expenditure includes the costs of transportation and special education, which may not be provided by private schools.

22. Data taken from the U.S. Department of Education (2000).

three percent of the private school parents reported such a program in their school, compared with 71 percent of the control group parents. Similarly, 75 percent of the private school parents reported their school had a nurse's office, as compared to 94 percent of public school parents. Public schools are also larger. In some instances, either no significant differences were detected or private school parents reported more services. The two groups of parents did not differ in their reports of the availability of a gym, a computer laboratory, art and music programs, and special programs for advanced learners. Private school parents, meanwhile, were more likely to say their school had individual tutors and an after-school program.

Despite the more limited financial resources of the private school, parents reported that their children attended classes with an average of twenty students, as compared to twenty-three in public schools (Peterson, Myers, and Howell 1998, table 5). However, the reduction in class size was only three students, considerably less than the amount generally thought to be necessary to achieve significant gains from class size reduction.[23] As estimated by parents, the effect of choosing the private sector was to reduce the average size of the school by 172 students or nearly 40 percent—from an average of 450 students to 278 students.

4.6.2   School Climate

In their study of public and private schools, John Chubb and Terry Moe (1990) found that the educational environment of private schools was more conducive to learning than that of public schools. They pointed out that public schools are governed by state laws, federal regulations, school board requirements, and union-contract rules that impose multiple and not always consistent obligations on teachers and principals. Because they must respond to numerous legal and contractual requirements, school administrators and teachers focus more on rule compliance than on educational mission, undermining the morale of educators whose original objective was to help children learn.

The problem, Chubb and Moe say, is particularly prevalent in big-city schools. Urban private schools operate with greater autonomy, focus more directly on their educational mission, and, as a result, achieve a higher degree of internal cohesion. To do otherwise would jeopardize their survival as fragile institutions dependent upon the annual recruitment of new students. As a consequence, principals and teachers in the private sector enjoy higher morale. Their interactions with one another and with their students are more positive, fostering a more effective learning environment.

Our findings confirm Chubb and Moe's. If parent reports are accurate, the

---

23. The reduction in class size in the Tennessee experiment was an average of approximately seven to eight students (Krueger 1999). For further discussion of this point, see Howell et al. (2002, 158–64).

Table 4.9   Parents' Perceptions of School Climate, One Year After Beginning of Voucher Programs (%)

Reported by Parents as Serious Problem	Switched to Private School (1)	Public School Control Group (2)	Programmatic Impact (3)
Fighting	32	63	–31***
Kids missing class	26	48	–22***
Tardiness	33	54	–21***
Kids destroying property	22	42	–20***
Cheating	26	39	–13***

Notes: See notes to table 4.7.

Table 4.10   Homework, One Year After Beginning of Voucher Programs (%)

Reported by Parents	Switched to Private School (1)	Public School Control Group (2)	Programmatic Impact (3)
Child has more than one hour of homework	72	56	16***
Difficulty of homework appropriate for child	90	72	18***

Notes: See notes to table 4.7.

scholarship programs in New York, D.C., and Dayton had a major impact on the daily life of students at school. As table 4.9 shows, public school parents were more likely to report that the following were serious problems at their school: students destroying property, tardiness, missing classes, fighting, cheating, and racial conflict. For example, 32 percent of the private school parents thought that fighting was a serious problem at their school versus 63 percent of the control group. Thirty-three percent of parents perceived tardiness as a problem, as compared to 54 percent of the control group. No more than 22 percent of private school parents, but 42 percent of the control group, said that destruction of property was a serious problem at their school.

4.6.3   Homework and Parental Communication

Thomas Hoffer, Andrew Greeley, and James Coleman (1985) have attributed the higher level of student performance in private schools to the amount of homework expected of students and to the frequency of communication between schools and parents. The reports by parents are consistent with their interpretation.[24] Table 4.10 shows that 72 percent of private school parents reported that their child had at least an hour of

24. For very similar first-year results, see Peterson, Myers, and Howell (1998), table 9.

Table 4.11   School Communication with Parents, One Year After Beginning of Voucher Programs (%)

Reported by Parents	Switched to Private School (1)	Public School Control Group (2)	Programmatic Impact (3)
Parents receive newsletter	88	68	20***
Parents participate in instrument	68	50	18***
Parents notified of disruptive behavior	91	77	14***
Parents receive notes from teacher	93	78	14***
Parents speak to classes about jobs	44	33	11**
Parents regularly informed about student grades	93	84	9**
Parent open houses held at school	95	90	5**
Regular parent-teacher conferences	95	90	5**

Notes: See notes to table 4.7.

homework a day, whereas only 56 percent of the control group parents reported a similar amount of homework. Private school parents were also more likely to say the homework was appropriate for their child. Seventy-two percent of the control group parents gave this response, as compared to 90 percent of private-school parents.

Compared with control-group parents, parents of students in private schools also said that they received more communication from their school about their child. The results presented in table 4.11 indicate that a higher percent of private school parents versus control group parents reported the following: being more informed about student grades halfway through the grading period; being notified when their child is sent to the office the first time for disruptive behavior; speaking to classes about their jobs; participating in instruction; receiving notes about their child from the teacher; receiving a newsletter about what is going on in school; and regular parent-teacher conferences.

4.7   Conclusions

Because random assignment to test and control groups assures that all significant effects may be attributed to the intervention, and not to the students' initial abilities or their family backgrounds, randomized field trials are the best available tool for detecting the effects of an educational intervention. Nonetheless, when one interprets the findings from the evaluation of any one program in a particular city, generalizations to a larger universe are problematic. Conditions specific to that place or minor fluctuations in testing conditions might skew results in one direction or another.

Still, when similar results emerge from evaluations of school voucher programs in three sites in different parts of the United States, they provide a stronger basis for drawing conclusions and generalizing to larger populations. Thus, the average impact across the three sites may provide a reasonable estimate of the likely initial impact of a school voucher initiative elsewhere.

In the three cases, taken together, we found effects of school vouchers only on the average test performance of African American students. African American students who switched from public to private schools in the three cities scored after two years, on average, approximately 6.3 percentile points higher on the ITBS than comparable African Americans who remained in public schools. After three years, private school attendance in two cities had an impact of 6.6 percentile points, an effect of 0.30 standard deviations.

At this point we do not know why the gains from switching to a private school are evident for African American students after two and three years, but not for students from other ethnic backgrounds. However, parents reported that private schools are smaller in size, maintain a better disciplinary climate, ask students to do more homework, maintain closer communication with families, and have somewhat smaller classes (about 3 fewer pupils). These school characteristics may be particularly helpful to students who are African American.

One must qualify any generalizations from the results of this pilot program to a large-scale voucher program that would involve all children in a large urban school system. Only a small fraction of low-income students in these three cities' schools were offered vouchers, and these voucher students constituted only a small proportion of the students attending private schools in these cities. A much larger program could conceivably have quite different program outcomes.

Still, slightly larger voucher programs initially directed at low-income families would attract those families with the greatest interest in exploring an educational alternative, exactly the group that applied for a voucher in these three cities. Thus, positive consequences of school choice reported herein may prove encouraging to those who seek to extend and expand school choices for low-income, inner-city families, and negative findings may indicate problems that need to be addressed. It is hoped that additional careful research will accompany larger programs established by private philanthropists and public authorities.

Appendix A
Response Rates

To promote high response rates, voucher program operators either required or strongly urged recipients to participate in testing sessions if they wished to have their voucher renewed for the next school year. In addition, evaluation teams offered financial incentives and new opportunities to win a voucher to encourage members of the control group and members of the treatment group who remained in public schools to return for follow-up testing.[25] Still, substantial numbers of students were not tested at the end of one, two, and three years.

Response rates were 100 percent at baseline, because families and students were not entered into the lottery unless they provided baseline information. Response rates after one year were 82 percent in New York, 56 percent in Dayton, and 63 percent in Washington, D.C. After two years, response rates in the three cities were 66 percent, 49 percent, and 50 percent, respectively. After three years, response rates were 67 percent in New York and 60 percent in Washington, D.C. Response rates were similar for treatment and control groups in all three cities.[26] The largest difference was in New York City in the second year, where the treatment group's response rate was 7 points higher than the control group rate.[27]

Comparisons of baseline test scores and background characteristics reveal only minor differences between respondents and nonrespondents in all three cities. Table 4A.1 presents, for example, baseline data on respondents and nonrespondents in the treatment and control groups after two years in the three cities; separate comparisons for African Americans are included in table 4A.2. Some differences in race, welfare, and religious orientation were detected, but they point in different directions in different cities and do not appear to systematically produce a more advantaged group of respondents in the treatment group or a particularly disadvantaged control group. In all three cities, inter-group differences in test scores, religious identification, residential mobility rates, church attendance, and family size were essentially nonexistent.

To adjust for the bias associated with nonresponse, in each year and city we generated weights for parents and students in the treatment and control

25. In New York City and Washington, D.C., families in the control group were entered in a new lottery if they attended follow-up testing in years one and two. In Dayton, control group families were entered in a new lottery after the first year of the program; in year two, they were offered higher compensation instead. Families that began the study as members of a control group were dropped from the evaluation if they subsequently won a follow-up lottery. Although this was necessary to preserve the random design of the evaluation, excluding such families had the effect of reducing the size of the control groups slightly. Although families that did complete the surveys may be systematically different from those that did not, dropping the randomly selected subset of survey respondents should only decrease the efficiency of the estimates, not bias the findings. In D.C. in year three, all control group families and all those that did not use the initial vouchers offered them were offered a voucher.

26. The one exception here concerns the year-two evaluation in New York City, in which the treatment group's response rate was 7 points higher than the control group's rate.

27. These response rates are similar to those in other randomized field trials that follow students over time. In his reanalysis of data from the Tennessee class size study, for example, Krueger (1999), while not providing annual attrition rates, reports that "only half the students who entered the project in kindergarten were present for all grades K-3" (506).

Table 4A.1   **Baseline Characteristics of Respondents and Nonrespondents in Treatment and Control Groups in Year Two**

	Treatment		Control	
	Attended Year Two	Didn't Attend Year Two	Attended Year Two	Didn't Attend Year Two
New York City				
% African American	42.4	48.3	41.4	47.2
% welfare recipients	53.2	64.5	59.4	62.3
% Catholic	54.7	46.4	53.7	43.2
% protestant	34.3	39.4	35.0	38.8
Average overall test scores	20.1	19.5	22.8	22.6
Average family size	2.6	2.6	2.4	2.9
Average residential mobility	3.7	3.6	3.7	3.7
Average church attendance	3.6	3.3	3.4	3.5
Average mother's education	2.4	2.4	2.4	2.5
Dayton				
% African American	74.0	65.2	71.9	69.3
% welfare recipients	16.7	13.8	16.2	16.7
% Catholic	5.8	14.0	13.4	18.1
% protestant	65.2	58.1	64.6	56.9
Average overall test scores	26.3	26.3	27.2	26.2
Average family size	3.0	3.0	3.0	3.1
Average residential mobility	3.4	3.3	3.3	3.6
Average church attendance	3.4	3.3	3.6	3.7
Average mother's education	5.6	5.4	5.3	5.6
D.C.				
% African American	90.4	92.1	90.9	92.1
% welfare recipients	38.0	34.1	32.1	30.3
% Catholic	15.5	12.6	16.0	13.8
% protestant	72.7	69.9	65.6	70.6
Average overall test scores	26.5	26.4	26.9	26.7
Average family size	3.1	3.1	3.3	3.0
Average residential mobility	3.4	3.5	3.5	3.4
Average church attendance	3.7	3.5	3.7	3.7
Average mother's education	5.4	5.0	5.3	5.2

Notes: Averages refer to the unweighted mean scores of responses on the parent surveys. Mother's education was scaled slightly differently in New York City than in Dayton and Washington, D.C., making intercity comparisons on that item inappropriate.

groups. Because those invited to participate in the follow-up studies had provided information about their family characteristics at baseline, it was possible to calculate the probability that each participant in the baseline survey would attend a follow-up session. To do so, we estimated simple logit regressions that used a set of variables assembled from baseline surveys to predict the likelihood that each student would attend a follow-up session. Covariates included mother's education, employment status, marital status, and religious affiliation; family size; whether the family received welfare

Table 4A.2   Baseline Characteristics of African American Respondents and Nonrespondents in Treatment and Control Groups in Year Two

	Treatment		Control	
	Attended Year Two	Didn't Attend Year Two	Attended Year Two	Didn't Attend Year Two
New York City				
% welfare recipients	55.3	63.5	65.8	65.8
% Catholic	17.8	18.0	19.5	8.6
% protestant	66.9	67.3	66.8	65.2
Average overall test scores	20.6	19.1	21.2	23.8
Average family size	2.6	2.8	2.5	3.1
Average residential mobility	3.8	3.7	3.7	3.7
Average church attendance	3.4	3.4	3.2	3.3
Average mother's education	2.5	2.5	2.5	2.6
Dayton				
% welfare recipients	15.9	15.0	17.9	20.7
% Catholic	7.6	12.4	8.7	4.7
% protestant	66.1	61.9	76.5	69.8
Average overall test scores	24.3	21.6	23.2	22.0
Average family size	2.7	2.6	2.8	2.9
Average residential mobility	3.4	3.2	3.3	3.6
Average church attendance	3.8	3.7	3.9	4.0
Average mother's education	6.1	5.8	5.5	5.4
D.C.				
% welfare recipients	38.8	31.6	34.7	27.9
% Catholic	13.0	15.1	13.7	16.0
% protestant	76.2	69.4	67.8	67.7
Average overall test scores	26.2	28.3	26.1	28.4
Average family size	3.1	3.0	3.3	2.9
Average residential mobility	3.5	3.5	3.5	3.5
Average church attendance	3.7	3.6	3.7	3.8
Average mother's education	5.4	5.2	5.3	5.4

Notes: See notes to table 4A.1.

benefits; whether the student was African American; the student's baseline math score; whether the student had a learning disability; and whether the student had experienced disciplinary problems.[28]

To allow for as much flexibility as possible, separate logit models were estimated for treatment and control group members. For illustrative purposes, table 4A.3 reports the results in Washington, D.C. after two years. Similar results were obtained for other cities and other years.[29] For the most part, the family and student characteristics had a similar impact on re-

28. When baseline information was missing, means were imputed.
29. In each study (in New York City and Washington and in Dayton after Year I) the models include slightly different independent variables.

Table 4A.3   **Logit Estimates Used to Construct Weights For Treatment and Control Groups in Washington, D.C. in Year Two**

	Treatment Group	Control Group
Family characteristics		
Catholic	−0.5*	−0.8***
Family size	0.2**	0.2**
Employment status	−0.6**	−0.1
Married	−0.6***	−0.3
Mother's education	0.0	−0.1**
Welfare	−0.3	0.2
African American	0.8***	0.6***
Student characteristics		
Learning disabled	0.7**	−1.0**
Disciplinary problems	0.7**	0.7**
Math	−0.0	−0.0**
Constant	−1.1**	−0.6
Pseudo R^2	0.07	0.07
Log-likelihood	−353.11	−479.83
N	580	866

Notes: The dependent variable is coded 1 if the student attended the year-two follow-up session in Washington, D.C., and 0 otherwise. The treatment group consists of all students who were offered a voucher and participated in the baseline study; the control group consists of all students who were not offered a voucher.
***Significant at the 1 percent level, two-tailed test.
**Significant at the 5 percent level.
*Significant at the 10 percent level.

sponse rates for both treatment and control group members. Catholics were less likely to attend follow-up sessions, as were mothers who were employed full time or were married. Larger families were more likely to attend follow-up sessions, as were African American families and families of students with disciplinary problems. Mother's education, welfare benefits, and math scores had a small or insignificant impact for both treatment and control group members. The most striking difference between the two models concerned students with learning disabilities. Although learning disabled students in the treatment group were significantly more likely to attend follow-up sessions, such students in the control group were significantly less likely to attend follow-up sessions.

The models generated a set of predicted values that represent the probability that individuals, given their baseline characteristics, would attend the follow-up session. The weights are simply the inverse of these predicted values, that is,

$$W_j = \frac{1}{F(X\beta)},$$

where $F(\ )$ is the model's logistic distribution function. The range of possible values for W_j was then capped so that the highest weight was four times the value of the lowest. (This restriction affected only a handful of observations.) The weights were then rescaled so that the sum of the weights equaled the sum of the total number of actual observations.[30]

To generate the weights, we could use only observable characteristics as recorded in parent surveys. To the extent that there were unmeasured or unobservable characteristics that encouraged some families, but not others, to attend follow-up sessions, the weights may not have eliminated the bias associated with nonresponse. However, in order for response bias to explain our findings, three conditions would have to hold. First, respondents would need to differ from nonrespondents on an unmeasured factor that influenced test performance. Second, the difference would have to be larger for one group (treatment or control) than for the other. Third, the difference would have to hold for black students but not for students of other ethnic groups. Although we cannot rule out the possibility that all three conditions existed in our study, we find it unlikely enough to be reasonably confident that response bias did not artificially generate the results we report.

It is possible that change in academic performance over time rather than baseline characteristics affected the likelihood that different subgroups within the treatment and control groups would attend subsequent testing sessions. If treatment group families that did not benefit from vouchers dropped out of the study while control group families that were suffering most in public schools continued to attend follow-up sessions consistently, then observed impacts may be somewhat inflated.

Three questions deserve consideration. Did gains in test scores from baseline to year one (two) decrease the probability that members of the control group would attend the year-two (-three) testing session? Did gains increase the probability that members of the treatment group would attend the year-two (-three) testing session? And were the differences in observed impacts on response rates for the treatment and control groups statistically significant?

Table 4A.4 estimates a series of logistic regressions that answer these questions. The dependent variable identifies whether a student attended the year-two (-three) follow-up session. The covariates include baseline math and reading test scores, the change in the total test score from baseline to year one (two), and the change interacted with treatment status. Separate models were run for African Americans and members of other ethnic groups. At the bottom of each column we report the probability that we can reject the following three null hypotheses: (a) Changes in test scores have a statistically insignificant effect on attendance at subsequent testing sessions for the control group; (b) the effect for the treatment group is statistically insignificant; and (c) the differences in observed effects for the two groups are not statistically significant.

---

30. Weights for New York City, as provided by Mathematica Policy Research.

Table 4A.4   Effect of Change in Test Scores from Baseline to Year One and Two on the Likelihood That Students Attend Subsequent Testing Sessions

| | New York City | | | | Washington, D.C. | Dayton | |
| | Year Two Attendance | | Year Three Attendance | | Year Two Attendance | Year Two Attendance | |
	Blacks	Latinos	Blacks	Latinos	Blacks	Blacks	Whites
Y1-baseline	-0.005	-0.001	...	0.002	-0.012	0.001	
Y2-baseline	...	...	-0.023*	-0.004	...	...	...
(Y1-B)*treat	0.004	0.006	...	...	0.002	0.023*	-0.004
(Y2-B)*treat	...	0.012*	0.031*	0.004	...	...	...
Baseline math	-0.003	...	0.007	0.002	-0.001	0.001	-0.003
Baseline reading	0.007	-0.004	0.006	-0.008	-0.001	0.003	0.004
N	623	709	497	612	891	298	108
Log-likelihood	-355.81	-355.68	-212.40	-191.13	-580.55	-189.52	-70.39
Pseudo-R^2	0.00	0.01	0.02	0.00	0.00	0.01	0.00
P for H_0: $B_1 = 0$	0.63	0.91	0.09	0.76	0.79	0.21	0.94
P for H_0: $B_1 + B_2 = 0$	0.90	0.57	0.50	0.96	0.50	0.28	0.79
P for H_0: $B_2 = 0$	0.77	0.46	0.07	0.78	0.79	0.07	0.79

Notes: Logit regression models performed on unweighted data. Y1-baseline refers to the change in the total math and reading test scores from baseline to year one; Y2-baseline refers to change from baseline to year two. (Y1-B)* offered voucher is an interaction term between one variable that is the difference between year one and baseline test scores and another variable that indicates whether a student was offered a voucher. The dependent variable is coded 1 if the student attended either the second- or third-year follow-up session.

***Significant at the 1 percent level, two-tailed test.

**Significant at the 5 percent level.

*Significant at the 10 percent level.

On the whole, the signs of the coefficients are in the expected direction. Gains in test scores from baseline to years one and two increased the probability that members of the treatment group attended the subsequent testing session and decreased the probability for members of the control group. The only models that generated statistically significant impacts, however, were for African Americans in New York after three years and for African Americans in Dayton after two years. None of the observed impacts for Hispanics were statistically significant in any year or city.

The model that predicts year-three attendance for African Americans in New York City generated the largest effects. Holding all variables at their means, the model predicted that 83 percent of the students who attended the year-two session would attend the year-three session. An increase of 10 NPR points from baseline to year two translated into a 3 percentage point drop in the probability that a control group member would attend the year-three testing session and a 1 percentage point increase in the probability that a member of the treatment group would attend the year-three follow-up session. Unless weighting adjusted for these differences, this response pattern may have marginally contributed to the positive estimate of voucher impacts on test scores.

In New York City, eighty-two African American students who had attended the year-two testing session failed to show up in year three. The data presented above suggest that those individuals consisted disproportionately of control group members whose scores decreased from baseline to year two and treatment group members whose scores increased, possibly inflating the estimated impact of attending a private school. To further explore their influence on estimated impacts, we imputed year-three test scores for those individuals based on their treatment status, baseline test scores, test score changes between baseline and year two, and the year-three weights. Although the observed impacts do drop in magnitude, they remain statistically significant. When we examined only those African American students who attended the year-three follow-up session, the estimated impact of switching from a public to a private school at year three was 5.4 NPR points, with 515 observations and a *t*-statistic of 3.7. When we looked at the same population but then imputed year-three test scores for those students who showed up in year two but not in year three, the size of the estimated impact of attending a private school dropped to 8.0 NPR points, with a *t*-statistic of 3.0.[31]

Another way of estimating the effects of response rates on outcomes is to distinguish between earlier and later respondents. Not all participants came

31. King et al. (2001). The point estimates reported come from weighted regressions: Imputed weights for missing observations in year three were constrained to have positive values. Impacts generated from unweighted regressions using imputed values and observables also are comparable.

to the first testing session to which they were invited. Given that we know the dates when students came in for testing, we can generate exact estimates of the impact of attending a private school for smaller response rates. In year one in New York City, for instance, we had an 82 percent response rate. By successively dropping the portion of students who attended later testing sessions, we can readily calculate the impacts for lower response rates.

If observed positive impacts derive from imperfect response rates, we should expect the estimated impact of attending a private school to increase as response rates decline. Presumably, those students who benefit most from treatment should come earlier to the testing sessions, along with those students in the control group who were performing most poorly in public schools. Impacts of attending a private school, then, should be quite large for lower response rates. The differences between the two groups, however, should attenuate (and may actually switch signs) as response rates increase.

Table 4A.5 reports the estimated impact of attending a private school for African American students for variable response rates. In each row, the first column represents the estimated impact for the full sample of African American students who attended testing sessions. Subsequent columns provide estimates of impacts for lower response rates, based on when students came in for testing.

As can be seen in table 4A.5, the New York City estimates remained remarkably stable for different response rates. Had we stopped testing students in year one after the first 30 percent of the sample showed up, we would have recovered almost exactly the same findings that we did after another 52 percent participated: The point estimate for the first 30 percent of students to be tested was 5.7 percentile points, and it was 5.4 for the full sample. In New York City in years two and three, rather than decreasing as response rates improved, the estimated impacts actually became larger.

Table 4A.5   **Estimated Impacts of Attending a Private School for African Americans in New York City for Variable Response Rates (% of Respondents Attending Follow-Up Sessions)**

	30	40	56	60	66	70	82
Year one impact	5.7***	4.4***	4.2***	4.8***	5.0***	5.3***	5.4***
Year two impact	3.6	2.7	4.4**	3.2*	4.3**	. . .	. . .
Year three impact	4.2	6.9***	7.1***	8.3***	9.2***a	. . .	. . .

Notes: Weighted two-stage least squares regressions performed; treatment status used as instrument. Differential response rates calculated by including in the analysis only the relevant percentage of students to initially attend testing sessions.

aThis is the test score impact for the full sample, at a 67 percent response rate.

***Significant at the 1 percent level.

**Significant at the 5 percent level.

*Significant at the 10 percent level, two-tailed test.

Moving from a 30 percent response rate to a 66 percent rate, the estimated test score impact of attending a private school increased by roughly 1 NPR point and became statistically significant. From these findings, at least, there is little to suggest that we would have observed significantly different impacts had we managed to test a greater number of students in the treatment and control groups. If anything, these results suggest that we may have underestimated the true effects of switching from a public to a private school.

Appendix B
The Effects of the Offer of a Voucher

Tables 4B.1, 4B.2, and 4B.3 report estimated effects of a voucher offer on student test score performance in each city. These ITT effects are smaller than actual treatment effects, because many students who were offered vouchers did not make use of them, and others who were not offered vouchers found alternative ways of financing a private education. The percentages using a voucher in each city are reported in the text of this chapter.

Table 4B.1   Impact in New York of Being Offered a Voucher on Test Score Performance

Test Score Performance	Year One (Percentiles)	N	Year Two (Percentiles)	N	Year Three (Percentiles)	N
African Americans						
Overall	4.5**	622	3.3**	497	5.5***	519
	(1.2)		(1.5)		(1.4)	
Math	5.7***	622	3.1*	497	7.0***	519
	(1.5)		(1.9)		(1.7)	
Reading	3.3**	622	3.4**	497	4.0**	519
	(1.5)		(1.7)		(1.7)	
All other ethnic groups						
Overall	–1.3	812	–1.0	699	–2.3	729
	(1.3)		(1.5)		(1.5)	
Math	–2.4	812	–2.2	699	–1.7	729
	(1.7)		(2.0)		(1.9)	
Reading	–0.9	812	0.1	699	–2.9*	729
	(1.4)		(1.6)		(1.7)	

Notes: Weighted ordinary least squares regressions performed. All models control for baseline test scores and lottery indicators. Impacts expressed in terms of national percentile rankings. Standard errors reported in parentheses.
***Significant at the 1 percent level, two-tailed test.
**Significant at the 5 percent level.
*Significant at the 10 percent level.

Table 4B.2	Impact in Washington, D.C. of Being Offered a Voucher on Test Score Performance					
Test Score Performance	Year One (Percentiles)	N	Year Two (Percentiles)	N	Year Three (Percentiles)	N
African Americans						
Overall	-0.3	891	3.8***	668	-0.5	656
	(1.1)		(1.2)		(1.2)	
Math	2.9**	891	4.3***	668	0.3	656
	(1.3)		(1.4)		(1.4)	
Reading	-3.6**	891	3.3**	668	-1.3	656
	(1.5)		(1.4)		(1.5)	
All other ethnic groups						
Overall	4.7	39	-0.1	42	-0.9	31
	(5.6)		(5.6)		(6.6)	
Math	5.5	39	4.1	42	-4.7	31
	(7.2)		(7.4)		(7.7)	
Reading	4.0	39	-4.3	42	2.9	31
	(8.0)		(5.7)	(9.1)		

Notes: Weighted ordinary least squares regressions performed. Standard errors reported in parentheses. All models control for baseline test scores; in year one models also control for initial testing session. Impacts expressed in terms of national percentile rankings.
***Significant at the 1 percent level.
**Significant at the 5 percent level.
*Significant at the 10 percent level.

Table 4B.3	Impact in Dayton of Being Offered a Voucher on Test Score Performance			
Test Score Performance	Year One (Percentiles)	N	Year Two (Percentiles)	N
African Americans				
Overall	1.9	296	3.5*	273
	(2.0)		(2.0)	
Math	0.2	296	2.8	273
	(2.3)		(2.3)	
Reading	3.5	296	4.1*	273
	(2.4)		(2.3)	
All other ethnic groups				
Overall	0.7	108	-0.1	96
	(4.1)		(4.0)	
Math	-0.5	108	0.0	96
	(4.8)		(4.7)	
Reading	1.8	108	-0.2	96
	(4.5)		(4.4)	

Notes: Weighted ordinary least squares regressions performed. Standard errors reported in parentheses. All models control for baseline test scores. Impacts expressed in terms of national percentile rankings.
***Significant at the 1 percent level.
**Significant at the 5 percent level.
*Significant at the 10 percent level.

References

Angrist, Joshua D., Guido W. Imbens, and Donald B. Rubin. 1996. Identification of causal effects using instrumental variables. *Journal of the American Statistical Association* 91:444–62.
Bridge, R. J., and J. Blackman. 1978. *Family choice in education.* Vol. 4 of *A study of alternatives in American education.* Santa Monica, Calif.: RAND Corporation.
Chaplin, Duncan D. 1998. Raising standards: The effects of high school math and science courses on future earnings. *Virginia Journal of Social Policy and Law* 6 (1): 111–26.
Chubb, John E., and Terry M. Moe. 1990. *Politics, markets, and America's schools.* Washington, D.C.: Brookings Institution.
Coerper, Lois H., and Shirley W. Mersereau. 1998. *Independent school guide for Washington, D.C. and surrounding area.* 11th ed. Chevy Chase, Md.: Independent School Guides.
Coleman, James S., Thomas Hoffer, and Sally Kilgore. 1982. *High school achievement.* New York: Basic Books.
Coulson, Andrew J. 1999. *Market education: The unknown history.* New Brunswick, N.J.: Social Philosophy and Policy Center and Transaction Publishers.
Elmore, Richard. 1990. Choice as an instrument of public policy: Evidence from education and health care. In *Choice and control in American education,* Vol. 1: *The theory of choice and control in American education,* ed. W. Clune and J. Witte, 285–318. New York: Falmer.
Evans, William N., and Robert M. Schwab. 1993. Who benefits from private education? Evidence from quantile regressions. University of Maryland, Department of Economics. Working Paper.
Figlio, David, and Joe Stone. 1999. Are private schools really better? In *Research in labor economics,* vol. 16, ed. Soloman W. Polachek and John Robst, 115–40. Stamford, Conn.: JAI Press.
Flanagan, Ann, Jennifer Kawata, and Stephanie Williamson. 2000. *Improving student achievement: What NAEP test scores tell us.* Santa Monica, Calif.: RAND Corporation.
Goldberger, Arthur S., and Glen G. Cain. 1982. The causal analysis of cognitive outcomes in the Coleman, Hoffer, and Kilgore report. *Sociology of Education* 55 (April–July): 103–22.
Greene, Jay P., William G. Howell, and Paul E. Peterson. 1998. Lessons from the Cleveland scholarship program. In *Learning from school choice,* ed. Paul E. Peterson and Bryan C. Hassel, 357–92, Washington, D.C.: Brookings Institution.
Greene, Jay P., Paul E. Peterson, and Jiangtao Du. 1998. School choice in Milwaukee: A randomized experiment. In *Learning from school choice,* ed. Paul E. Peterson and Bryan C. Hassel, 335–56. Washington, D.C.: Brookings Institution.
Hill, Jennifer, Donald B. Rubin, and Neal Thomas. 1998. The design of the New York school choice scholarship program evaluation. Paper presented at the American Political Science Association annual meeting. 31 August, Boston, Massachusetts.
Hoffer, Thomas, Andrew Greeley, and James Coleman. 1985. Achievement growth in public and Catholic schools. *Sociology of Education* 58 (April): 74–97.
Howell, William G., and Paul E. Peterson. 2000. School choice in Dayton, Ohio: An evaluation after one year. Harvard University, Program on Education Policy and Governance. Occasional paper, February.
Howell, William G., Paul E. Peterson, Patrick J. Wolf, and David Campbell. 2002.

The education gap: Vouchers and urban schools. Washington, D.C.: Brookings Institution.

Jencks, Christopher, and Meridith Phillips, ed. 1999. *The black-white test score gap.* Washington, D.C.: Brookings Institution.

King, Gary, James Honaker, Anne Joseph, and Kenneth Scheve. 2001. Analyzing incomplete political science data: An alternative algorithm for multiple imputation. *American Political Science Review* 95 (1): 46–69.

Krueger, Alan. 1999. Experimental estimates of education production functions. *Quarterly Journal of Economics* 114:497–533.

Krueger, Alan, and Diane Whitmore. 2000. Would smaller classes help close the black-white achievement gap? Paper presented at conference entitled Closing the Gap: Promising Strategies for Reducing the Achievement Gap. February, Washington, D.C.

Metcalfe, Kim K., William J. Boone, Frances K. Stage, Todd L. Chilton, Patty Muller, and Polly Tait. 1998. A comparative evaluation of the Cleveland scholarship and tutoring grant program: Year one: 1996–97. Bloomington, Ind.: Indiana University School of Education, Smith Research Center.

Murname, Richard, John B. Willet, Yves Duhaldeborde, and John H. Tyler. 2000. How important are the cognitive skills of teenagers in predicting subsequent earnings? *Journal of Policy Analysis and Management* 19 (4): 547–68.

Myers, David, Paul E. Peterson, Daniel Mayer, Julia Chou, and William P. Howell. 2000. School choice in New York City after two years: An evaluation of the school choice scholarships program. Harvard University, Program on Education Policy and Governance. Occasional paper, September.

Neal, Derek. 1997. The effects of Catholic secondary schooling on educational achievement. *Journal of Labor Economics* 15 (1): 98–123.

Peterson, Paul E. 1998. School choice: A report card. In *Learning from school choice,* ed. Paul E. Peterson and Bryan C. Hassel, 3–32. Washington, D.C.: Brookings Institution.

Peterson, Paul E., Jay P. Greene, William G. Howell, and William McCready. 1998. Initial findings from an evaluation of school choice programs in Dayton, Ohio and Washington, D.C. Harvard University, Program on Education Policy and Governance. Occasional paper, October.

Peterson, Paul E., and Bryan C. Hassel, ed. 1998. *Learning from school choice.* Washington, D.C.: Brookings Institution.

Peterson, Paul E., David E. Myers, Josh Haimson, and William G. Howell. 1997. Initial findings from the evaluation of the New York school choice scholarships program. Harvard University, Program on Education Policy and Governance. Occasional paper, November.

Peterson, Paul E., David E. Myers, and William G. Howell. 1998. An evaluation of the New York City school choice scholarships program: The first year. Harvard University, Program on Education Policy and Governance. Occasional Paper, October.

Peterson, Paul E., David E. Myers, William G. Howell, and Daniel P. Mayer. 1999. The effects of school choice in New York City. Chap. 12 in *Earning and learning: How schools matter,* ed. Susan B. Mayer and Paul E. Peterson. Washington, D.C.: Brookings Institution.

Rouse, Cecilia. 1997. Private school vouchers and student achievement: An evaluation of the Milwaukee parental choice program. Princeton University, Department of Economics. Working Paper.

Schneider, Mark, Paul Teske, Melissa Marschall, and Christine Roch. 1998. Tiebout, school choice, allocative and productive efficiency. Paper presented at the annual meeting of the American Political Science Association. 3–6 September, Boston, Mass.

U.S. Department of Education, Office of Educational Research and Improvement, National Center for Education Statistics. 2000. *Common core of data, school years 1993–94 through 1997–98.* Washington, D.C.: U.S. Department of Education.

West, Martin R., Paul E. Peterson, and David E. Campbell. 2001. School choice in Dayton, Ohio after two years. Harvard University, Program on Education Policy and Governance. Occasional paper, August.

Wilms, Douglas J. 1985. Catholic school effects on academic achievement: New evidence from high school and beyond follow-up study. *Sociology of Education* 58: 98–114.

Witte, John F. 1996. School choice and student performance. In *Holding schools accountable: Performance-based reform in education,* ed. Helen F. Ladd, 149–76. Washington, D.C.: Brookings Institution.

———. 1997. Achievement effects of the Milwaukee voucher program. Paper presented at the annual meeting of the American Economics Association. January, New Orleans, La.

Wolf, Patrick J., William G. Howell, and Paul E. Peterson. 2000. School choice in Washington, D.C.: An evaluation after one year. Harvard University, Program on Education Policy and Governance. Occasional paper, February.

Wolf, Patrick J., Paul E. Peterson, and Martin R. West. 2001. Results of a school voucher experiment: The case of Washington, D.C. after two years. Harvard University, Program on Education Policy and Governance. Occasional paper, August.

5

Introducing School Choice into Multidistrict Public School Systems

Thomas J. Nechyba

5.1 Introduction

School choice is a contentious issue in part because of the lack of agreement on many of the important empirical issues surrounding the policy debate.[1] Evidence regarding the role of such factors as peers and parents, class size and teacher quality, competition and bureaucracy, unionization and curriculum design remains hotly debated, and the impact of increased choice on many of these elements of school quality is still controversial. However, we do have decades of experience with school choice of a kind somewhat different from what is pondered in many choice-based policy proposals, and it is within this current system of school choice that at least some agreement can be found. Although it may therefore be difficult to fully predict the impact of new choice-based initiatives, information arising from the choices made by households in the current system may yield important evidence regarding some neglected empirical issues that are critical for policymakers to consider.

This paper begins by providing evidence regarding one such issue: the linkage between housing and school consumption, and the impact that private schools (and private school vouchers) can have by severing this linkage and thus setting off a series of general equilibrium effects that are quite independent from many of the more controversial issues surrounding

Thomas J. Nechyba is the Fuchsberg-Levine Family Professor of Economics and Public Policy Studies at Duke University and a research associate of the National Bureau of Economic Research.

The author is grateful to the NBER as well as the National Science Foundation (SBR-9905706) for research support, and to participants of the NBER School Choice Conference (22–24 February 2001), particularly Charles Manski, Richard Romano, and Caroline M. Hoxby.

1. Voucher experiments in the United States are still sparse, with only limited empirical investigations possible (see, for instance, Rouse 1998).

school choice. The intuition behind these results is quite straightforward: In a residence-based public school system, the location of a family's residence directly determines which public school that family's children are eligible to attend. Housing markets are typically such that low-income families may not be able to afford housing in high-quality public school districts, which implies that choice among public schools is greater for some than for others. By bringing choice into low-income school districts, private school vouchers sever the link between school quality and residential location, thus increasing the value of living in poor public school districts and lowering the value of living in wealthy districts. Such voucher proposals therefore tend to benefit lower-income households (through a variety of channels) more than high-income households that are already exercising choice in the present system. The research summarized in this paper provides evidence on the potential magnitude of these benefits as well as the likely channels through which they might emerge under a variety of different assumptions regarding empirical factors that remain controversial.

In addition, the paper proceeds to predict the impact of private school choice on school quality. Whereas results regarding residential segregation are rather unambiguous and robust, implications for school quality are more dependent on the precise underlying assumptions regarding the impact of competition within schools. Results indicate that, under the most pessimistic assumptions, increasing school choice may lead to surprisingly small declines in average public school quality and in the overall level of inequality in the system, whereas it may yield substantial gains under more optimistic assumptions. The first of these results is surprising because previous theoretical and simulation approaches have tended to compare the outcome under private school vouchers to a rather idealized outcome where all public schools provide equal educational quality, and these approaches have arrived at the conclusion that increased private school choice must necessarily lower public school quality and raise inequities in an otherwise equitable public school system.[2] Furthermore, these approaches have tended not to model the political process through which public school spending is determined and have thus ignored potential offsetting public school spending effects as some students leave the public system.[3] The ap-

2. To be fair, the models used to arrive at these analyses were not intended to arrive at predictions of the overall impact of vouchers but rather to demonstrate some of the trade-offs involved (Manski 1992) as well as explore such issues as the efficiency of pricing policies of private schools (Epple and Romano 1998; Caucutt 2001). Furthermore, it should be noted that previous approaches have investigated inequities within the public school system (Fernandez and Rogerson 1996, 1999, for instance) but not in the presence of private school alternatives and/or vouchers.

3. Political economy models have been used extensively to analyze school finance issues (as in, for example, Fernandez and Rogerson 1999) as well as voting on vouchers (Bearse, Glomm, and Ravikumar 2000; Glomm and Ravikumar 1998), but political economy models have not previously been combined with multidistrict models of public school finance, as is done here.

proach taken here differs fundamentally in that it incorporates from the start the very forces that have led to the inequities within the public system and in that it models explicitly an underlying political process within this environment. The approach then exploits the semi-competitive nature of the current public school system (and the resulting observed inequities across school districts) in order to model the structural parameters underlying the decisions made by households. This allows for a calibration of the model that can replicate current features of the data and then come to conclusions about extending competition to private schools in an environment where political and household choices are endogenously determined. It is then possible to compare these predictions to actual rather than idealized prevoucher outcomes.

Section 5.2 provides a basic overview of the methodological approach taken throughout the paper. Although this approach is different from the reduced-form regression analysis typically employed by empirical researchers, it is an approach particularly well suited for the kinds of issues that are central to the school choice debate. Section 5.3 goes on to provide a nontechnical summary of the details of the theoretical assumptions employed in the model, and section 5.4 provides the results from a number of policy simulations under different assumptions. The remainder of the paper considers the empirical justification for the model's key assumptions and the evidence for some of its testable implications (section 5.5) as well as some policy implications arising from the simulation results (section 5.6). Finally, section 5.7 concludes.

5.2 Predicting the Impact of Increased Choice from the Current Choice System

Whereas some have proposed marginal choice-based reforms to the current system, others advocate making choice the central theme around which to reform primary and secondary education. Conventional empirical approaches may be well suited to predicting some of the likely effects of small changes to the system, but one becomes less confident in such predictions as policy reforms get large and affect incentives, actions, and prices throughout the system. Put differently, large and discrete policy changes in an area as central to people's lives as primary and secondary education may change incentives in a way that brings to light forces that are unlikely to be important with small policy changes and impossible to pick up with many of the commonly employed empirical techniques. The approach taken in this paper therefore uses data on outcomes under the current limited-choice system to infer preference and production parameters in a very general model that incorporates forces likely to be important under large-scale reforms. Before that model is presented in section 5.3, section 5.2.1 begins with a brief discussion of how household choices under the current system lead to observable outcomes; section 5.2.2 then argues that these observable outcomes can be used as the basis of an approach that can analyze the likely impact of large policy changes; and section 5.2.3 arrives at some of the basic features that must be modeled in order to implement this approach.

5.2.1 Choice under the Current System Leads to Observable Outcomes

Choice has been a pervasive feature of school systems in most U.S. states for the past half century. Parents can participate in the local political process that shapes their schools, and they can choose among tens of thousands of school districts or neighborhood school areas in which to reside. At least in principle, choice among many public schools is therefore pervasive. Elite private schools as well as more common parochial schools offer additional options for those unhappy with the public system, and choice is clearly being exercised. Approximately 12 percent of U.S. schoolchildren attend private schools; a small but growing number are homeschooled; and, most significantly, many of those households that remain within the public system consider public school quality carefully when choosing where to purchase or rent a home. Real estate agents typically come armed with information regarding public school quality associated with different neighborhoods, and such information is increasingly accessible through less formal channels. It is therefore no surprise that measures of perceived school quality can consistently explain at least a portion of the pattern of residential location that we observe, and house prices in good school districts are consistently higher than those in bad school districts.[4]

At the same time, differing constraints faced by different households clearly imply that some have more choice than others. Career and job constraints, for instance, are likely to narrow the number of possible public school districts that are feasible for different households. Furthermore, either due to historical forces or because of deliberate zoning policies, lower-income parents may find little or no affordable housing in some of the otherwise feasible school districts and neighborhoods.[5] Elite private schools are available only in some areas and are similarly unaffordable for low-income families, and even parochial schools are likely to be too expensive for many. Although some parents therefore clearly enjoy many school options, choice for others may be quite constrained by job considerations, housing markets, and lack of affordable private school alternatives.

The combination of the exercise of these constrained political, residential, and school choices then results in various outcomes that we can measure and observe. House prices differ both within and across school dis-

4. See, for example, Nechyba and Strauss (1998) and Bayer (1999) for discrete choice approaches, as well as a long literature on education and house prices with recent contributions such as Black (1999).
5. Even when lower-quality housing is available in good school districts, capitalization of public school quality will tend to inflate the prices of such houses substantially.

tricts, and markets incorporate both house/neighborhood quality and school quality considerations into these prices. Differing house quality and community amenity levels result in some mixing of different income groups within districts as well as some stratification by income across districts, both of which can generally be observed in the data. Commonly reported spending levels in schools reflect the result of an aggregation of preferences (however imperfect) through political institutions and thus give an indication of the value of per-pupil spending in household preferences. Finally, private school attendance rates in different districts give a measure of discontent within these districts with local public schools, spending levels, and other features such as the quality of peer interactions within those schools.

5.2.2   Using Observable Outcomes Today to Predict the Impact of Increased Choice Tomorrow

Although the choices that households make under the current school system—and the observed outcomes that result from these choices—are interesting in and of themselves, they also give rise to several research opportunities and challenges for those interested in predicting the impact of expanding school choice. One possible strategy takes as its starting point the empirical observation of varying degrees of choice within the current school system (across, say, metropolitan areas) and then attempts to link specific observed features of current public or private schools to the degree of competition faced by those schools.[6] A second strategy begins with a theoretical model that encompasses the forces we think are important for analyzing school competition, then tries to calibrate that model to replicate the most important outcomes (income and house price heterogeneity within and across districts, per-pupil spending levels, private school attendance rates) observed in the data under the current school system, and finally introduces new policies into the calibrated model to see how such policies would change outcomes. The first of these approaches therefore attempts to infer the impact of increased choice directly from current data and is most appropriate for predicting changes resulting from marginal policy adjustments. The second approach, on the other hand, uses the data to generate parameters within a structural model and then asks that model to simulate the impact of new policies assuming that the underlying structural parameters (in preferences and production functions) remain unchanged. Since economists generally are comfortable with the notion that preferences and production functions themselves are exogenous, the latter approach allows a full unfolding of all the forces within a general equilibrium setting where everything else is endogenous. This approach is potentially most useful for predicting the impact of large and discrete changes in policy, and it is the approach taken in this paper.

6. This approach is exemplified in Hoxby (1994, 2000a,b), McMillan (1999), and others.

5.2.3   Important Features to Be Modeled under This Approach

In order to implement this approach successfully, however, one must begin by convincingly identifying the core features of the current school choice environment (as well as specifying functional forms for preferences and production processes whose parameters are then to be dictated by the data). It is therefore worthwhile to pause and ask precisely what features a model would have to have in order to serve as an effective tool for the proposed analysis.

Given the important role of residential location and mobility in the current choice environment, one must start with a model that contains a heterogeneous housing market, with some locations inherently more desirable (apart from school considerations) than others. When applied to a specific context, such heterogeneity in housing within and across school districts is important because it serves as one of the limiting factors in school district choice. Second, in order for a relationship between housing and school choices to emerge under certain types of school financing, the heterogeneous houses must somehow be classified into different political jurisdictions. More precisely, it must be specified whether school finance decisions are made at the central level or more locally by regional or district governments; and it must be made clear how children gain access to particular schools (i.e., whether this is by living in a given jurisdiction or by some other rationing mechanism). Third, a meaningful analysis requires the model to incorporate different types of households that face different constraints, where the most important distinction between them is their wealth and ability. Fourth, in order for parents to be able to choose a school within their constrained choice set, they must have a way of evaluating school quality based on observable features within the model. Thus, an education production process—or at least a parentally perceived production process—must be formulated, a task made particularly challenging by the continuing disagreement in the literature regarding what matters in this process. Finally, both private and public schools can potentially enter the constrained choice sets of each household, and these choice sets could be expanded by policies such as private school vouchers. Therefore, we must model the private school market carefully, allowing for supply responses in case of changing demand for private schools.

5.3   The Model

The first challenge, then, is to construct a tractable and internally consistent model with (a) heterogeneous housing, (b) multiple jurisdictions describing how political choices regarding funding of public schools and admissions requirements are made, (c) households with different wealth and ability levels, (d) a specification of the education production process, and (e) a description of the private school market. The second challenge is to use available data on outcomes in the current choice environment to infer parameters of preferences and production processes. A nontechnical discussion of the elements of such a model (detailed more precisely elsewhere) is offered in section 5.3.1 and is followed by a discussion of how an equilibrium arises in such a model (section 5.3.2) and how the various parameters can be matched to important features of the data (section 5.3.3).[7] Once matched to the data, the model is then shown to be relatively successful in replicating the outcomes we currently observe (section 5.3.4).

5.3.1   Components of the Model

The policy simulations in later sections are based on a model in which 1,500 types of households that differ in their wealth level and child ability simultaneously choose where among three school districts and fifteen neighborhoods (or house types) to live, which school to attend, and how much public school spending to support at the ballot box. The overall number of houses available in the three districts is assumed to be equal to the total number of households in the model. Thus, there is exactly one house per household, but just as households differ in wealth and ability, houses differ in quality. More precisely, the three school districts contain five house types (or neighborhoods) each, and the total quantity of houses is the same in each of the three districts. The quality of housing, however, differs among the three districts, with average quality lowest in district 1 and highest in district 3. In addition, housing quality varies both within and across districts, and some house types in district 1 are of higher quality than some house types in district 3 despite the fact that average quality is highest in district 3.

The house quality of a type h house in district d is indexed by a parameter k_{dh}, and this parameter enters directly into the utility function that all households (regardless of wealth and ability) share.[8] In particular, households are assumed to value consumption c and school quality s as well as house quality k_{dh}. The utility of living in district d and house type h while consuming school quality s and private consumption c is given by

(1) $$u(d, h, s, c) = k_{dh}s^{\alpha}c^{\beta},$$

and the fifteen house quality parameters as well as α and β are derived from the data in a way described below. For now it should simply be noted that, since house prices are used to calibrate the house quality parameters, any-

---

7. The earliest theoretical development of the local public finance portion of this model is due to Dunz (1985).

8. An alternative way for a model to generate heterogeneity of housing and household types within districts is to assume housing to be fully malleable and household preferences to differ in school quality (Epple and Platt 1998). The relative merits of that approach as compared to the one taken here (in which houses are assumed to not be malleable and preferences are assumed to be identical) are discussed in section 5.5.

thing that is captured in house prices is also captured in these parameters. Specifically, in addition to standard housing quality measures, these parameters would capture non-school-related local amenities as well as non-school-related neighborhood externalities.

School quality s depends on whether the household has chosen a private school or the local public school. Two inputs are assumed to matter: (a) per-pupil spending and (b) average peer quality in the school. Per-pupil spending in the public school is determined through the political process of local voting (on property taxes) combined with an exogenously specified state aid formula (financed through state income taxes), whereas spending in the private schools is set by the school in order to maximize profit. Similarly, the public school has no control over peer quality but must admit all students who reside in the district and choose to attend the public school, whereas private schools are able to set a lower bound on peer quality. (Peer quality itself is specific to each household type and is a combination of child ability and parental income.[9]) Either type of school then takes its per-pupil spending x and combines it with average peer quality q to produce s through the production process given by

(2) $s = f(x, q) = \phi x^{(1-\rho)} q^{\rho}$ where $0 \leq \rho \leq 1.$

The parameter ρ is derived from the data in a way described below, and ϕ is a function that depends on how the impact of competition is modeled.[10]

More precisely, current researchers differ on whether public and private schools face different types of production technologies. For many of the initial simulations reported in the next section, we will therefore assume that $\phi = 1$, and public and private schools face the same production technology regardless of the nature of the competitive environment they face.[11] Under such an assumption, the data *require* that both per-pupil spending and peer quality enter the production process. If only spending mattered, the model

9. More specifically, peer quality for household n is given by $q(n) = [z(n)^{\theta} a(n)^{(1-\theta)}]/7.5$, where $z(n)$ is household income and $a(n)$ is child ability. The inclusion of both household income and child ability arises from different notions of peer effects. Some view the school peer effect as operating primarily through parents and their involvement and monitoring of schools (which we know increases in income; McMillan 1999), whereas others see peer effects as operating through child ability. The empirical literature offers little guidance as to the appropriate value for θ, which is set to 0.5 in the simulations in this paper. Sensitivity analysis with respect to different values suggests that the precise value of θ is not critical for the results.

10. Note that, for purposes of predicting changes in behavior of households, it is unimportant whether per-pupil spending actually matters in generating better outcomes such as test scores—a proposition that continues to be surrounded by controversy (Hanushek 1999; Krueger 1999; Hoxby 2000b). Rather, what matters is whether households value additional spending in schools, for whatever reason, and it is rather uncontroversial to say that they might. Just how much households value spending as opposed to peer quality is determined by the parameter ρ as it is set in a way to replicate the data. This is described in more detail subsequently.

11. Different levels of inputs will of course nevertheless generally result in different levels of school quality among the various schools, both public and private.

would predict zero private school attendance even for high levels of vouchers. On the other hand, if only peer effects mattered, no public school could survive in the model even without any vouchers.[12] The assumption of identical production processes for private and public schools therefore necessarily entails a production process that places weight on both spending and peers: That is, ρ falls strictly between 0 and 1 and is dictated rather precisely by the data. In later simulations, however, we will allow technologies between schools to differ through the function ϕ in ways that will be made more precise in the section "School Quality When Public Schools Respond to Competition." These alternative models of school production essentially permit private schools the additional advantage of more efficient resource use. However, here again the data will restrict just how much private schools can differ from public schools while still permitting the model to predict accurately the levels of private school attendance that are observed. Specifically, as private schools gain a competitive advantage in terms of efficient resource use, their other large competitive advantage (being able to select peers) must take on less importance: That is, ρ decreases as resource use is assumed to be more efficient in private schools. Since ρ cannot fall below zero, the data therefore place a natural bound on how large the efficiency advantage of private schools can be in the model. The "assumption" that either peer effects play an important role or private schools are more efficient (or some combination of the two) is therefore not an assumption at all. Rather, it is an empirical conclusion that arises from the need to accurately predict current private school attendance rates.

A second concern in modeling school production is that researchers currently know little regarding the precise way in which peer effects enter school production or parentally perceived school production. The most common assumption in the literature is that such peer effects are of the form modeled in equation (2), where the mean of peer quality enters school production, and where mixing of peers consequently benefits lower peer quality children at the expense of high peer quality children. Alternatively, it may be the case that, under certain types of curriculum arrangements, not just the mean but also the variance of peer quality is important. This form of peer effects is incorporated into the model through the function ϕ in the Section on "School Quality When Public Schools Respond to Competition" under the heading of "curriculum targeting."[13] As is illustrated in that

12. This is because the main competitive advantage a private school has in the model when production technologies are identical to those of public schools is the ability to select its inputs, particularly the peer composition. When peer composition is assumed not to matter, then there is simply not enough of a competitive advantage for private schools to convince anyone to pay for them. On the other hand, if that competitive advantage is too large—that is, if peers matter too much—then private school markets can attract all students away from public schools.

13. One way of distinguishing these two views of peer effects would be to call the former the "American view" and the latter the "European view." More precisely, in the United States there

section, the latter formulation of peer effects tends to produce substantially more favorable impacts of vouchers on school quality. Finally, the degree of tracking that is present in public schools clearly affects the way in which peer effects matter. Although tracking is not included explicitly in the model, it should be pointed out that—conditional on whatever level of mixing occurs in public schools—parents *must* still have preferences that place weight on peers in order for any model of this kind to replicate private school attendance levels we actually observe in the data. Thus, the presence of tracking would not in fact alter the initial calibration of the model, but it would cause us to expect an increase in tracking as competition increases, a process that is modeled in the section "School Quality When Public Schools Respond to Competition" as an increase in curriculum targeting within public schools.

5.3.2 Defining an Equilibrium in the Model

An equilibrium in the model occurs when each actor is doing the best he or she can given the features of the economy that can be observed, and when those features are consistent with the underlying political and production processes. Thus, an equilibrium must specify those aspects that everyone can see—house prices, tax rates, public and private school quality levels—and these must be such that (a) no private school or potential private school could increase its profits by exiting or entering the market, or by changing its pricing or admissions policy; (b) no household wants to move or change schools; (c) all tax rates are consistent with majority rule yielding balanced government budgets; and (d) public school quality in each district arises from the inputs allocated to the public schools through the decisions of households to attend (thus determining peer quality) and the decisions resulting from the public choice process (which determines per-pupil funding levels). Although the formal definition of equilibrium and the necessary mathematical proof of its existence is given elsewhere (Nechyba 1997a, 1999), this section provides a brief overview of the issues involved. In essence, we can view a full equilibrium as consisting of equilibrium in three different areas: the private school market, the housing market, and the political market. I discuss each in turn.

---

tends to be an effort to teach a relatively similar curriculum to all ability types within the same school through the age of eighteen, when a sharp ability-based separation takes place, whereas in Europe students are typically separated into different schools based on ability at a much earlier age and then taught very different subjects intended to prepare them for very different tasks. Under the U.S. system, it may well be the case that the presence of higher-ability students benefits lower-ability students that are being taught similar subjects, whereas in Europe such mixing would simply get in the way of the rather different missions of schools that are targeting curricula to different ability types. Some have argued that the introduction of competition may tend to lead to a more European peer effect because schools would differentiate themselves horizontally by targeting to different types of students.

The Private School Market

Recall that private schools compete along two dimensions: They set both a per-pupil spending level and a minimum peer quality admissions level. The assumption of perfect competition in the private school market then leads to a relatively straightforward private school hierarchy. Specifically, private schools (to the extent that they exist in equilibrium) are composed of children from the same type of household, and the tuition charged to each household is equal to the most preferred per-pupil spending level of that household. To see this, suppose either of these conditions were not satisfied in equilibrium. If the school consisted of several types of peer groups, then a new school could enter, set a higher minimum peer admissions level while charging the same tuition, and make the same profit as the existing school. Similarly, if tuition were greater than per-pupil spending, a school with the same admissions rule and per-pupil spending level but slightly lower tuition could enter and make positive profits. Thus, equilibrium in the private school market simply means that, if a particular household type demanded a private school with that household's peer quality and that household's most preferred level of spending, then such a private school will be available.[14] As a result of perfect competition, private schools make zero profits.[15]

The Housing Market

When households in the model evaluate which house type (or neighborhood) in which school district to choose, they can then check easily how much utility each option offers. For example, in evaluating the utility from house h in district d, a household would calculate both the utility of resid-

---

14. The equilibrium prediction of homogeneity of peer quality within each private school is, of course, somewhat extreme and not meant to be a perfectly realistic outcome. It arises from two particular assumptions in the model. First, the production process assumes no economies of scale in school production, thus permitting small schools in the model to arise easily. Even if economies of scale were explicitly introduced, however, the model would still predict relative homogeneity given the discrete number of household types, and unless such scale economies were substantially larger than is indicated by any of the available empirical estimates, the simplifying assumption of no scale economies does not result in substantial qualitatively or quantitatively different implications. Second, I am explicitly not allowing price discrimination within a school such as that used in Epple and Romano (1998) and Caucutt (2001). If private schools can observe peer effects, these papers have demonstrated that pricing of these peer effects is profit-maximizing and efficient—and results in a different form of cream skimming. Although it is unclear from the current empirical literature to what extent such differential pricing is actually practiced in private schools, it is certain that at least some does indeed take place, although probably not as much as predicted by Epple and Romano (1998). To whatever extent this would occur, some heterogeneity within private schools would, however, emerge.

15. An observationally equivalent set of assumptions for the model employed here would be that private schools, rather than being profit maximizers constrained to charge a single price, are exclusionary clubs of parents who agree to an equal cost-sharing rule (Nechyba 1999).

ing there while attending the district's public school and the utility of residing there and attending the private school offered by the market (i.e., a
private school with that household's peer quality and most preferred level
of tuition). The utility household n obtains from living in this house and attending public school is given by $u(d, h, s_d, c_{dhn})$ where s_d is district d's public
school quality and c_{dhn} is the level of private consumption that is equal to
household n's after-tax income minus the property tax–inclusive house payment required to live in house (d, h). The utility from living in the same
house and attending private school, on the other hand, is given by $u(d, h, s_n,$
$c_{dhn} - \tau_n)$, where s_n is the private school quality offered to household n by the
market, and τ_n is the private school tuition required of household n. Thus,
for a given location, public schools have the advantage that they permit
higher private consumption, whereas private schools might offer higher
school quality (due to their ability to tailor tuition to household demand,
due to their ability to restrict access to lower peer quality students, and—in
some specifications of the model—due to their more efficient use of resources).

Given house prices, tax rates, and public school quality levels, a household can therefore determine the utility of a house h in district d as simply
the higher of $u(d, h, s_d, c_{dhn})$ and $u(d, h, s_n, c_{dhn} - \tau_n)$. The housing market is in
equilibrium (given public school quality and tax rates) if every household
chooses its most preferred location at the prevailing house prices and, as a
result, all houses are occupied.

The Political Market and Full Equilibrium

Finally, residents of each district are assumed to vote on local property
tax rates knowing that local tax revenues, supplemented by state funds
through a prespecified state aid formula, will translate to spending on
public education.[16] Alternatively, for versions of the model in which funding of public schools is equalized and centralized, residents of all districts
vote on a state income tax rate with the understanding that revenues support equal levels of per-pupil spending in all districts. Households that send
their child to public school have single peaked preferences over property tax
rates (Nechyba 1997a), as do those who send their child to private school
(Nechyba 1999) under certain voter myopia assumptions. For any given distribution of the population into districts, a political (voting) equilibrium
therefore exists.[17] A full equilibrium is then a partition of households into

16. In addition, a state income tax rate sufficient to fund state aid (and vouchers in later simulations) is imposed.
17. These myopia assumptions are relatively standard in the literature and roughly assume
that households hold a variety of factors fixed when voting. The assumptions essentially require voters to hold expectations that, although accurate in equilibrium, are not accurate out
of equilibrium. For details on the required voter myopia assumptions to insure this single-
peakedness of preferences, see Nechyba (1999). It should also be noted, however, that single-
peakedness is actually a stronger condition than what is required for a voting equilibrium to

house types and school districts, a price for each house type, a local property tax rate for each district, a state income tax rate, and an indication of who goes to public and who goes to private school, such that private school markets and housing markets as well as the political market are in equilibrium.

5.3.3 Matching Parameters to Data

The three school districts in the model are intended to be representative of the several hundred low-income, middle-income, and high-income school districts located in four New Jersey counties (Bergen, Hudson, Essex, and Union Counties) that include the suburbs of New York City. More specifically, using the *1990 School District Data Book* (National Center for Education Statistics 1995) and census (Bureau of the Census 1992) data from all districts in these four counties, school districts in these counties were divided into three categories by median household income such that each category ends up with roughly equal numbers of households. The features of the model to be matched to these data are (a) the income/wealth and ability distributions; (b) the parameters in utility and production functions of equations (1) and (2); and (c) the formula of state aid that is taken as given by voters.

Income/Wealth and Ability Distributions

The simulation model begins with twenty different income levels endowed with fifteen different types of houses, yielding a total 300 different endowment or wealth levels. Incomes in the model range from 1 (corresponding to $10,000) to 20 (corresponding to $200,000) and represent a discretized version of the actual household income distribution in the data, and house values (which are properly interpreted as annualized flows of housing services) range from 0.3 to 3.5. Since income types are initially spread uniformly across the fifteen house types, the addition of housing endowments has the effect of smoothing the income distribution in the model.[18] In addition, ability endowments take on five different possible discrete values, which are set to range from 1 to 10. Empirical estimates of the correlation of parental and child income of 0.4 (Solon 1992; Zimmerman 1992) are used as a proxy for the correlation of parental income and child ability.[19] The addition of five ability endowments to the 300 income/wealth

---

exist when voters have a private alternative to the publicly provided service (Epple and Romano 1996; Glomm and Ravikumar 1998), although weaker conditions are difficult to guarantee easily within the present setup.

18. It is important to note that, although this implies that some low-income households in the model are initially endowed with expensive houses, this is not the case once the equilibrium has been calculated, when such houses would have been traded at market prices.

19. One can also interpret the correlation between parental and child income of 0.4 as an upper bound on the correlation between parental income and child ability because of the correlation of school quality and parental income. Sensitivity analysis with versions of the model

endowments then yields a total of 1,500 different types of households in the model.

Parameters in Utility and Production Functions

More challenging is the process of setting the parameters in the utility and production functions. These parameters include the housing quality parameters $(k_{11}, \ldots, k_{dh}, \ldots k_{35})$, the preference parameters α and β, and the production parameter ρ. The methodology used to calibrate these parameters builds on that of Nechyba (1997b, 2000) and is outlined more fully in Nechyba (forthcoming). The method translates a near-continuum of house qualities observed for each district type into five discrete quality intervals (neighborhoods) of equal sizes. It starts by assuming an underlying utility function $u(h, s, c) = h^\delta s^\alpha c^\beta$ where h jointly captures housing and neighborhood quality and is interpreted as the annualized flow of housing/neighborhood services. Substituting equation (2) for s, this utility function can be rewritten as

$$u(h, x, c; q) = h^\delta [x^{(1-\rho)} q^\rho]^\alpha c^\beta = \gamma h^\delta x^{(1-\rho)\alpha} c^\beta,$$

where q is equal to peer quality and $\gamma = q^{\rho\alpha}$. When h, x, and c are treated as choice variables in an ordinary maximization problem, the exponents δ, $(1 - \rho)\alpha$, and β can then, without loss of generality, be normalized to sum to 1 and interpreted as budget shares. Thus, I calculate the budget shares for h, x, and c for a hypothetical "median household" that consumes the imputed median annualized flow of housing/neighborhood services (in the data), earns the median income, and chooses the mean school spending level observed in the New Jersey districts, and these budget shares become our estimates of δ, $(1 - \rho)\alpha$, and β (equal to 0.22, 0.12, and 0.65, respectively).[20]

Of course, housing in the model is not a continuous variable h, but rather consists of a discrete number of house/neighborhood quality levels denoted by $(k_{11}, \ldots, k_{dh}, \ldots k_{35})$ in equation (1). I therefore combine the housing value distribution data from the *School District Data Book* with our estimate for δ to calibrate the fifteen values for k_{dh} across the three representative school districts. In particular, I take the housing distribution for all houses in districts of a particular type (i.e., low-, middle-, or high-income as defined above), find house values at the 10th, 30th, 50th, 70th, and 90th percentile (corresponding to neighborhoods 1 through 5 in district 1) and con-

---

that drive the correlation to 0, however, suggest that this makes little difference for the results I report. In particular, changing the correlation to 0.2, for instance, results in essentially no change in the results of tables 5.4 and 5.7. Results in tables 5.5 and 5.6 are affected slightly in that public school quality levels in the poor district are slightly lower, and the impact of vouchers on public school levels is slightly less favorable. Overall, however, these differences in results are minor and therefore go unreported.

20. Given data on house prices rather than flows of housing services, the median annualized flow of housing/neighborhood services is calculated for the median house value in the data assuming a 5.5 percent interest rate.

vert these to annualized housing flows (using a 5.5 percent interest rate). I then combine these annualized flow values with the exponent δ to arrive at the five housing (or neighborhood) quality parameters for this representative district.[21] As noted in an earlier section, this methodology—because it employs all the information contained in housing prices—is quite general in that it incorporates not just house quality measures but also non-school-related neighborhood amenities and non-school-related peer effects into the k_{dh} quality parameters.[22]

Finally, although the calibration procedure above has placed a restriction on the values of ρ and α (given that $[1 - \rho]\alpha = 0.12$ from the budget share exercise), the precise values of ρ and α are set to match private school attendance rates. Recall from equation (2) that ρ is the weight on peer quality (as opposed to per-pupil spending) in the school production function. When ρ is set to 0, school quality differences are determined solely by per-pupil spending differences, which, in this model, yield zero private school attendance even if private school vouchers are introduced at relatively high levels. On the other hand, if ρ is set close to 1, public schools cannot survive even without private school vouchers. As ρ rises from 0 to 1, private school attendance increases monotonically, and ρ is set to replicate as closely as possible the level of private school attendance observed in the data (yielding ρ = 0.475). Given the restriction that $(1 - \rho)\alpha = 0.12$, this also determines the value of α (= 0.229). When an additional efficiency advantage of private schools is introduced in the section on "School Quality When Public Schools Respond to Competition" through the function φ, ρ is adjusted (downward) so as to continue to allow the model to accurately predict private school attendance rates.

State Aid Formula

As argued in MaCurdy and Nechyba (2001), it is difficult to construct state aid formulas from statutory language because of the fungibility of aid and the subtle trade-offs that local policy makers are aware of but that are unobservable to the outsider. Rather than attempting to mimic a statutory

21. More precisely, suppose that for houses in districts falling into district category 3 (i.e., high-income districts), the annualized flow of housing services for a house at the 50th percentile of the distribution is 1.5 (corresponding to $15,000). The housing quality parameter for neighborhood 3 (the median neighborhood) in district 3 is then just equal to $(1.5)^\delta$, i.e. $k_{23} = (1.5)^\delta = (1.5)^{0.22} = 1.093$. This procedure is then similarly applied to other district types to arrive at housing quality parameters for all neighborhoods in all representative districts. These parameters are reported in Nechyba (forthcoming).

22. It should be noted, however, that these neighborhood quality measures are assumed to stay constant throughout the policy simulations. This implies that, although the benchmark equilibrium presented below accurately captures current neighborhood externalities, the simulations do not allow for a *change* in these externalities as populations migrate. However, as I have argued elsewhere (Nechyba forthcoming) and will argue again in what follows, this actually implies that the migration results highlighted in the paper are *understated* and would probably be stronger if neighborhood externalities were endogenized.

Table 5.1   Benchmark Equilibrium to Replicate New Jersey Data

	Average Income	Average Property Values	Fraction Private	Per-Pupil Spending	School Quality
District 1	3.1120	0.6121	0.2000	0.6652	0.4322
District 2	4.6216	1.0720	0.2250	0.7910	0.6178
District 3	6.5863	1.5248	0.1250	0.8621	0.7803

Table 5.2   Predictions versus Data

	Representative School Districts		
	Low Income ($d = 1$)	Middle Income ($d = 2$)	High Income ($d = 3$)
Mean house value	$157,248	$192,867	$271,315
Predicted mean land value[a]	$117,412	$205,629	$292,484
Median household income	$30,639	$45,248	$67,312
Predicted mean household income	$31,120	$46,216	$65,863
Per-pupil spending	$6,702	$7,841	$8,448
Predicted per-pupil spending	$6,652	$7,910	$8,621
Fraction choosing private school	0.21	0.23	0.20
Predicted fraction in private school	0.20	0.23	0.13
Fraction raised locally	0.52	0.77	0.87
Fraction raised locally in model	0.52	0.77	0.87

[a]Calculated from static values assuming 5.5 percent interest rate.

formula, I therefore implement a state aid formula that combines block grant and matching grant elements (as defined in Nechyba 1996) in such a way as to allow the model to replicate the levels of per-pupil spending observed in the data.

5.3.4   The Calibrated New Jersey Equilibrium

With the distributional properties and functional parameters chosen, the computer model is then asked to generate an equilibrium. If the calibration is successful, the stylized facts in the data should be approximately replicated by the computer simulation. Table 5.1 provides numbers for key equilibrium values generated by the computer model when $\phi = 1$, and table 5.2 translates these to be comparable to the numbers in the data employed to calibrate the model. Overall, the match between the predicted values from the computer model and those found in the data seems reasonably close (with some exceptions).[23] The remaining simulations then employ the same

23. The generated data also match well in terms of other moments of the within-district distributions of house values and income levels. In fact, the calibration method seeks to match not only the means but also the variances of these distributions. For space considerations, these details go unreported here.

income/wealth/ability distributions for the 1,500 household types, and the same parameters for utility and production functions (with adjustments made only to ρ as ϕ is altered in the section on "School Quality When Public Schools Respond to Competition." The New Jersey specific state aid formula, however, is not employed in all simulations because some are intended to reflect results in more stylized state-financed or locally financed systems.

5.4   Policy Simulations

Two types of predictions arise from the policy simulations reported in this section. First, a substantial portion of the current level of income-based residential segregation can be attributed to the limits on competition inherent in the current public school system, and the fostering of additional private school choice has the potential to dramatically reduce this kind of segregation. This prediction is robust to the inclusion of various controversial assumptions regarding other forces unleashed by increased competition. On the other hand, assumptions regarding the impact of competition on school behavior do matter for predicting the degree to which increased competition from private schools may affect school quality. Such policies may create winners and losers while leaving average school quality roughly unchanged, or they may create substantial increases in school quality. Section 5.4.1 focuses on the first of these predictions, and section 5.4.2 discusses the second.

5.4.1   Public Schools, Residential Segregation,
and Private School Choice

It is apparent, both in the data and the benchmark equilibrium (which is relatively consistent with the data) that there is a substantial degree of residential segregation by income across school districts. Given the interdistrict distribution of housing quality, this is of course no surprise. The simulation results reported in this section, however, suggest an additional role played by the rules inherent in different types of school systems, and they suggest a large potential for private school vouchers to change the degree of residential segregation. In the following section, I begin by investigating the school-related causes of segregation in the absence of vouchers, and the subsequent section builds on these intuitions and investigates the role of vouchers.

The Role of Private and Public Schools without Vouchers

The results of five simulations are reported in the five rows of table 5.3, which is taken from Nechyba (2002). The first row establishes a benchmark for the degree of residential segregation implied simply by the housing market absent any distortion through the public school sector. This is accom-

Table 5.3   Schools and Residential Segregation

Public Financing	Income				Property Values			
	Average Income ($)			Ratio: Dist. 3 Avg./ Dist. 1 Avg.	Average Property Values ($)			Ratio: Dist. 3 Avg./ Dist. 1 Avg.
	Dist. 1	Dist. 2	Dist. 3		Dist. 1	Dist. 2	Dist. 3	
None[a]	25,700	50,175	67,325	2.62	8,254	11,844	13,892	1.68
No private schools								
Local tax[b]	17,628	39,647	85,925	4.87	5,301	10,639	20,457	3.86
State tax[c]	19,875	42,250	81,075	4.08	5,322	11,507	20,204	3.80
Private schools								
Local tax[d]	29,725	50,262	63,212	2.13	6,424	11,038	15,370	2.39
State tax[e]	29,891	51,309	62,000	2.07	6,177	11,800	16,490	2.67

Note: Property values are expressed as annualized flows.
[a]This simulation sets public spending to zero and assumes only private schools operate.
[b]This simulation prohibits private schools and assumes all funding for public schools comes from local voting on a proportional local property tax. All tax revenues within a district are assumed to be spent on schools in that district.
[c]This simulation prohibits private schools and assumes all funding for public schools comes from voting on a proportional state income tax. Under this state system, all public schools receive the same per-pupil funding.
[d]This simulation allows a full private school market and assumes that all funding for public schools comes from local voting on a proportional property tax. All tax revenues within a district are assumed to be spent on schools in that district.
[e]This simulation allows for a full private school market and assumes that all funding for public schools comes from voting on a proportional state income tax. Under this state system, all public schools receive the same per-pupil funding.

plished by setting public school spending to zero in all districts, thus causing all households in the model to choose private schools. Housing price differences now reflect solely the house/neighborhood quality differences embodied in the k_{dh} values in equation (1), and no public choices regarding schooling interfere with where households choose to live.

Next, the second row reports simulation results in which private schools are prohibited and all public schools are financed at the local level through a local property tax. The difference is striking: The residence-based public school system (in the absence of private schools) introduces a substantial degree of segregation, as evidenced in both average incomes and average property values across the three districts. For instance, the ratio of average income in district 3 to average income in district 1 rises from 2.62 to 4.87, and the ratio of average property values in district 3 over those in district 1 rises from 1.68 to 3.86. Capitalization of public schools (which is absent in the first row but not the second) raises average housing values in the wealthy district by nearly 50 percent while lowering them in the poor district by similar magnitudes.

One natural reaction to this comparison might be to suspect that the dramatic difference in the first two rows of the table is due to the decentralized nature of public school financing in the second row. The third row therefore reports simulation results from a state income tax–supported equalized public school system, with private schools again prohibited. Somewhat surprisingly, the results are rather similar to those of the second row, implying that the increase in segregation from row 1 to row 2 is due primarily to the switch from a purely private to a purely public system and only secondarily due to the level of decentralization of public financing.

Finally, the fourth and fifth rows repeat the previous two simulations but this time permit the emergence of a private school market. Again, the results are striking: Not only does the emergence of the private school market alleviate the segregation observed in the purely public systems, but it actually produces less income segregation than exists in the purely private system, in which public schools played no role in where households chose to reside. Given that public school quality continues to increase with community wealth, however, capitalization of school differences must—and does—persist in equilibrium. Thus, under local public financing, capitalization still raises average property values in district 3 by 11 percent and lowers them in district 1 by 28 percent.[24] This yields the curious outcome that the district 3 to district 1 ratio of average district income actually falls below the pure private simulations (first row), but the similar ratio of average property values settles well above the pure private benchmark (first row).

These seemingly contradictory results on income segregation and capitalization, however, are closely linked. Consider a relatively high income household that resides in district 3 under both the purely public and the purely private systems. Under the public system the household chooses district 3 because this is the only way to consume high-quality education. Under the private system, on the other hand, there is no reason for a household to choose any particular district: The only factor that matters is housing/neighborhood quality. When a private market is introduced into a public system, however, an important effect emerges for households considering private schooling: The difference in public school quality is capitalized into house prices (albeit at a lesser rate than under pure public financing), thus making the same house (if it exists in both districts) substantially cheaper in the poor district than in the rich district. In the case of local public financing, this results in an average price difference of approximately 40 percent for the same type of house in district 3 versus district 1. Unlike the case of a purely private system, this capitalization of public school differences then gives rise to rather strong incentives for those choosing private schools to choose a house in the poor district—even if that house is of suboptimal

24. These capitalization differences appear even higher in the last column (under state funding) for reasons addressed elsewhere (Nechyba forthcoming).

164   Thomas J. Nechyba

quality. Households with high-ability children receive the biggest payoff from opting out of the public system, as do middle- to high-income households. Thus, the introduction of private schools into a public system— whether state- or locally financed—provides incentives to middle- and high-income families (with high-ability children) to settle in poor districts. As a result, average income differences narrow substantially more than property value differences that continue to capitalize public school quality.[25]

Vouchers and Segregation

Tables 5.4, 5.5, and 5.6 report simulation results for three different public school finance regimes (local, state, and the system calibrated to the New Jersey data) and three types of vouchers: The top portion of each table simulates vouchers that are universally available; the middle portion simulates vouchers targeted only to residents of district 1; and the lowest portion reports results from the introduction of vouchers targeted only to households earning below $25,000. Vouchers simply allow eligible households to redeem the face value for that level of private school tuition, and they can freely supplement the voucher amount.

The impact of private school vouchers on segregation then follows straightforwardly from the logic behind the previous results. To the extent that a voucher causes someone who previously chose public schools to switch to private schools, the same price incentive to settle in the poor rather than the rich district applies. At the same time, however, interdistrict housing price differences narrow as more households choose private schools in poor districts and as voucher levels increase the value of housing in those districts. Thus, two opposing effects emerge as vouchers are introduced: First, the capitalization-induced price incentive for private school attending households to reside in poorer communities applies to a larger number of households, thus causing households with incomes above the average for district 1 to immigrate and raise average income. Second, this price incentive declines as housing price differences narrow and as only lower-quality housing remains for private school immigrants in district 1—thus causing lower-income households with high-ability children to compose the additional private school–attending population. Since vouchers are taken up primarily by households that are not at the lowest end of the income distribution, however, these effects are either absent or modest when vouchers are small in size or targeted only to low-income households (as opposed to low-income districts).

25. A cautionary note is perhaps in order: Although the results in table 5.3 suggest that segregation would be greater in a purely private system than in mixed private/public system, it would be stretching the bounds of the model to take this implication too literally. Specifically, linking public schooling to housing for decades causes housing stocks to evolve endogenously, whereas private schooling introduces no such distortions. Because housing is fixed at its present quality levels in this paper, the model cannot be used to infer where the segregation would have ended up under public versus private financing. Rather, the model suggests that, conditional on housing markets fixed at present levels and not being allowed to change, a purely private system would lead to higher levels of income segregation.

Table 5.4   Private School Vouchers under Local Public Financing[a]

Voucher Amount	Average Income ($)		Property Values ($)		Ratio: Dist. 3/Dist. 1		Private (%)	
	Dist. 1	Dist. 3	Dist. 1	Dist. 3	Income	Property	Dist. 1	Dist. 3
All Eligible for Voucher[b]								
$0	29,725	63,212	6,424	15,370	2.1266	2.3926	30	10
$1,000	31,925	59,800	7,122	14,654	1.8731	2.0576	40	10
$2,500	33,425	58,000	9,097	14,468	1.7352	1.5904	62.5	25
$4,000	33,125	57,425	8,256	13,339	1.7336	1.6157	87.5	30
$5,000	32,900	56,425	8,027	11,816	1.7150	1.4720	100	37.5
Voucher Targeted to District 1[c]								
$0	29,725	63,212	6,424	15,370	2.1266	2.3926	30	10
$1,000	34,050	59,950	7,124	14,974	1.7606	2.1019	37.5	10
$2,500	37,125	54,125	9,979	14,804	1.4579	1.4835	70	10
$4,000	43,275	52,950	13,741	15,141	1.2236	1.1019	100	17.5
$5,000	44,624	53,632	14,282	15,041	1.2019	1.0531	100	19.84
Voucher Targeted Families with Income below $25,000[d]								
$0	29,725	63,212	6,424	15,370	2.1266	2.3926	30	10
$1,000	29,725	63,212	6,424	15,370	2.1266	2.3926	30	10
$2,500	30,185	62,320	6,513	15,220	2.0646	2.3369	45	10
$4,000	32,325	60,340	7,012	15,184	1.8667	2.1654	82.5	7.5
$5,000	32,675	62,250	9,187	15,589	1.9051	1.6969	100	10

Note: Property values are expressed as annualized flows.

[a]These simulations introduce vouchers funded by the state through an increase in the state income tax sufficient to balance state budgets. No local sources of revenues are used to fund vouchers. A household can redeem the value of the voucher as part or all of tuition at any private school that will accept the household's child. All public schools are locally funded through proportional property taxes set through local voting with all revenues staying within the district.

[b]This set of simulations assumes that vouchers are not restricted; that is, regardless of where a household lives and how much income that household earns, the household is eligible for the voucher.

[c]This set of simulations assumes that vouchers are restricted to households who reside in district 1—the poorest district. Within district 1, all households are eligible regardless of household income.

[d]This set of simulations assumes that only households with incomes below $25,000 are eligible for vouchers.

First, consider the top portions of the tables 5.4, 5.5, and 5.6 (which do not restrict voucher eligibility). For low levels of such vouchers, the first effect dominates, thus causing decreases in income segregation as households with incomes above district 1's average immigrate to take advantage of lower house prices while sending their children to private school. For higher levels of such vouchers, on the other hand, the second effect dominates, thus causing increases in income segregation.[26] The impact of uni-

26. If vouchers were to get high enough to cause all public schools to collapse, the degree of residential segregation would settle to what appears in the purely private system in row 1 of table 5.3.

Table 5.5   Vouchers under Central Public Financing[a]

Voucher Amount	Average Income ($)		Property Values ($)		Ratio: Dist. 3/Dist. 1		Private (%)	
	Dist. 1	Dist. 3	Dist. 1	Dist. 3	Income	Property	Dist. 1	Dist. 3
All Eligible for Voucher[b]								
$0	29,891	62,000	6,177	16,490	2.0742	2.6696	22.5	15
$1,000	33,375	60,350	6,215	15,599	1.8082	2.5099	30	25
$2,500	34,188	58,254	6,431	15,851	1.7039	2.4648	35	27.5
$4,000	33,500	61,225	7,710	14,908	1.8276	1.9336	62.5	30
$5,000	28,775	64,875	8,327	14,016	2.2546	1.6832	100	100
Voucher Targeted to District 1[c]								
$0	29,891	62,000	6,177	16,490	2.0742	2.6696	22.5	15
$1,000	33,400	59,645	6,242	15,711	1.7858	2.5170	30	12.5
$2,500	39,326	59,825	6,720	15,940	1.5213	2.3720	42.5	11.25
$4,000	43,202	53,861	8,652	16,805	1.2467	1.9423	70	10
$5,000	44,225	58,850	12,509	16,100	1.3307	1.2871	100	37.5
Voucher Targeted Families with Income below $25,000[d]								
$0	29,891	62,000	6,177	16,490	2.0742	2.6696	22.5	15
$1,000	29,891	62,000	6,177	16,490	2.0742	2.6696	22.5	15
$2,500	29,891	62,000	6,177	16,490	2.0742	2.6696	22.5	15
$4,000	30,281	61,348	6,091	16,573	2.0260	2.7209	37.5	12.5
$5,000	31,644	60,858	5,910	16,940	1.9232	2.8663	52.5	10

Note: Property values are expressed as annualized flows.

[a]These simulations introduce vouchers funded by the state through an increase in the state income tax sufficient to balance state budgets. A household can redeem the value of the voucher as part or all of tuition at any private school that will accept the household's child. All public schools are equally funded through a proportional income tax.

[b]This set of simulations assumes that vouchers are not restricted; that is, regardless of where a household lives and how much income that household earns, the household is eligible for the voucher.

[c]This set of simulations assumes that vouchers are restricted to households who reside in district 1—the poorest district. Within district 1, all households are eligible regardless of household income.

[d]This set of simulations assumes that only households with incomes below $25,000 are eligible for vouchers.

versally available vouchers on income segregation is, therefore, U-shaped in the size of the voucher.

Now consider the middle parts of tables 5.4, 5.5, and 5.6—results for vouchers targeted solely to residents of district 1. For such vouchers, it appears that the second effect never materializes. Since vouchers are available only to residents in district 1, migration of private school–attending households into district 1 continues despite the fact that price differences are narrowing, with higher-income immigrants out-competing others for the houses that ensure voucher eligibility despite the fact that some of these houses are not of high quality. In the middle portions of tables 5.4, 5.5, and 5.6, income segregation therefore continues to decline as houses in district 1 become increasingly valuable to those interested in private education. At

Table 5.6   **Vouchers under New Jersey Financing System**[a]

Voucher Amount	Average Income ($)		Property Values ($)		Ratio: Dist. 3/Dist. 1		Private (%)	
	Dist. 1	Dist. 3	Dist. 1	Dist. 3	Income	Property	Dist. 1	Dist. 3
All Eligible for Voucher[a]								
$0	31,120	65,863	6,121	15,248	2.1164	2.4911	20	12.5
$1,000	32,845	63,100	6,534	14,921	1.9211	2.2836	32.5	15
$2,500	35,525	60,050	8,692	14,312	1.6904	1.6466	40	22.5
$4,000	33,350	61,340	9,342	13,164	1.8393	1.4091	67.5	30
$5,000	32,533	61,788	8,210	12,329	1.8992	1.5017	100	32.5
Voucher Targeted to District 1[c]								
$0	31,120	65,863	6,121	15,248	2.1164	2.4911	20	12.5
$1,000	33,250	61,125	6,623	15,120	1.8383	2.2830	35	12.5
$2,500	38,466	56,380	9,922	14,792	1.4657	1.4908	47.5	15
$4,000	43,620	52,890	12,331	14,910	1.2125	1.2091	82.5	15
$5,000	44,130	54,210	12,910	14,225	1.2284	1.1019	100	17.5
Voucher Targeted Families with Income below $25,000[d]								
$0	31,120	65,863	6,121	15,248	2.1164	2.4911	20	12.5
$1,000	31,120	65,863	6,121	15,248	2.1164	2.4911	20	12.5
$2,500	31,120	65,863	6,121	15,248	2.1164	2.4911	20	12.5
$4,000	31,833	64,421	6,223	15,005	2.0237	2.4112	40	12.5
$5,000	32,960	63,184	7,325	15,225	1.9170	2.0785	67.5	10

Note: Property values are expressed as annualized flows.

[a]These simulations introduce vouchers funded by the state through an increase in the state income tax sufficient to balance state budgets. A household can redeem the value of the voucher as part or all of tuition at any private school that will accept the household's child. All public schools are funded through a mix of local property and state income taxes under a formula replicating the New Jersey finance system in 1987.

[b]This set of simulations assumes that vouchers are not restricted; that is, regardless of where a household lives and how much income that household earns, the household is eligible for the voucher.

[c]This set of simulations assumes that vouchers are restricted to households who reside in district 1—the poorest district. Within district 1, all households are eligible regardless of household income.

[d]This set of simulations assumes that only households with incomes below $25,000 are eligible for vouchers.

the $5,000 voucher level, the decline in segregation is most dramatic, with district 3's average income now only 20 percent higher than district 1's average income for the local financing simulation and property values (despite higher housing quality) only 5 percent higher.

Both types of vouchers—those that are not targeted and those targeted to the poorest district—can therefore reduce segregation. However, universally available vouchers, by privatizing the system at high enough voucher levels, eventually lead to the level of segregation that would occur in a purely private system (which is higher than the segregation in the present mixed system). For universally available vouchers, residential income desegregation then occurs only at lower levels of vouchers. Vouchers targeted to poor districts, on the other hand, have the potential to increase significantly these desegregating effects by preventing a complete privatization of the public system and instead making the poor district increasingly attractive to those seeking private education at high voucher levels.

Finally, the lowest portions of tables 5.4, 5.5, and 5.6 report simulation results for vouchers targeted only to households that earn below $25,000 per year. These households can be grouped into two broad conceptual categories: those that have high-ability children and those that have low-ability children. Whatever migration is caused by such vouchers is then primarily migration of relatively low income families (who are eligible for the voucher) with high-ability children that locate in the poor district and send their children to private schools. As a consequence, relatively little change in the degree of interdistrict income segregation arises (with the ratio of average income in district 3 to average income in district 1 falling by a modest 5 to 10 percent for high levels of the voucher). Furthermore, the voucher is actually not used until it reaches at least the $2,500 level.[27] Cases between universally available vouchers and household-targeted vouchers of the kind modeled here are of course also possible, and results for such vouchers fall predictably between those reported in the top and bottom portions of the table panels. For instance, vouchers might be set high for low-income households and phased out as incomes rise. This would then introduce some (but not all) of the migration forces unleashed by universally available vouchers.

Finally, it should be noted that the assumption that housing quality is fixed (i.e., k_{dh} does not change) tends to bias the mobility results emphasized in this section *downward*. In the discussion of the calibration of the model, for instance, I emphasized that the methodology (using housing prices) employed to calibrate house/neighborhood quality parameters incorporates not just housing quality but also non-school-related neighborhood amenities and externalities. Holding the k_{dh} parameters fixed as migration takes place then assumes that housing qualities as well as non-school-related neighborhood amenities and externalities are also unchanged. Because the migration that takes place primarily involves relatively higher income households moving from middle- and high-income districts to the low-income district, one would expect k_{dh} values to increase in district 1 (as these households expand houses and add to neighborhood amenities and externalities) and to decrease in district 3 (as the converse happens there). This

27. It should be noted that, in voucher experiments in some cities, the demand for low levels of vouchers targeted to low-income families has been higher than predicted here. Since the "low-income district" in this model is an aggregation of the lowest one-third of all districts, the model clearly does not capture desperate conditions in the worst public schools and thus the demand for vouchers in such districts. It is in such primary inner-city districts, however, that voucher demand by low-income families has been surprisingly high even when voucher levels were relatively low. We should therefore expect voucher take-up rates for low levels of vouchers targeted to the poor in very poor districts to be higher than what is predicted by this model.

would make district 1 even more attractive, thus causing even less segregation and a further narrowing of property values. Thus, the explicit exclusion of adjustments in the k_{dh} values yields lower-mobility results than what the model would otherwise tend to predict.

5.4.2 School Choice and School Quality

Previous models of vouchers have ignored the implications of voucher policies on residential mobility and have instead focused on single-community settings in which private schools compete with a homogeneous public school sector. The purpose of these models is to study the effect of vouchers on average school quality as well as the distribution of school quality across different types of students, and to investigate the likely workings of private school markets in a voucher environment. The problem with comparing pre- and postvoucher outcomes within single-district models of this kind, however, is that they abstract away from one of the defining characteristics of the U.S. public school system—the degree of inequality in existing public schools—and thus analyze the issue of vouchers from an empirically incorrect benchmark. We therefore now revisit the competition forces analyzed in single-district models here in the context of the multidistrict model with heterogeneous public schools.

These competition forces are of two general kinds: First, it is argued by voucher opponents that a policy of private school vouchers will drain the public system of resources and thus leave it worse off. The term "resources" needs to be interpreted loosely to include not only financial resources (which may in fact increase on a per-pupil basis[28]) but also peer quality (including whatever part of peer quality is due to parental involvement [McMillan 1999]) and political support. Second, it is argued by proponents of vouchers that the increased competition for students will lead to greater effort by public schools and that the greater variety of education options will lead to a better matching of resources with student needs.[29] The loss of resources would, of course, lead to a decline in public school quality, whereas the competition-induced efficiency gains through more efficient resource uses and better matching of resources with students would lead to an increase.[30]

The next section begins with the version of the model (outlined in section 5.3) that incorporates only the first of these forces—that is, the cream-

---

28. If the voucher amount is below per-pupil spending in the public school, then, assuming no change in overall government spending on education (including spending on vouchers), per-pupil spending in public school would increase as students depart with vouchers. If vouchers also go to those currently attending private schools, then the increase in per-pupil spending would occur only if the number of students departing the public system is sufficiently large.

29. Chubb and Moe (1990), for instance, argue such points, as do others.

30. Manski (1992) formalizes this type of trade-off in a single-district context. Epple and Romano (1998) and Caucutt (2001) add a different type of efficiency gain when they allow private schools to price peer externalities, a point I do not investigate here.

skimming by private schools of top students from the public schools. Again, three types of vouchers are analyzed: universally available vouchers, vouchers targeted only to residents of district 1, and vouchers targeted to the poorest families (i.e., those earning below $25,000 per year). Naturally, without the second counteracting force, the presence of just private school cream-skimming implies that vouchers will have a tendency to lower public school quality, although—perhaps surprisingly—not always and not primarily in the district in which vouchers are being taken up. The subsequent section then considers two types of potential efficiency-enhancing forces resulting from increased competition—forces that will tend to produce results more favorable for those interested in promoting vouchers.

School Quality in the Absence of School Responses to Competition

Tables 5.7, 5.8, and 5.9 present public school variables as well as private school attendance rates for each of the districts under different levels of the three types of vouchers for different public school funding systems (local, state, and a system calibrated to New Jersey). The cream-skimming effect of private schools is evident in the peer quality columns of these tables: Higher peer quality students tend to leave the public school system as vouchers are introduced, thus decreasing the average peer quality in the public sector. However, because of the mobility forces described above, the declines in public school peer quality are not as concentrated in school districts that experience a decline in public school enrollment and an increase in private school attendance. Rather, private schools are drawing high peer quality students from all public schools even though marginal private school–attending households reside in poorer districts as a result of moving to take advantage of more favorable housing prices. For the same reason, vouchers targeted to the poor district have impacts similar to untargeted vouchers so long as voucher levels are modest: Because marginal households who take up vouchers tend to move to the better neighborhoods in the poor district, the targeted nature of the voucher is relatively nonbinding as long as voucher levels are not too high.[31]

Whether or not public school quality declines, however, depends on whether or not the declines in average peer quality are offset by increases in per-pupil spending. In table 5.7 (under local financing), public school quality shrinks relatively uniformly in all three districts, whereas in table 5.8 (under state financing), public school quality is relatively unchanged in all districts (until voucher levels become high). The intuition for these results is straightforward: As vouchers push high peer quality households into private

31. The differences and similarities between district-targeted and universal vouchers are discussed in detail in Nechyba (2000). That paper also demonstrates formally the clear intuition emerging from the exercise that household income targeting has significantly different policy implications from district targeting, again because of the mobility forces that arise in a multi-district public school environment. I return to this point in section 5.6.

Voucher Amount	Peer Quality[c]			Per-Pupil Spending[d] ($)			School Quality[e]			Attending Private (%)		
	Dist. 1	Dist. 2	Dist. 3	Dist. 1	Dist. 2	Dist. 3	Dist. 1	Dist. 2	Dist. 3	Dist. 1	Dist. 2	Dist. 3
	All Eligible for Voucher[b]											
$0	0.2613	0.5142	0.6404	5,000	7,326	10,215	0.36737	0.61922	0.8183	30	20	10
$1,000	0.2292	0.4745	0.6000	5,000	7,593	9,768	0.34519	0.60734	0.77494	40	27.5	10
$2,500	0.2211	0.3036	0.5419	5,000	7,645	9,555	0.33934	0.49302	0.72985	62.5	40	12.5
$4,000	0.1054	0.1370	0.3373	5,000	5,000	9,388	0.23868	0.27033	0.57731	87.5	82.5	30
$5,000	—	—	0.2626	—	—	9,696	—	—	0.5321	100	100	37.5
	Voucher Targeted to District 1 Residents Only[f]											
$0	0.2613	0.5142	0.6404	5,000	7,326	10,215	0.36737	0.61922	0.8183	30	20	10
$1,000	0.2097	0.4026	0.4943	5,000	7,065	9,539	0.33092	0.54088	0.69805	37.5	25	10
$2,500	0.2015	0.2984	0.4944	5,000	6,346	8,333	0.32471	0.44345	0.65029	70	40	10
$4,000	—	0.2174	0.3993	—	5,000	7,774	—	0.33663	0.56651	100	40	17.5
$5,000	—	0.2152	0.3937	—	5,000	7,777	—	0.33501	0.56283	100	40	19.8
	Voucher Targeted to Families with Incomes below $25,000[g]											
$0	0.2613	0.5142	0.6404	5,000	7,326	10,215	0.36737	0.61922	0.8183	30	20	10
$1,000	0.2613	0.5142	0.6404	5,000	7,326	10,215	0.36737	0.61922	0.8183	30	20	10
$2,500	0.2104	0.4718	0.6404	5,000	7,381	10,146	0.33144	0.59675	0.8154	45	20	10
$4,000	0.1054	0.4142	0.6307	5,000	7,269	9,801	0.23868	0.55648	0.79494	82.5	25	7.5
$5,000	—	0.3993	0.6298	—	7,132	9,657	—	0.54144	0.78825	100	25	10

Note: Dashes indicate that figure cannot be computed given results elsewhere in row.

[a] These simulations introduce vouchers funded by the state through an increase in the state income tax sufficient to balance state budgets. A household can redeem the value of the voucher as part or all of tuition at any private school that will accept the household's child. All public schools are funded through local property taxes, and all local tax revenues go to only public schools. This set of simulations assumes cream-skimming by private schools and no responses from public schools to increased competition.

[b] This set of simulations assumes that vouchers are not restricted; that is, regardless of where a household lives and how much income that household earns, the household is eligible for the voucher.

[c] Peer quality is the average of peer characteristics (with parental income and child ability weighted equally) within the public school in a district.

[d] Per-pupil spending refers to spending within the public school in the district. A minimum level of $5,000 per pupil is assumed. The spending level is determined by majority rule voting on local property taxes in each district, with tax revenues in each district going solely to public schools in that district.

[e] School quality refers to public school quality as determined by the production function that incorporates both peer quality and per-pupil spending.

[f] This set of simulations assumes that vouchers are restricted to households who reside in district 1—the poorest district. Within district 1, all households are eligible regardless of household income.

[g] This set of simulations assumes that only households with incomes below $25,000 are eligible for vouchers.

Table 5.8   Vouchers and Public School Quality under State Financing and Cream-Skimming[a]

Voucher Amount	Peer Quality[c]			Per-Pupil Spending[d] ($)			School Quality[e]			Attending Private (%)		
	Dist. 1	Dist. 2	Dist. 3	Dist. 1	Dist. 2	Dist. 3	Dist. 1	Dist. 2	Dist. 3	Dist. 1	Dist. 2	Dist. 3
				All Eligible for Voucher[b]								
$0	0.2826	0.5469	0.6470	7,195	7,195	7,195	0.46158	0.63161	0.6841	22.5	17.5	15
$1,000	0.2619	0.5688	0.5727	7,363	7,363	7,363	0.45063	0.65134	0.65346	30	10	25
$2,500	0.2570	0.5040	0.5652	7,781	7,781	7,781	0.45974	0.63306	0.66848	35	22.5	27.5
$4,000	0.2055	0.3117	0.4713	8,831	8,831	8,831	0.44182	0.53849	0.65535	62.5	40	30
$5,000	—	—	—	—	—	—	—	—	—	100	100	100
				Voucher Targeted to District 1 Residents Only[f]								
$0	0.2826	0.5469	0.6470	7,195	7,195	7,195	0.46158	0.63161	0.6841	22.5	17.5	15
$1000	0.2762	0.5582	0.5962	7,336	7,336	7,336	0.46126	0.6443	0.66478	30	10	12.5
$2500	0.2529	0.5048	0.5969	7,416	7,416	7,416	0.44488	0.61776	0.66895	40	12.5	11.3
$4000	0.2208	0.3314	0.5447	7,904	7,904	7,904	0.43129	0.52304	0.66228	70	27.5	10
$5000	—	0.2301	0.3204	—	4,250	4,250	—	0.31755	0.37163	100	40	37.5
				Voucher Targeted to Families with Incomes below $25,000[g]								
$0	0.2826	0.5469	0.6470	7,195	7,195	7,195	0.46158	0.63161	0.6841	22.5	17.5	15
$1,000	0.2826	0.5469	0.6470	7,195	7,195	7,195	0.46158	0.63161	0.6841	22.5	17.5	15
$2,500	0.2826	0.5469	0.6470	7,195	7,195	7,195	0.46158	0.63161	0.6841	22.5	17.5	15
$4,000	0.2521	0.5348	0.6470	7,293	7,293	7,293	0.44032	0.62939	0.68898	37.5	17.5	12.5
$5,000	0.2347	0.5247	0.6662	7,456	7,456	7,456	0.43059	0.63099	0.70677	52.5	17.5	10

Note: Dashes indicate that figure cannot be computed given results elsewhere in row.

[a] These simulations introduce vouchers funded by the state through an increase in the state income tax sufficient to balance state budgets. A household can redeem the value of the voucher as part or all of tuition at any private school that will accept the household's child. All public schools are funded equally (on a per-pupil basis) through a state income tax determined by majority rule. This set of simulations assumes cream-skimming by private schools and no responses from public schools to increased competition.

[b] This set of simulations assumes that vouchers are not restricted; that is, regardless of where a household lives and how much income that household earns, the household is eligible for the voucher.

[c] Peer quality is the average of peer characteristics (with parental income and child ability weighted equally) within the public school in a district.

[d] Per-pupil spending refers to spending within the public school in the district. A minimum level of $5,000 per pupil is assumed. The spending level is determined by majority rule voting on state income taxes, with tax revenues distributed equally on a per-pupil basis to all public schools.

[e] School quality refers to public school quality as determined by the production function that incorporates both peer quality and per-pupil spending.

[f] This set of simulations assumes that vouchers are restricted to households who reside in district 1—the poorest district. Within district 1, all households are eligible regardless of household income.

Table 5.9 Vouchers and Public School Quality under New Jersey Funding System and Cream-Skimming

Voucher Amount	Peer Quality[c]			Per-Pupil Spending[d] ($)			School Quality[e]			Attending Private (%)		
	Dist. 1	Dist. 2	Dist. 3	Dist. 1	Dist. 2	Dist. 3	Dist. 1	Dist. 2	Dist. 3	Dist. 1	Dist. 2	Dist. 3
	All Eligible for Voucher[b]											
$0	0.2684	0.4701	0.6989	6,652	7,910	8,621	0.43224	0.61778	0.78031	20	22.5	12.5
$1,000	0.2422	0.4698	0.6521	6,923	7,734	8,354	0.42038	0.61034	0.74267	32.5	22.5	15
$2,500	0.2212	0.4110	0.5910	7,054	7,221	8,111	0.40663	0.55251	0.69786	40	27.5	22.5
$4,000	0.1124	0.3302	0.4127	5,000	6,939	7,781	0.24608	0.48764	0.57573	67.5	40	30
$5,000	—	0.1425	0.2921	—	5,000	8,004	—	0.27544	0.49587	100	82.5	32.5
	Voucher Targeted to District 1 Residents Only[f]											
$0	0.2684	0.4701	0.6989	6,652	7,910	8,621	0.43224	0.61778	0.78031	20	22.5	12.5
$1,000	0.2416	0.4623	0.5881	6,992	7,812	8,572	0.42207	0.60889	0.71673	35	22.5	12.5
$2,500	0.2183	0.3945	0.4916	6,859	7,696	8,210	0.39819	0.56029	0.6435	47.5	30	15
$4,000	0.1058	0.2772	.04122	5,000	7,102	8,114	0.23911	0.45426	0.5882	82.5	42.5	15
$5,000	—	0.2294	0.4097	—	6,910	7,761	—	0.40927	0.57297	100	47.5	17.5
	Voucher Targeted to Households with Incomes below $25,000[g]											
$0	0.2684	0.4701	0.6989	6,652	7,910	8,621	0.43224	0.61778	0.78031	20	22.5	12.5
$1,000	0.2684	0.4701	0.6989	6,652	7,910	8,621	0.43224	0.61778	0.78031	20	22.5	12.5
$2,500	0.2684	0.4701	0.6989	6,652	7,910	8,621	0.43224	0.61778	0.78031	20	22.5	12.5
$4,000	0.1988	0.4365	0.6922	6,832	7,892	8,638	0.38009	0.59568	0.77755	40	22.5	12.5
$5,000	0.1438	0.4022	0.6856	5,000	7,834	8,551	0.27663	0.57076	0.76991	67.5	20	10

Note: Dashes indicate that figure cannot be computed given results elsewhere in row.

[a] These simulations introduce vouchers funded by the state through an increase in the state income tax sufficient to balance state budgets. A household can redeem the value of the voucher as part or all of tuition at any private school that will accept the household's child. All public schools are funded through a mix of local property and state income taxes under a formula replicating the New Jersey finance system in 1987. This set of simulations assumes cream-skimming by private schools and no responses from public schools to increased competition.

[b] This set of simulations assumes that vouchers are not restricted; that is, regardless of where a household lives and how much income that household earns, the household is eligible for the voucher.

[c] Peer quality is the average of peer characteristics (with parental income and child ability weighted equally) within the public school in a district.

[d] Per-pupil spending refers to spending within the public school in the district. A minimum level of $5,000 per pupil is assumed. The spending level is determined using the New Jersey financing system with voting taking place at the local level.

[e] School quality refers to public school quality as determined by the production function that incorporates both peer quality and per-pupil spending.

[f] This set of simulations assumes that vouchers are restricted to households who reside in district 1—the poorest district. Within district 1, all households are eligible regardless of household income.

[g] This set of simulations assumes that only households with incomes below $25,000 are eligible for vouchers.

schools, the political constituency for public school funding declines. At the same time, the exit of some into the private sector implies that those remaining in public schools now receive more per-pupil funding for any given tax rate—that is, voting for public school spending has just become cheaper. All else being equal, the first effect causes the median voter to prefer less public school spending, whereas the second effect causes him to prefer more. Under state funding, the latter effect outweighs the former, causing increases in per-pupil funding in public schools as voucher levels increase. The argument that vouchers result in a decrease in public school resources therefore holds only for peer quality and not for school spending once the political economy forces are taken into account under state financing, and the net effect is relatively unchanged public school quality. In table 5.7, on the other hand, public school quality in the poor district falls because per-pupil spending is determined by the constitutional minimum rather than the median voter and thus does not change to offset the decrease in peer quality. Effects in the other districts differ, with some experiencing an increase in quality and others a decrease. Finally, table 5.9 presents school outcomes for the New Jersey calibrated state funding system, a hybrid system that includes both local and state funding. Implications for public school quality are closer to those under the state system, primarily because of the fact that state aid in New Jersey insures that the poor district is not at some constitutionally minimum spending level but, rather, determined in a local public choice equilibrium. Only when more than 50 percent of the population attends private school in the poor district does public school quality suffer considerably.

Including both the multidistrict nature of public schools and a political economy model for the setting of public school spending therefore casts doubt on the common perception emerging from single-district, non-political-economy models that public schools are bound to decline in quality unless competition itself produces considerable efficiency gains. Here, the two additions to the model undo much of the negative effect of cream-skimming private schools by allowing those remaining in the public school system to free-ride on the contributions of others and to benefit from mobility forces that insure declines in peer quality will not be concentrated in only those districts that experience the biggest declines in public school attendance. While the model certainly does not rule out the possibility that public schools will suffer in the absence of competitive efficiency gains, it does suggest this effect to be smaller and less concentrated than one might have imagined. Variances in school outcomes (not reported in the tables) similarly do not change significantly.

School Quality When Public Schools Respond to Competition

The simulation results in the absence of a competitive efficiency effect can then serve as a benchmark, and any efficiency-enhancing impact of competition would be expected to improve the impact of vouchers (as in the single-district models; Manski 1992). Efficiency-enhancing effects could in principle come in many forms, but I focus in this section on two types of possible competition-induced changes in the production relationship. Essentially, the production function has two inputs, and competition could affect either one of these. In the case of peer quality, we have assumed thus far that only average peer quality matters. It is conceivable, however, that the variance matters as well. If two schools are identical in every way (i.e., average peer quality and average spending) except that school A has a greater variance in peer quality than school B, school B may well be able to more effectively target its resources to the student population's needs because those needs are more uniform across the student population. I will refer to this effect as *curriculum targeting*. In the case of spending, on the other hand, it is often argued that the marginal product of a dollar of spending will rise in public schools as those schools face greater competition. This effect will be referred to as *competitive efficiency gain*. Each of these effects is included in separate simulations reported below.

More precisely, tables 5.10, 5.11, and 5.12 present simulation results for universal, district-targeted, and household-targeted vouchers, respectively, for the case of both curriculum targeting and competitive efficiency gains. The curriculum-targeting effect is modeled as a constant ϕ in front of the school production function (2) that declines as the variance of peer quality increases,[32] and the competitive efficiency effect is modeled as a similar constant in the public school production function that rises in the percentage of private school attendance in all three districts combined.[33] Both of these changes in production functions affect only public schools, but each does so in a different way. The curriculum targeting is public school–specific in that it affects the production functions in different districts differently as school population variances changed. The competitive gain, on the other hand, affects all public school production functions similarly in that it provides an overall measure of the competitive pressures faced by the public system. These changes of course require recalibrations of various parameters of the model in order to replicate something close to the benchmark quantities in table 5.2. For the sake of brevity, I forgo a detailed discussion of this calibration process and instead simply note that the size of the two types of public school responses

32. This constant is $\phi = (1 - \lambda_1 * \text{variance})$ for all schools, where λ is calibrated jointly with ρ to match private school attendance rates in the absence of vouchers. Given zero variance in peer quality for private schools, the private school production function is effectively unchanged by this (i.e., $\phi = 1$ in equilibrium for all private schools).

33. This constant is $\phi = (1 - \lambda_2 * \text{PUB}^2)$ for public schools and $\phi = 1$ for private schools, where PUB is the fraction of the population attending public schools and λ_2 is calibrated jointly with ρ to match private school attendance rates in the absence of vouchers.

Table 5.10   School Quality and Vouchers under New Jersey Calibration and Universally Available Vouchers[a]

Voucher Amount	Public School Quality[c]			Average Private School Quality	Variance After/ Variance Before[d]	Attending Private School (%)
	Dist. 1	Dist. 2	Dist. 3			
Schools Become More Efficient through Curriculum Targeting[b]						
$0	0.4167	0.5922	0.7761	1.1628	—	18.67
$1,000	0.4528	0.6012	0.7705	1.1167	0.9721	23.50
$2,500	0.4770	0.6216	0.7679	1.0335	0.9512	29.25
$4,000	0.4833	0.6277	0.7802	0.9411	0.9481	36.33
$5,000	0.4551	0.6014	0.7522	0.8623	0.9551	46.66
Schools Become More Efficient through More Efficient Resource Utilization[e]						
$0	0.4023	0.6121	0.7629	1.1711	—	19.25
$1,000	0.4127	0.6233	0.7771	1.1018	0.9891	24.33
$2,500	0.4273	0.6421	0.7849	1.0911	0.9821	27.25
$4,000	0.4351	0.6591	0.8033	1.0300	0.9755	32.66
$5,000	0.4391	0.6718	0.8116	1.0029	0.9812	33.00

[a]These simulations introduce vouchers funded by the state through an increase in the state income tax sufficient to balance state budgets. A household can redeem the value of the voucher as part or all of tuition at any private school that will accept the household's child, and all households—regardless of residence and income—are eligible for the voucher. All public schools are funded through a mix of local property and state income taxes under a formula replicating the New Jersey finance system in 1987. This set of simulations assumes cream-skimming by private schools and some responses from public schools to increased competition.

[b]The simulations involving "curriculum targeting" assume that school quality is related inversely to the variance in peer quality—that is, all else being equal, a lower variance in peer quality is better because teaching can be more targeted to particular student needs.

[c]Public school quality in this set of simulations is not only a function of public school spending and average peer quality, but also a function of the variance in peer quality within the school.

[d]This column reports the overall variance in school quality consumed by all children—those in public and private schools.

[e]Simulations invoking efficiency of resource utilization assume that the marginal product of a dollar in per-pupil spending in public schools increases with the level of private school competition (attendance). Private schools are assumed to use resources efficiently regardless of the level of private school attendance. Public school quality in this set of simulations is a function not only of per-pupil spending and average peer quality but also of the degree of private school competition (attendance).

modeled in the simulations I report represents the midpoint of a feasible range of such effects.[34]

34. The λ constants in the curriculum-targeting and the competitive gain formulations of production functions can of course be set at various levels and thus introduce competitive effects of various magnitudes. As alluded to earlier, the recalibration requires primarily a change in the value ρ—the strength of the peer quality as opposed to spending in production. More precisely, for any λ constant that is chosen for either the curriculum-targeting or the competitive gain specification, public school quality falls while private school quality remains constant. Maintaining benchmark levels of private school attendance requires lowering the value of peer quality in production, the factor that gives private school their other competitive advantage. There is, however, an upper bound to how high λ can be and still produce only

Table 5.11 **School Quality and Vouchers under New Jersey Calibration and District 1 Targeted Vouchers**[a]

Voucher Amount	Public School Quality[c]			Average Private School Quality	Variance After/ Variance Before[d]	Attending Private School (%)
	Dist. 1	Dist. 2	Dist. 3			
Schools Become More Efficient through Curriculum Targeting[b]						
$0	0.4167	0.5922	0.7761	1.1628	—	18.67
$1,000	0.4613	0.5892	0.7783	1.1218	0.9721	23.25
$2,500	0.4852	0.5923	0.7811	1.0613	0.9512	26.12
$4,000	0.4925	0.6011	0.7734	1.0015	0.9481	26.12
$5,000	0.4727	0.5985	0.7692	0.9476	0.9551	35.25
Schools Become More Efficient through More Efficient Resource Utilization[e]						
$0	0.4023	0.6121	0.7629	1.1711	—	19.25
$1,000	0.4096	0.6186	0.7685	1.1102	0.9932	24.25
$2,500	0.4111	0.6322	0.7774	1.1033	0.9906	26.00
$4,000	0.4171	0.6556	0.7813	1.0731	0.9843	29.50
$5,000	0.4219	0.6555	0.7938	1.0663	0.9892	30.25

[a]These simulations introduce vouchers funded by the state through an increase in the state income tax sufficient to balance state budgets. A household can redeem the value of the voucher as part or all of tuition at any private school that will accept the household's child, but only households who reside in district 1 qualify for the voucher. All public schools are funded through a mix of local property and state income taxes under a formula replicating the New Jersey finance system in 1987. This set of simulations assumes cream-skimming by private schools and some responses from public schools to increased competition.

[b]The simulation involving "curriculum targeting" assume that school quality is related inversely to the variance in peer quality—that is, all else being equal, a lower variance in peer quality is better because teaching can be more targeted to particular student needs.

[c]Public school quality in this set of simulations is not only a function of public school spending and average peer quality, but also a function of the variance in peer quality within the school.

[d]This column reports the overall variance in school quality consumed by all children—those in public and private schools.

[e]Simulations invoking efficiency of resource utilization assume that the marginal product of a dollar in per-pupil spending in public schools increases with the level of private school competition (attendance). Private schools are assumed to use resources efficiently regardless of the level of private school attendance. Public school quality in this set of simulations is a function not only of per-pupil spending and average peer quality but also of the degree of private school competition (attendance).

Table 5.10 focuses on curriculum targeting where improvements in public school production processes hinge on each school's variance in peer quality. Since migration patterns are similar to those discussed in section 5.4.1, this effect is most pronounced in district 1, which experiences the greatest decline in student population and with it the greatest increase in peer quality homogeneity. As a result, public school quality rises most in district 1,

---

modest private school attendance levels in the absence of vouchers. The simulations reported here set the λ constants in both the curriculum-targeting and the competitive gain specification of production processes to be the midpoint between this upper bound and the lower bound of zero.

Table 5.12   School Quality and Vouchers under New Jersey Calibration and Vouchers Targeted to Households with Incomes below $25,000[a]

Voucher Amount	Public School Quality[c]			Average Private School Quality	Variance After/ Variance Before[d]	Attending Private School (%)
	Dist. 1	Dist. 2	Dist. 3			
Schools Become More Efficient through Curriculum Targeting[b]						
$0	0.4167	0.5922	0.7761	1.1628	—	18.67
$1,000	0.4167	0.5922	0.7761	1.1628	1.000	18.67
$2,500	0.4167	0.5922	0.7761	1.1628	1.000	18.67
$4,000	0.4439	0.5881	0.7734	1.0872	0.9822	21.85
$5,000	0.4623	0.5793	0.7702	0.9763	0.9719	27.33
Schools Become More Efficient through More Efficient Resource Utilization[e]						
$0	0.4023	0.6121	0.7629	1.1711	—	19.25
$1,000	0.4023	0.6121	0.7629	1.1711	1.000	19.25
$2,500	0.4023	0.6121	0.7629	1.1711	1.000	19.25
$4,000	0.3827	0.6281	0.7774	1.1005	1.041	23.50
$5,000	0.3540	0.6411	0.7829	1.0324	1.0720	26.67

[a]These simulations introduce vouchers funded by the state through an increase in the state income tax sufficient to balance state budgets. A household can redeem the value of the voucher as part or all of tuition at any private school that will accept the household's child, but only households whose income is below $25,000 qualify for the voucher. All public schools are funded through a mix of local property and state income taxes under a formula replicating the New Jersey finance system in 1987. This set of simulations assumes cream-skimming by private schools and some responses from public schools to increased competition.

[b]The simulations involving "curriculum targeting" assume that school quality is related inversely to the variance in peer quality—that is, all else being equal, a lower variance in peer quality is better because teaching can be more targeted to particular student needs.

[c]Public school quality in this set of simulations is not only a function of public school spending and average peer quality, but also a function of the variance in peer quality within the school.

[d]This column reports the overall variance in school quality consumed by all children—those in public and private schools.

[e]Simulations invoking efficiency of resource utilization assume that the marginal product of a dollar in per-pupil spending in public schools increases with the level of private school competition (attendance). Private schools are assumed to use resources efficiently regardless of the level of private school attendance. Public school quality in this set of simulations is a function not only of per-pupil spending and average peer quality but also of the degree of private school competition (attendance).

although other districts experience a narrowing of the variance in their student population as well even though the total population in those schools does not decrease by as much. Average private school quality falls with increasing private school enrollment because the marginal private school choosers have lower peer quality and thus enjoy lower private school quality. Moreover, although those switching to private schools increase the overall variance in school outcomes, those remaining in public schools now experience higher school quality and thus bring about a counteracting narrowing in the overall variance of outcomes. Finally, since the public school responds under these simulations, private school attendance does not rise as quickly with increases in voucher amounts as it does in previous simulations without competitive effects. Results are similar for district-targeted vouchers (table 5.11) as they are for universal vouchers, although private school take-up rates are predictably smaller when eligibility is restricted solely to one district. Similar forces also operate in table 5.12 for household-targeted vouchers, although changes are modest (or absent for low levels of vouchers) given the limited impact on migration discussed in the previous section.

The lower portions of tables 5.10, 5.11, and 5.12 offer simulation results under the assumption of a competitive effect. Here, the effect on public school production functions is the same across all public schools because the competitive pressure on the entire public school system is modeled, rather than school-specific effects (as under curriculum targeting). Thus, improvements in public schools are more uniform across all districts, and private school take-up rates are lower. Again, for the same reasons as under curriculum targeting, average private school quality falls as more households choose private schools. Moreover, the overall variance in educational outcomes falls slightly. A comparison of results for targeted versus universal vouchers gives rise to predictable differences in take-up rates under higher levels of the voucher.

The broad conclusion regarding school quality under vouchers in this model, is then, that the impact on average educational opportunities as well as the variance in such opportunities depends on what assumptions are made regarding the responses by public schools. In the base case in which cream-skimming by private schools was permitted but no competitive response on the part of public schools was assumed, average public school quality remains relatively constant under some public financing and declines slightly under others (unless voucher levels become very high).[35] When different types of competitive effects are included, on the other hand, both average public school quality and overall average school quality can rise substantially, and the variance in outcomes may drop somewhat. Impacts tend to be strongest for vouchers that induce large migrations, which occurs under universally available vouchers and even more so under district targeted voucher. Such migrations are, however, significantly more muted when vouchers are targeted to low-income households.

5.4.3   Robustness of Results on Segregation and School Quality

Finally, we return to the issue of residential segregation. In section 5.4.1, it was demonstrated that residential segregation can be affected significantly by the introduction of vouchers, especially vouchers targeted to poor districts. These results were arrived at in simulations that ignored any

35. Overall average quality, including private schools, was not reported but stays relatively constant or falls slightly in the benchmark cases. Overall variances rise as well.

potential competitive effects. Table 5.13 then provides comparisons of indicators of residential segregation for both centralized and decentralized public school systems when the two types of competitive effects we introduced in section 5.4.2 are included. These results indicate that the segregation effects raised in section 5.4.1 are robust to the inclusion of such effects.[36]

5.5 Empirical Foundation and Testable Implications

The simulations reported in section 5.4, and the model structure of section 5.3 that gives rise to these simulation results, offer a variety of predictions regarding the policy impact of expanded private school choice. Although it is difficult to test these predictions directly (due to the current lack of a sufficiently large policy experiment of this kind in the United States), the model itself does have testable implications that can be analyzed with current data, and some of the key foundations of the model can be empirically challenged. This section provides a brief discussion of both the empirical foundations and the testable implications arising from the model, and some of the available empirical evidence that speaks to these.

5.5.1   Foundations of the Model: Tastes, Housing Markets, and Mobility

In arriving at a model that has the potential to replicate both the current interdistrict differences in public school quality and the heterogeneity of income and property values within jurisdictions, two possible avenues are available to the economic theorist: First, he could model the outcome as a result of taste differences, where household tastes differ over housing or school quality, and both high- and low-income households settle in jurisdictions with similar school quality as a result.[37] This approach is put forth by Epple and Platt (1998), empirically implemented by Epple and Sieg (1999), and will henceforth be called the Epple-Platt-Sieg (EPS) approach. A second alternative approach—and the one taken in this paper—is to assume that households share preferences but the housing market, whether because of zoning regulations or historical evolution, offers only limited bundles of school quality and housing combinations. In particular, this approach assumes that low-quality housing is relatively more concentrated in some districts, which then results endogenously in relatively worse public schools in those districts. Both approaches can be reconciled with the data, but both contain underlying assumptions that are problematic for policy analysis. Below we discuss several of these as they relate to some other literature.

36. Results for public school finance systems calibrated to results for New Jersey show similar robustness but are not reported explicitly.
37. Without heterogeneity in preferences, this model results in perfect stratification of incomes across districts (Epple, Filimon, and Romer 1993).

Table 5.13   District 3/District 1 Variables for Different Assumptions Regarding School Quality

	No Private School Markets Permitted		Private School Markets Permitted[a]									
			Nontargeted Vouchers[a]						District-Targeted Vouchers[b]			
			No Vouchers		Voucher = $2,500		Voucher = $5,000		Voucher = $2,500		Voucher = $5,000	
	Local[c]	Central[d]	Local[c]	Central[d]	Local[c]	Central[d]	Local[c]	Central[d]	Local[c]	Central[d]	Local[c]	Central[d]
	School Quality Assuming No Adjustments from Public Schools											
Income[e]	4.874	4.079	2.126	2.074	1.735	1.704	1.715	2.255	1.458	1.521	1.202	1.331
Property[f]	3.859	3.796	2.392	2.667	1.590	2.465	1.472	1.683	1.484	2.372	1.053	1.287
	Public Schools Become More Efficient through Curriculum Targeting											
Income[e]	4.505	4.188	2.076	2.033	1.798	1.921	1.832	2.119	1.397	1.510	1.193	1.279
Property[f]	3.791	3.586	2.222	2.512	1.553	2.213	1.394	1.762	1.427	2.181	1.081	1.231
	Public Schools Become More Efficient through More Efficient Resource Utilization											
Income[e]	4.771	3.892	2.231	2.100	1.751	1.691	1.802	2.387	1.424	1.478	1.249	1.414
Property[f]	3.712	3.603	2.469	2.702	1.539	2.568	1.528	1.732	1.329	2.292	1.103	1.302

[a] Vouchers that are available for all households regardless of income or place of residence. Voucher amounts can be used as part of private school tuition, with parents able to pay additional tuition out of household funds.

[b] Vouchers that are available only to households residing in district 1—the poorest district. Voucher amounts can be used as part of private school tuition, with parents able to pay additional tuition out of household funds.

[c] Local financing through a property tax, with all revenues staying in the district.

[d] State financing through an income tax, with all public schools receiving equal per-pupil funding.

[e] Ratio of average income in district 3 (the wealthiest district) to average income in district 1 (the poorest district).

[f] Ratio of average property values in district 3 (the wealthiest district) to average property values in district 1 (the poorest district).

Housing Markets

The EPS approach treats housing as a good similar to other types of goods in that, at any particular location, consumption of the good can be changed in either direction as conditions change. From the urban economics literature we know, of course, that housing is a rather durable good, and although it is often possible to increase housing quantity or quality at a particular location, it is not similarly possible to decrease these (except through depreciation in the long run). The approach taken in this paper, on the other hand, models housing as entirely fixed and thus does not permit quality improvements of the kind that might be made under certain policy changes while precluding the unrealistic decreases in housing quantity allowed under the EPS model. Thus, one model seems to err in the direction of allowing too many types of changes in housing consumption at a particular location, whereas the other errs in the direction of permitting too few.

Empirical discussion of this issue is primarily embedded in the literature on local property taxation, with the "New View" of the property tax arguing for the EPS model of housing markets and the "Benefit View" arguing for a model similar to that in this paper.[38] As a result, the New View suggests that taxation of residential property is primarily taxation of all forms of capital because higher property taxes simply imply a fleeing of capital from housing to other uses, whereas the Benefit View argues that the local property tax, through both direct payments and capitalization effects, approximates a local benefits tax. Unfortunately, different versions of both these views are difficult to empirically distinguish, and much of the debate therefore centers on the degree to which zoning in fact keeps housing stocks at particular locations fixed. Thus, the literature offers little guidance as to which model is more correct.[39]

For purposes of analyzing the forces discussed in this paper, however, the latter approach has one distinct advantage over the EPS approach. First, to whatever extent a bias in the policy prediction is introduced, it is predictable that the bias is in the direction of making the forces weaker rather than stronger. In particular, the model predicts that vouchers, by disentangling housing and schooling choices and resulting in various general equilibrium price effects, will tend to cause middle- to high-income households to settle in poorer districts to send their children to private schools. High-quality housing in these districts is, of course, limited, and were these migrants to change housing stocks, they would be likely to improve them. This additional flexibility would cause migration forces to become more pronounced, thus causing predictions regarding mobility to represent a con-

---

38. Recent expositions of this debate can be found in Fischel (2001) and Zodrow (2001).
39. For a discussion of the difficulty in finding testable implications that distinguish between these views, see Nechyba (2001).

servative lower bound. It is not clear that a similar direction for the bias introduced by the EPS housing model could be determined were a similar policy exercise undertaken in such a model. In addition, the model employed in this paper allows for a calibration of housing quality to include various other neighborhood features (through the use of market prices in the calibration exercise) even though it then holds these features fixed as policies change. Here again, however, the assumption of fixed neighborhood features biases the predictions downward by not allowing middle- to high-income immigrants to low-income districts to improve local neighborhoods in ways other than schooling.

Differences in Tastes

Second, because of the perfect flexibility of housing choices at each location, the EPS model requires preferences to vary in order to generate heterogeneity of household income and house prices within districts.[40] Because housing markets themselves are calibrated to yield this within-district heterogeneity in this paper, no heterogeneity in tastes is required. Although taste heterogeneity could easily be introduced into the model used in this paper, it is preferable of course not to do so unless it is either necessary in order for the model to match the important features of the data or unless there is strong empirical evidence suggesting how such heterogeneity should be introduced. The empirical literature in this area is still evolving, although recent work by Bayer (1999) suggests that the hypothesis of persistent taste differences for education in different income or racial/ethnic groups can be largely rejected.

Mobility and School Choice

Much of what is reported in this paper would be of little value if school choice and residential choice were not indeed closely linked. However, the empirical evidence in this regard is overwhelming (and discussed in part earlier in the paper). Capitalization studies, starting with Oates (1969) and continuing with recent papers such as Black (1999), have consistently confirmed the importance of school quality in housing prices, thus providing evidence that housing choices are based in part on perceptions of local public schools. Even more recently, Figlio and Lucas (2000) provide fascinating evidence of how quickly this process happens as perceptions of public school quality change when new information is provided.[41] Similarly, discrete choice studies have linked residential location choices more di-

---

40. In the absence of such heterogeneity in tastes, households segregate perfectly into districts (Epple, Filimon, and Romer 1993).

41. The state of Florida began assigning grades to school in order to determine who qualifies for school-targeted vouchers under the new statewide voucher initiative. Figlio and Lucas demonstrate the immediacy with which seemingly new information that is revealed affects prices, and how these prices change as additional information becomes available.

rectly to the costs of living in particular school districts and the benefits from local public school quality.[42] The notion that households consider school quality when choosing residences is therefore rather uncontroversial, and the model in this paper simply assumes that this consideration of school quality does not change under new policy regimes. The only remaining issue is the speed with which it is reasonable to assume mobility to play out, an issue difficult to analyze in the static model of this paper. It is unlikely, for instance, that households would respond immediately by changing residences, but with mobility rates (for non-school-related reasons) as high as they are in the United States, the process may be shorter than otherwise expected.

5.5.2 Testable Implications

Section 5.5.1 was concerned with direct challenges to the foundations of the model underlying the simulation results. We now turn to consider more directly the testable implications of this model. A variety of such implications regarding mobility, segregation, private school formation, and school quality changes from increased choice policies arise from the simulations in section 5.4, but these cannot be tested directly without a large policy experiment. Several other related implications, however, are testable and are discussed below.

Voting on Voucher Initiatives

The model has rather straightforward predictions regarding the distribution of benefits from voucher policies. Benefits arise in two areas: First, households with high peer quality can more easily improve the school quality of their children by choosing private schools, and other households may benefit from better public schools if a competitive effect of the types incorporated into some simulations arises. Second, every household—whether in the public or private system—is affected through changes in household wealth as housing prices change dramatically. Results from the model suggest that, for most households, the latter effect may outweigh the former—at least for versions of the model that do not include a large competitive efficiency improvement from increased choice. More precisely, the model predicts that homeowners in good public school districts will tend to experience large capital losses, whereas homeowners in poor school districts will tend to experience large capital gains.

The empirical implication for homeowners is therefore straightforward: One would expect support for broad-based private school vouchers to vary inversely with local public school quality. Of course, a similar implication for homeowners arises from a different model that simply generates a greater desire for vouchers in districts with worse public schools because

---

42. See Nechyba and Strauss (1998) and references therein as well as Bayer (1999).

parents in those districts are more dissatisfied with public education. The two models can be empirically distinguished, however, by drawing a distinction between renters and owners who are similarly affected by public schools but differently affected by changes in property values. In particular, renters in poor school districts would be adversely affected by higher rents resulting from vouchers under the model in this paper, whereas renters in good school districts would benefit from lower rents. At the same time, renters and homeowners go to the same public schools and thus would not differ in their support for vouchers under the alternative model.

Thus, the testable implication arising from this model is that renters and homeowners will differ in their support for vouchers, with homeowners in good districts opposing vouchers due to the fear of capital losses and homeowners in poor districts favoring vouchers due to anticipated capital gains. Renters would be expected to exhibit the reverse preferences, with those in good school districts looking forward to lower rents and those in poor districts anticipating higher rents. These implications are formalized by Brunner, Sonstelie, and Thayer (2000) and tested for the case of the California statewide voucher initiative that was defeated in the election of 1994. Their results provide strong evidence for the hypothesis that homeowners in good districts voted against vouchers to protect their property values. When implications regarding renters versus homeowners are tested against an alternative hypothesis, the analysis provided no additional conclusive evidence one way or another.

Residential Location, School Choice, and Family Size

Although the model assumes each family has a single child, the implications of the model for families with different numbers of children is straightforward but, to my knowledge, remains untested. In particular, the choice of private school is one that brings with it a relatively constant marginal cost per child, whereas this may not be the case for the choice of high-quality public schools to which a family can gain access by residing in that school's district. A family with three children, for instance, must pay roughly the same private school tuition for each of its children if private schools are chosen, whereas the same family pays a lump-sum "capitalization fee" when choosing a house in the good public school district. Of course, house size also increases with family size, and thus the marginal cost of sending an additional child to public school is not zero. Nevertheless, it is likely to be less than private school tuition,[43] which gives the implication that, all else being equal, families with more children would choose good public schools whereas families with few children would more likely choose private schools in poorer public school districts.

---

43. In principle this can also be tested, and, were it not the case, the implication would run in the opposite direction.

Evidence from Current Experiments

Although private school choice experiments in the United States at this point are too small to give rise to effects such as those simulated in this paper, there are other types of choice arrangements for which the model has similar testable implications. For instance, large numbers of charter and magnet schools in various states do not use the residence-based admissions criteria so common in the rest of the public school system. Although clearly different from private school choice in that no tuition requirements are made of parents and various regulations inhibit the more extreme forms of cream-skimming, the introduction of such choice vehicles within the public system does weaken the link between residential and school choices. If such arrangements are widespread in a given geographic region, then mobility and price effects similar to those predicted in the simulations of section 5.4 should emerge.

Similarly, public school choice programs (such as those in Minnesota)— to the extent that they offer true choice rather than having good public schools close their doors by claiming capacity constraints—similarly alter the link between residential location and school choice. As a result, a model similar to that applied to private school choice in this paper would suggest capitalization effects that reflect this change. Research on this topic, to my knowledge, has been limited, although Reback (2002) provides evidence that mobility forces of the type raised in section 5.4.1 may play an important role.

Finally, the model offers predictions regarding private school formation, residential segregation, housing price differences, and so on for different types of state funding systems for public schools, but these are explored elsewhere (Nechyba 1999, forthcoming). Given the diversity of such state systems as well as their changing nature over the past few decades, such state differences provide yet another opportunity to test predictions other than those related to increasing choice. One notable test comes out of the 1970s California experience, when school finance changed rapidly and gave rise to a large number of private schools in a relatively short period of time. Downes and Greenstein (1996) present evidence on these private school formations and particularly the location of new private schools. Consistent with predictions arising from the model in this paper, they show that private schools tended to form in lower-income districts and near poorly performing public schools.

5.6 Policy Implications

The large policy implication emerging not only from the simulations reported in this paper but also from the broader research project referenced throughout is that, given the evidence that the links of residential, political, and school choices are strong in the current system, these links are potentially important for a variety of school finance policies, including the proposal of expanding choice through vouchers. When models abstract away from these links, the debate on vouchers becomes a stylized argument over which of two forces—the cream-skimming of private schools or the efficiency enhancements of increased choice—is likely to dominate. As a matter of theoretical exploration, limiting models to considering only some forces in isolation is, of course, extremely valuable and has provided numerous insights, some of which are included in the simulation exercises above. However, as a matter of policy analysis, forces that are best analyzed in isolation for conceptual clarification must ultimately be analyzed in a single framework.

The exercise in this paper is therefore one of expanding the framework within which we analyze the merits of vouchers to include components that move us away from a narrow debate and toward utilizing empirical facts that are less controversial than those asserted in much of the debate. These facts include (a) the current public school system is far from a homogeneous ideal and full of inequities that are commonly acknowledged in the literature; (b) these inequities are due largely to a linkage of residential and school choices that offer real school choice to only those who can afford to live in multiple types of school districts; (c) the forces that have shaped current schools under the current choice environment are unlikely to change as choice is expanded; (d) political processes are important and will probably continue to be important in setting school spending and thus school quality differences; and (e) private schools arising from voucher policies are likely to search out high peer quality students over low peer quality students. It is only after finding implications from these primitives that we have moved on to consider additional forces that are more controversial.

5.6.1 Winners and Losers from Vouchers

Most policies have clear winners and losers. In the case of private school vouchers, however, the problem of identifying precisely who wins and who loses is not an easy one. The analysis in this paper offers an opportunity to suggest which households are likely to definitely win, which might win under different assumptions, and which are most likely to lose. The gains and losses to households in the model arise from two different effects: First, most households will experience some change in the school quality consumed by their children, and, second, homeowners are likely to experience capital gains or losses as changing school choice affects market prices.[44] We can discuss each of these in turn.

---

44. A third avenue through which households are affected is through changing tax burdens, but we forgo a detailed analysis of these effects here. Furthermore, households already attending private schools benefit from lump-sum transfers through the voucher.

Winners and Losers in School Quality

With respect to winners and losers in terms of educational quality, the intuitions arising from this model are similar to those in the current single-district literature. Because private schools are assumed to gain a competitive advantage through their ability to exclude low peer quality students, it is clearly high peer quality students that are most likely to experience improvements in their school quality. In the context of the model in this paper, peer quality arises from both family income and child ability. Thus, relatively high ability children from high-income households who do not choose private schools before vouchers are put in place are the first to benefit from higher private school quality. Conversely, low-ability children from low-income households are likely to see little benefit or modest declines in their school quality as either public schools decrease in quality or they are forced to choose a private school with only their peer type. Similarly, low-ability children from higher-income households do not switch to private schools unless voucher amounts become high, and they, too, experience similar modest declines in their public school quality. The main additional insight offered by the model here over previous single-district models is that declines in public school quality are likely to be spread across districts even if private schools themselves arise primarily in poor districts, and because of this they are not likely to be as large as might otherwise be predicted (or may in fact be absent for some school financing systems). An important caveat to this, however, is that a restriction of vouchers to only poor households (as opposed to a targeting to poor districts) gives rise to sharper losses for public schools in poor districts once vouchers are taken up at high rates, and competitive effects are not readily spread to other districts whose populations do not qualify for the voucher regardless of where they move.

The prediction becomes significantly more rosy, however, as competitive effects are introduced. Since public school quality now generally increases, all children can in principle benefit from the introduction of vouchers. The precise nature of this competitive effect is, of course, important, as is the nature of the voucher itself. Particular concern for children who remain in poor public schools is warranted both because they are most likely to suffer in the absence of a competitive effect within the context of this model, and because of empirical evidence from abroad suggesting the possibility that choice may leave those children behind even when benefiting most other children.[45] Furthermore, the simulations suggest that vouchers limited only to low-income families (as opposed to low-income districts) carry with them a bigger potential threat to public schools in the poorest districts. The ambiguity regarding the likely impact of vouchers on those children that re-

---

45. In particular, Fiske and Ladd (2000) present compelling evidence that this has occurred under the public school choice reforms in New Zealand.

main in low-income public school districts therefore suggests that voucher initiatives—especially those motivated by concerns for poor children—ought to be accompanied by strong efforts to independently improve public schools in those districts. Additionally, the insights regarding migration effects that are uncovered in this model suggest that district targeting is a much more effective way of limiting eligibility than household targeting, both on efficiency grounds (because district targeting spreads the competitive effect throughout the public school system) and on equity grounds.

Winners and Losers in Housing Markets

Winners and losers in housing markets are more easily identified. As already discussed in the section on "Voting on Voucher Initiatives," and despite the fact that renters are not specifically included in the model of this paper, we can predict from the results in this model that homeowners and renters are affected differently.[46] In particular, homeowners in good districts experience relatively large capital losses while homeowners in poor school districts experience capital gains. Renters, of course, do not experience such gains and losses. Finally, to the extent that neighborhood effects may spread beyond school buildings, the desegregating effect of vouchers may have additional benefits for poor districts that are not modeled in this paper.

5.6.2   Implications for Targeting Vouchers

After the failure of broad-based vouchers to pass the political test in several state referenda, it now seems likely that voucher policies, to the extent that they will be enacted, will be targeted in some way. Current experiments at the city level are following that pattern with only low-income families qualifying for vouchers, and the only statewide plan to pass a legislature and be enacted (in Florida) has targeted vouchers to underperforming schools, as does the Bush proposal at the national level. However, the two kinds of targeting—toward low-income households or low-income or underperforming schools—are predicted to have very different implications within the framework of this paper.

More precisely, vouchers targeted to low-income families have little impact in the context of this model unless the voucher amount is set quite high. The reason for this is that household-targeted vouchers do not unleash similar mobility and capitalization effects because moving would have little value to anyone whose income is too high to receive the voucher. District targeting, on the other hand, creates the incentive to move in order to take advantage of private schools. Vouchers targeted to low-income households would therefore not give rise to the forces that a multidistrict model picks

---

46. Including renters does not alter the positive predictions of the model significantly because the capital gains and losses for homeowners (which are absent for renters) produce only income effects that do not alter behavior in major ways. Renters would have similar incentives to settle in poor districts if they choose private schools.

up, and single-district models illustrating the trade-offs between cream-skimming private schools and benefits from competition would give predictions similar to models of the kind employed in this paper. The clear policy implication, then, is that higher response rates are to be expected from district targeting than from household targeting, and these are likely to have greater efficiency and equity-enhancing consequences.

5.6.3 Designing Politically Feasible Vouchers

The difference in implications for different types of targeting thus rests on the fact that district targeting takes advantage of mobility forces whereas household targeting does not, and this may lead policymakers to view district targeting as a more effective tool to infuse competition into the public school system. On the other hand, this difference makes district targeting considerably less politically palatable to the population as a whole unless large competitive gains in public schools are expected. More specifically, district targeting affects homeowners in ways very similar to no targeting at all, with homeowners in wealthy districts suffering and homeowners in poor districts gaining. If voters are aware of such effects when expressing political preference for or against vouchers (as Brunner, Sonstelie, and Thayer 2000 suggest California voters were in 1994), homeowners in good school districts are almost as likely to be opposed to district-targeted vouchers as they are to universal vouchers. Put differently, targeting to households instead of districts would in effect isolate homeowners in such districts from capital losses.

Thus, the same factors that cause district targeting to be a more potent policy tool are likely to make it politically more difficult to implement. A trade-off between policy impact and political feasibility therefore emerges for policymakers. This trade-off is unlikely to be optimally resolved at either extreme (i.e., pure district targeting or pure household targeting) and is more likely to involve a combination of district targeting with income phaseouts. To the extent that higher-income households are ineligible for vouchers, this reduces the mobility and capitalization effects but may increase their willingness to agree to the proposal. On the other hand, if competitive effects are sought, these too are diminished as income phaseouts become more severe. A detailed analysis of this trade-off is, however, beyond the scope of this paper.

5.6.4 Short Run versus Long Run

A final issue worth raising involves the timing of changes and their impact. The model in this paper has little to offer in regard to this because it does not include a multiperiod analysis during which households adjust to policies. Rather, the model provides a snapshot of the prevoucher world and another of the postvoucher prediction but is not equipped to analyze the transition. The most critical issue is, of course, that of the speed at which mobility forces come into play. Although I have cited evidence that price adjustment to new education-related information are relatively fast, residential moves are typically undertaken for multiple reasons, with education being only one. Thus, a likely transition would include household relocations for a variety of job- or family-related reasons, where the considerations related to schools come into play once the decision to move has been made on other grounds. As a result, those predictions related to mobility are likely to take some time to unfold and require reasonable confidence on the part of households that policy changes are not just transitory.

In the short run, it may therefore be prudent to place some weight on results emerging from single-district models in which residential location is, in effect, assumed to be fixed. As is mentioned throughout this paper, this would imply considerably more negative short-run effects of vouchers because the more positive effects arise primarily from multidistrict considerations. In addition, voucher take-up rates would be considerably more muted in the short run, and decreases in public school quality more concentrated. Therefore, although the model has little to offer in terms of predicting the length of time between short-run and long-run effects, it does suggest that a full evaluation of the impact of large-scale voucher programs will require a considerable period of maintaining the policy in place.

5.7   Conclusion

In summary, this paper has placed the previously analyzed forces related to private school vouchers into a multidistrict context that is capable of more accurately establishing a prevoucher benchmark from which to conduct policy analysis. I have then argued that this gives rise to a number of general equilibrium effects that are important to such an analysis. Two main conclusions emerge: First, most voucher policies have profound implications for how the broader set of choices that households make are undertaken and how residential districts are likely to evolve, with vouchers offering a large potential for reducing income segregation across district boundaries. Second, the likely impact of private school vouchers on public school quality depends on a number of assumptions regarding public school responses, assumptions that all remain controversial. Under the more pessimistic set of assumptions, public school quality may suffer as a result of vouchers, although this decline would not be as large or as concentrated as predicted by a narrower single-district analysis. Under more positive assumptions, on the other hand, public school quality may improve through private school competition. In one case, overall school quality (including private schools) remains relatively unchanged, with clear winners and losers (in terms of educational opportunities), whereas in the other cases both average quality and the variance in quality can improve significantly. Since the potential losers (in terms of school quality) under the more pessimistic assumptions of the model are the very poorest children who remain in public schools in poor districts, an important implication arising from these simulations is that caution would dictate that strong efforts to independently improve public schools in poor districts accompany any vouchers intended to help poor children. Similarly, the simulations suggest a more hopeful picture for vouchers targeted to districts rather than vouchers that are targeted to households. More empirical analysis is, of course, required in order to narrow the range of likely school quality outcomes under different types of voucher policies.

References

Bayer, Patrick. 1999. An empirical analysis of the equilibrium in the education market. Ph.D. diss., Stanford University.
Bearse, Peter, Gerhard Glomm, and B. Ravikumar. 2000. On the political economy of means-tested education vouchers. *European Economic Review* 44:904–15.
Black, Sandra E. 1999. Do better schools matter? Parental valuation of elementary education. *Quarterly Journal of Economics* 114 (2): 577–99.
Brunner, Eric, Jon Sonstelie, and Mark Thayer. 2000. Capitalization and the voucher: An analysis of precinct returns from California's Proposition 174. *Journal of Urban Economics* 50 (3): 517–36.
Bureau of the Census. 1992. *1990 census of population and housing.* Washington, D.C.: Bureau of the Census.
Caucutt, Elizabeth. 2001. Peer-group effects in applied general equilibrium. *Economic Theory* 17 (1): 25–51.
Chubb, John, and Terry Moe. 1990. *Politics, markets, and America's schools.* Washington, D.C.: Brookings Institution.
Downes, Thomas, and Shane Greenstein. 1996. Understanding the supply decision of nonprofits: Modeling the location of private schools. *RAND Journal of Economics* 27 (2): 365–90.
Dunz, Karl. 1985. Existence of equilibrium with local public goods and housing. Department of Economics Discussion Paper no. 201. Albany: State University of New York.
Epple, Dennis, Radu Filimon, and Thomas Romer. 1993. Existence of voting and housing equilibrium in a system of communities with property taxes. *Regional Science and Urban Economics* 23:585–610.
Epple, Dennis, and Glenn Platt. 1998. Equilibrium and local redistribution in an urban economy when households differ in both preferences and income. *Journal of Urban Economics* 43 (1): 23–51.
Epple, Dennis, and Richard Romano. 1996. Ends against the middle: Determining public service provision when there are private alternatives. *Journal of Public Economics* 62 (3): 297–325.
———. 1998. Competition between private and public schools, vouchers, and peer group effects. *American Economic Review* 88 (1): 33–62.
Epple, Dennis, and Holger Sieg. 1999. Estimating equilibrium models of local jurisdictions. *Journal of Political Economy* 107 (4): 645–81.
Fernandez, Raquel, and Richard Rogerson. 1996. Income distribution, communi-

ties, and the quality of public education. *Quarterly Journal of Economics* 111 (1): 135–64.

————. 1999. Education finance reform and investment in human capital: Lessons from California. *Journal of Public Economics* 74 (3): 327–50.

Figlio, David, and Maurice Lucas. 2000. What's in a grade? School report cards and house prices. NBER Working Paper no. 8019. Cambridge, Mass.: National Bureau of Economic Research.

Fischel, William. 2001. Municipal corporations, homeowners, and the benefit view of property taxation. In *Property taxation and local public finance,* ed. Wallace Oates, 33–77. Cambridge, Mass.: Lincoln Institute Press.

Fiske, Edward, and Helen Ladd. 2000. *When schools compete: A cautionary tale.* Washington, D.C.: Brookings Institution.

Glomm, Gerhard, and B. Ravikumar. 1998. Opting out of publicly provided services: A majority voting result. *Social Choice and Welfare* 15 (2): 187–99.

Hanushek, Eric. 1999. Some findings from an independent investigation of the Tennessee STAR experiment and from other investigations of class size effects. *Educational Evaluation and Policy Analysis* 21 (2): 143–63.

Hoxby, Caroline M. 1994. Do private schools provide competition for public schools? NBER Working Paper no. 4978. Cambridge, Mass.: National Bureau of Economic Research.

————. 2000a. Does competition among public schools benefit students and taxpayers? *American Economic Review* 90 (5): 1209–38.

————. 2000b. The effects of class size on student achievement: New evidence from population variation. *Quarterly Journal of Economics* 115 (4): 1239–86.

Krueger, Alan. 1999. Experimental estimates of education production functions. *Quarterly Journal of Economics* 114 (2): 497–532.

MaCurdy, Thomas, and Thomas Nechyba. 2001. How does a community's demographic composition alter its fiscal burdens? In *Demographic change and fiscal policy,* ed. A. Auerbach and R. Lee, 101–48. Cambridge, England: Cambridge University Press.

Manski, Charles. 1992. Educational choice (vouchers) and social mobility. *Economics of Education Review* 11 (4): 351–69.

McMillan, Robert. 1999. Parental involvement and competition: An empirical analysis of public school quality. Stanford University, Department of Economics. Working Paper.

National Center for Education Statistics. *School district data book.* Washington, D.C.: U.S. Department of Education.

Nechyba, Thomas. 1996. A computable general equilibrium model of intergovernmental aid. *Journal of Public Economics* 62:363–97.

————. 1997a. Existence of equilibrium and stratification in local and hierarchical public goods economies with property taxes and voting. *Economic Theory* 10: 277–304.

————. 1997b. Local property and state income taxes: The role of interjurisdictional competition and collusion. *Journal of Political Economy* 105 (2): 351–84.

————. 1999. School finance induced migration patterns: The impact of private school vouchers. *Journal of Public Economic Theory* 1 (1): 5–50.

————. 2000. Mobility, targeting, and private-school vouchers. *American Economic Review* 90 (1): 130–46.

————. 2001. The benefit view and the new view: Where do we stand 25 years into the debate? In *Property taxation and local public finance,* ed. Wallace Oates, 113–21. Cambridge, Mass.: Lincoln Institute Press.

————. 2002. School finance, spatial income segregation, and the nature of communities. Department of Economics Working Paper no. 02-17. Duke University.

———. Forthcoming. Centralization, fiscal federalism, and private school attendance. *International Economic Review.*

Nechyba, Thomas, and Robert Strauss. 1998. Community choice and local public services: A discrete choice approach. Regional Science and Urban Economics 28 (1): 51–74.

Oates, Wallace. 1969. The effects of property taxes and local public spending on property values: An empirical study of tax capitalization and the Tiebout hypothesis. *Journal of Political Economy* 77 (6): 957–71.

Reback, Randall. 2002. Capitalization under school choice programs: Are the winners really the losers? University of Michigan, Department of Economics. Mimeograph.

Rouse, Cecilia. 1998. Private school vouchers and student achievement: An evaluation of the Milwaukee parental choice program. *Quarterly Journal of Economics* 113 (2): 553–602.

Solon, Gary. 1992. Intergenerational income mobility in the United States. *American Economic Review* 82:393–409.

Zimmerman, David. 1992. Regression toward mediocrity in economic stature. *American Economic Review* 82:409–29.

Zodrow, George. 2001. Reflections on the new view and the benefit view of the property tax. In *Property taxation and local public finance,* ed. Wallace Oates, 78–112. Cambridge: Lincoln Institute Press.

School Vouchers as a Redistributive Device
An Analysis of Three Alternative Systems

Raquel Fernández and Richard Rogerson

6.1 Introduction

Two broad movements can be identified in the public policy debates over financing and provision of K-12 education. The first movement began in the early 1970s with the landmark ruling by the California Supreme Court that found California's system of financing public K-12 education to be unconstitutional. This movement sought to bring about greater equality in educational opportunities by reducing disparities in spending per student across communities. The main method used to accomplish this was changing the rules used by states to redistribute funding across districts. The second movement began in the 1980s and was largely an outgrowth from a collective sense that the quality of public K-12 education in the United States was low, especially in lower-income neighborhoods. This second movement has advocated increasing the choice of schools available to students with the hope of increasing competition across schools and enhancing efficiency.

An important theme in our previous research has been the observation that parents' inability to borrow against the future income of their children (to allow them to, say, move to a neighborhood with better schools) may result in inefficiently low investment in the human capital of children from poorer families in a quantitatively significant manner (see, e.g., Fernández and Rogerson 1996, 1997, 1998). We will refer to this as the imperfect capital markets perspective on school financing. School choice also relates to this market failure, because policies that facilitate the access of lower-

Raquel Fernández is professor of economics at New York University, a research fellow at the Center for Economic Policy Research, and a research associate of the National Bureau of Economic Research. Richard Rogerson is the Rondthaler Professor of Economics at Arizona State University and a research associate of the National Bureau of Economic Research.

income students to higher-quality schools and thereby increase the efficiency of schools in low-income neighborhoods will also raise the human capital investment in children of poorer families.

Redistribution and other policies that promote greater access to high-quality schools can therefore be seen as operating to overcome similar problems. The school choice movement, though, on the whole tends to stress the potential inefficiencies that arise from the provision of school services in a system with a public monopoly (see, e.g., Hoxby 2000). The capital markets approach stresses the unequal educational opportunities individuals may face as a consequence of parental income and imperfect capital markets.

It is important to note that even if schools functioned efficiently, as long as they responded to parental income either as a result of local funding (with wealthier parents living in wealthier communities able to fund higher-quality schools) or as a result of profit maximization on the part of private schools (with higher-quality schools charging higher prices), then the inefficiency associated with imperfect markets would remain. The objective of this chapter is to examine the consequences of this source of market failure by abstracting away from inefficient provision per se. We do this by assuming that all schools are private and operate in a competitive market. Consequently, the provision of these services is efficient, in the sense that a dollar of education expenditures can buy the same services regardless of family income, holding other potential inputs constant.

We examine the consequences of several voucher programs that serve to redistribute income in a manner that affects the distribution of the quality of education across students. We consider three voucher programs: a lump-sum voucher program in which all households are given a voucher of equal value, a means-tested voucher program in which all households below some threshold are given a voucher of equal value, and a "means-equalizing" voucher program, which gives all households below some income a voucher that depends both on their income and the amount of their funds they devote to education. Because the inefficiency associated with imperfect capital markets is dynamic—there exist profitable investments that are not undertaken because of financing constraints—we examine the consequences of these different education finance systems in a dynamic framework. By relating quality of education to future earnings, our framework allows us to analyze the effects of voucher programs on the distribution of income, in both the short and the long run. We can also evaluate the dynamic welfare consequences of these programs. Our main finding is that voucher programs can have a large positive impact on income and welfare.

Our analysis concludes with the consideration of endogenously determined parameters in each of the voucher programs. We do this by allowing the specification of the voucher system to be determined by a process of majority vote. Here we find that the outcomes vary quite widely across systems.

In particular, the means-tested voucher system leads to very little redistribution relative to the two other systems we analyze.

6.2 Benchmark Model

An analysis of the effects of different voucher systems is a complex undertaking. Parents can differ in their preferences, education levels, number of children, and marital status. Children can differ in ability, temperament, and family background. Here we choose to abstract away from these potentially important elements to better focus attention on the short- and long-run consequences of the redistribution implicit in alternative voucher systems.

In this section we describe the model that will serve as a benchmark in our analysis. Our benchmark model is chosen with an eye toward the objective of our analysis as outlined in the introduction. In particular, it is common in current policy debates for proponents of voucher programs to argue that one of the positive effects of vouchers is to increase competition in the provision of educational services and hence raise efficiency. Although we believe this may be one of the important consequences of voucher programs in the context of the current institutional context, our objective here is to argue that even in a world in which provision of educational services is efficient, the potential for vouchers to redistribute educational resources is also economically important. With this in mind, our benchmark model is one in which educational services are provided efficiently to all families, but there is a complete absence of other mechanisms in place that serve to transfer educational resources across families.

One interpretation of this benchmark corresponds to the well-known Tiebout model of local public good provision. In this model, education services are provided at the local level and are financed entirely by local taxation, and individuals sort themselves perfectly into communities. A second interpretation is that there is no public provision of education services, but there is a private market in which all individuals purchase educational services. In both interpretations, of course, the assumption of efficient provision of education services is maintained.[1]

Regardless of which interpretation one adopts, it should be clear that the benchmark is not an attempt to model the current state of education finance and provision in the United States, although the first interpretation does capture some of its elements. In particular, although the existing system in the United States does involve local provision of education, it is not entirely financed at the local level. Most states have systems of education finance

---

1. Note that what matters for our results is not that the provision of education is efficient but, rather, that the degree of inefficiency is invariant to the voucher programs analyzed.

that effectively transfer some resources from wealthier districts to less wealthy districts, although the extent to which this happens varies from state to state. Another feature of reality is that local revenues come largely from the taxation of property, whereas the state-level resources tend to come from the taxation of income or consumption. Also, although there is sorting of individuals across communities, the sorting is much less than perfect.[2] Finally, there is substantial evidence to suggest that the efficiency with which educational services are provided varies widely across schools and communities.

The benefit of our simplified setting is that it allows us to focus on the redistributive role of vouchers without concerning ourselves with how different redistributive programs may affect one another or with the complex interactions among these programs, housing prices, preferences, and incomes. Although a fully developed analysis of the impact of a voucher program should incorporate all these elements, we think that such a benchmark is too difficult an undertaking and that a more computational approach would obscure some of the more salient features of the workings of a voucher program. A word of caution is warranted, however: To the extent that the current system of finance does involve some redistribution, one should not interpret our results as indicating that vouchers are required to provide redistribution. We note, however, that there is an important distinction between redistributing using vouchers versus redistributing in the existing framework of school finance. Vouchers are targeted to individuals, whereas interdistrict redistribution is targeted to districts. Because of imperfect sorting of families across districts, redistribution across districts is likely to be less effective in transferring funds to poor individuals. However, perhaps precisely because of this feature, vouchers may be less effective when endogenously determined than a system of transfers across districts.

We next turn to a description of the formal structure of the model and of our choice of functional forms and parameter values to be used in the quantitative analysis in subsequent sections. Our choice of parameter values, such as fraction of income devoted to education, is guided by data for the U.S. economy over the last forty or so years. We have also conducted an extensive sensitivity analysis and found our main findings to be robust to what would be viewed as large deviations in these values, so the reader should not be overly worried about disagreements in the literature about the exact values of these numbers.

Following Fernández and Rogerson (1997, 1998), we consider the following structure. At any point in time there are a large number of families, each of which (for simplicity) is assumed to consist of one adult and one

2. For example, Epple and Sieg (1999) analyze communities within the Boston metropolitan area and find that sorting according to income is very imperfect. See Fernández (2002) for a review of the literature on sorting, education, and inequality.

child. One period later, the adult will be deceased and hence leave the model, whereas the child will be in the period of adult life in which he or she heads a family that also has one child. The only distinction between families is that they differ in their level of income, which we denote by y. In each period a family has one decision to make: how to allocate its income between expenditures on consumption and expenditures on the child's education. We assume that parents make all the decisions and have identical preferences over current consumption and their child's future income described by

$$(1) \qquad\qquad u(c) + Ez(y'),$$

where c is the household's consumption in the current period and y' is next period's income of the household's child. We include the expectations operator E in front of the function $z(y')$ because, as we will see shortly, the child's future income is stochastic viewed from the perspective of the current period. In general, we assume that the two functions u and z are increasing and concave. The essence of our preference specification is to say that parents care about both their standard of living and the expected standard of living that their children will attain. To simplify matters we assume that parents use the future income of their children as a proxy for the standard of living that they will attain.

In the first period of life, the child attends school and obtains the quality of education q. In the second period, the now old child receives a draw from the income distribution. This income draw depends on the quality of schooling the child received when young and an independently and identically distributed (i.i.d.) shock ξ whose distribution $\psi(\xi)$ is assumed to be independent of q. Thus, $y' = f(q, \xi)$. In adopting this specification we are assuming that although there is a link between quality of education and future income, the link is not perfect. There are a number of additional factors, which we assume to be random, that will also affect the ultimate level of income that one achieves. These factors could include how one gets along with one's superiors, landing a good first job, or working for a company that becomes very successful.

Calibrating the model requires choosing an education production function. Unfortunately, there is very little consensus on the form the latter should take; indeed, a large and controversial literature surrounds this topic. Guided primarily by simplicity, a convenient specification is

$$y' = Aq^\theta\xi,$$

which yields an elasticity of future income with respect to education quality that is constant and equal to θ: That is, for every percent increase in the quality of education, future earnings will increase by θ percent. We assume that ξ is lognormally distributed such that $\log \xi$ has zero mean and standard deviation σ_ξ.

An important (and controversial) empirical issue is what determines school quality. There is a substantial amount of work that suggests that many schools do not use resources effectively. Moreover, one of the chief motivations for the school choice proponents is that increased choice will spur competition and hence lead to more efficient use of resources in providing education services. As discussed previously, in order to focus our analysis on the finance side of school choice, we have chosen to examine the role for redistributional finance in a world in which educational resources are used efficiently. In addition to school resources, it is also plausible that peer effects and parental attributes also matter.[3] To focus the analysis on the different incentives associated with alternative voucher schemes, we assume that peer effects and parental attributes do not affect school quality. We also assume that there are no scale effects in providing education. Hence, in the analysis that follows we will assume that spending on education and quality of education are in fact synonymous.

Evidence presented by Card and Krueger (1992), Wachtel (1976), and Johnson and Stafford (1973) suggests an elasticity of earnings with respect to education expenditures close to 0.2. This analysis would suggest that we set $\theta = 0.2$ in our benchmark specification. One potentially problematic issue with this procedure is that it abstracts from the potential inefficient use of resources. An alternative approach to calibrating the value of the parameter θ is to target a rate of return to spending on education. A large volume of empirical work suggests that the rate of return to spending on education lies in the range of 5 to 15 percent. In our model this return will vary with the level of spending, but it turns out that a value of $\theta = 0.2$ implies a rate of return that varies from 4 to 11 percent depending on an individual's spending (and hence income).[4] In view of this we think the choice of $\theta = 0.2$ is a reasonable one.

The adult's decision is a choice of the fraction of income to spend on consumption relative to the child's education. In formulating this decision it is convenient to define $w(q) \equiv \int_0^\infty z(f(q, \xi))d\psi$. The function $w(q)$ represents the expected utility that a parent receives from spending q dollars on the child's education. We can now write the decision problem facing a parent as one of choosing how to allocate income y between c and q so as to maximize

$$U(c,q) = u(c) + w(q)$$

Not surprisingly, the consequences of various redistributive programs will depend upon the income and substitution effects implicit in the utility function U. It is thus instructive to ask whether there are some reasonable

3. Several authors have studied peer effects. See de Bartolome (1990) for a survey of the empirical literature and a theoretical model incorporating peer effects. See also Benabou (1993, 1996), Durlauf (1996), Epple and Romano (1996, 1998), and Caucutt (2002) for other studies incorporating peer effects.
4. See Fernández and Rogerson (1997), table 5, for more detail.

restrictions that can be placed upon preferences in order to discriminate among the many possible specifications. As is true in many other contexts, we think that longer-run evidence provides some important information to guide choices. Fernández and Rogerson (2001) show that across the United States the share of personal income devoted to public elementary and secondary education has remained roughly constant over the 1970–90 period at the same time that income per capita almost doubled. This property will be satisfied if the function U takes the form

$$(2) \qquad \frac{c^{\alpha}}{\alpha} + B\frac{q^{\alpha}}{\alpha}$$

for some parameters α and B. This implies a utility function of the form

$$(3) \qquad \frac{c^{\alpha}}{\alpha} + \frac{b}{\alpha}E(y'^{\gamma})$$

for some parameter values γ and b together with the restriction that $\theta\gamma = \alpha$ and $B = bE(\xi^{\gamma})$. In the analysis that follows, we impose these preferences and assume as well that α is nonpositive.

Having chosen the functional form for preferences, we must assign values to b and α. Given values for all the other parameters, there is a monotone relationship between b and the fraction of income an individual would choose to devote to education. In our benchmark model we choose a value of b so that this fraction equals 0.041, which is roughly the fraction of aggregate income devoted to K-12 education in the United States over the last forty years. This requires b to be given by $b = \{[(1 - t^*)/t^*]^{\alpha-1}\}/[A^{\gamma}E(\xi^{\gamma})]$, where $t^* = 0.041$ is the fraction of income devoted to education. Choosing a value of α is somewhat more difficult. Fernández and Rogerson (1999a) survey several different approaches to picking this value and conclude that values in the range of $[-2, 0]$ are most reasonable. We choose $\alpha = -1$ for our benchmark model.

In order to analyze the model described above, we need to specify an initial distribution of income. We denote the initial period by period 0 and let the initial income distribution be described by a density function denoted by $g_0(y)$. Letting $g_t(y)$ be the income distribution of old individuals in period t, an equilibrium generates an income distribution for period $t + 1$, g_{t+1}. Denote this mapping from the income distribution of a given period into the income distribution of the next period by the function $F[g(y)]$. A steady state in this model is given by a distribution of income for the next generation that is the same as the distribution of income for the current generation. Note that this does not presume that each child will have the same income as the parent. Because income when old contains a random element, this will not be the case. Rather, in a steady state, for each individual whose income is greater than that of his or her parent, there is another individual who experiences the opposite movement, and vice versa. Of course, to the extent that educational expenditures are related to parental income, there will be a positive correlation between a parent's income this period and the child's income next period. From a formal perspective, a steady state in this model then consists of an income distribution $g^*(y)$ such that $g^*(y) = F[g^*(y)]$. In the analysis of alternative voucher systems that follows, we will take the starting position of the economy to be the steady state for the model just described. We will be interested in solving for the steady states of the model with different voucher schemes as well as examining the transition path to these steady states.

The final element of the calibration exercise that remains concerns two parameters of the educational production function: A, the constant term in front of the production function, and σ_ξ, the standard deviation of the idiosyncratic income shock. Intuitively, the larger the value of A, the greater we expect everyone's income to be next period, because it implies a higher expected value of income for any given level of spending on education. The larger the value of σ_ξ, the more spread out we expect income to be, because this variable determines the spread of the random component of income. If this parameter were set to zero, then children's incomes would be perfectly determined by their educational expenditures.

Given the functional forms described above, one can show that the steady-state distribution of income in the benchmark model is also lognormally distributed, with mean and standard deviation determined by the values of A and σ_ξ. To see this, consider the decision problem solved by a particular individual with income y_i. Let t_i be the fraction of income devoted to education. Then, they solve the following problem:

(4)
$$\max_{t_i} u[(1 - t_i)y_i] + w(t_i y_i)$$

Thus, each individual's value for t_i is given by the first-order condition

(5)
$$-u'[y_i(1 - t_i)] + w'(t_i y_i) = 0$$

Note that equation (5) has individuals set spending on education to equate the marginal utility of consumption with the marginal utility of education quality—that is, $u'(c) = w'(q)$.

It is then easy to solve for the dynamic evolution of the economy. One can show that the preferences specified in equation (2) imply a constant and identical value of t_i across individuals, $t^* = 1/(1 + \kappa)$, where $\kappa = (bA^\gamma E(\xi^\gamma))^{1/(\alpha - 1)}$. That is, all individuals spend the same fraction of their income on education. To solve for the dynamics of the system, note that if a parent's income in period 0 is y_0, the child's income, y_1, is given by $\log y_1 = \log A + \theta \log t^* + \theta \log y_0 + \log \xi_1$. Given $\theta < 1$, it follows that $\log y_t$ has a limiting distribution that is normal with mean and standard deviation

(6)
$$\mu_\infty = \frac{\log A + \theta \log t^*}{1 - \theta} \qquad \sigma_\infty = \frac{\sigma_\xi}{(1 - \theta^2)^{1/2}}$$

We choose A and σ_ξ such that μ_∞ and σ_∞ are reasonable in view of U.S. data over the last forty years. Specifically, we match the mean and median of the U.S. family income distribution as measured in the 1980 census, respectively 23.1 and 19.9, measured in thousands of dollars.

A key feature of our benchmark model is that the educational expenditures for a given child must be financed out of the income of the parent. In particular, we are ruling out the possibility that a parent or a child could borrow against the child's future income in order to have greater expenditure on education when young. We believe this is the most natural assumption to make in the context of K-12 education, but we wish to stress it because of its importance to our analysis.

We next turn to the determination of the distribution of education expenditures across individuals under different voucher systems.

6.3 Voucher Programs

In this section we describe three different types of voucher programs. We focus on the outcomes for the distribution of education expenditures achieved in a given period under each of the voucher systems taking the initial income distribution as given.

6.3.1 A Lump-Sum Voucher System

In this section we consider a voucher system that we refer to as a lump-sum voucher system. Under this system all households receive a voucher of size v_l, which they can use only to fund expenditures on education. They are, however, free to spend more than this amount by supplementing this voucher with their own funds.

For any system, we need to describe how the voucher is financed. We assume that this is achieved by proportional (income) taxation at rate τ_l. Requiring the budget to be balanced in every period, we obtain

$$(7) \qquad v_l = \tau_l \mu_y,$$

where μ_y is mean income in the economy. In this section we assume that the size of the voucher is fixed over time, and hence omit time subscripts to simplify notation.

Consider the choices facing an individual parent in an economy that offers this type of voucher program. Letting t_i denote the fraction of income that individual i devotes to education over and above the voucher level, we have

$$(8) \qquad c_i = (1 - t_i - \tau_l)y_i$$

$$q_i = v_l + t_i y_i$$

Note that because of the balanced budget requirement the voucher program in a given period is effectively summarized by one parameter, either

τ_l or v_l. Given a tax rate, τ_l, an individual's preferred choice of t_i is the solution to

$$(9) \qquad \max_{t_i} u[(1 - t_i - \tau_l)y_i] + w(v_l + t_i y_i), \quad t_i \geq 0,$$

yielding the first-order condition

$$(10) \qquad -u'[(1 - t_i - \tau_l)y_i] + w'(v_l + t_i y_i) \leq 0,$$

with strict equality for $t_i > 0$.

With the restriction on preferences described earlier, one can show that the values of the t_i are increasing in y_i. Moreover, there will be some cutoff value of y, which we call $\hat{y}_l$, such that all individuals with $y \leq \hat{y}_l$ choose $t_i = 0$; that is, all households with income below $\hat{y}_l$ have spending on education that is exactly equal to the size of the voucher. Furthermore, the level of this cutoff value is increasing in the size of the voucher. These results are intuitive. The voucher provides a minimum value of spending on education. If this level is sufficiently large it will exceed the amount that the lowest-income families wish to spend on education (at a marginal cost of y_i), and hence they may choose not to devote any additional funds to education. Of course, families with more income may still wish to increase their education expenditures. The larger the size of the voucher, the greater the number of families that will choose not to spend any additional resources on education.

We can also say something about how this program affects the distribution of education expenditures across the income distribution. For example, it is easy to show that anyone who chooses $t_i = 0$ will have a larger expenditure on education under this lump-sum voucher system than in the benchmark model. More generally, one can show that there exists some level of income $\overline{y} > \hat{y}_l$ such that everyone below this value spends more than in the benchmark model and everyone above this level will end up spending less than in the benchmark model.

The properties of this system come from noting that in a system of proportional taxation, all households with income less than mean income pay less in taxes than the value of the voucher they receive. This induces households with income less than mean income to increase their spending on education relative to the benchmark model. The same reasoning does not hold for individuals with income above the mean, because the voucher on net redistributes income away from them. Of course, if the voucher level is set sufficiently high—say, higher than the maximum amount being spent by anyone in the benchmark model—then spending on education by everyone would increase.

It follows that a lump-sum voucher system tends to compress the distribution of educational expenditures, and (for any voucher amount below the maximum spending on education observed in the benchmark system) this compression will come about both by raising spending at the bottom of the distribution and by lowering spending at the top of the distribution. We will see later that the extent of compression from above turns out to be quite small quantitatively, so that the primary effect is to generate compression from below.

6.3.2 A Means-Tested Voucher

In this subsection we describe a second voucher system, which we refer to as a means-tested voucher. This system is similar to the lump-sum voucher but differs in one feature. Rather than assuming that all families receive a voucher of value v_m, we now assume that the voucher is received only by those households that have income below some cutoff level denoted by y_m. As before, households are free to supplement the voucher if they wish to spend more on education, but the voucher must be used only for spending on education. As above, the voucher program is financed by a proportional tax on income, and the budget is assumed to balance in each period.

The mechanics of this voucher system are quite similar to that described above. The problem faced by a household with income less than the means-tested cutoff y_m is now

(11) $$\max_{t_i} u[(1 - t_i - \tau_m)y_i] + w(v_m + t_i y_i), \quad t_i \geq 0,$$

yielding the first-order condition

(12) $$-u'[(1 - t_i - \tau_m)y_i]y_i + w'(v_m + t_i y_i)y_i \leq 0,$$

with strict equality for $t_i > 0$.

On the other hand, an individual with income that lies above the means-tested cutoff y_m faces the problem of

(13) $$\max_{t_i} u[(1 - t_i - \tau_m)y_i] + w(t_i y_i), \quad t_i \geq 0,$$

yielding the first-order condition

(14) $$-u'[(1 - t_i - \tau_m)y_i]y_i + w'(t_i y_i)y_i \leq 0,$$

with strict equality for $t_i > 0$.

Assuming that y_m is binding (i.e., some households are not eligible), a voucher of the same size as in the lump-sum system (i.e., $v_i = v_m$) will require a smaller tax to finance it because not all households are receiving the voucher.

Several basic results follow easily. Relative to the benchmark model, all households that have income above the means-tested cutoff will now spend less on education. This is entirely because the tax to support the voucher plan reduces their after-tax income. As in the case of the lump-sum voucher system, even conditional on receiving a voucher, a given household's spending on education may either increase or decrease. However, any household that receives the voucher and has income below mean income will necessarily spend more on education.

As above, we conclude that this type of voucher system will also tend to compress the distribution of educational spending. Once again, however, we will see in the quantitative work that the compression from above tends to be quite small.

6.3.3   A Means-Equalizing Voucher

Lastly, we turn to an analysis of another voucher that depends on individual characteristics, which we refer to as a means-equalizing voucher system. Like the previous case, this system excludes individuals with income greater than some prespecified level, but it avoids a troubling aspect of the previous system. In particular, in the means-tested voucher system two families with very similar incomes but that fall on opposite sides of the means-tested cutoff level will be treated very differently—one of them receives a potentially significant transfer, whereas the other receives nothing. To avoid this type of discontinuity in the value of the voucher, the means-equalizing system presents individuals with a voucher payment that depends both on their income and on the fraction of their income devoted to education. In particular, as we explain in more detail below, this voucher plan will guarantee that a poor family that devotes a certain fraction of its budget to education will end up with the same level of total educational expenditure as a richer family that devotes the same fraction of its budget to educational expenditures. The term "means-equalizing" is used because this voucher guarantees that families that devote the same fraction of their income to education will end up with equal educational expenditures, thus equalizing their means in terms of generating education expenditure through a given tax effort. There are, of course, many ways to alter the means-tested voucher system in order to remove the discontinuity, but we focus on this one because it has parallels with many redistributive tax programs and it has a close analogue in the school finance system literature. Another aspect of this voucher system that differs from those considered previously is that in this system the size of the voucher is dependent on the actions of the family. In particular, a family that devotes no resources to education expenditures is not eligible for a voucher, independent of their income.

We now describe this plan more formally. Let y_e be the cutoff level of income in this system. Consider a household with income y_i and suppose this household chooses to devote a fraction t_i of its income to education. The voucher system is set up to guarantee all households a minimum base from which to obtain their total expenditures on education that is given by

$$q_i = t_i \max\{y_i, y_e\}$$

It follows that the actual voucher received by a household with income y_i that allocates a fraction t_i of its income to education is given by

$$\upsilon_e = \max \, [t_i(y_e - y_i), 0].$$

Obviously, anyone with income greater than the cutoff level y_e will not receive any voucher. Note that although the system does not guarantee any particular level of education spending, it does provide a common base for all individuals.

We assume, as in the previous case, that the required education funds are generated by a state income tax, τ_e, so that private consumption is given by

(15) $c_i = (1 - t_i - \tau_e)y_i$

and the tax rate must satisfy the budget constraint

(16) $\tau_e\mu_y = \int\limits_{y < y_e} t_i(y_e - y)g(y)dy.$

Once again we can characterize how this type of voucher system will affect the distribution of education expenditures relative to the benchmark model. It is straightforward to show that any household with income greater than the means-tested cutoff y_e will have lower spending on education than in the benchmark model. Moreover, similar to the situations considered above, any individual with income below the minimum of y_e and mean income will necessarily increase his or her spending on education. Once again, this type of voucher program serves to compress the distribution of educational expenditures.

We mentioned above that this voucher scheme has parallels in other redistributive programs. One such parallel is a negative income tax program that seeks to guarantee a "reasonable" level of income for someone who satisfies a work requirement. By way of comparison, the voucher program just described attempts to provide everyone who devotes a specified fraction of income to education a "reasonable" level of educational expenditures.

6.3.4   Parallels with the School Finance Literature

Before turning to an analysis of the quantitative impact of the various voucher programs just described, we think it is useful to note some parallels between these and several programs that are commonly studied in the literature on school finance. As noted in the introduction, the issue of redistributing resources across school districts has been prominent in public policy discussions of education at least since the landmark Serrano decision in California in 1971. Many states have been forced to restructure their systems of school finance as a result of court orders. The common issue raised in all of these court cases is that children who grow up in poor school districts (where *poor* is defined as low property value per person) do not receive an adequate education because of the shortage of funding. In an attempt to deal with this situation, various types of programs have been used to redistribute resources from property-rich districts to property-poor districts.

In addressing this issue, a common benchmark is a system of pure local finance in which all school districts are solely responsible for financing their own schools: That is, there is no redistribution across districts. As previously mentioned, this system has its parallel with our benchmark model, except that in our model there is no longer an entity known as a school district. Instead, each individual is solely responsible for financing his or her educational expenditures: That is, there is no redistribution across individuals. Just as property-poor districts are at a significant disadvantage in terms of financing an adequate education in the district system, in our benchmark model it is the income-poor individuals who are at a disadvantage in terms of financing an adequate education.

One popular redistributive school finance system is what is known as a foundation system. In this system, each district is given a fixed amount of money per student in order to help all districts ensure a minimum level of quality. This type of system closely parallels our lump-sum voucher system, in which all households are given a fixed amount of money per child in order to help all households afford an education of some minimum level of quality.

Another popular redistributive measure is means-tested transfers to school districts, through which all districts whose property base per student lies beneath some cutoff value receive a given grant per student. Our means-tested voucher is obviously the analogous program in our context.

Lastly, the Serrano ruling in California in the early 1970s prompted Coons, Clune, and Sugarman (1970) to devise a school finance system known as a power-equalizing system. The basic idea underlying this system was targeted specifically to the nature of the problem identified by the California Supreme Court—namely, that even if families in districts with different property value per student chose to tax themselves at the same rate, the children would end up with very different qualities of education because a given tax effort yielded such different revenues in different districts. To remedy this, Coons suggested a scheme whereby districts would be guaranteed a given revenue per unit of tax effort. Although such a system does not guarantee a given level of spending in a particular district, it does offer that district a guaranteed yield for its tax effort. Obviously, our means-equalizing voucher system is the analogue of this system.

To summarize, the issue of redistribution in the context of education appears both in a world in which education is publicly provided and children attend district level schools and in a world in which education is privately provided and children can attend any school subject to paying the tuition. Many of the schemes used to redistribute in one context are likely to have interesting counterparts in the other context as well.

6.4   Results with Exogenous Policy

In this section we examine the quantitative impact of introducing vouchers of the types discussed previously. We assume that the parameters of

Table 6.1   Income Distribution of Families

Income Threshold	% of Families below Threshold
0.25 × mean income	1.6
0.4 × mean income	9.72
0.5 × mean income	18.9
0.75 × mean income	44.2
Mean income	64.4

these voucher systems are set exogenously and contrast how various parameter values affect the outcomes. Specifically, in the lump-sum voucher plan we consider different settings for the size of the voucher. In the case of the power-equalizing voucher program, we consider different levels for the guaranteed tax base, which is also the cutoff level of income at which households qualify for some voucher. In the case of the means-tested voucher, the program is characterized by two values: the cutoff level of income that determines who receives the voucher, and the value of the voucher. Because this system is characterized by two parameters, there are obviously many more possibilities to consider when setting parameters exogenously. To simplify matters, in what follows we will report results for a particular one-dimensional family of specifications. We will look at means-tested vouchers that are introduced into the benchmark model with the following characteristic: Let v_m be the size of voucher. Then we assume that the income threshold is set such that all households that in the steady state of the benchmark model spent less than v_m will be eligible for the voucher.[5]

Before we proceed with the results, it is of interest to first consider some aspects of the benchmark steady-state equilibrium, in particular the distribution of educational expenditures across families. In considering the impact of various voucher systems it is instructive to see the original distribution of expenditures in order to gauge the number of families that will be directly affected by a given size of voucher system. Recall that in the benchmark steady state all families are spending the same fraction (0.041) of their income on education. Hence, the steady-state distribution of education spending mimics the properties of the steady-state income distribution. Table 6.1 provides a breakdown of the income distribution of families by reporting the percentage that fall below certain threshold values relative to mean income.

So, for example, if we consider a lump-sum voucher of size equal to 25 percent of average educational expenditures in the original steady state, fewer than 2 percent of families will be directly affected in the sense that the voucher exceeds their spending in the original steady state. This is signifi-

5. This formulation obviously introduces a discrete downward jump in spending as a function of income, because those who spend $v_m + \varepsilon$, $\varepsilon > 0$ do not get a voucher and hence in aggregate will end up having lower education spending (despite having higher income).

cant because, as we shall see in the case of a lump-sum voucher program, the impact of the voucher on families whose original spending exceeded the size of the voucher is minimal. A similar point also applies to the case of the means-tested voucher.

In what follows we will report results about both allocations and welfare, looking at static (initial-period) effects, steady-state effects, and the transition. We begin by analyzing the effects on allocations.

6.4.1   Allocations

Static Effects

We begin our analysis by examining the static or first-period effects of the voucher programs on education spending. Specifically, we take the income distribution corresponding to the steady state of the benchmark model and ask what will happen to the distribution of education expenditures in that period if various voucher programs are introduced. In the case of the lump-sum and the means-tested voucher systems, it is useful to measure the size of the voucher relative to mean spending on education in the benchmark steady state. In the case of the power-equalizing voucher, it is useful to measure the value of the cutoff relative to mean income in the benchmark steady state. We let $\bar{\mu}_e$ represent mean spending on education in the benchmark steady state and let $\bar{\mu}_y$ represent mean income in the benchmark steady state. Recall that these values are $(0.0410)(23.08) = 0.946$ and 23.08 respectively, measured in thousands of dollars. Table 6.2 reports results for each of the three voucher systems for several cases distinguished by the magnitudes of the program.

The first column in each section of the table reports the size of the voucher system, relative to mean educational spending (or mean income) in the initial steady state. The second column reports total spending on education, expressed as a fraction of total income (i.e., E/y). The third column reports a measure of inequality in education spending, in particular the coefficient of variation (cv_e) for the distribution of education spending, which is the ratio of the standard deviation of education spending to average education spending. In what follows we will use this as our measure of inequality. The final column in each case reports the tax rate that is required to finance the specified voucher system. Note that the first row in each section of the table corresponds to the case in which there is no voucher system and hence simply reproduces the distribution of education spending in the original steady state.

A few basic patterns emerge. In each case as the magnitude of the voucher system is increased we see an increase in the fraction of income devoted to education and a decrease in the inequality of education expenditures. These qualitative results are really not that surprising. One of the key impacts of both voucher systems is to raise expenditures on education at the bottom of

Table 6.2   **First-Period Effects on Education Spending**

Size of Voucher Relative to Mean Educational Spending	Education Spending Relative to Total Income	Education Inequality	Tax Rate (%)
A. Lump-Sum Voucher System			
0.00	0.0410	0.594	0.0
0.10	0.0410	0.592	0.4
0.25	0.0410	0.588	1.0
0.40	0.0412	0.577	1.6
0.50	0.0416	0.562	2.1
0.60	0.0423	0.541	2.5
0.75	0.0437	0.501	3.1
1.00	0.0474	0.421	4.1
B. Means-Tested Voucher System			
0.00	0.0410	0.594	0.00
0.10	0.0410	0.592	0.00
0.25	0.0410	0.588	0.01
0.40	0.0412	0.577	0.13
0.50	0.0416	0.562	0.33
0.60	0.0422	0.541	0.63
0.75	0.0436	0.501	1.24
1.00	0.0471	0.421	2.50

C. Means-Equalizing Voucher System

Equalizing Factor Relative to Mean Income	Education Spending Relative to Total Income	Education Inequality	Tax Rate (%)
0.00	0.0410	0.594	0.00
0.10	0.0410	0.594	0.00
0.25	0.0410	0.593	0.00
0.40	0.0411	0.590	0.02
0.50	0.0413	0.582	0.06
0.60	0.0416	0.572	0.13
0.75	0.0424	0.548	0.28
1.00	0.0441	0.504	0.64
1.25	0.0463	0.456	1.09

the distribution. Not surprisingly, this raises overall spending on education and decreases inequality in education spending. However, the quantitative results also produce some findings that are of interest and that are not necessarily expected. For example, in the case of the lump-sum voucher, the above results indicate that unless the size of the voucher exceeds the initial spending for a substantial fraction of the population it has very small effects on total spending on education. To see this, consider the second row of the first section, which corresponds to a voucher that is equal to 10 percent of average spending. This is seen not to have an effect on education expenditures, either by way of changing total expenditure or by changing inequality. However, from table 6.1 we know that this voucher exceeds initial spending for less than 2 percent of the households, and even for them it raises their spending by relatively little on average. The basic message is that in order for a lump-sum voucher (or a means-tested voucher) to have any sizable impact, it must be of a magnitude that exceeds education spending for a significant fraction of the population. Otherwise it simply amounts to a small program of income redistribution. A similar point holds in the case of the means-equalizing voucher.

It is also of interest to draw a few comparisons across the three systems. One point that the table makes quite clear is that the consequences of the lump-sum voucher and the means-tested voucher are virtually identical for education spending. The one difference between the two, not surprisingly, is that the means-tested voucher requires a smaller tax to finance the system. This is a pattern that will be repeated in the remainder of the results as well. Two other important differences are that offering a voucher equal to the expenditure of, say, the mean-income household will reduce inequality in spending by a much greater amount than will guaranteeing everyone a tax base equal to mean income. The other is that the means-equalizing system seems to provide a steeper drop in inequality per dollar of tax revenue raised than does either of the other two systems.

In order to more fully appreciate the different consequences of the three systems for the distribution of educational expenditures, it is of interest to look at these distributions in more detail. In table 6.3 we report average spending on education by deciles of the income distribution for each of the three systems.

In each section the first column repeats the results without a voucher program; thus, it simply describes the distribution of spending in the steady state of the benchmark model. Reading across each section allows one to examine how increasing the magnitude of a given voucher program affects spending at various deciles of the income distribution. A general pattern is that as each voucher program becomes more generous, spending at the bottom part of the income distribution increases, whereas spending at the higher end of the distribution tends to decrease. However, the relative magnitudes of these two changes are noteworthy. Whereas spending at the bottom of the distribution may double or even triple as we move to the columns at the far right of each section, the spending at the top of the distribution is decreasing on the order of 1 percent. Hence, although each of the voucher programs is decreasing inequality in spending by compressing the distribution of spending, this compression is almost entirely acting from below.

Next we compare the lump-sum voucher and the means-tested voucher. We noted previously that both vouchers had virtually identical aggregate effects. If we look at the distributions more carefully, we see that the two vouchers do produce some differences across the distribution but that these effects tend to roughly cancel in aggregate. For example, consider the case of a voucher that is 75 percent of mean spending in the benchmark steady

Table 6.3   **First-Period Effects on the Distribution of Education Spending**

Decile	0.00	0.10	0.25	0.40	0.50	0.60	0.75	1.00
				Size of Voucher Relative to Mean Spending				
				A. Lump-Sum Vouchers				
1st	0.315	0.317	0.323	0.382	0.473	0.568	0.710	0.946
2nd	0.456	0.458	0.461	0.464	0.483	0.568	0.710	0.946
3rd	0.559	0.560	0.563	0.565	0.567	0.580	0.710	0.946
4th	0.656	0.658	0.659	0.661	0.662	0.664	0.710	0.946
5th	0.758	0.759	0.760	0.761	0.762	0.763	0.764	0.946
6th	0.870	0.871	0.871	0.872	0.872	0.872	0.873	0.946
7th	1.004	1.004	1.004	1.003	1.002	1.003	1.002	1.002
8th	1.181	1.180	1.178	1.177	1.176	1.175	1.174	1.171
9th	1.448	1.446	1.443	1.440	1.438	1.436	1.433	1.427
10th	2.196	2.191	2.183	2.176	2.171	2.165	2.158	2.145
				B. Means-Tested Vouchers				
1st	0.315	0.315	0.320	0.381	0.473	0.568	0.710	0.946
2nd	0.456	0.456	0.456	0.455	0.480	0.568	0.710	0.946
3rd	0.559	0.559	0.559	0.558	0.557	0.576	0.710	0.946
4th	0.656	0.656	0.656	0.656	0.654	0.652	0.710	0.946
5th	0.758	0.758	0.758	0.757	0.756	0.754	0.750	0.946
6th	0.870	0.870	0.870	0.869	0.868	0.865	0.860	0.946
7th	1.004	1.004	1.004	1.003	1.001	1.000	0.992	0.9832
8th	1.181	1.181	1.180	1.179	1.177	1.173	1.166	1.151
9th	1.447	1.447	1.448	1.446	1.443	1.439	1.430	1.412
10th	2.196	2.196	2.196	2.193	2.189	2.182	2.169	2.141

C. Means-Equalizing Vouchers

Equalizing Factor Relative to Mean Income

	0.00	0.10	0.25	0.40	0.50	0.60	0.75	1.00	1.25
1st	0.315	0.315	0.317	0.345	0.386	0.424	0.475	0.549	0.612
2nd	0.456	0.456	0.456	0.456	0.468	0.510	0.572	0.661	0.737
3rd	0.559	0.559	0.559	0.559	0.558	0.567	0.631	0.729	0.814
4th	0.656	0.656	0.656	0.656	0.656	0.656	0.682	0.788	0.881
5th	0.758	0.758	0.758	0.758	0.758	0.757	0.756	0.845	0.944
6th	0.870	0.870	0.870	0.870	0.870	0.869	0.868	0.903	1.009
7th	1.004	1.004	1.004	1.004	1.003	1.003	1.001	0.998	1.081
8th	1.181	1.181	1.181	1.181	1.180	1.179	1.178	1.173	1.182
9th	1.447	1.447	1.447	1.447	1.447	1.446	1.444	1.439	1.432
10th	2.196	2.196	2.196	2.196	2.195	2.193	2.190	2.182	2.172

state: That is, $v_t = v_m = 0.75\bar{\mu}_e$. For the means-tested case this voucher is available to the bottom 44 percent of households. In both cases the bottom 40 percent of the population spends only the amount of the voucher. However, note that the next decile spends more under the lump-sum voucher than under the means-tested voucher. This reflects the fact that in the means-tested case everyone with income above 75 percent of mean income is receiving no voucher, and hence the only effect on their education spending is due to the imposition of the income tax needed to finance the voucher. In contrast, in the case of the lump-sum voucher, those households with income slightly higher than 75 percent of mean income still receive a voucher that is large relative to their spending in the benchmark model. This, of course, must all be allocated to education. However, they still choose to supplement this with a small amount of their own funds. They also face a larger income tax, but for these families the effect of the subsidy to education exceeds the effect associated with the tax rate. However, as we move to higher deciles in the income distribution we see that the relative spending levels are reversed. For the highest decile, spending is greater under the means-tested voucher than under the lump-sum voucher. The reason for this is that for this group the voucher is relatively small compared to education spending in the benchmark model, and the loss in income due to taxation is much larger. Thus, the net effect of the tax is much greater for this group. Since the tax is much smaller under the means-tested program, they spend more under this program.

Next we compare the means-tested voucher with the means-equalizing voucher. The differences are more apparent for larger values of the voucher programs, so once again we focus on the cases in which the means-tested voucher is 75 percent of mean spending and the cutoff level is 75 percent of mean income. What is particularly striking is how different the spending is in the lower part of the distribution. For the lowest decile the means-tested voucher yields spending on education that is more than one-third larger than spending under the means-equalizing voucher. The reason for this difference is that under the means-tested voucher these households are receiving a voucher in the amount of 0.071 that must be used for education. In contrast, under the power-equalizing system these households are told that they can raise money for education as if they had a tax base equal to 75 percent of mean income, but every dollar they devote to education reduces their consumption. However, all families that have income above the 50th percentile have greater spending under the power-equalizing system than under the means-tested system. None of these households is eligible for a voucher, so the differences are due entirely to the fact that the tax rate is lower under the means-equalizing system. These two observations go hand in hand: The reason that taxes are lower in the means-equalizing system is that less money is being redistributed to low-income households to be used for education. The key point that this table illustrates, however, is that the largest difference between the two systems has to do with the differential extent to which the means-tested program will lift the spending of the lowest-income households. The difference in levels of spending among the richer households is in fact less than 1 percent.

Steady-State Effects

The results in the last section focused on what would happen to current education spending as a result of introducing various voucher systems. However, changes in the level or distribution of current education expenditures will also have impacts on the future level and distribution of income. In fact, one of the main motivations for public concern over the distribution of education spending is that this spending plays a key role in the human capital accumulation of children and thus in the future productive capacity of the economy. In this section we focus on the long-run implications for the distribution of income associated with the various voucher programs analyzed previously—that is, we look at the resulting steady-state distributions. Table 6.4 provides the information.

As before, the first column reports the size of the voucher system. The next two columns report some properties of the steady-state income distribution. The second column reports mean income, and the third column reports the coefficient of variation of income, which we will again use as our measure of income inequality. The final three columns present the same information that was presented in the previous subsection where we focused on the static effects on education spending. Once again, the first row of each section considers the case of no voucher and hence simply reproduces the benchmark steady state.

Perhaps the most striking result to note here is the size of the potential increases in income that are associated with some of the programs considered above. A lump-sum voucher that was equal to average expenditures in the benchmark steady state leads to an increase in income of roughly 10 percent! A means-equalizing voucher that assisted everyone with income below the mean would raise income by more than 6 percent. Note, moreover, that the tax rate needed to support this voucher system is just slightly more than one-half of 1 percent. These gains in income are large and point to the potential gains to be obtained by a redistributive education finance system even in a world where all individuals have access to schools that use resources efficiently. We will show later that these large gains in income also represent large gains in average welfare.

Considering the results in more detail, if education expenditures increase and the inequality of those expenditures decreases, we would expect to see that these two properties show up in the distribution of income as well. The previous table reveals this to be the case. It is interesting to note, however, that the magnitudes of these two effects are quite different. Consider, for example, the two extreme cases represented in section A of table 6.3, one in which the lump-sum voucher is zero and one in which the lump-sum voucher is equal to mean spending on education in the benchmark steady state. In the expenditure on education there is an increase of roughly 15 percent, and in

Table 6.4   Steady-State Implications of Vouchers

Size of Voucher Relative to Mean Education Spending	Mean Income	Income Inequality	Education Spending Relative to Total Income	Education Inequality	Tax Rate
A. Lump-Sum Voucher					
0.00	23.08	0.594	0.0410	0.594	0.0
0.10	23.09	0.594	0.0410	0.592	0.4
0.25	23.13	0.594	0.0410	0.587	1.0
0.40	23.32	0.591	0.0412	0.572	1.6
0.50	23.55	0.589	0.0416	0.554	2.0
0.60	23.84	0.587	0.0423	0.527	2.4
0.75	24.36	0.585	0.0437	0.480	2.9
1.00	25.29	0.583	0.0474	0.390	3.7
B. Means-Tested Voucher					
0.00	23.08	0.594	0.0410	0.594	0.00
0.10	23.08	0.594	0.0410	0.594	0.00
0.25	23.11	0.594	0.0410	0.592	0.01
0.40	23.29	0.591	0.0412	0.580	0.13
0.50	23.52	0.589	0.0416	0.562	0.30
0.60	23.82	0.587	0.0422	0.534	0.56
0.75	24.34	0.585	0.0437	0.486	1.05
1.00	25.27	0.583	0.0471	0.393	2.03

C. Means-Equalizing Voucher

Equalizing Factor Relative to Mean Income	Mean Income	Income Inequality	Education Spending Relative to Total Income	Education Inequality	Tax Rate
0.00	23.08	0.594	0.0410	0.594	0.00
0.10	23.08	0.594	0.0410	0.594	0.00
0.25	23.09	0.594	0.0410	0.593	0.00
0.40	23.18	0.593	0.0411	0.588	0.02
0.50	23.30	0.591	0.0413	0.578	0.06
0.60	23.46	0.590	0.0416	0.564	0.12
0.70	23.64	0.589	0.0421	0.547	0.20
0.75	23.73	0.588	0.0424	0.537	0.25
1.00	24.21	0.587	0.0441	0.486	0.56
1.25	24.68	0.585	0.0462	0.437	0.93

the decrease in inequality in the distribution of educational spending there is a decrease of roughly 33 percent. However, whereas the increase in mean income is roughly 10 percent, the decrease in inequality in the income distribution is only about 1.5 percent. The reason that inequality in the income distribution decreases by so little relative to the decrease in inequality in the education spending distribution is that differences in education spending account for very little of the variance in the income distribution. Most of the variance is accounted for by the stochastic earnings term ξ. In fact, one can

Table 6.5   **Long-Run Effects of Given Expenditure Levels**

Required Revenue (% of Total Income)	% Increase in Long-Run Income		
	Lump-Sum	Means-Tested	Means-Equalizing
0.25	0.00	1.60	2.60
0.50	0.04	2.69	4.07
1.00	0.21	4.55	6.54

ask what would happen to inequality in the income distribution even if inequality were completely removed from the education spending distribution. Holding mean spending constant, the resulting steady-state income distribution would have a coefficient of variation of 0.58.

It is also of interest to contrast the differing fiscal requirements of these voucher systems from the perspective of their implications for aggregate income. Table 6.5 shows the long-run consequences in terms of percent increase in aggregate income as a function of the initial (first-period) fiscal requirement also expressed as a percentage of aggregate income.

As can be seen, the differences are striking. Holding the fiscal requirement constant, the lump-sum voucher system produces substantially smaller long-run increases in income as compared with the other two systems. The means-equalizing voucher system produces the largest increase per dollar of tax revenue required.

Transition Effects

What is the nature of the transition from the initial steady state to the final steady state? The transition turns out to be very fast—the economy moves most of the way to the new steady-state income distribution one period after the introduction of the voucher programs. Rather than presenting a long list of results for all of the various cases, we simply present one case for each of the lump-sum and means-equalizing voucher systems (the results for the means-tested voucher are similar to those for the lump-sum voucher). For the lump-sum voucher we consider the case in which the voucher is equal to mean spending on education, and for the means-equalizing voucher we consider the case in which the equalizing factor is mean income. Period 0 indicates the period in which the voucher is introduced, so that in period 0 the income distribution corresponds to that of the benchmark steady state. Table 6.6 reports the results for several of the variables considered above.

As already indicated, it is clear that most of the change in the income distribution actually occurs by period one. Subsequently there are relatively minor increases in both mean income and mean educational expenditures (note that even if education spending stays constant as a fraction of mean income, mean income continues to increase), and minor decreases in in-

Table 6.6   Transition Paths

Period	Mean Income	Income Inequality	Education Spending Relative to Total Income	Education Inequality	Tax Rate
		A. Lump-Sum Voucher Equal to Mean Education Spending			
0	23.081	0.594	0.0474	0.421	4.10
1	25.166	0.582	0.0474	0.391	3.76
2	25.286	0.583	0.0474	0.390	3.74
3	25.294	0.583	0.0474	0.390	3.74
4	25.294	0.583	0.0474	0.390	3.74
5	25.294	0.583	0.0474	0.390	3.74
		B. Means-Equalizing Voucher with Equalizing Factor Equal to Mean Income			
0	23.081	0.594	0.0441	0.504	0.64
1	24.039	0.586	0.0441	0.489	0.57
2	24.190	0.586	0.0441	0.486	0.56
3	24.210	0.586	0.0441	0.486	0.56
4	24.212	0.586	0.0441	0.486	0.56
5	24.213	0.586	0.0441	0.486	0.56

equality in both distributions. Given that mean income is increasing, required tax rates are decreasing over time.

6.4.2   Welfare

Having analyzed the effects on allocations, we now analyze the welfare effects associated with these changes. In a model such as this, in which families are heterogeneous with regard to income and policies have differential effect on households, there is no definitive choice for a measure of welfare. If some families are made better off while others are made worse off, then one needs to take a stand on what weight to attach to each of the two groups. We adopt as a welfare measure the expected utility of a family where the weight on each type of family's utility is its proportion in the population. This is equivalent to a utilitarian welfare criterion: that is, one that puts equal weight on all families. We then compute the extent to which the income distribution in the benchmark model would have to be scaled in order to equalize welfare across the comparisons. We make this comparison for each of several periods following the adoption of the various voucher programs.

We should expect that welfare comparisons at different dates will look quite different because income is changing over time. In particular, given that steady-state income is sometimes significantly higher in the economy with vouchers, we would expect welfare to also be substantially higher. Such a comparison, of course, ignores the fact that in order to get the higher income some redistribution was required (with a welfare cost for some). This element is particularly significant in the first period (period 0) because at that point in time there has not been any increase in mean income and more resources are being devoted to education. Of course, families do take into

Table 6.7   **Welfare Effects**

	Voucher Relative to Initial Mean Education Spending						
Period	0.10	0.25	0.40	0.50	0.60	0.75	1.00
	A. Lump-Sum Voucher						
0	1.006	1.014	1.020	1.023	1.024	1.023	1.019
1	1.007	1.018	1.036	1.051	1.067	1.094	1.137
2	1.007	1.019	1.037	1.053	1.071	1.098	1.142
3	1.007	1.019	1.038	1.054	1.072	1.099	1.142
4	1.007	1.019	1.038	1.054	1.072	1.099	1.142
5	1.007	1.019	1.038	1.054	1.072	1.099	1.142
	B. Means-Tested Voucher						
0	1.000	1.006	1.019	1.027	1.032	1.034	1.033
1	1.000	1.008	1.033	1.053	1.074	1.105	1.152
2	1.000	1.009	1.034	1.056	1.078	1.110	1.156
3	1.000	1.009	1.035	1.056	1.078	1.110	1.157
4	1.000	1.009	1.035	1.056	1.078	1.110	1.157
5	1.000	1.009	1.035	1.056	1.078	1.110	1.157

	C. Means-Equalizing Voucher						
	Equalizing Factor Relative to Initial Mean Income						
	0.25	0.40	0.50	0.60	0.75	1.00	1.25
0	1.001	1.005	1.008	1.011	1.015	1.019	1.020
1	1.002	1.012	1.022	1.033	1.050	1.076	1.098
2	1.003	1.013	1.024	1.036	1.054	1.083	1.107
3	1.003	1.014	1.024	1.036	1.055	1.083	1.108
4	1.003	1.014	1.024	1.036	1.055	1.084	1.108
5	1.003	1.014	1.024	1.036	1.055	1.084	1.108

account the fact that their children will end up with higher incomes when they assess the utility that they receive from a given voucher program.

Table 6.7 presents the welfare results.

In interpreting these numbers, note that a value of 1.020 for a particular period, for example, indicates that income in the benchmark economy would have to be scaled upward by 2 percent in order to make individuals indifferent between the steady state in the no-voucher world versus having the allocation of resources be given to that in the world with a voucher in the particular time period considered.

A striking finding is that welfare gains are positive in all periods for all voucher plans considered (as indicated by the fact that all numbers are equal to or greater than one). Moreover, the effects are large; in several cases the steady-state welfare gain exceeds 10 percent. As suggested above, it is in fact the case that welfare gains in the initial period are quite a bit less than the welfare gains associated with later periods. However, the size of the welfare gain in the period following the introduction of the voucher is already close to the steady-state welfare gain. Another finding of some interest is that for the lump-sum voucher the size of the first-period gain is not monotone in the size of the voucher. For the values considered in the table it reaches its maximum value for a lump-sum voucher equal to 60 percent of mean spending. Steady-state welfare gains are monotone over the range of voucher programs considered here.

6.4.3   Sensitivity Analysis

The results presented above are for one set of the model's parameter values. To what extent are these results robust? We have carried out an extensive sensitivity analysis of this issue. Rather than providing numerous additional tables, we attempt to summarize the main findings. In our calibration we picked the preference parameter α to be equal to -1, although we stated that the reasonable range was the interval $[-2, 0]$. It turns out that choosing α to be some other value within this interval has very little effect on the quantitative results. We also calibrated the model so that educational expenditures accounted for 4.1 percent of income in the benchmark model. Changing this value within the interval of 3 percent to 5 percent had very little effect on the results.

One parameter value that does affect the results in a significant manner is the educational production function parameter θ. For the results above we assumed $\theta = 0.2$. Recall that a larger value of θ will imply that additional educational resources have a larger effect on future income. It should come as no surprise that this parameter is important. For example, consider the extreme case in which $\theta = 0$, which implies that educational resources do not matter at all for income. In this case there is no issue of inefficiently low investment by poor families because education ceases to be an investment. Conversely, larger values of θ imply that education offers a higher rate of return and hence is more important as an investment. We find, not surprisingly, that the effects of vouchers are increased as the value of θ is increased. Moreover, in terms of our income gains and welfare gains, we found that these measures are roughly linear in θ. Thus, if we were to decrease θ to 0.1, the income gains and welfare gains would be cut roughly in half, whereas if we were to increase θ to 0.3, these gains would be increased by 50 percent. We note that if one considers a value of $\theta = 0.1$, for example, the implied rate of return to education will be less than 5 percent, which lies below the accepted range of estimates for this return.

It is also of interest to discuss an alternative model specification. We have assumed that there are no channels that generate intergenerational correlations other than spending on education. In reality one may consider it likely that other channels may also give rise to positive intergenerational correlations of income, such as genetics, or family connections. If, for example, ability is partially heritable, then this may give rise to a correlation of the random draws of ξ across generations. The main effect of this modification is that it increases the desire of richer families to invest in their children's education because it raises the rate of return to their education. Similarly, it decreases the rate of return to investing in the education of children from poorer families. However, it remains true that poor families tend to under-invest in education relative to what is efficient because of their inability to borrow against the income of future generations. The new feature that this adds to the analysis is that compressing spending at the top of the distribution becomes more costly, since these are the children with the highest rates of return. Recalling, however, that in our simulations we found that vouchers induced very little compression from above, we conclude that allowing for some degree of ability to be heritable across generations is not likely to have a large effect on our findings.

6.5   Endogenous Choice of Vouchers

In the previous section we traced out the consequences of various voucher programs for allocations and welfare in both the short and long run. In tracing out these consequences, however, we have simply taken the parameters of a given voucher system as exogenous. In reality, once a voucher program is put in place, its parameters are likely to ultimately be chosen through the political process. In view of this it is also important to try and assess the likely outcome of the political process for the magnitude of various voucher programs. This is the issue that we address in this section.

Modeling the political process is of course a challenging endeavor. As is common in the political economy literature, the benchmark that we adopt for our study is that of majority voting. Hence, we will assume that all households participate and are given equal weight in the process. In each period, agents are assumed to choose the parameter that governs the size of the voucher. The analytics of this problem for the lump-sum voucher and the means-equalizing voucher have been studied previously by Fernández and Rogerson (1999b).[6] We refer the reader to that reference for analytical details on the voting problem.

Here we focus on the outcomes that result from majority voting. In our previous analysis we considered vouchers that were of constant value over time. Once we endogenize the determination of the voucher, this will in general not be the case, because changes in the income distribution over time may lead to changes in the political outcome over time as well.

---

6. That paper considers several school finance systems rather than voucher systems, but, as discussed previously, there is a mapping between the two.

Table 6.8   Endogenous Choice of Vouchers: Lump-Sum Vouchers

Period	Mean Income	Tax Rate	Size of Voucher Relative to Mean Education Expenditure	Education Inequality	Education Expenditure Relative to Total Income	Welfare
0	23.081	2.75	0.671	0.523	0.0429	1.024
1	23.950	2.75	0.696	0.502	0.0431	1.080
2	24.142	2.75	0.702	0.496	0.0432	1.088
3	24.183	2.76	0.705	0.495	0.0432	1.090
4	24.202	2.76	0.706	0.495	0.0432	1.091
5	24.202	2.76	0.706	0.495	0.0432	1.091

We begin with the case of the lump-sum voucher. Results are presented in table 6.8.

The table shows that in the initial period, majority vote leads to a voucher whose value is a fraction 0.671 of average household education expenditure in the benchmark steady state. The consequences of this for education expenditures can be inferred from the earlier tables that indicate the consequences of a given voucher. Hence, the results here lie somewhere between those reported in table 6.2 for a lump-sum voucher of 60 and 75 percent of mean spending. As before, we still find that the transition to a steady state is quite rapid. The one feature that could potentially be different in this case is that it could be that there are more dynamics introduced by the endogenous choice of the voucher each period. In particular, the size of the voucher increases over time, but otherwise these additional dynamics are not too significant quantitatively. Hence, the economy is most of the way to the new steady state income distribution one period after the introduction of the voucher. As the final column indicates, there are substantial welfare gains associated with the introduction of the voucher plan, both in the short run and the long run. The long-run gain exceeds 9 percent when expressed relative to steady-state income in the benchmark economy.

Next consider the case of the means-tested voucher. The political economy of this system is more complicated than the other two systems. The reason for this is that whereas the other two systems were completely summarized by a single parameter, this system is summarized by two parameters. As is well known in the social choice literature, two-dimensional problems are much more difficult. In considering the political economy of this system we assume a two-stage process. In the first stage the cutoff level y_m is chosen, and in the second stage the size of the voucher is chosen given the value of y_m chosen in the first stage. We find that a majority voting equilibrium exists and takes the form of having the cutoff level y_m being equal to median income, so that half of the population receives the voucher. The size of the voucher is then decided as the preferred choice of the lowest-income indi-

Table 6.9   Endogenous Choice of Vouchers: Means-Tested Voucher

Period	Mean Income	Tax Rate	Size of Voucher Relative to Mean Education Expenditure	Education Inequality	Education Expenditure Relative to Total Income	Welfare
0	23.081	0.62	0.299	0.593	0.0410	1.021
1	23.156	0.62	0.300	0.593	0.0410	1.028
2	23.179	0.62	0.300	0.593	0.0410	1.029
3	23.184	0.62	0.300	0.593	0.0410	1.030
4	23.185	0.62	0.300	0.593	0.0410	1.030
5	23.185	0.62	0.300	0.593	0.0410	1.030

Table 6.10   Endogenous Choice of Vouchers: Means-Equalizing Voucher

Period	Mean Income	Tax Rate	Equalizing Factor Relative to Mean Income	Education Inequality	Education Expenditure Relative to Total Income	Welfare
0	23.081	1.45	1.44	0.432	0.0481	1.019
1	24.755	1.45	1.55	0.394	0.0490	1.112
2	25.132	1.45	1.57	0.387	0.0492	1.129
3	25.208	1.45	1.57	0.385	0.0493	1.133
4	25.223	1.45	1.57	0.385	0.0493	1.133
5	25.226	1.45	1.57	0.384	0.0493	1.133

vidual. We take this individual to be someone with income of $1,000. This turns out to generate a relatively small amount of redistribution. Results are reported in table 6.9.

As the table indicates, the size of the voucher is relatively small—only 30 percent of average educational spending in the original steady state. As we know from table 6.1, this voucher exceeds spending for only about 2 percent of all households and, not surprisingly, has a fairly negligible effect on the economy.

Lastly, consider the case of the power-equalizing voucher. Table 6.10 presents the results.

An interesting finding here is that majority vote leads to a very high value of the equalizing factor y_e: As can be seen, this level is 1.44 times mean income. As a result, this system brings about considerably more compression in the distribution of education spending than does the lump-sum voucher system. The increase in steady-state income is now almost 10 percent, and the increase in steady state welfare exceeds 13 percent. Note that although y_e increases over time relative to initial mean income, it is actually quite stable relative to mean income over time. As a result of the increase in y_e, the convergence to the new steady state is somewhat slower here than in the case of exogenous policy considered earlier.

It is interesting to note that the political economy of these three systems is quite different. We saw earlier that a means-tested voucher is able to increase education spending among poorer households equally well as the other two systems, given appropriate choice of program parameters. However, the striking finding in the foregoing analysis is that when choices are made by a process of majority vote, poorer households end up with very little increase in their spending on education relative to the other two systems.

Although this finding is significant, it is important to note some qualifications. Majority vote is one mechanism that can be used to generate a solution to a social choice problem. Also, we have abstracted from some features that may generate additional support for redistribution. For example, we have assumed that greater education for poorer households has no benefits for other households. In reality, the additional skills accumulated by these households may benefit others as well.[7] With this in mind, it is probably best to interpret our results as showing that political economy considerations may imply that the three systems generate quite different outcomes.

References

Benabou, R. 1993. Workings of a city: Location, education, and production. *Quarterly Journal of Economics* 108 (3): 619–52.
———. 1996. Heterogeneity, stratification, and Growth. *American Economic Review* 86:584–609.
Card, D., and A. Krueger. 1992. Does school quality matter? Returns to education and the characteristics of public schools in the U.S. *Journal of Political Economy* 100:1–40.
Caucutt, E. 2002. Educational vouchers when there are peer effects: Size matters. *International Economic Review* 43:195–222.
Coleman, J., E. Campbell, C. Hobson, J. McPartland, A. Mood, F. Weinfeld, and R. York. 1966. *Equality of educational opportunity*. Washington, D.C.: U.S. Government Printing Office.
Coons, J., W. Clune III, and S. Sugarman. 1970. *Private wealth and public education.* Cambridge, Mass.: Belknap Press of Harvard University.
de Bartolome, C. 1990. Equilibrium and inefficiency in a community model with peer group effects. *Journal of Political Economy* 98 (1): 110–33.
Durlauf, S. 1996. A theory of persistent income inequality. *Journal of Economic Growth* 1:75–93.
Epple, D., and R. Romano. Ends against the middle: Determining public service provision when there are private alternatives. *Journal of Public Economics* 62:297–325.
———. 1998. Competition between private and public schools, vouchers, and peer-group effects. *American Economic Review* 88 (1): 33–62.

---

7. See Benabou (1996) for a model that incorporates this possibility.

Epple, D., and H. Sieg. 1999. Estimating equilibrium models of local jurisdictions. *Journal of Political Economy* 107:645–81.

Fernández, R. 2002. Sorting, education, and inequality. In *Advances in economic theory,* ed. M. Dewatripont, L. Hansen, and S. Turnovsky. Cambridge, England: Cambridge University Press, forthcoming.

Fernández, R., and R. Rogerson. 1996. Income distribution, communities, and the quality of public education. *Quarterly Journal of Economics* 111 (1): 135–64.

———. 1997. Education finance reform: A dynamic perspective. *Journal of Policy Analysis and Management* 16 (1): 67–84.

———. 1998. Public education and income distribution: A dynamic quantitative evaluation of education finance reform. *American Economic Review* 88:813–33.

———. 1999a. Education finance reform and investment in human capital: Lessons from California. *Journal of Public Economics* 74:327–50.

———. 1999b. Equity and resources: An analysis of education finance systems. NBER Working Paper no. 7111. Cambridge, Mass.: National Bureau of Economic Research.

———. 2001. The determinants of public education expenditures: Longer-run evidence from the States, 1950–1990. *Journal of Education Finance* 27:567–83.

Hoxby, C. 2000. Does competition among public schools benefit students and taxpayers? *American Economic Review* 90:1209–38.

Johnson, G., and F. Stafford. 1973. Social returns to quantity and quality of schooling. *Journal of Human Resources* 8:139–55.

Wachtel, P. 1976. The effects on earnings of school and college investment expenditures. *Review of Economics and Statistics* 58:326–31.

7 Neighborhood Schools, Choice, and the Distribution of Educational Benefits

Dennis Epple and Richard Romano

7.1 Introduction

In this chapter, we examine the implications of a neighborhood system of public schooling and compare it to provision that allows districtwide open enrollment or choice. We also contrast these policy regimes with the most decentralized form of direct public educational provision, in which neighborhoods constitute their own school districts. This study is part of a research agenda that investigates school choice and finance policies. We begin by outlining our research findings to date in order to place the results developed below in the broader context of our conception of alternative educational policies and their consequences.

Our research emphasizes differences in attributes of students and their households (especially in student ability and household income), peer groups in schools and in the classroom, equilibrium sorting of types of students within the schooling system, and the consequences for school qualities and the distribution of educational benefits. Although variation in schooling expenditure plays a role, because schooling quality is substantially determined by student peer groups, we find that significant hetero-

Dennis Epple is the Thomas Lord Professor of Economics at Carnegie Mellon University and a research associate of the National Bureau of Economic Research. Richard Romano is the Gerald L. Gunter Professor of Economics at the University of Florida.

An earlier version of this paper was titled "Public School Choice and Finance Policies, Neighborhood Formation, and the Distribution of Educational Benefits." The authors thank David N. Figlio, Jon Hamilton, Eric A. Hanushek, Caroline M. Hoxby, Michael Kremer, Steve Slutsky, David E. Wildasin, two anonymous referees, and seminar participants at the University of British Columbia, the University of Montreal, Stanford University, the 1995 National Bureau of Economic Research (NBER) School Finance Workshop, and the 1996 American Association Meetings for comments. This research is supported by NBER, the National Science Foundation, and MacArthur Foundation, with our gratitude.

geneity in schools and outcomes results even under policies that equalize finance or if expenditure variation has small effects.

In our research, we have developed a theoretical model of students and their households and of related educational institutions that makes simple assumptions. For example, we presume that households with a school-age child obtain higher utility as their child's educational achievement increases, and attendance at a higher-quality school increases that achievement. Our model is detailed below. Our intent in focusing on simple characteristics in developing the model is to allow the flexibility to analyze the variety of educational policy alternatives that exist and have been proposed. Given a policy regime, we predict consequences for schooling qualities and educational outcomes. We quantify and illustrate these predictions with a computational model that complements the theoretical model. The computational model specifies functional forms for components of the model like the household utility function, and its parameters are calibrated to a variety of empirical findings.

Most of the theoretical components of our model are part of received theory. However, we must make assumptions about what the crucial elements of the educational process are, including assumptions about issues lacking definitive empirical evidence, and, in calibrating the computational model, we can rely only on the best available estimates. The most important of these assumptions we make is that a student's educational achievement is influenced by the student's peer group in school. For these reasons, it is important that predictions of the model be tested. Although Epple, Figlio, and Romano (forthcoming) provide evidence that supports the basic model, more such testing remains to be done. We focus on developing predictions in this chapter.

Our research predicts that the nature of student sorting into schools and the consequences for school qualities and educational outcomes are dramatically influenced by public policy. This is illustrated by the three panels of figure 7.1, which depict student sorting into schools under three different policy regimes. Abstracting from detail that is developed later in the chapter, our model characterizes households as having exogenous income (y) and one student with ability level denoted b. Households value the educational achievement of their child, which rises with the quality of the school attended and the child's own ability. School quality is determined at least in part by the distribution of student ability in the school, with higher-ability students improving school quality for all through a peer-group effect. Higher-income households are willing to pay more for increases in their child's educational achievement and hence are willing to pay more for increases in the quality of their child's school. The set of households is characterized by a joint distribution over income and ability, which we will usually assume to exhibit positive correlation (for several reasons to be discussed).

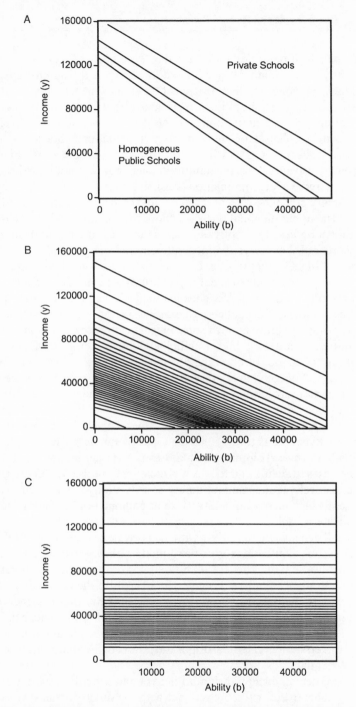

Fig. 7.1 *A,* Admission spaces with no voucher; *B,* admission spaces with a flat-rate per-student voucher of $4,200 (all private schools); *C,* admission spaces for a neighborhood school system

The panels of figure 7.1 show how the "type space of students," that is, the ability-income plane, is partitioned into schools in equilibrium under three different policy regimes. In each of these cases there is only one (large) school district, or a single political jurisdiction, that determines educational expenditure per student in public schools. In panel A, there is open enrollment in the public sector, meaning that students may choose any (free) public school so long as they live in the district, and there is a competitive (free entry) private sector. In equilibrium, here public schools are homogeneous and serve a large population consisting of relatively nonaffluent and lower-ability students, those that make up the triangle with vertex at the origin. The upper diagonal lines, which we call "boundary loci," delineate the student bodies of four private schools that arise in the equilibrium. The private school that serves the most affluent and highest-ability set of students is of highest quality, due to its having the highest-ability peer group (and perhaps higher per-student expenditure). The private schools as one moves southwest in panel A decline in quality, but all are of higher quality than the homogeneous public-sector schools. Private schools charge tuition that varies with ability and, to some extent, with income. Private schools give tuition discounts to higher-ability students because they increase the quality of the school through the peer-group effect on education, thus allowing the school to charge everyone higher tuition. Very high ability students may pay zero tuition or receive fellowships. The discounting to ability combined with increased demand for quality with income leads to a cross-subsidization within schools from the relatively higher-income and lower-ability students to the opposite types of students—hence the partition with downward-sloping boundary loci. As either income or ability itself increases, students find themselves in better schools. We refer to the latter respectively as income and ability stratification. Students must be of sufficiently high income or ability (or some combination) to find themselves in a private school.

Panel B depicts an equilibrium with only private schools serving students. Such a system would obviously arise if public policy provides no public option, but it also would arise if all households have access to a voucher of magnitude equal to at least average school cost. In the latter case, no students choose the public option. Private schools behave as in panel A, the difference being that there are many private schools and a wider distribution of schooling qualities. The differences in peer groups and school qualities between students near the origin and far out in the ability-income plane are substantial.

Panel C depicts an equilibrium with no private schools (as if they are illegal or unable to cover their costs), but with the single district divided into small neighborhoods, each of which has its own school. Here, public policy requires that a household send its child to school in the neighborhood in which the household resides. This equilibrium presumes, as could be in the other cases in figure 7.1, that demand for schooling quality is independent of student ability but that household income and student ability are positively correlated. Although per-student expenditure is the same across the schools since this is within one district, the income stratification and income-ability correlation lead to a hierarchy of public school qualities via the peer effect. The quality hierarchy is supported by rising housing prices across neighborhoods with school qualities, and selection of higher-income households into neighborhoods with better schools. Although it appears that households are stratified only by income in panel C, *average* student ability rises as neighborhoods become more wealthy due to the correlation between income and ability.

We see that the three policy regimes have substantially different predictions about the equilibrium allocation. These three policy alternatives vividly illustrate that the effects of school choice policies vary dramatically with the specifics of the policy. Panel A presumes open enrollment in the public sector, or that there is public-school choice. Panel B corresponds to a universal voucher system with vouchers of sufficient magnitude that everyone chooses a private school. There are many other "choice policies," several of which are discussed later, also with different predicted outcomes. It bears emphasis that school choice policies can be expected to have (sometimes) radically different implications for equilibrium provision of schooling, a theme of this paper and volume.

From a research standpoint, differences in predictions across educational policies provide a means to test the model: Although both a neighborhood schooling regime and private schooling are associated with income stratification across schools, only the latter exhibits ability stratification for given income. Hence, for example, our model predicts that vouchers or lower entry barriers on private schools will increase ability stratification.

Detailed analysis of the regimes in panels A and B are in Epple and Romano (1998, 1999). Epple and Romano (1998) develop the analysis with no vouchers and with flat-rate (or universal) vouchers. Epple and Romano (1999) investigate voucher design, allowing vouchers to be conditioned on student attributes and, perhaps, characteristics of the school attended. In this chapter we develop properties and attendant predictions of the equilibrium that is depicted in panel C, as well as investigating the effects of a public-school choice policy.[1] We will also in section 7.6 return to a more detailed comparison of neighborhood public schooling provision to voucher-induced private provision.

This chapter proceeds as follows. The next section motivates our study of neighborhood schooling and public-school choice, provides an overview of

---

1. Epple, Newton, and Romano (2002) investigate the equilibrium causes and consequences of ability tracking in schools, hence the interaction of sorting of students within and across schools.

the related results, and discusses related literature. Section 7.3 presents the theoretical model, and section 7.4 develops the theoretical predictions. Section 7.5 details the computational analysis, including normative findings. Section 7.6 further contrasts the neighborhood equilibrium with the private-provision alternative. Section 7.7 draws conclusions. Some of the more technical analysis is in the appendix.

7.2 Neighborhood Schooling, the Choice Movement, and an Overview

Public education in the United States is increasingly characterized by centralized finance but with schools determined by neighborhood of residence. Within jurisdictions, households frequently may choose among neighborhoods in which to reside and send their children to school, but with limited opportunity to choose alternative tax-expenditure schooling packages. In 1998, nine states had school districts that were coterminous with counties or very nearly so, and the ratio of school districts to counties was 2 or below in four more states.[2] Since counties are relatively large geographic entities, county districts are typically multischool districts. Moreover, these thirteen states do not include a number of states that have the lowest variation among districts in expenditure per student due to relatively centralized finance systems. Examples are Delaware, Colorado, and California, whose ratios of 95th percentile to 5th percentile district expenditures in 1994 were, respectively, 1.26, 1.31, and 1.34.[3] Although uneven and of limited success, a central theme in educational finance reform over the last several decades has been expenditure equalization.[4] For example, the same district expenditure ratios in 1972 for the three states just mentioned were, respectively, 1.81, 1.61, and 1.95.[5] Most students live in districts with multiple schools: In 1993–94, 91 (66) percent of elementary- (high-)school students lived in districts with multiple elementary (high) schools (U.S. Department of Education 1994). Although there is a growing trend toward centralization of finance in the United States, centralization of finance is al-

---

2. The first nine states are Hawaii, Maryland, West Virginia, Nevada, Florida, Louisiana, Georgia, Virginia, and North Carolina, and the second four states are Tennessee, Utah, Alabama, and Mississippi. These data are from the *Common Core of Data* for 1998.

3. These calculations use data from the Census of Governments for 1972 and the Common Core of Data for 1994. The ratios for these years have been calculated for forty-five states, excluding Hawaii (whose ratio is 1), Alaska, Arkansas, Montana, and Vermont. Districts are nonunified in the latter three states and were exempted from the calculations. Special thanks to David Figlio for providing access to his database.

4. See Gold, Smith, and Lawton (1995) for state-by-state description of their school finance system and summary of reforms and initiatives.

5. Among the forty-five states for which calculations were made (see footnote 3), the change from 1972 to 1994 of the 95th percentile to 5th percentile district expenditure ratio exceeded 10 percent (of the 1972 ratio) in eighteen states. In sixteen of these states the ratio declined. The exceptions are Maine and Missouri. See Murray, Evans, and Schwab (1998) for evidence that court cases have substantially reduced expenditure inequality.

ready well established in many other countries (Benabou 2000). Analysis of the provision of education using a standard Tiebout model with community-level finance of education is inappropriate in such settings. One purpose of this chapter is to examine neighborhood formation and schooling provision when no choice among political jurisdictions is practical but choice among neighborhoods within the jurisdiction can be exercised. Here any neighborhood sorting of households and variation in school quality that result are driven solely by peer-group effects.

As school finance is under reform in the United States, a school choice movement is gaining momentum.[6] Choice policies and proposals include inter- and intradistrict open enrollment, formation of magnet and charter schools, and vouchers for private schools. The United States is by no means at the forefront of this movement. For example, broad school choice reforms were adopted in the United Kingdom in the early 1980s. It remains to be seen how the school choice movement will evolve, but it seems likely that some form or forms of increased school choice will play a role in the future. Another purpose of this chapter is to investigate the effects of public-school choice. We examine the consequences of elimination of territorial (neighborhood) restrictions on school attendance in our model, with and without friction in the exercise of school choice.[7]

We develop a theoretical and complementary computational model to study equilibria in the aforementioned policy regimes, with attention to the distribution of educational benefits. School quality is presumed to depend both on per-student educational expenditure and on the makeup of the student body, the latter measured by mean student ability. Households differ continuously by income and student ability, with normal demand for educational quality. The economy is made up of an exogenous number of neighborhoods, each having a school and with given housing supply. Households choose in which neighborhood to reside and where to send their child to school as constrained by policy, and vote over the economy's tax expenditure package. With neighborhood schooling, students must attend school in their neighborhood of residence. With choice, students may attend school in another neighborhood, which may or may not entail a private (transportation) cost. We also compare these equilibria to that of the tradi-

---

6. Probably the biggest recent story is Florida's statewide voucher program for students in failing public schools introduced in the 1999–2000 academic year. However, there are a myriad of choice programs and initiatives. See Rees (2000) for a recent state-by-state summary.

7. The U.S. Department of Education National Center for Educational Statistics (1996) estimated that 13.8 percent of U.S. school districts had intradistrict open enrollment policies and 28.6 percent of districts were subject to interdistrict open enrollment policies in 1993–94. Participation of students subjected to the respective policies was 24.5 percent and 1.6 percent respectively. The estimated rate of "participation" in intradistrict policies must be interpreted with care, because some programs require households to choose their school, with then 100 percent participation rate. More generally, programs differ in limitations and requirements. See Rees (2000) for details and sources for more information.

tional Tiebout environment, where neighborhoods provide schooling only to their residents, who then also collectively determine their neighborhood's tax-expenditure package.

The main predictions are as follows. Neighborhood schooling is enough to lead to stratified equilibrium and a school-quality hierarchy if ability and income are positively correlated or if demand for school quality rises with student ability. Thus, a stratified outcome typically arises even though there is no variation in per-student expenditure across schools. Why? Peer student abilities are a key determinant of school quality in our model. Thus, households who demand higher school quality will pay a housing price premium to live in neighborhoods with schools having a higher-ability student peer group. If demand for educational quality rises with income, as we assume, then households will stratify by income across schools, with higher-income households occupying neighborhoods with higher-quality schools. This income sorting in turn sustains the school quality hierarchy via the positive correlation between income and student ability. If demand for school quality also rises with ability, as in some specifications we consider, equilibrium continues to be characterized by a hierarchy of school qualities, and there is stratification by both income and ability across the school hierarchy.

The equilibrium described in the preceding paragraph is supported by housing prices that ascend across neighborhoods in the same order as school quality. If we introduce intradistrict choice across public schools and there are no costs of exercising this choice (e.g., if transportation costs are paid by the government), then schooling qualities will be equalized in equilibrium. With the linkage between residence and school severed, housing prices cannot ration access to higher-quality schools. Equilibrium is characterized by equal-quality schools, each with the same student peer groups, and no housing price differences across neighborhoods. There are also secondary effects on the equilibrium school expenditure level, and results vary some when costs of exercising choice are present, as we will later show.

The (former) single-district equilibrium with neighborhood schools of different qualities is comparable to another no-choice policy in which neighborhoods constitute their own districts that individually select school tax-expenditure levels. Although this alternative does lead to differences in expenditure levels across neighborhoods, it does not alter much (if at all) the sorting of households and students into neighborhoods and schools. Given that peer effects are important, what is fundamental to sorting into neighborhoods and schools is a residence requirement for school placement, which characterizes both a single-district neighborhood system and a multidistrict local-finance system. An implication that we emphasize is that expenditure equalization, a popular reform intended to equalize schooling quality, will itself fail miserably to "equalize" peer groups and thus school qualities (given the importance of peer effects). Moreover, we will provide clear evidence that sorting across neighborhoods and schools within large districts is extreme.

School choice engendered by a universal and laissez-faire voucher system with vouchers of sufficient magnitude that all schooling is provided privately also eliminates any role that residence has on school attendance. However, such a voucher system is predicted to yield a highly stratified equilibrium, much closer to the multidistrict public equilibrium than to the single-district, public-school choice equilibrium. Here the market will provide households with what they want, *given their incomes* (and the voucher supplement), while rewarding student ability because it is an input to educational quality through the peer effect. Higher-income households with lower-ability students will buy their way into private schools by supplementing the voucher. Higher-ability students, whether of high or low income, will be drawn into private schools with tuition subsidies provided by schools on top of the voucher, including fellowships in some cases. The result will be an equilibrium stratified by both income and ability across schools (but not neighborhoods), with more ability stratification than under the no-choice, public-schooling equilibria because of the latitude of the private schools to use financial aid to attract higher-ability students. As will be discussed further, limits on the practices of private schools that may be associated with alternative voucher systems can radically alter the predicted allocation. This is but another example of the truism "all choice programs are not alike."

Before turning to the analysis, we comment briefly on related literature. Our analysis is in the tradition of multicommunity models of local public good provision begun by Tiebout (1956).[8] A number of papers study provision of public education in such a framework, including Inman (1978), de Bartolome (1990, 1997), Glomm and Ravikumar (1992), Benabou (1993, 1996), Silva and Sonstelie (1995), Durlauf (1996), Fernandez and Rogerson (1996, 1997a, 1997b, 1998), and Nechyba (1999, 2000). Central to our model are peer effects, which play a role only in de Bartolome (1990), Benabou (1993, 1996), Durlauf (1996), and Nechyba (1999, 2000) among the latter list. Further narrowing the overlap, only Benabou (1993, 1996) has an analogue to neighborhood provision of schooling within a jurisdiction.[9] In results similar to one of "our" findings, he shows that complementarities in

---

8. See Ellickson (1971); Westhoff (1977); Epple, Filimon, and Romer (1984); Goodspeed (1989); Epple and Romer (1991); Fernández (1997); Brueckner (2000); and the papers that focus on schooling discussed next.

9. Nechyba's jurisdictions are divided into neighborhoods that differ by their qualities of housing, but public school students in all neighborhoods within a jurisdiction attend the same school. Hence, he finds stratification by income across neighborhoods within jurisdictions but not across public schools within a jurisdiction. Stratification in public schooling quality across jurisdictions arises, however, including when there is statewide finance. In the latter case, the role of a jurisdiction is similar to the role of a neighborhood in our paper, and school-quality stratification arises similarly.

individual and group characteristics can lead to community stratification without expenditure differences. The models and emphasis differ substantially. Other related research is noted at various points during the chapter.

7.3 The Model

Each household has one child of ability b who will attend public school. Household income is denoted y. The population of households is normalized to one and characterized by joint probability density function $f(b, y)$, with $f(b, y)$ continuous and strictly positive on its support $S \equiv [b_m, b_x] \times [y_m, y_x] \subset R^2_+$. Whether income and ability are correlated in the population is important. To simplify, we assume that $E[b|y]$ is either strictly increasing in y or independent of y, implying either positive or zero correlation.

Household utility depends on numeraire and housing consumption, and the educational achievement of the child denoted a. Every household consumes exactly one unit of housing at price denoted p, the simple housing market discussed further later. The student's educational achievement depends on the quality, q, of the school attended, and on the student's ability: $a = a(q, b)$. School quality depends on per-student educational expenditure in the school, X, and on the mean ability of the school's peer group, denoted θ. The latter peer-group effect in education is central to our model and will be discussed further. Educational expenditure is financed by a proportional income tax, t. Given that a unit of housing is consumed, utility is then given by $U = U[y(1 - t) - p, a(q(X, \theta), b)]$, with all functions increasing, continuous, and differentiable. Demand for educational quality is assumed normal:

(1) $\dfrac{U_q}{U_y}$ increases with y.

In much of the analysis we employ a Cobb-Douglas utility-achievement specification:

(2) $U = [y(1 - t) - p]X^\alpha\theta^\gamma b^\beta;$ $q = X^\alpha\theta^\gamma;$ $a = qb^\beta;$ $\alpha,\gamma,\beta > 0.$

The economy consists of $N \in \{2, 3, \ldots\}$ neighborhoods, with exogenously defined boundaries and with one school in every neighborhood. Each neighborhood has a backward-L housing supply, horizontal at magnitude c until neighborhood land capacity is reached. Interpret c to be the construction cost of a unit of housing, with each housing unit requiring one lot of land. For now, assume the economy land capacity is exactly enough to house the population. We offer a more appealing interpretation later, but it can introduce additional equilibria that we wish to avoid initially.

Households make a residence choice, choose a school for their child, and participate in a vote over tax rates. The nature of these choices depends on a binary policy parameter that we vary exogenously. The choice of school

Residence Choices   →   Schools Chosen   →   Voting Over
& Housing Markets   Proportional
      Clear   Income Tax

Fig. 7.2   Order of activities

may or may not be restricted by a neighborhood residence requirement. A residence requirement implies that attendance is restricted to one's neighborhood school so that the school's peer group corresponds to that of the children of neighborhood residents. Of course, the absence of such a requirement permits real school choice, and this is what we mean by a school-choice or open-enrollment policy. We will consider the effects of a school choice policy with and without any frictions (costs of exercising choice).

As motivated above, we focus on the case in which school finance is centralized. A single income tax rate is determined by majority preference in the entire economy here under centralized finance. Constant returns to scale in schooling are assumed, implying that per-student expenditure in the economy is invariant in this case. This conforms to cases with district-level finance and large enough districts that nonschool factors determine district choice, or to some cases with statewide finance.[10] For purposes of comparison, we will also examine the more traditional Tiebout public finance problem with multiple political jurisdictions by assuming that neighborhoods correspond to jurisdictions.

Equilibria are determined assuming the timing of activities summarized in figure 7.2. In the first stage, (atomistic) households make neighborhood residence choices as price takers and the housing markets clear. Households then choose a school, although a residence requirement renders this choice a given. Voting over taxes takes place last, voters taking the (now committed) residences and schools as given.[11] The model has a single period; no real time elapses between the stages. Households correctly anticipate the ensuing properties of equilibrium when making choices, of course.

---

10. The model applies precisely to statewide finance if households are exogenously assigned to regions (e.g., by employment opportunities), and regions are homogeneous with regard to their distribution of household types and their neighborhoods' housing supplies. Alternatively, the model applies precisely if choice of neighborhood in the entire state is determined by schooling. These are obviously very strong assumptions, but they are needed only to be consistent with the model's determination of voting equilibrium. Key results like stratification across neighborhoods require only that expenditure is constant across neighborhoods, and then would hold for appropriately modified determination of voting equilibrium.

11. Perhaps surprisingly, if voting occurs in the second stage and school choice is last, all results below are correct as long as equilibrium exists under this alternative. This is because, for one subset of cases we study, the exercise of choice does not vary with the tax; and, for the remaining cases, the preferred tax of voters is (locally) independent of anticipated variation in the exercise of choice. The problem with the alternative timing is that existence of voting equilibrium is not guaranteed in the latter cases, leading us to adopt the timing in figure 7.1. We developed the results with the alternative timing in an earlier version of this paper (Epple and Romano 1995) while simply assuming existence.

Some elements of the model warrant further discussion. School quality is determined in part by a peer-group externality, which influences neighborhood formation and school choice. Ability-based peer effects in the classroom are confirmed by numerous studies, but this is not without controversy.[12] This aspect of the model can be given a more generic interpretation. Any household variable that positively affects both the performance of the child and the child's school conforms to the model.[13] Parental input in the education process that entails both helping the child and the school is an example. Parental input in the school might come in the form of direct participation in education (e.g., classroom volunteer work) or in monitoring and disciplining teachers and administrators.[14] McMillan (2000) provides evidence of positive parental effects on school quality operating through parent-teacher associations with parental involvement predicted by income and educational level. For all these interpretations of household characteristic b, it is likely to be positively correlated with parental educational attainment, hence also with household income. We show when and why positive correlation between b and y is important. We will continue to refer to b as student ability for expositional ease.[15]

12. The influence of ability on own educational achievement is well documented and not controversial (see Hanushek 1986). In the economics literature, Henderson, Mieszkowski, and Sauvageau (1978); Summers and Wolfe (1977); Toma (1996); Zimmer and Toma (1999); Sacerdote (2000); and Hoxby (2000b) find significant peer group effects. Evans, Oates, and Schwab (1992) adjust for selection bias in the formation of peer groups and show that it eliminates the significance of the peer group in explaining teenage pregnancy and dropping out of school. They are careful to point out that their results should not be interpreted as suggesting that peer group effects do not exist, but that scientific demonstration of those effects is inadequate. Note, too, that their work supports the notion that peer group variables enter the utility function, because a selection process does take place. See also Cullen, Jacob, and Levitt (2000). The psychology literature on peer group effects in education also contains some controversy. See Moreland and Levine (1992) for a survey that concludes: "The fact that good students benefit from ability grouping, whereas poor students are harmed by it, suggests that the mean level of ability among classmates, as well as variability in their ability levels, could be an important factor. The results from several recent studies . . . support this notion."
    Theoretical models of education that incorporate peer group effects include Arnott and Rowse (1987); Manski (1992); Eden (1992); Rothschild and White (1995); Epple, Newlon, and Romano (2002); Epple and Romano (1998, 1999); and Caucutt (2002), in addition to the papers discussed in section 7.2.
    13. In fact, many of the results are independent of b's positive impact on the child's own achievement. This is so when the assumption in equation (3), presented below, holds.
    14. The monitoring interpretation of the public school input suggests that teacher-administrator contracts should reflect school quality. This interpretation of our model embraces the belief that in fact users of a school are the primary enforcers of (implicit) contracts, and they vary in their ability and willingness to enforce them. McMillan (1999) develops a related theoretical model. For a study of the effects of centralized versus decentralized school finance systems on the effectiveness of explicit incentive contracts with school administrators, see Hoxby (1995).
    15. We should also note that measuring the peer quality with the mean of b in the school is less restrictive than it may appear. Relevant to the student ability interpretation, some researchers have argued that reduced variation in ability in the classroom facilitates curriculum specialization, thus improving the quality of instruction. Our model and qualitative results generalize to measuring peer quality as the mean in the school of any increasing function $h(b)$

That housing prices serve as screens to accessing neighborhoods is not controversial (see Black 1999 and Barrow 1999). We think it is important to introduce housing markets into the model, but have adopted a simple specification. We examine income taxation rather than property taxation so that tax liabilities rise continuously with income. The model can be varied to examine property taxation, with results that are qualitatively the same.

7.4 School Policy and Equilibrium

7.4.1 Equilibrium with Neighborhood Schooling

This model applies whenever the political jurisdiction encompasses multiple neighborhoods, each providing schooling for its own residents, if household entry into and exit from the jurisdiction can reasonably be ignored. This analysis also provides a basis for investigating cases with multiple districts consisting of multiple neighborhoods, as we discuss in the concluding section. Toward developing the properties of equilibrium, note first that here the school choice stage is trivial, committed in the initial residential choice stage. Providing conditions for and describing a voting equilibrium are not problematic except for one minor issue. We must guarantee that equilibrium permits everyone to purchase a house. Later we explicitly address this issue and develop voting equilibrium properties for the case of Cobb-Douglas preferences (equation [1]). For now, take as given the existence of a unique voting equilibrium in the third stage, with everyone able to afford a house. By definition, centralized finance implies a single tax rate and $X_1 = X_2 = \ldots = X_N$, where, here and henceforth, subscripts indicate the neighborhood.

We focus now on the residential choices. Although the voting equilibrium depends on the residential allocation, it is not influenced by individual (atomistic) household choice, implying that households treat the anticipated voting outcome as a given in the residential-choice stage. Our primary concern is with the nature of equilibria having differentiated neighborhoods, school peer groups, and school qualities. An issue relevant to the equilibrium allocation of households about which there is little evidence is how student ability affects the demand for school quality. We restrict consideration to two possibilities:

(3) $\dfrac{U_q}{U_y}$ is invariant to ability;

---

of ability (i.e., $\theta = Eh[b]$ in the school). If $h(b)$ is concave, for example, then decreases in Rothschilde-Stiglitz variability of student ability increase peer quality, accommodating the curriculum-specialization hypothesis. See Epple, Newlon, and Romano (2002) and Epple and Romano (1999) for more detail about this generalization of the model. For expositional ease, we present the results here using the simple mean of b.

(4) $\dfrac{U_q}{U_y}$ increases with ability.

In the latter case, the demand for school quality is normal in student ability. The case in equation (3) is neutral on this issue and is a property of the Cobb-Douglas specification.

The first proposition describes some necessary properties of any equilibrium with differentiated schools or neighborhoods.

PROPOSITION 1. *For $K \leq N$, suppose $q_1 < q_2 < \ldots < q_K$. (If $K < N$, then some neighborhoods have schools of the same quality.) Then the following will occur: (a) Housing prices ascend: $p_1 < p_2 < \ldots < p_K$. (b) The allocation exhibits income stratification: If household with income y_1 chooses neighborhood having school quality q_i and household with child of the same ability but income y_2 necessarily chooses neighborhood having higher school quality q_j ($j > i$), then $y_2 > y_1$. (c) If assumption (4) holds, the allocation exhibits ability stratification analogously defined.*[16] *Under equation (3), household residential choice is invariant to the student's ability. (d) The allocation exhibits boundary indifference and strict preference within boundaries: Type space (the [b, y] plane) is partitioned into neighborhoods by (measure zero) boundaries along which the corresponding households are indifferent to adjacent neighborhoods, and for which interior households have strict preference for their neighborhood over differentiated neighborhoods.*

PROOF. Since everyone pays the same tax rate, part (a) follows simply. Housing price must be lower if school quality is lower to attract any residents. Given part (a), the converse of part (b) contradicts equation (1). Part (c) is proved analogously. Part (d) is implied by continuity of $U(\cdot)$.

Figure 7.3 illustrates a potential equilibrium allocation for a case with $K = N = 3$ and assuming equation (3). Stratification by income arises but not by ability, households with incomes y_1 (y_2) are indifferent to residing in neighborhoods 1 or 2 (2 or 3), and all other households strictly prefer their neighborhood of residence. For preferences instead satisfying equation (4), the boundary loci in type space separating differentiated neighborhoods are downward sloping, exhibiting stratification by both ability and income.

The next proposition establishes conditions for existence of equilibrium with differentiated neighborhoods and schools (continuing to take as given existence and uniqueness of voting equilibrium).

PROPOSITION 2. *(a) Equilibrium with differentiated schools exists if preferences satisfy equation (3) and $E[b|y]$ is increasing in y. (b) Equilibrium with differentiated schools sometimes exists if preferences satisfy equation (4) and*

16. For any given income, only higher-ability students attend higher-quality schools.

Income (y)

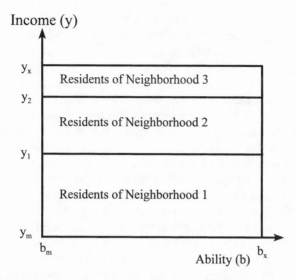

Fig. 7.3   **Residences and peer groups in neighborhood equilibrium**

either $E[b|y]$ is increasing in y or constant. (c) Constancy of $E[b|y]$ and preferences satisfying equation (3) are inconsistent with existence of equilibrium having differentiated schools.

PROOF. We show part (a) in the appendix by construction (see the proof of proposition A1). We have worked out examples demonstrating part (b), which are available on request. Regarding part (c), under equation (3), proposition 1 shows that an equilibrium with differentiated schools must exhibit stratification by income but not by ability (e.g., as in figure 7.3). However, constancy of $E[b|y]$ then implies equal θs in all schools, hence schools of equivalent quality—a contradiction.

School qualities can vary due only to variation in peer groups because expenditures are equalized across neighborhoods. Access to neighborhoods with better peer groups is rationed by higher housing prices. This rationing must be consistent with differentiated peer groups for such an equilibrium. If willingness to pay for school quality depends only on income (i.e., under equation [3]), then stratification across neighborhoods will be determined solely by income, as in figure 7.3. Income and ability must then be positively correlated to produce the school quality hierarchy. The mean ability or peer-group measure in any neighborhood i ($i = 1, 2, \ldots, N$) can be written thus:

$$(5) \qquad \theta_i \equiv \frac{\int_{y_{i-1}}^{y_i} \int_{b_m}^{b_x} bf(b, y)dbdy}{\int_{y_{i-1}}^{y_i} \int_{b_m}^{b_x} f(b, y)dbdy} = \frac{\int_{y_{i-1}}^{y_i} E[b|y] \cdot \left[\int_{b_m}^{b_x} f(b, y)db\right]dy}{\int_{y_{i-1}}^{y_i} \int_{b_m}^{b_x} f(b, y)dbdy},$$

where y_{i-1} is the minimum income type of household residing in neighborhood i and y_i is the maximum. Hence, given that $E[b|y]$ is increasing in y, the income stratification implies school quality stratification.

Alternatively, if willingness to pay for school quality also increases with the child's ability (i.e., under equation [4]), then positive correlation between ability and income is unnecessary for a differentiated equilibrium. In these equilibria, the (b, y) plane is partitioned into neighborhoods by downward-sloping boundary loci, with relatively high-income and low-ability households mixing with relatively low-income and high-ability households. Although the existence of equilibrium with differentiated neighborhoods cannot generally be shown under equation (4), we have consistently found such equilibria in simulations of specific cases.

In all that follows (and without constant repetition), we adopt the assumption in equation (3) and thus also assume that $E[b|y]$ is increasing in y. With N neighborhoods, equilibrium can have N different neighborhood peer groups and school qualities. In fact, proposition A1 in the appendix shows that a multiplicity of such equilibria exists if neighborhoods differ in size. We henceforth assume that school administrators choose neighborhood boundaries so that schools are of the same size, thus eliminating this multiplicity. This is a natural simplifying assumption because differentiated equilibria arise whether or not schools are of equal size, and no new issues arise in extending the results to schools of unequal size. We also anchor the housing price in the poorest neighborhood at c, as must arise in the variation of the model with elastic housing supply in one neighborhood, eliminating a degree of freedom in housing prices that arises otherwise. Other equilibria exist as well, with subsets of neighborhoods having the same peer groups, school qualities, and housing prices, including the allocation with no neighborhood differentiation. Such equilibria are unstable under reasonable adjustment assumptions.[17] This instability and the empirical evidence (see below), including evidence on school-driven housing price dif-

---

17. The argument that an equilibrium that is not maximally stratified will tend to be unstable is as follows. An arbitrary finite perturbation of the residences across neighborhoods beginning with $\theta_1 = \theta_2$ would generally imply differences in the peer measures. Households would relocate toward the higher-quality neighborhood and bid up its relative housing price, implying that the relocation pattern would satisfy income stratification (as in proposition 1[b]). In turn, the relocations and the assumption in equation (1) would imply greater quality differential, and so on. To formalize this argument, one needs to make assumptions about the rates at which types relocate and what they anticipate would change, if anything. Consider an example. Suppose that there are two neighborhoods, initially homogeneous with $p_1 = p_2 = c$. Perturb their residences so that θ_2 is a little higher than θ_1. Now let an arbitrarily selected positive measure of types relocate and suppose that they anticipate no changes in variables due to their own relocations. The housing market price that clears their housing exchanges must have $p_2 > p_1$ (the latter price might be anchored at c), and the relocation pattern must satisfy income stratification among those moving. However, then θ_2 would rise further and θ_1 would decline further, these implied by equation (1) and the assumption that the measure permitted to move was selected arbitrarily (i.e., the θs would change as stated with probability one).

ferentials within jurisdictions (Black 1999; Barrow 1999), lead us to ignore such equilibria.

Hence, we study the equilibrium with each neighborhood having a differentiated school and with a housing price of c in the poorest neighborhood. We emphasize that all stable equilibria in our model, whether or not schools are of equal size, have every neighborhood school differentiated.

Central cities in the United States are typically served by a single school district, as is assumed in our model, and provide evidence supporting our predictions. Income stratification across central-city neighborhood schools of the form we have described is quite evident in cities. Data from high schools in the city school district of Los Angeles (i.e., the Los Angeles Unified District) provide an illustration of the extent of income stratification. Although direct measures of household income by school are unavailable, data are available on the percentage of students in each school who are from low-income households—children who qualify for free or reduced-price lunch.

In panel A of figure 7.4 we plot the percentage of low-income students in each of the fifty-five "regular" high schools in the city of Los Angeles for the 1997–98 school year. We exclude schools classified in the *Common Core of Data* as "special educational" or "alternative," mainly because they frequently have much smaller enrollments, although their inclusion would not alter the message. In this plot, schools are ordered by their percentage of low-income students. This figure reveals that there is substantial income stratification. As a benchmark for comparison, consider random assignment of students to schools. We also show in panel A of figure 7.4 the 95 percent confidence bounds for the mean number of low-income students per school under random assignment of this population of students to schools.[18] The narrowness of these bounds stands in dramatic contrast to the observed variation across schools, confirming that there is a high degree of income stratification across neighborhood schools. In addition to peer effects in schools, there is no doubt that other factors support the observed stratification. These include incentives to interact regularly with others of similar background (educational, socioeconomic, and racial), incentives to locate near employment, and a durable and somewhat stratified existing housing stock. Our analysis of neighborhood equilibria attributes all stratification to school-based peer effects, which is clearly an exaggeration.

Research on local jurisdictions, following Tiebout, has traditionally emphasized sorting across rather than within jurisdictions. Most of the high schools in the other 110 districts in metropolitan Los Angeles have just one or a few high schools. In 1997–98, 41 percent of these districts had one (reg-

---

18. We use the normal approximation to the binomial distribution in calculating these confidence bounds, which is quite accurate given that the smallest school has 212 students and all but three schools have over 1,000 students. The fluctuation in the boundaries reflects differences in the sizes of the schools.

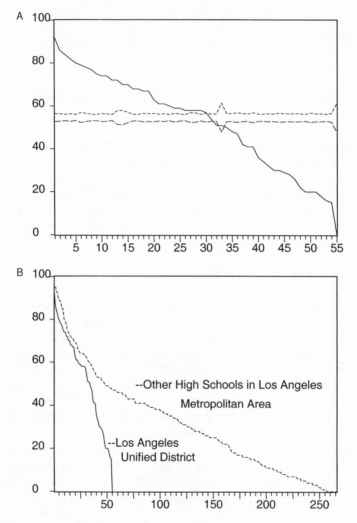

Fig. 7.4   *A,* Percent low-income students and 95 percent confidence bounds for high schools in Los Angeles unified district; *B,* percent low-income students in high schools in the Los Angeles metropolitan area

ular) high school, 62 percent had two or less, and 78 percent had three or less. Thus, jurisdictions in suburban Los Angeles accord reasonably well with the kind of structure presumed in most prior research. In light of this, it is of interest to compare stratification patterns between the 53 city high schools and the 266 suburban high schools in the Los Angeles metropolitan area. This is done in panel B of figure 7.4. The solid curve in the plot reproduces panel A of figure 7.4, and the new curve contains the percentage of low-income students for the suburban schools, with these also ordered by their percentages of low-income students. There is, as expected, stratification by income between city and suburbs. The mean of the proportion of low-income students in the city schools is 0.525, whereas it is 0.312 in the suburban schools. Of more interest, however, is the degree of stratification among suburban (Tiebout) schools relative to the degree of stratification among city (neighborhood) schools. Inspection of panel B suggests that the pattern of stratification among the city schools is not dramatically different from that of the suburban schools. The standard deviations of percentage of low-income students in the city and the suburbs are 0.222 and 0.230, respectively. Although it is not clear what is the right metric for comparing stratification in the two cases, the data for Los Angeles high schools reveal a high degree of income stratification across all schools and point to the need for more extensive investigation of the sorting of households within jurisdictions.

We now discuss voting equilibrium. To obtain precise results, we restrict consideration henceforth to the Cobb-Douglas utility specification (1).[19] We also set $N = 2$ in what follows for simplicity. Hence, the neighborhood housing capacities are $1/2$, and we know that the equilibrium partition of households has $y_1 = y_{med}$ as the boundary locus, y_{med} denoting the median income. Number the poorer neighborhood 1 and the wealthier neighborhood 2. Using equation (2) and setting $p_1 = c$, find p_2 from the fact that the median-income household is indifferent to residence in equilibrium (proposition 1[d]):

$$(6) \qquad p_2 = c + [y_{med}(1 - t) - c]\left[1 - \left(\frac{\theta_1}{\theta_2}\right)^{\gamma}\right].$$

Since the partition implies $\theta_1 < \theta_2$ (and assuming the median-income household can afford a house), inspection of equation (6) confirms that $p_2 > p_1$. We also see that housing prices are independent of per-student expenditure, due to the Cobb-Douglas specification.

One can find voting equilibrium following the methodology used in Epple and Romer (1991). The detailed analysis is in the appendix. Here we summarize the logic and results. Assume for simplicity that only tax rates that allow the poorest type to purchase homes can be adopted: $t \le (y_m - c)/y_m$.[20] It turns out that preference for higher-expenditure tax pairs increases with y/p. That is, households with a higher ratio of income to housing price favor more educational expenditure, although this requires a higher tax

19. Voting equilibrium can be shown to exist much more generally. See Roberts (1977), Epple and Romer (1991), and Gans and Smart (1996).
20. We have in mind an income policy that precludes equilibrium taxation such that the poorest household cannot afford housing in so restricting feasible taxes. A specific policy that yields this without direct restriction on the tax rate dictates no additional tax liability once a household is driven down to subsistence: Household with income y pays a maximum of $y - c$ in taxes. One can confirm that proposition 3 continues to apply without its tax ceiling under our assumption below that problem (8) has an interior solution.

rate. The tax rate most preferred by households with median value of y/p is then majority preferred. The latter tax and implied per-student educational expenditure is the equilibrium pair because it would defeat any other feasible pair in a tax referendum.

With one minor technical assumption on the income distribution (see equation [A1] in the appendix), there are median-preference households residing in (the poorer) neighborhood 1 having income denoted y_{p1} and median-preference households residing in neighborhood 2 having income $y_{p2} \equiv (p_2/c)y_{p1}$. Letting F_y denote the marginal cumulative density function (c.d.f.) of income, y_{p1} solves

$$(7) \qquad F_y(y_{p1}) + \left[F_y\left(\frac{p_2}{c}y_{p1}\right) - 0.5 \right] = 0.5.$$

We have the following proposition:

PROPOSITION 3. *The solution to*

$$(8) \qquad \max_{t,X}[y_{p1}(1 - t) - c]X^\alpha$$

$$\text{s.t. } X = t\bar{y}; \quad t \le \frac{y_m - c}{y_m}$$

is the unique majority voting equilibrium, where $\bar{y}$ denotes the mean income in the population.

The solution to problem (8) is

$$(9) \qquad t^* = \frac{\alpha}{1 + \alpha}\left(1 - \frac{c}{y_{p1}}\right) \quad \text{and} \quad X^* = \frac{\alpha}{1 + \alpha}\left(1 - \frac{c}{y_{p1}}\right)\bar{y},$$

provided it is not on the upper bound of t, which is easily ruled out.[21] Comparison to other policy outcomes and numerical examples are provided below.

To summarize to this point, for Cobb-Douglas preferences, $E[b|y]$ increasing in y, and two neighborhoods of equal size, equilibrium splits households by income at the median into the two neighborhoods, with the wealthy neighborhood having higher θ (equation [5]). With $p_1 = c$, the remaining equilibrium variables are described by equations (6), (7), and (9). In addition to the pivotal voters in neighborhood 1, those with income $p_2 y_{p1}/c$, who reside in neighborhood 2, also have median voting preferences.

Equilibrium is characterized by income stratification across neighborhoods, with differences in school quality deriving from differences in peer groups. More neighborhoods would increase stratification and the spread of schools' peer qualities. Although stratification affects expenditure levels

---

21. This requires $\alpha(1 - c/y_{p1})/(1 + \alpha) < (y_m - c)/y_m$. One set of sufficient conditions is $\alpha < 1$ and $y_m > 2c$.

(as will be discussed further), differences in school qualities obviously have nothing to do with expenditures. All that is needed is that a positive externality in schooling is correlated with household income. The preponderance of research concerning differences in quality of public schools emphasizes expenditure differences. However, equalization of finance will not itself create equal-quality schools. The emphasis on expenditure in most of the literature as well as in policy reform misses a crucial element of the equilibrium determination of schooling quality. The concern for the implications of peer-group effects in schooling is further heightened by the evidence indicating that expenditure per se matters little (e.g., see Hanushek 1986). We return to this discussion after clarifying the implications of alternative policies and welfare effects.

7.4.2   Equilibrium with School Choice

The analysis of school choice with no frictions is straightforward. Households select schools without constraint in the second stage of figure 7.2. We assume schools face no capacity constraints and must admit all comers.[22] School finance continues to entail an allocation of funds to schools so as to equalize expenditure per student. Those who send their child to school in the "other neighborhood" bear no transportation or other transactions costs (introduced later).[23] Lacking evidence on productivity effects of intradistrict choice, we hold fixed the schooling production function $q(\cdot)$.

The immediate implication is that the exercise of school choice must lead to equal school qualities in equilibrium, and, since expenditures are equalized, $\theta_1 = \theta_2$. Further, indifference to residence is implied, so that $p_2 = p_1$ ($= c$). Voting equilibrium continues to reflect the preference of a household with median ratio of income to housing price. Because housing prices do not vary, only one type of household has median preference: those families with median income (who can live in either neighborhood). The solution to equation (9) substituting y_{med} for y_{p1} is the outcome of the voting equilibrium.[24] We have established the following proposition:

PROPOSITION 4. *Equilibrium values with frictionless choice are given by*

$$(10)\, p_1 = p_2 = c; \quad \theta_1 = \theta_2 = \overline{\theta}; \quad \text{and} \quad X_1 = X_2 = \frac{\alpha}{1 + \alpha}\left(1 - \frac{c}{y_{med}}\right)\overline{y},$$

where $\overline{\theta}$ denotes the mean ability in the entire population. Households with median income are pivotal in the voting equilibrium. The residential allocation

---

22. The same results obtain if there are capacity constraints, but every applicant, independent of residence, has the same probability of admittance. Aggregate uncertainties disappear because of the atomism of households.

23. We also ignore any possible changes in transportation costs borne by taxpayers. Explicit consideration of transportation costs borne by taxpayers would not effect the set of equilibrium residential and school choices, since these costs are invariant to individual choices.

24. The parameter restrictions provided in footnote 21 continue to be sufficient.

is indeterminate. Any allocation assigning half the population to each neighborhood is an equilibrium. Any set of school choices resulting in $\theta_1 = \theta_2$ is an equilibrium set.

Comparing equilibria, introduction of (frictionless) school choice leads to higher θ_1 and lower θ_2. Using equations (9) and (10) and that $y_{med} > y_{p1}$, the tax rate and expenditure are higher under choice. This is explained by an income effect on voting from a lower p_2. The strongest implication is that households with income below the median attend better schools unambiguously. Further normative and quantitative analysis is in section 7.5.

Interneighborhood Transportation Costs

We now introduce friction in the exercise of school choice. We assume that it costs any household T to send its child to school in the other neighborhood. Hence, for example, intraneighborhood transportation is costless (or provided), but households bear a private cost of T to transport their children between neighborhoods as across a "Hoxby river" (Hoxby 2000a).

Transportation costs effectively prohibit the exercise of choice if T exceeds the housing price differential that arises without choice. Here equilibrium is as though choice is not allowed. Letting p_2^* denote neighborhood 2's housing price in the equilibrium without choice, we then suppose

(11) $T < p_2^* - c,$

which is clearly the more realistic case.

We describe an "interior equilibrium," one in which some but not all households exercise choice. Figure 7.5 depicts an interior equilibrium allocation.[25] A threshold income below the median, y_1, divides households according to the neighborhood where their children attend school. Those with income below y_1 live in neighborhood 1, and their children attend school there. Those with higher income send their children to the better school in neighborhood 2 but are indifferent to their neighborhood of residence. A number of households equal to one-half the population drawn from the latter group must live in neighborhood 2 for housing-market clearance. Their residential indifference is supported by a housing price differential equal to the transportation cost:

(12) $p_2 - c = T.$

Living in neighborhood 1 and paying the transportation cost is equivalent to avoiding it but paying the higher housing price in neighborhood 2.

25. Cullen, Jacob, and Levitt (2000) provide evidence of sorting due to public school choice among high schools in Chicago that is consistent with the equilibrium we describe. When instrumenting for peer groups to correct for potential endogeneities they fail, however, to find evidence of peer effects on graduation rates.

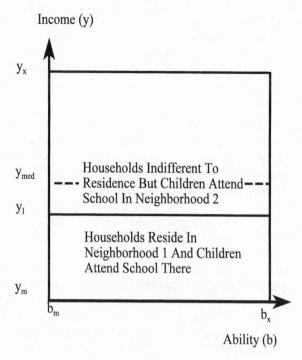

Income (y)

y_x

y_{med}
y_I

Households Indifferent To
Residence But Children Attend
School In Neighborhood 2

Households Reside In
Neighborhood 1 And Children
Attend School There

y_m

b_m b_x

Ability (b)

Fig. 7.5   Residences and peer groups with public-school choice and transport cost

Let $\theta_i^*(y_i)$, $i = 1, 2$, denote the implied mean ability in neighborhood i. Since $E[b\,|\,y]$ is increasing, $\theta_2^* > \theta_1^*$ for all y_i, although housing-market clearance requires $y_i < y_{med}$. Indifference to transporting one's child from neighborhood 1 to 2 for schooling identifies y_i:

(13) $$T = [y_i(1 - t) - c][1 - R(y_i)^\gamma],$$

where $R(y_i) \equiv \theta_1^*/\theta_2^*$.

Voting equilibrium can be determined analogously to the previous models with $T + c$ replacing the housing price for those who live in neighborhood 1 and transport their child to school in neighborhood 2. All those with $y > y_i$ pay "effective housing price" equal to p_2. There is always a median preference voter with $y > y_i$, whose income we denote y_{p2} (and there may or may not be one having $y < y_i$). By ordering households according to their income divided by effective housing price, one can identify y_{p2} as detailed in the appendix. Replacing y_{p1} with y_{p2} in equation (9), we compute[26]

(14) $$t = \frac{\alpha}{1 + \alpha}\left(1 - \frac{p_2}{y_{p2}}\right); \quad \text{and} \quad X = t\overline{y}.$$

26. The parameter restrictions in footnote 21 remain sufficient.

PROPOSITION 5. *Assume equation (11) is satisfied and any voting equilibrium permits everyone to afford housing. A solution (p_2, y_l, t, y_{p2}, X) with $y_l <$ y_{med} to equations (12) through (14), with y_{p2} as calculated in the appendix, and with $\theta_i = \theta_i^*(y_l)$, $i = 1, 2$, is an interior equilibrium with allocation depicted in figure 7.5 (and with any mass equal to one-half of households having $y > y_l$ living in neighborhood 2).*

Although existence and uniqueness of an interior equilibrium are not guaranteed, we find unique interior equilibrium for a range of T in our computational model of section 7.5. Another possibility is a "boundary equilibrium" having $p_2 = T + c$, but where everyone attends school in neighborhood 2. Here T is low enough that choice induces everyone to get the same schooling.

Relative to the no-choice equilibrium, the exercise of choice by those with below-median income is on average associated with a negative peer-group externality to both those who stay behind and attend school in neighborhood 1, and to those with above-median income. Both θ_1 and θ_2 decline because $E[b|y]$ is an increasing function of y. The decline in neighborhood 1, borne by the poorest segment of the population, supports the concerns of some critics of choice: Those least equipped to exercise choice suffer from its introduction. Because the outcome of the voting equilibrium changes, we must quantify effects to pursue further normative analysis, which is taken up later in section 7.5.

7.4.3   Multiple Jurisdictions: Tiebout Equilibrium

It is of interest to compare the single-district equilibria above to the more decentralized provision regime, in which education finance is highly localized. Here the two neighborhoods are assumed to correspond to two political jurisdictions for the determination of the tax rate and per-student expenditure. Policy dictates that households' children must attend school in their neighborhood-district of residence. Otherwise, we maintain the properties of the model including Cobb-Douglas preferences (hence equation [3]), the same housing capacities of 1/2 in each now-jurisdiction, and $E[b|y]$ increasing in y. As in the single-district model without choice, the school-choice stage is trivial because, again, school is dictated by residence. This version of our model is akin to an environment with small school districts that is fairly densely populated as in areas of Pennsylvania, New Hampshire, Ohio, and Vermont, for example.[27]

We focus again on equilibrium with differentiated schools for the same reasons as above. First, we have the following proposition:

---

27. The 1993–94 respective ratios of high schools to districts in these states were 1.20, 1.03, 1.27, and 1.02 (U.S. Department of Education 1994).

PROPOSITION 6. *Any equilibrium with differentiated schools exhibits the following: (a) stratification by income (independent of ability); and (b) boundary indifference and strict preference within boundaries.*

PROOF. Using equation (2), calculate the sign of the utility difference (Δ) from residing in neighborhood 2 versus 1: sgn Δ = sgn $\{[(1 - t_2)q_2 - (1 - t_1)q_1]y + (p_1q_1 - p_2q_2)\}$. Housing market clearance implies that one-half the population lives in each neighborhood. Linearity of Δ in y then implies either income stratification (that is independent of ability) and differentiated schools or that Δ vanishes for every income. The latter case is an unstable equilibrium having everyone indifferent. Given that Δ does not vanish for some y, boundary indifference for $y = y_{med}$ and strict preference otherwise are then implied by the linearity.

Residential choices and peer groups are then the same as in the single-jurisdiction model without choice. Each neighborhood or jurisdiction chooses its own tax rate, however. Households within a neighborhood face the same housing price, and voting equilibrium is calculated as above. The households with median preferences in neighborhoods 1 and 2 have first-quartile income (y_{q1}) and third-quartile income (y_{q3}), respectively. The voter's problems are analogous to equation (8) with the obvious substitutions:[28]

(15)
$$t_1 = \frac{\alpha}{1 + \alpha}\left(1 - \frac{p_1}{y_{q1}}\right); \quad X_1 = t_1\bar{y}_1;$$

(16)
$$t_2 = \frac{\alpha}{1 + 1}\left(1 - \frac{p_2}{y_{q3}}\right); \quad \text{and} \quad X_2 = t_2\bar{y}_2,$$

where $\bar{y}_i$, i = 1, 2, denotes mean income in neighborhood i. Note that it is not immediately clear where tax rates are higher and where per student expenditure is higher. Boundary indifference implies that prices satisfy

(17)
$$[y_{med}(1 - t_2) - p_2]q_2 = [y_{med}(1 - t_1) - p_1]q_1,$$

which allows us to demonstrate the following:

PROPOSITION 7. $q_2 > q_1$ *in equilibrium.*

PROOF. If $p_2 \leq p_1$, then $t_2 > t_1$ and $X_2 > X_1$, both by equations (15) and (16). The better peer group in neighborhood 2 then implies the result. For the case of $p_1 < p_2$, suppose to the contrary that $q_2 \leq q_1$. From equation (17), then, $[y_{med}(1 - t_2) - p_2] \geq [y_{med}(1 - t_1) - p_1]$, implying $p_2 - p_1 \leq (t_1 - t_2)y_{med}$. Substitute from equations (15) and (16) for the ts in the latter, yielding

(18)
$$p_2 - p_1 \leq \frac{\alpha}{1 + \alpha}\left(p_2\frac{y_{med}}{y_{q3}} - p_1\frac{y_{med}}{y_{q1}}\right).$$

---

28. Again we assume that t is not at its upper bound, and again the conditions in footnote 21 continue to be sufficient, assuming $p_1 = c$.

Since $\alpha/(1 + \alpha) < 1$ and $y_{q3} > y_{med} > y_{q1}$, equation (18) contradicts $p_2 > p_1$.

Proposition A2 in the appendix provides conditions for existence of differentiated equilibrium. These conditions also imply that the housing price will be lower in the poorer district, hence $p_1 = c$. They are satisfied in realistic cases, including our computational analysis in the next section.

Relative to the single-jurisdiction, multineighborhood environment without choice, one would expect here lower per-student expenditure in the poor neighborhood-district and the opposite in the wealthy neighborhood-district due to the changes in the tax base. A wider dispersion in school quality under multiple jurisdictions is then implied. The theoretical analysis is, however, obscured by changes across the equilibria in the identities of the pivotal voters and housing prices. We explore this issue computationally in section 7.5.

For our Cobb-Douglas specification with fixed housing capacities, residential choices and thus peer groups are exactly the same, with no school choice whether or not neighborhoods are also political jurisdictions. This illustrates a central result of this paper: Peer-group effects alone can lead to income-stratified equilibrium and school quality differences, as in a Tiebout equilibrium with local public finance.[29] If we depart from a Cobb-Douglas specification or assume upward-sloping housing supplies, then the residential allocation will vary somewhat across the two regimes. However, this is only to the extent that educational expenditure is important to school quality. In the Cobb-Douglas case with upward-sloping housing supplies, for example, the allocations converge as $\alpha \to 0$. If educational expenditure has small effects at the margin, as most evidence indicates (see Hanushek 1986, 1997 and Betts 1996), then policies that more evenly distribute educational funds will not much reduce stratification absent school choice.[30]

Interjurisdictional school choice is also worthy of study.[31] The analysis of interjurisdictional school choice depends on how the choice policy implements school finance when choice is exercised. Here we briefly summarize some results, because space constraints prevent a complete presentation. In an early version of this paper (Epple and Romano 1995), we analyzed frictionless interjurisdictional choice assuming that those who cross district boundaries bring with them their own jurisdiction's locally determined per-student expenditure. This policy leads to a nonstratified outcome and ho-

29. As discussed in section 7.2, an alternative version of this result can be found in Benabou (1993, 1996).

30. It is correct to observe that even for small α in the Cobb-Douglas case, stratification may result with multiple jurisdictions if $E[b \mid y]$ is invariant to y, and equilibrium will not be stratified in the single-jurisdiction model. Note, however, that only slightly rising $E[b \mid y]$ gets back stratification in the latter model. Moreover, for utility specifications satisfying equation (4) and $E[b \mid y]$ flat, near equivalence holds as expenditure effects disappear.

31. In 1993–94, 28.6 percent of school districts had interdistrict choice policies (U.S. Department of Education 1996). However, only 1.6 percent of public school students residing in these districts attended school outside of the district where they resided.

mogeneous schools, but with a severe free-rider problem in school finance: Voting to raise one's local tax would attract outsiders (or reduce exit), and this externality would lead to substantially lower schooling expenditure. Anticipating this, an interjurisdictional choice policy might require that a household exercising choice become a member of its chosen school's jurisdiction for purposes of school finance. That is, it pays its chosen district's tax rate while being allowed to vote there on the school budget.[32] We show in the appendix that this policy would frequently lead to the same outcome as does choice in a single jurisdiction if there are no frictions (i.e., nontax costs) to exercising choice. The logic is that housing prices must be equalized in equilibrium, and potential differences in tax rates will frequently not alone be enough to support an outcome with stratified schools. However, as we discuss more fully below, potential recipient districts generally have an incentive to resist accepting students from outside the district, casting doubt on the extent to which choice is likely to be frictionless.

7.5 Computational Analysis and Welfare Effects

We begin with a general discussion of welfare issues that will facilitate the interpretation of the computational results that follow. Although much of our analysis concerns traditional efficiency measures, this is presented with serious caveats. First, education is regarded by many as a primary means to lessen equity problems, and we are not unsympathetic to this view. Second, equity aside, long-term social externalities associated with low educational achievement or wide variance in educational achievement may exist (e.g., crime and resentment). For both these reasons, it is important to also consider the distribution of educational achievement.

A third caveat concerns education as an investment rather than a consumption good. If education is an investment good, then our model implicitly assumes imperfect opportunities for borrowing on future earnings, which constrains all households. This follows from our assumption that household demand for educational quality increases with income.[33] Such credit constraints are also consistent with Peterson et al.'s findings (chap. 4 in this volume) that small partial vouchers are *needed* to induce poor families to switch to private schools in spite of relatively large educational gains. The standard static analysis does not properly measure welfare changes under the investment interpretation; one must measure and value changes in aggregate achievement and factor this into the welfare measure. Our belief is that education has both investment and consumption value.

32. Whether outsiders are allowed to vote or not does not matter to equilibrium.
33. Actually, our equilibrium results do not require a binding borrowing constraint on high-income households, specifically those with income above the maximum income of any pivotal voter. If demand ceases to increase with income above this threshold, all our equilibrium results continue to hold.

With these reservations in mind, we turn to standard efficiency analysis. Understanding properties of Pareto efficient (PE) allocations provides perspective for understanding the variation in welfare (producer surplus plus compensating variation) across the policy regimes analyzed below. In examining PE allocations, we assume that there are at most two schools and that an allocation entails an assignment of all students to a school (i.e., no schooling is not an option). Let $A_i(b, y) \in [0,1]$ denote the proportion of students of type (b, y) attending school i, $i = 1, 2$, so that $A_1(b, y) + A_2(b, y) = 1$ for all (b, y). For the applications we study, A_i will equal 0 or 1 for all types: That is, efficient student bodies entail no overlap of types. We assume no transportation costs so that neighborhood residence is irrelevant to efficiency. Set $p_i = c$, $i = 1, 2$, giving the anonymous land owners no rents. Proposition 8 is the main result in Epple and Romano (2000). It includes a description of the "social marginal cost" of a student attending school i, which we denote SMC_i. Also, let $r_i(b, y)$ denote the "regulated price" that a social planner charges type (b, y) to attend school i. Actually, $r_i(b, y)$ will turn out to be a function only of b at the optimum as we will see.

Proposition 8 is a variant of the Second Fundamental Welfare Theorem in economics.

PROPOSITION 8. *If appropriate lump-sum transfers of income are arranged, then every PE allocation can be achieved by utility-maximizing school choices, with, for all (b, y), students paying prices*

$$(19) \qquad r_i(b, y) = \text{SMC}_i \equiv X_i + \frac{q_\theta(X_i, \theta_i)}{q_X(X_i, \theta_i)}(\theta_i - b), \quad i = 1, 2,$$

with X_i satisfying

$$(20) \quad \int_s \int A_i(b, y) \frac{\partial U^i(b,y)/X_i}{\partial U^i(b,y)/\partial y} f(b, y) db dy = \int_s \int A_i(b, y) f(b, y) db dy, \quad i = 1, 2;$$

$$(21) \quad U^i(b, y) \equiv U[y - c + R(b, y) - r_i(b, y), a(q(X_i, E_i), b], \quad i = 1, 2;$$

$R(b, y)$ denoting the lump-sum transfer function; and, finally, θ_i, $i = 1, 2$, and $A_i(b, y)$ as implied by utility-maximizing choices.
PROOF. See Epple and Romano (2000).

Here we provide only intuition for this result, with formal proof in the paper cited. With prices that reflect the peer externality in schools (and efficiently chosen expenditure levels), individual school choice will yield an efficient allocation. The social cost of type (b, y) entering school i is given by SMC_i, which equals the per-student expenditure plus the dollar value of the peer-group externality. The value of the peer externality is the last term in equation (19). q_θ/q_X equals the cost of maintaining quality as θ changes, which is multiplied by $(\theta_i - b)$, the change in θ_i that results due to student type b's attendance at i. Note that the peer-group cost of attendance is negative for students having ability higher than the student body's mean ($b >$ θ_i), and their SMC can then be negative. Note, too, that the social cost depends on b, but not y. Hence, efficient prices depend on ability but not income.

The efficient expenditure levels satisfy the within-school "Samuelsonian conditions" in equation (20) that equate the sum of marginal values of educational expenditure to marginal expenditure cost. Note that school budgets balance: Integrating r_i over the student body in i yields total expenditure in school i. The lump-sum transfers that are considered must also satisfy budget balance.

We next consider implications in the case of Cobb-Douglas utility that we have adopted. A natural benchmark allocation presumes no income transfers, so set $R(b, y) = 0$ for all (b, y). We have the following proposition:

PROPOSITION 9. *For Cobb-Douglas utility/achievement, the no-transfer PE allocation has (a)* $q_2 > q_1$; *(b) stratification by income with linear boundary locus*

$$(22) \quad y = \left[c + \frac{(X_2 + \eta_2 \theta_2)q_2 - (X_1 + \eta_1 \theta_1)q_1}{q_2 - q_1} \right] - \left(\frac{\eta_2 q_2 - \eta_1 q_1}{q_2 - q_1} \right) b,$$

where $\eta_i \equiv (q_\theta / q_X)_i$, $i = 1, 2$; *(c)*

$$(23) \quad X_i = \frac{\alpha}{1 + \alpha} (\bar{y}_i - c), \quad i = 1, 2; \quad \text{and}$$

$$(24) \quad \eta_i = \frac{\gamma}{(1 + \alpha)} \frac{(\bar{y}_i - c)}{\theta_i}, \quad i = 1, 2,$$

where $\bar{y}_i$ *and* θ_i *are the school means implied by the efficient allocation. Further,* $E[b|y]$ *invariant to* y *is sufficient for (d)* $\theta_2 > \theta_1$; *and (e) stratification by ability (hence, a downward-sloping boundary locus). If, also,* $\gamma < 1$, *then (f)* $X_2 > X_1$.

PROOF. See the appendix.

Figure 7.6 illustrates a typical PE allocation, calculated for the baseline case of our computational model (parameter values match those in table 7.1, discussed later). It is notable that a strict hierarchy ($q_2 > q_1$) is efficient even if expenditure is not permitted to vary (see Epple and Romano 1998). This is because relatively low-ability and high-income types are willing to subsidize relatively low-income and high-ability types to attend the same school. This necessarily leads to a downward-sloping boundary between the student bodies if b and y are independently distributed (results [d] and [e] in proposition 9). However, the efficient boundary locus will typically be downward sloping when $E[b|y]$ is increasing in y as well, as we have found consistently in numerous computations (e.g., figure 7.6 has $E[b|y]$ increasing in y). Similarly, the condition in part (f) of proposition 9 that $\gamma < 1$ for

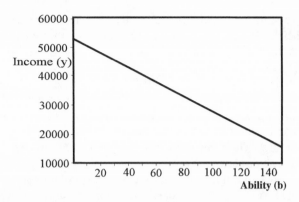

Fig. 7.6   Boundary locus for efficient allocation (parameter values are as in table 7.1)

$X_2 > X_1$ is unnecessary, but neither is it very restrictive. As discussed further in section 7.6, a private schooling equilibrium also results in a (nearly) PE allocation.

This PE benchmark reveals sources of inefficiency in the equilibrium outcomes above. Welfare gains would result on average from partitioning the population into schools as in figure 7.6. We then expect that the introduction of public-school choice will tend to reduce aggregate welfare, because the neighborhood-school partition is a better approximation to the efficient partition when $E[b|y]$ is increasing. The neighborhood-equilibrium partition is not, however, efficient in general. The implicit pricing of schools in neighborhood equilibrium through housing prices is independent of ability, hence, incorrectly accounts for the peer-group effect. As the correlation in (b, y) increases, partitioning only according to income as in the neighborhood equilibrium becomes a perfect substitute for partitioning by income and ability. While the point of partition in the neighborhood equilibrium will not generally be the efficient one since it is driven by neighborhood lines and their housing supplies, this line of argument suggests that welfare losses from choice will rise with the correlation in (b, y).

Proposition 9-f indicates that expenditure "typically" rises with school quality in the efficient allocation. Consider centralized versus decentralized finance (Tiebout equilibrium) without school choice. Comparing equations (15) and (16) to equation (23), we see decentralized finance provides a first approximation to the efficient outcome. A standard voting bias from median (neighborhood) income differing from mean income arises, as does another voting bias from the distorted housing price in neighborhood 2. Nevertheless, we expect that centralization of finance (absent choice) will lower welfare.

Tables 7.1 through 7.7 present representative results from our equilibrium computations, with table 7.1 the "baseline case." Throughout, we set the minimum population ability $b_m = 0$ and assume

$$\begin{bmatrix} \ln b \\ \ln(y-y_m) \end{bmatrix}$$

is distributed bivariate normal with covariance matrix

$$\begin{bmatrix} \sigma_b^2 & \rho\sigma_b\sigma_y \\ \rho\sigma_b\sigma_y & \sigma_y^2 \end{bmatrix}.$$

We set y_m = \$5,000 and use 1989 U.S. annual mean (\$36,360) and median (\$28,860) income to set the mean and variance of $\ln(y - y_m)$. We use the Cobb-Douglas utility achievement function, which (not obviously) implies that the mean of ability is irrelevant to our calculations.

We calibrate the distribution of ability so that it has the same median and mean as income. This may be motivated as follows. Consider a steady state and suppose that income is proportional to achievement. This provides a cardinalization of achievement, and this, coupled with the educational production function, induces a distribution on ability. For simplicity we calibrate ability for a case in which all students receive the same educational quality. In this case, the Cobb-Douglas achievement function implies that the logarithm of achievement is a linear function of the logarithm of ability. Hence, in this case, the steady-state lognormal distribution of income and the assumption that income is proportional to achievement imply that ability has a lognormal distribution as well. It is then convenient to choose the unit of measurement of ability so that the mean and median of ability for this case of equal school qualities equals the mean and median of income.

Two papers (Solon 1992; Zimmerman 1992) provide evidence on the correlation between fathers' and sons' income, and they are in agreement that the best point estimate of this correlation is approximately 0.4. Hence, we set $\rho = 0.4$ in the baseline case. This completes the calibration of $f(b, y)$.

We have set $\alpha = 0.06$ because this implies that a household's educational expenditure would be approximately 5.6 percent $= \alpha/(1 + \alpha)$ percent of its income, the actual U.S. educational percentage expenditure in 1989. Lacking evidence on the relative importance of peer group and expenditure, we also set $\gamma = 0.06$ in the baseline case. The value of β is irrelevant to our calculations, again due to the Cobb-Douglas specification.

We set the annual amortized construction cost of a house, c, equal to \$2,500. Last, we set the transportation cost of exercising interneighborhood choice equal to \$300 for the baseline case of choice with friction. We have computed equilibria with all parameters varied and report representative results here.

In addition to the equilibrium values in the four policy regimes, each table presents welfare changes relative to the neighborhood-school, one-district equilibrium. CV_i, $i = 1, 2$, denotes the mean compensating variation resulting from the policy change of those who reside in neighborhood i in the neighborhood-school, one-district equilibrium. Adding to $(1/2)(CV_1 +$

Table 7.1   Equilibrium Properties of Four Policy Regimes

	Neighborhood Schools, One District	Choice, One District ($T = 0$)	Neighborhood Schools, Two Districts	Choice, One District ($T = 300$)
θ_1	28,565	36,360	28,565	18,450
θ_2	44,154	36,360	44,155	36,777
t_1	0.051	0.052	0.049	0.051
t_2	0.051	0.052	0.051	0.051
X_1	1,858	1,880	958	1,865
X_2	1,858	1,880	2,706	1,865
p_2	3,142	2,500	4,569	2,800
q_1	2.91	2.95	2.79	2.83
q_2	2.98	2.95	3.05	2.95
y_I				10,434
CV_1		228	−612	−59
CV_2		87.2	−352.0	−181.0
Δp_2		−642	1,428	−342
ΔW		−163	232	−291

Notes: Peer measure of school $i = \theta_i$; tax rate in neighborhood i = t_i; per-student expenditure of school $i = X_i$; housing price in neighborhood 2 = p_2; quality of school $i = q_i$; minimum income attending school 2 in fourth equilibrium = y_I; mean compensating variation relative to first equilibrium in neighborhood $i = CV_i$; per capita welfare change relative to first equilibrium = ΔW; cost of exercising choice when feasible = T. Parameters of utility/cost function: $\alpha = 0.06$; $\gamma = 0.06$; $c = 2,500$. Parameters of distribution function: $\rho = 0.40$; $\bar{y} = 36,360$; $y_{med} = 28,860$; $\bar{b} = 36,360$; $b_{med} = 28,860$.

CV_2) the per capita change in the housing price in neighborhood 2 ($p_1 = c$ always), $\Delta p_2/2$, one obtains the per capita welfare change (denoted ΔW) equal to per capita producer surplus plus compensating variation. We have calculated equilibrium values without redistributing the land rents for simplicity and because it is not likely to have much effect on equilibrium. In so doing, we also avoid having to specify land ownership.[34]

Frictionless public-school choice lowers aggregate welfare in every simulation (including all unreported ones): That is, ΔW is consistently negative. Noting that per-student expenditure changes little from the benchmark (one-district, neighborhood) equilibrium, and in fact rises (because of the positive income effect on voting from the reduction in p_2), it is clear the welfare loss is explained by the homogenization of peer groups. Comparing table 7.1 to 7.2, the latter having a higher (lower) γ (α), one sees that the welfare loss rises with increased weight placed on the peer group in educational achievement. (See also table 7.3.) The reason that CV_2 is usually positive

34. In our computations, if all land is owned by those with income above the 3rd quartile, our equilibrium calculations would be unchanged. Skewing the top end of the net income distribution has no effect on equilibrium because no such households are ever pivotal decision-makers in our computations.

Table 7.2   **Equilibrium Properties of Four Policy Regimes**

	Neighborhood Schools, One District	Choice, One District ($T = 0$)	Neighborhood Schools, Two Districts	Choice, One District ($T = 300$)
θ_1	28,565	36,360	28,565	14,392
θ_2	44,155	36,360	44,155	36,390
t_1	0.043	0.043	0.042	0.043
t_2	0.043	0.043	0.043	0.043
X_1	1,561	1,581	806	1,564
X_2	1,561	1,581	2,283	1,564
p_2	3,254	2,500	4,456	2,800
q_1	2.96	3.01	2.87	2.82
q_2	3.05	3.01	3.11	3.01
y_I				7,598
CV_1		268.0	−512.0	−29.8
CV_2		101.8	−296.0	−196.6
Δp_2		−754	1,202	−554
ΔW		−192	196	−340

Notes: For definitions of variables, see notes to table 7.1. Parameters of utility/cost function: $\alpha = 0.05$; $\gamma = 0.07$; $c = 2,500$. Parameters of distribution function: $\rho = 0.40$; $\bar{y} = 36,360$; $y_{med} = 28,860$; $\bar{b} = 36,360$; $b_{med} = 28,860$. Change from table 7.1: α lower; γ higher.

Table 7.3   **Equilibrium Properties of Four Policy Regimes**

	Neighborhood Schools, One District	Choice, One District ($T = 0$)	Neighborhood Schools, Two Districts	Choice, One District ($T = 300$)
θ_1	28,565	36,360	28,565	22,074
θ_2	44,155	36,360	44,155	38,078
t_1	0.059	0.060	0.057	0.060
t_2	0.059	0.060	0.059	0.060
X_1	2,152	2,173	1,107	2,184
X_2	2,152	2,173	3,119	2,184
p_2	3,031	2,500	4,681	2,800
q_1	2.86	2.89	2.73	2.82
q_2	2.92	2.89	3.00	2.90
y_I				14,528
CV_1		188.4	−708.0	−62.8
CV_2		72.6	−406.0	−117.2
Δp_2		−530	1,650	−230
ΔW		−135	268	−205

Notes: For definitions of variables, see notes to table 7.1. Parameters of utility/cost function: $\alpha = 0.07$; $\gamma = 0.05$; $c = 2,500$. Parameters of distribution function: $\rho = 0.40$; $\bar{y} = 36,360$; $y_{med} = 28,860$; $\bar{b} = 36,360$; $b_{med} = 28,860$. Change from table 7.1: α higher; γ lower.

Table 7.4   Equilibrium Properties of Four Policy Regimes

	Neighborhood Schools, One District	Choice, One District ($T = 0$)	Neighborhood Schools, Two Districts	Choice, One District ($T = 500$)
θ_1	28,844	36,360	28,844	14,857
θ_2	47,876	36,360	47,876	37,630
t_1	0.051	0.052	0.049	0.051
t_2	0.051	0.052	0.050	0.051
X_1	1,849	1,880	958	1,862
X_2	1,849	1,880	2,686	1,862
p_2	3,461	2,500	4,870	3,000
q_1	2.88	2.95	2.77	2.80
q_2	3.00	2.95	3.07	2.96
y_I				12,352
CV_1		358.0	−612.0	−99.8
CV_2		178.2	−340	−224
Δp_2		−960	1,410	−460
ΔW		−212	229	−392

Notes: For definitions of variables, see notes to table 7.1. Parameters of utility/cost function: $\alpha = 0.06$; $\gamma = 0.06$; $c = 2,500$. Parameters of distribution function: $\rho = 0.60$; $\bar{y} = 36,360$; $y_{med} = 28,860$; $\bar{b} = 36,360$; $b_{med} = 28,860$. Change from table 7.1: ρ higher; T higher.

when choice is introduced is because the housing price p_2 declines—but someone bears this loss.

Although choice causes an overall welfare loss, those residing initially in neighborhood 1 consistently gain on average from its introduction. This holds when we assign to this group a proportion of the loss in producer surplus in the housing market from choice equal to its income share (these calculations not shown in the tables).

Absent public-school choice, decentralizing the finance decision by going from one jurisdiction (or district) to two consistently increases welfare, but it also increases the dispersion of school qualities. Since peer groups in schools are unchanged, these result because of changes in educational expenditures. Not surprisingly, the housing price in neighborhood 2 rises substantially. Those initially residing in neighborhood 1 lose out on average from decentralization of finance, and this persists if they are assigned their income-proportional share of the increased producer surplus in the housing market (not shown). Hence, again, the poor are affected in the direction opposite to the average.

For the case of choice with a transport cost, we set $T = 300$ in the computations, letting it vary once ($T = 500$ in table 7.4). With one exception (table 7.5), we find $T = 300$ (or 500) induces a large percentage of those with income below the median to exercise choice and attend school in neighborhood 2, that percentage ranging from about 72.0 to 99.7. Compare this equilibrium to frictionless choice with one district (ignoring table 7.5 for the

Table 7.5   Equilibrium Properties of Four Policy Regimes

	Neighborhood Schools, One District	Choice, One District ($T = 0$)	Neighborhood Schools, Two Districts	Choice, One District ($T = 300$)
θ_1	32,427	36,360	32,427	32,102
θ_2	40,293	36,360	40,293	39,923
t_1	0.051	0.052	0.049	0.051
t_2	0.051	0.052	0.051	0.051
X_1	1,869	1,880	958	1,863
X_2	1,869	1,880	2,727	1,863
p_2	2,822	2,500	4,268	2,800
q_1	2.93	2.95	2.82	2.93
q_2	2.97	2.95	3.04	2.97
y_I				26,966
CV_1		108.60	−612.0	−8.44
CV_2		27.60	−362.00	−4.84
Δp_2		−322	1,446	−22
ΔW		−92.9	236.0	−17.7

Notes: For definitions of variables, see notes to table 7.1. Parameters of utility/cost function: $\alpha = 0.06$; $\gamma = 0.06$; $c = 2,500$. Parameters of distribution function: $\rho = 0.20$; $\bar{y} = 36,360$; $y_{med} = 28,860$; $\bar{b} = 36,360$; $b_{med} = 28,860$. Change from table 7.1: ρ lower.

moment). The voting equilibria are not much different, so expenditures vary little. The welfare loss from choice with transport costs exceeds that from frictionless choice by about the amount of the transportation costs expended. Assigning the losses in producer surplus again by income shares (not shown in the tables), we find that the greater welfare loss under choice with transport costs is borne largely by those with below-median income. Those that exercise choice obviously pay the transportation costs. Those that choose not to commute face a substantially diminished peer group.

The exceptional case of table 7.5 has low correlation of income and ability. The per capita welfare loss relative to the benchmark equilibrium equals only $17.65. Because the peer group difference is small in the neighborhood equilibrium, little incentive to exercise choice is present, and less than 9 percent of those with below median income do so. Note, too, that the price difference between neighborhoods ($p_2 - c$) is only $322 in the benchmark equilibrium for the parameter settings in table 7.5. This is another manifestation of the limited value of the peer quality gain to migration in this case. By contrast, for the other cases we report in the tables, the housing price differential in the benchmark case is much larger, ranging between $530 and $960. Table 7.6 has a higher construction cost of housing than in the baseline case. This has a negative income effect, manifest in lower schooling expenditures in all equilibria and less exercise of choice when there is a transportation cost.

Table 7.7 has a more right-skewed income distribution, holding constant

Table 7.6   **Equilibrium Properties of Four Policy Regimes**

	Neighborhood Schools, One District	Choice, One District $(T = 0)$	Neighborhood Schools, Two Districts	Choice, One District $(T = 300)$
θ_1	28,565	36,360	28,565	21,416
θ_2	44,155	36,360	44,155	37,748
t_1	0.048	0.049	0.045	0.049
t_2	0.048	0.049	0.049	0.049
X_1	1,752	1,773	873	1,790
X_2	1,752	1,773	2,612	1,790
p_2	4,605	4,000	5,952	4,300
q_1	2.90	2.94	2.78	2.85
q_2	2.97	2.94	3.05	2.95
y_I				13,644
CV_1		208.0	−556.0	−50.4
CV_2		47.0	−298.0	−126.6
Δp_2		−606	1,346	−306
ΔW		−166	247	−241

Notes: For definitions of variables, see notes to table 7.1. Parameters of utility/cost function: $\alpha = 0.06$; $\gamma = 0.06$; $c = 4,000$. Parameters of distribution function: $\rho = 0.40$; $\bar{y} = 36,360$; $y_{med} = 28,860$; $\bar{b} = 36,360$; $b_{med} = 28,860$. Change from table 7.1: c higher.

Table 7.7   **Equilibrium Properties of Four Policy Regimes**

	Neighborhood Schools, One District	Choice, One District $(T = 0)$	Neighborhood Schools, Two Districts	Choice, One District $(T = 300)$
θ_1	28,565	36,360	28,565	22,860
θ_2	44,155	36,360	44,155	38,534
t_1	0.051	0.052	0.048	0.053
t_2	0.051	0.052	0.051	0.053
X_1	2,300	2,326	839	2,365
X_2	2,300	2,326	3,708	2,365
p_2	3,142	2,500	5,139	2,800
q_1	2.94	2.99	2.77	2.91
q_2	3.02	2.99	3.11	3.00
y_I				12,905
CV_1		200.0	−824.0	−31.4
CV_2		−126.4	−134.8	−192.0
Δp_2		−642	1,996	−342
ΔW		−284	519	−283

Notes: For definitions of variables, see notes to table 7.1. Parameters of utility/cost function: $\alpha = 0.06$; $\gamma = 0.06$; $c = 2,500$. Parameters of distribution function: $\rho = 0.40$; $\bar{y} = 45,000$; $y_{med} = 28,860$; $\bar{b} = 36,360$; $b_{med} = 28,860$. Change from table 7.1: variance y higher.

the median income. This is associated with greater inframarginal demand for segregation by the relatively wealthy. This amplifies the aggregate welfare loss from frictionless choice and the aggregate welfare gain from neighborhoods becoming jurisdictions.

An important warning concerning our normative analysis is that our model abstracts from potential productivity gains from increased competition among schools for students. Hoxby (2000a) finds such gains when district competition for students increases, as would occur with finance decentralization. Increased school choice within districts might have similar effects. Our model emphasizes the likely sorting effects of such policies. Although we do *not* by any means believe our welfare findings to be definitive, we think it crucial in policy design to anticipate potential changes in school composition.

7.6 Vouchers and Private Schooling

We have examined the consequences of introducing public-school choice into a school district. One can interpret this choice policy as a voucher equal to the average cost of schooling that can be used at any public school. Now we examine the consequences of allowing vouchers to be used at a private school. We focus on a voucher policy that will eliminate the public sector, where the comparison will be between the allocations in panels B and C of figure 7.1.

The choice program we examine provides a voucher of exogenous amount to any student who chooses to attend a school other than his neighborhood public school, the voucher financed out of the income tax (adjusted to cover the cost of the voucher). Importantly, private schools admitting voucher students are unconstrained in all regards. Private schools can pursue whatever admission and tuition policies they would like, including selective admissions, tuition on top of the voucher, and giving of scholarships and fellowships. Hence, we examine a laissez-faire voucher system as described by Friedman (1962). Because of the free reign of the market (and the magnitude of the voucher), the voucher equilibrium can also be interpreted as an equilibrium with only private provision allowed, but with a linear income tax that redistributes income so everyone can pay the average cost of schooling. As we will discuss further, alternative voucher policies that place restrictions on schools accepting voucher students may have different effects.

We modify the model above in two ways. Because private schools have incentives to become very specialized in the student bodies they serve, we introduce economies of scale into the provision of schooling, and this keeps them from becoming infinitely specialized. We do this by making an element of school cost independent of quality-producing inputs, and these "custodial costs" are first rising and concave in the number of students, then rising and convex. Expenditure on quality-producing inputs (X) is in addition to the latter costs and continues to exhibit constant returns to scale. For any per-student expenditure on quality, the average cost is then U-shaped in the number of students with the same efficient scale.

The second modification of the model is to simplify by exogenously fixing the expenditure per student on quality in every school, public or private, at the same level. All variation in school quality is then due to variation in the peer group. This simplification does not affect the qualitative nature of sorting in equilibrium. We note the expected quantitative effects of allowing expenditure variation. The production function of educational quality q continues to be as in equation (2), does utility, except now X is fixed exogenously in all schools. Other than through effects on the tax rate, none of our following welfare calculations are affected by the level of X because of the Cobb-Douglas specification of utility and achievement. Later we consider differences in productivity of public and private schools, but we assume initially that they are equally productive.

Details of the modified calibration are in Epple and Romano (1998). We calibrate the cost function of schooling so that the efficient scale of operation is 3.03 percent of the population, with schooling cost of approximately $4,200 per pupil. How these costs break down between custodial costs and expenditure on quality-enhancing inputs is irrelevant to the calculations we do (again due to the Cobb-Douglas specification). The calibrated utility function is the same as in the benchmark model above. We use the same calibration of the income distribution but with the simplification that minimum income equals 0. Hence, we also set $c = 0$. Again we set the correlation between income and ability equal to 0.4. We calibrate the ability distribution using the same (steady-state) strategy as above, but here we take account of the fact that the ratio of workers to school-age children is 2.6, implying a tighter ability distribution with mean 13,600 and median 11,300.

Private schools are modeled as in Epple and Romano (1998). They choose tuition and admission policies to maximize profits, and there is free entry and exit. They can determine a student's ability and his or her household income, implying that they can condition tuition and admission on these characteristics as competition allows. They take as given every student type's willingness to pay for school quality. Assuming there is adequate demand for quality of schooling for private schools to arise, equilibrium satisfies some basic properties, which we briefly summarize.[35]

Refer to panel A of figure 7.1, which depicts the case in this calibration with public school choice and no voucher, where four private schools then

---

35. Precise equilibrium fails to exist due to a variant of the integer problem, so we calculate an approximate equilibrium. See Epple and Romano (1998) for details.

enter and each earns (approximately) zero profits. The private schools serve nonoverlapping student sets as delineated by the four boundary loci in the figure. Private schools each serve student bodies of size below the efficient scale (the density of types is low in the upper right of the $[b, y]$ plane), in a fashion similar to that of Chamberlin monopolistically competitive equilibria. Within each private school, relatively lower-ability and higher-income types mix with relatively higher-ability and lower-income types. Equilibrium pricing entails cross-subsidization within a private school from the former to the latter students. Essentially, the higher-income types are purchasing the positive peer effect of the higher-ability types. In fact, the peer externality is fully internalized: Prices to all students on the margin of switching schools equal social marginal cost as in equation (19), with inframarginal students paying somewhat higher prices as schools take away consumer surplus.[36] A strict quality hierarchy of private schools always results. Because demand for schooling quality rises with income, the lack of entry barriers (other than a free public schooling alternative!) leads the private sector to refine the quality of schooling limited only by economies of scale. The internalization of the peer effect implies an efficient allocation of the private-school students among the private schools that enter. When public schools remain, they are of lower quality than any private school.

The equilibrium with the voucher has a $4,200 voucher with allocation of types into schools as depicted in panel B of figure 7.1. This voucher, equal to average educational cost at the efficient scale, wipes out public provision. Because we have fixed quality-enhancing expenditures and provided a voucher that can cover these costs, the pricing flexibility of private schools permits them to engender student bodies that are more efficient than a public school would attract. This is not, however, to suggest a Pareto improvement from introducing a $4,200 voucher relative to the no-voucher equilibrium of panel A. Private schools cream-skim high-ability students as they enter with negative externalities for those of lower abilities who end up in schools with weakened peer groups. Equilibrium properties are as in panel A of figure 7.1, but, obviously, there is substantially more income and ability stratification and variability in school qualities. There are thirty-four private schools, all serving less than (but close to) 3.03 percent of the population of students.

If expenditures are allowed to vary in public and private schools, the level of the voucher necessary to eliminate public provision depends primarily on the following factors. Although private schools have the increased advantage of being able to set expenditures as their clientele prefers, per-student expenditure in public schools is subsidized by taxation of private-school students (maintaining here the assumption of majority choice of tax-

---

36. Our warnings discussed in section 7.5 concerning efficiency measures apply here as well.

expenditure policy).[37] At the same time, as the voucher rises and students are drawn into the private sector, political support for taxation to finance private schools declines.[38] Due to the latter fact, the voucher need not be too high before the public sector is eliminated. Importantly, the qualitative nature of the equilibrium allocation—for example, the "diagonalized stratification across private schools"—remains with expenditure variation.

We now compare the voucher equilibrium to the neighborhood schooling equilibrium with neighborhood lines drawn to minimize schooling costs. Hence, the neighborhood equilibrium has thirty-three equally sized schools with allocation of types into schools as depicted in panel C of figure 7.1. Private schools would be unlikely to enter without any voucher.

The panels of figure 7.7 provide information by student type on the effects of a voucher that covers average schooling cost. The upper panel shows the welfare effect as a percentage of income, equal to the (negative of the) compensating variation from moving to the voucher equilibrium. Housing prices everywhere drop to their construction cost (0) in the voucher equilibrium. In the welfare calculation, we assume that households own the land where they reside in the initial equilibrium, so the declines in housing prices are irrelevant to welfare (i.e., households pay themselves less rent). The welfare change is then entirely due to changes in school quality and payments for school, with the latter being equal to any tuition after the voucher plus tax changes. Tax changes are close to zero, since the tax required to finance the voucher approximately equals the tax otherwise used to finance the public school system. Thus, tax changes can be ignored in the discussion. Keep in mind that tuition varies continuously with student ability and income in each private school. Thus, although the average after-voucher tuition is (approximately) equal to zero, virtually every student will pay a net positive or negative tuition in the voucher equilibrium.

Before discussing the welfare effects, it is useful to describe the lower panel of figure 7.7. This panel shows percentage changes in "normed achievement," which equals our achievement measure raised to the power $1/\beta$ (see equation [2] for achievement, a). Normed achievement can be given several interpretations. First, its changes are proportional to changes in school quality (with factor of proportionality $1/\beta$). Second, proportional changes in normed achievement due to changes in school quality have equivalent effects on utility and achievement as the same proportional change in own student ability. Third, related to the latter and given our calibration of the utility function, changes in normed achievement approximate changes in future earnings while employed.

37. The expenditure flexibility of private schools need not just imply relatively high expenditure levels. With our laissez-faire voucher policy, private schools may form that serve the poorest students and use some voucher money to provide all students with fellowships. Of course, the voucher policy might be modified to prevent this.
38. The effects of this on voting equilibrium are analyzed in Epple and Romano (1996).

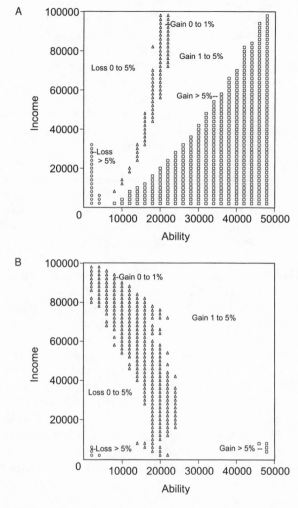

Fig. 7.7 *A,* **Welfare effects of voucher;** *B,* **achievement in private schools relative to public schools**

The average welfare change from the voucher is only about $55. It is positive because the student sorting is Pareto efficient in the voucher equilibrium. It is small in part because the neighborhood equilibrium has many schools that also sort students by ability and income to the extent that income and ability are correlated. For example, the average welfare gain in going from the equilibrium in panel A, which has little sorting, to the voucher equilibrium is larger (although still only about $185). If private schools could choose their expenditure levels, the average gain would be larger as well.

Although, on average, there are gains from moving to the voucher equilibrium from the neighborhood school equilibrium, the effects of the voucher are not distributed equally. Gains and losses for many are substantial relative to the average effect. Beginning at the lower right of panel A of figure 7.7 and moving counterclockwise, we see that the welfare gains decline and ultimately become negative. Students in the lower right triangle in this panel gain the most as a percentage of their household income. These are poor but relatively high-ability students. As one can see from panel B of this figure, most of these students are in better schools in the voucher equilibrium than in the neighborhood school equilibrium, because private schools sort students on ability to the benefit of higher-ability students. Comparing these two panels, we see that some of these students (e.g., those with low income and moderate ability) end up in lower-quality schools but nonetheless have a welfare gain. They are above-average students in the schools they attend, and they thus generate a positive peer externality. As a result, they obtain a negative net tuition (i.e., a scholarship), yielding a financial gain sufficiently large to offset the monetary value to them of their achievement loss.

More generally, tuition discounts are part of the gain to all relatively high-ability students. However, inspection of the right portion of panel A reveals that gains decline as income rises for a given ability. High-ability students gain less from switching to the voucher equilibrium primarily because they were in relatively high-quality neighborhood public schools.

Moving sufficiently counterclockwise in the (b, y) plane, one finds welfare losses. Thus, welfare losses accrue to relatively low-ability students. It is useful to consider separately the impacts on high- and low-income students in this low-ability group. As can be seen from panel B of figure 7.7, the high-income, low-ability students are in higher-quality schools in the voucher equilibrium. They nonetheless experience a welfare loss because they pay a tuition premium in the voucher equilibrium to gain access to schools with relatively high-quality peer group. Turning to low-income members of the low-ability group, we see from panel B that they attend lower-quality schools; they do not have high enough income to be willing to pay the tuition premium to attend a higher-quality school. From panel B, we see, not surprisingly, that they also experience a welfare loss. The poorest and lowest-ability students end up in worse schools and have to pay a positive net tuition.

Although the average welfare gain is positive, a majority equal to about 60 percent is worse off from the voucher. We emphasized earlier that our analysis abstracts from potential productivity gains from increased competition for students (see Hoxby, chap. 8 in this volume). On top of the evidence, there are several reasons to believe that competing private schools will more efficiently provide education (for given student body) than will schools in a neighborhood system. Most important, students attending a low-productivity private school can switch to a new efficient entrant at little or no cost. Neighborhood public schools are much more insulated from competition, because switching schools would require moving and paying a housing price premium. Households with children at different educational levels would be frequently forced to switch schools for every child when moving between neighborhoods, sometimes curtailing an incentive to do so. It is true that land owners in a neighborhood have incentives to foster efficient public schooling, but their control is limited at best. For these reasons, we now examine how our welfare results vary with increases in the relative productivity of private schools.

Specifically, we compute the average welfare change and the proportion that gains from the voucher as a function of the relative productivity of private versus public schools. Before discussing the results reported in the panels of figure 7.8, we provide several pieces of information for interpret-

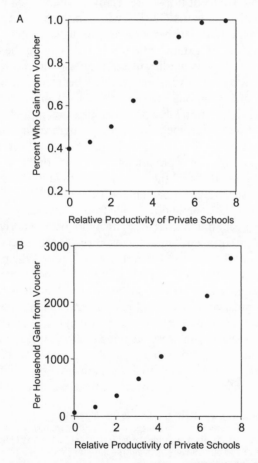

Fig. 7.8 *A,* **Percent who favor voucher as function of productivity of private relative to public schools;** *B,* **per-household gain from voucher as function of productivity of private relative to public schools**

ing the productivity measure on the horizontal axis. This scale can be interpreted as the percentage gain in earning power the student would acquire in private school relative to the earning power the student would acquire in an otherwise identical public school.[39] Thus, a productivity value of 2 implies that a student graduating from private school would earn 2 percent more than if the student graduated from a public school that expended the same resources and had the same peer group. With the available empirical evidence, this productivity measure can also be related to differences in achievement test scores. For example, Neal and Johnson (1996, 874) estimate that a 1 standard deviation improvement in the Armed Forces Qualification Test (AFQT) score translates into a 20 percent increase in wages. Thus, 2 on our productivity scale would be comparable to a test score improvement in private relative to public school of 1/10 of a standard deviation in the AFQT. Elsewhere in this volume, Peterson et al. (chap. 4) estimate that voucher experiments have improved student test scores by about 1/3 of a standard deviation. Assuming the Neal-Johnson coefficient on test scores applies to the tests used in the voucher experiments, the test score improvement in the voucher experiments would imply a value of roughly 6 on our productivity scale. Hoxby (2000a) estimates that a 1 standard deviation increase in her measure of public school choice would increase income at age thirty-two by 4 percent, a value of 4 on our productivity scale.[40]

Given the preceding interpretations of the horizontal axis in figure 7.8, we now turn to discussion of the results reported in those figures. The bottom panel translates a given percentage differential in earning power into an average annual household dollar gain from introducing the voucher. For example, a 4 percent differential in productivity between private and public schools translates into a difference in average household earning power of about $1,000 in 1990 dollars. The upper panel reports the proportion that gains from the voucher. With a productivity value of 2, a narrow majority of the population gains from the voucher. With a value of 4, roughly 80 percent of the population gains from the voucher. If relative productivity values exceed about 6, then everyone is better off in the voucher equilibrium.

The reader must, again, keep in mind that our predictions about the effects of a voucher depend on the particular voucher policy. Three types of variations in the voucher policy analyzed here have been considered by policymakers and enacted in some instances. First, we have analyzed a univer-

39. These calculations use the normed-achievement function previously discussed and the fact that normed achievement can be interpreted as future earnings, the latter implied by our calibration strategy. We can then multiply the achievement function in public schools by a constant greater than 1 to obtain an achievement function for private schools that conforms to a given percentage gain in earning power.

40. In table 4, Hoxby (2000a, 1227) reports that a regression of ln(income) on her school choice measure yields a coefficient of 0.151. A standard deviation of her school choice measure is 0.27. Multiplying the preceding two numbers yields the percentage reported in the text.

sal voucher of sufficient magnitude to cover average schooling cost, leading to elimination of the public sector. Universal vouchers that cover only part of schooling cost would be taken up only by those with sufficiently high demand for educational quality, with the rest still attending public schools. Nechyba analyzes such partial vouchers in a multidistrict setting in his chapter of this volume. He shows that (many) households taking up vouchers will relocate to districts with lower housing prices, with important local fiscal externalities on remaining public schools. In our single-district environment, partial vouchers would likewise lead to movement to initially poorer neighborhoods, but without such fiscal externalities since public school finance is not localized in our case. See Epple and Romano (1998, 1999) for analysis of partial vouchers in a single-district case with homogeneous public schools (e.g., due to public school choice).

Rather than being universally available, vouchers might be targeted to particular types of students. Nechyba (chap. 5 in this volume) also analyzes targeting to poor districts. Fernández and Rogerson (chap. 6 in this volume) examine the political economy of means- (income-) tested vouchers in their chapter. The three privately funded voucher programs evaluated in Peterson et al. (chap. 4 in this volume) are all targeted to low-income students (and are partial vouchers). Figlio and Page (chap. 2 in this volume) argue that school accountability plans that accurately measure school productivity and that make vouchers available to students in low-productivity schools will poorly target vouchers to the most disadvantaged. In Epple and Romano (1999), we ask whether appropriately targeted vouchers might yield benefits to everyone by maintaining or improving upon status quo stratification, while increasing productivity by injecting private-school competition into the education system.

The answer to the latter question depends on a third element of voucher policies. Rather than a laissez-faire voucher policy, participating private schools might face regulations, most importantly regarding their admission or tuition policies. The Florida voucher program, for example, requires participating private schools to accept exactly the voucher for tuition and to accept every voucher-financed student (or, if capacity-constrained, to admit from the pool of voucher-financed students with equal probabilities). Assuming enforceability of such regulations (a serious concern), they can be highly relevant to the effects of voucher system. In Epple and Romano (1999), we show that a laissez-faire voucher whose magnitude varies with student ability (from which the peer externality derives) will continue to lead to a highly stratified equilibrium. We show further, however, that a voucher properly targeted to ability combined with a requirement on participating schools to take exactly the voucher for tuition for any students the school chooses to admit can lead to significant private school entry and thus productivity gains, without significant effect on stratification. Everyone gains here.

7.7   Discussion and Conclusions

Many models of multijurisdictional equilibrium are structured so that differences in tax and expenditure policies across jurisdictions are the only force leading to stratification of population across jurisdictions. These models have been quite fruitful in studying a variety of policy issues related to state and local government finance. In investigating school finance policy issues, it is natural to turn to those models to understand the effects of changing the structure of school finance. In geographic areas in which students are served by a single school in each district, these models should give reasonable guidance, particularly in studying finance policies that entail only partial equalization across jurisdictions.

Unfortunately, these conditions are almost never met. As we noted in section 7.1, the vast majority of children in the United States go to school in multischool districts. Central-city districts are virtually all multischool districts. Thus, many students go to school in districts that have dozens of schools. The second difficulty with using the traditional model to study school policy is that it gives either no predictions or incorrect predictions in cases where there is full equalization of expenditure per student or in the study of intradistrict public school choice. The difficulty lies in the common assumption that stratification of the population across schools is driven by expenditure differences and that stratification does not arise when expenditures are equalized.

Even a cursory look at the stratification of households across neighborhood schools in large urban districts is sufficient to put to rest the notion that there is no stratification among schools in a district when expenditures are equalized. We have shown in this paper that there is likely to be little or no change in stratification when expenditures are equalized in neighborhood school systems. School quality differences arising from peer effects give rise to housing price differentials across neighborhoods that are sufficient to sustain stratification. Thus, although expenditure equalization may lead to some reduction of school quality differences, equalization of school quality will generally not arise when expenditures per student are equalized.

Our paper provides insights into public school choice programs and offers a foundation for addressing many issues related to public school choice. We noted earlier that, although many states have interdistrict school choice programs, few students participate in such programs. This is as our model would predict, because districts that are prospective recipients of choice students will resist accepting such students. To see why, consider two districts, D1 and D2, and a student from D1 who wishes to attend school in D2. For simplicity, suppose that each district has only one school. It is easy to see that D2 will resist if the funding the student brings from D1 is less than the expenditure per student in D2. Suppose then that the choice program compensates for any such funding disparities. Our model predicts that D2 will nonetheless resist. In the absence of funding disparities, students will wish to transfer from schools with low average peer ability to those with high average peer ability. The clientele of the prospective recipient school will resist accepting such students since, on average, they will be of lower peer ability than the incumbent students. In practice, in states where district participation in interdistrict choice programs is voluntary, high-income districts typically opt out. In states where such formal opting out is not permitted, de facto opting out is nonetheless likely to occur, as prospective recipient districts give priority to local residents and then "find" that they have little or no excess capacity to serve students from outside the district.

Of course, the same incentives to resist choice students arise within districts. Within-district programs often tackle this resistance by requiring schools to select at random from their applicant list if they are oversubscribed. Of course, a recipient school may still be less welcoming to students from outside the neighborhood than to students from inside the neighborhood, but such informal resistance is likely to be muted if district administrators are sufficiently committed to the choice program. Students exercising choice may then find that the gain in school quality is sufficient to justify living with any residual resistance. Such resistance may, however, be similar to the role of our transportation cost variable, T, in discouraging students from the lowest-income households from attending a higher-quality choice school.

Our model points to potential unintended consequences of public school choice programs. For example, suppose, again, that there are two districts, D1 and D2. Suppose now that D1 has two neighborhood schools, A and B, and D2 has one school, C. For simplicity, let the three schools be of equal size. Suppose that low- and high-income students are in district D1, and middle-income districts are in D2. Specifically, let the attendees of A be low-income students, with B serving high-income students, and C serving middle-income students. Thus, the ordering of school qualities is A, C, B. How could such an allocation be an equilibrium? One could easily construct realistic examples in which tax base per student in D1 would be comparable to tax base per student in D2, so that equilibrium would be characterized by little difference in spending per student in the two districts. With $E[b|y]$ increasing in y, the ordering of school qualities A, C, B would then primarily reflect differences in peer qualities.

Beginning with such an equilibrium, consider the effect of introducing a frictionless intradistrict choice program in D1. What are the possible equilibria with this choice program? The equalization of peer qualities in D1 means that there will no longer be stratification within districts. There will, however, be stratification across districts. Thus, one possible equilibrium is that the high-income households will remain in D1, middle-income households will move to D1, and the poor will move to D2. The other possible equilibrium is that the high-income households will move to D2 and the middle-income households will move to D1.[41] What are the effects on school quality? In the first case, students in poor households receive a worse education after introduction of the choice program. They face the same peer quality as before the change and reside in a district where the tax base is lower than in the original equilibrium. In addition, the pivotal voter is poorer than in the original equilibrium, so there will be a decline in spending due both to the lower tax base and to the lower willingness of the pivotal voter to tax in support of education. Middle-income students will probably gain because they move to a district with higher average tax base and higher average peer quality. The effect on high-income students is ambiguous, because their district's tax base per student rises but choice causes the quality of peer students to fall. In the second case, the effect of the change on students in low-income households is ambiguous, depending on whether peer effects or expenditure effects are more important. Students in high-income households will receive higher-quality education than before the change, and students in middle-income households will receive lower-quality education.

The preceding discussion illustrates the potential of our model for anticipating consequences of public school choice programs.[42] Because choice programs have been undertaken by a number of central-city districts, the possibilities raised in this example cannot be easily dismissed. Metropolitan areas typically contain suburban districts that have lower average income than average income in the wealthiest central-city neighborhoods. Thus, there is a very real possibility that introduction of choice programs in central-city districts will induce exodus from the city by the high-income households and entry by middle-income households. Of course, a central-city district may nonetheless decide that the choice program should be undertaken. The point of the example is to illustrate that our model provides a vehicle for thinking through the likely consequences of such policy changes.

Appendix

The Existence and Multiplicity of Differentiated Equilibria in the Neighborhood Model

Proposition A1 identifies the multiplicity of equilibria that arise in the neighborhood schooling model with N neighborhoods. It also proves existence of such equilibria, thus proving part (a) of proposition 2.

41. If one thinks of the multischool district as a central city, then the second is the more likely outcome, because forces not in our model lead the poor to live in cities (Glaeser, Kahn, and Rappoport 2000).
42. Incorporating a private schooling sector is obviously of interest, an extension that we are currently pursuing.

PROPOSITION A1. *Divide the N neighborhoods into k ($\leq N$) sets, each set consisting of all neighborhoods having the same housing capacity. Let m_i, i = 1, 2, . . . , k, equal the number of neighborhoods in set i. The maximum number of neighborhoods/schools having different peer groups in an equilibrium equals N. There are # $\equiv N!/(m_1! \cdot m_2! \cdots m_k!)$ distinct such equilibria.*

PROOF. Obviously, N is the maximum number of different school qualities that is feasible in an equilibrium. The number of distinct ways neighborhoods can be ordered by their housing capacities is #. We now show each distinct order is consistent with an equilibrium having N different school qualities by construction. Refer to figure 7.3 for an example. (Note that figure 7.3 has three neighborhoods but not necessarily with distinct housing capacities [population sizes], the latter depending on $f(b, y)$.)

Take any order of neighborhoods and number them 1, 2, . . . , N. Let $F_y(y)$ denote the marginal c.d.f. of y in the population. Set $y_0 \equiv y_m$ and find y_i, $i = 1, 2, \ldots, N-1$, such that $F_y(y_i) - F_y(y_{i-1})$ equals the land capacity of neighborhood i. Recalling that we normalized the population to 1 and also setting the aggregate housing capacity equal to 1, it is clear that the ordering of neighborhoods results in a unique vector $(\mathbf{y_1}, \mathbf{y_2}, \ldots \mathbf{y_{N-1}})$. These delineate the equilibrium partition. Set $y_N \equiv y_x$, and let

$$\theta_i \equiv \frac{\int_{y_{i-1}}^{y_i}\int_{b_m}^{b_x} bf(b, y)db\,dy}{\int_{y_{i-1}}^{y_i}\int_{b_m}^{b_x} f(b, y)db\,dy} = \frac{\int_{y_{i-1}}^{y_i} E[b|y] \cdot [\int_{b_m}^{b_x} f(b, y)db]dy}{\int_{y_{i-1}}^{y_i}\int_{b_m}^{b_x} f(b, y)db\,dy};$$

denote the implied peer quality measures. Since $E[b|y]$ is increasing, $\theta_1 < \theta_2 < \ldots < \theta_N$. Then, since X_i is constant across neighborhoods, the q_is also ascend. Let p_i denote the housing price in neighborhood i, and set $p_1 = c$. Find p_i, $i = 2, 3, \ldots, N$, recursively from

$$U[y_{i-1}(1 - t) - p_i, a(q_i, b)] = U[y_{i-1}(1 - t) - p_{i-1}, a(q_{i-1}, b)],$$

noting that equation (3) implies unique solutions independent of b. Since $q_i > q_{i-1}, p_i > p_{i-1}$. By equation (1) the assigned residential choices are utility maximizing, and the housing markets clear by construction. We have then described an equilibrium consistent with the given ordering of neighborhoods. A distinct equilibrium can be so constructed from each of the distinct orderings.

Voting Equilibrium

To solve for voting equilibrium, we follow the same methodology employed in Epple and Romer (1991). Take as given the household's residence and consider the preference mapping in the (X,t) plane for Cobb-Douglas utility function (see equation [2]). An indifference curve is defined: $U(X, t; y, p, b, \theta) =$ constant. Using equation (2), it is straightforward to confirm the following:

LEMMA 1. *(a) Indifference curves in the (X, t) plane are upward sloping and concave, with lower (southeasterly) indifference curves corresponding to higher utility. (b) The indifference curve mapping is independent of b and* θ, *depending only on y/p and* α. *(c) As we look across households, the slope of indifference curves through any point (X, t) increases with y/p. Hence, any pair of indifference curves cross once at most.*

Lemma 1 implies that households with higher y/p have a stronger preference for (X, t) in the following sense. If a household is indifferent to choices (X_2, t_2) and (X_1, t_1) where $X_2 > X_1$ and $t_2 > t_1$, then all households with higher (lower) y/p strictly prefer point (X_2, t_2) (point $[X_1, t_1]$) over the alternative. The latter can be verified using lemma 1 by drawing indifference curves in the (X, t) plane (see figure 7A.1 for example). It also follows that, whether or not the feasible choice set of (X, t) values voters face is well behaved (e.g., convex):

LEMMA 2. *A most preferred choice of a voter with median preference (i.e., median y/p) from the feasible choice set is a majority voting equilibrium. Only a most-preferred choice of a voter with median preference is a voting equilibrium if the density of the preference parameter y/p is positive in the vicinity of the median.*

PROOF. The argument follows the graphic technique of Epple and Romer (1991), and is presented here for the reader's convenience. Refer to figure 7A.1 where U_{med} is an indifference curve of a voter with median preference, and suppose point (X^*, t^*) is a most-preferred choice of this voter in the feasible choice set (not shown). We argue first that no feasible points in the

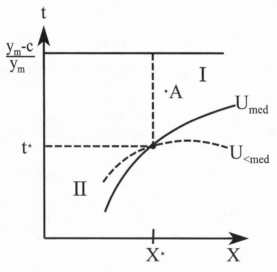

Fig. 7A.1   Illustration of proof of lemma 2

(X, t) plane are majority preferred to (X^*, t^*), establishing it is an equilibrium point. The indifference curve U_{med} and point (X^*, t^*) partitions the (X, t) plane into four regions. No points below U_{med} are feasible choices, because this would contradict the median voter's preference for (X^*, t^*). Point (X^*, t^*) is preferred unanimously over all points in the rectangle with lower right-hand corner at (X^*, t^*). Region I (see figure 7A.1) is made up of points above and including U_{med} and with $X > X^*$ (e.g., point A). Since those with below-median preferences have flatter indifference curves through point (X^*, t^*)—for example, U_{med} in figure 7A.1—they prefer (X^*, t^*) to all points in region I. Since the median voter prefers (X^*, t^*) or is indifferent (i.e., if the alternative point is on U_{med}), at least a weak majority prefers (X^*, t^*). By an analogous argument, (X^*, t^*) is not defeated by any points in region II. We have established that any most-preferred point of a voter with median preference is a majority voting equilibrium.

Any most-preferred point of the median voter is preferred by a strict majority over any other feasible point assuming a positive density of types in the vicinity of the median. A positive measure of households with y/p in the vicinity of y/p of the median voter will share the latter's strict preference, as will all those with lower or higher y/p (or both). Hence, only most-preferred points of a voter with median preference are voting equilibria.

Lemma 2 points toward two potential cases of multiple equilibria. One has a gap in the density of the preference parameter at the 50th percentile and two median preference voters with distinct preferences. The other has multiple most-preferred points of a unique median preference voter. The former is ruled out by the (reasonable) parameter restriction

(A1) $$y_x \geq \frac{p_2}{c} y_m,$$

and the latter will not arise in our model.

Applying lemma 2 to the neighborhood schooling case with no transportation cost and using equation (A1), one finds the pivotal voter in equation (7) of the text. For the case of choice with friction, it is straightforward to identify three exhaustive cases that identify income y_{p2} of a pivotal voter:

(A2)   For y^* defined in $F_y(y^*) - F_y(y_I) = 0.5,$

(A3) $$y_{p2} = y_{med} \text{ if } \frac{y_{med}}{p_2} \geq \frac{y_I}{c};$$

(A4) $$y_{p2} = y^* \text{ if } \frac{y_{med}}{p_2} < \frac{y_I}{c} \text{ and } \frac{y^*}{p_2} \leq \frac{y_m}{c};$$

or

(A5) $$y_{p2} \text{ satisfies } F_y(y_{p2}) - F_y(y_I) + F_y\left(\frac{c}{p_2}y_{p2}\right) = 0.5$$

$$\text{if } \frac{y_{\text{med}}}{p_2} < \frac{y_l}{c} \text{ and } \frac{y^*}{p_2} > \frac{y_m}{c}.$$

Existence of Equilibrium in the Two-Jurisdiction Model

PROPOSITION A2. *A sufficient condition for existence of differentiated equilibrium is*

$$(A6) \quad \left\{ y_{\text{med}} - c\left[1 + \alpha\left(1 - \frac{y_{\text{med}}}{y_{q3}} \right) \right] \right\} \left(1 - \frac{c}{y_{q3}} \right)^\alpha$$

$$> \left\{ y_{\text{med}} - c\left[1 + \alpha\left(1 - \frac{y_{\text{med}}}{y_{q1}} \right) \right] \right\} \left(1 - \frac{c}{y_{q1}} \right)^\alpha \Omega; \text{ where } \Omega \equiv \left(\frac{\theta_1}{\theta_2} \right)^\gamma \left(\frac{\overline{y}_1}{\overline{y}_2} \right)^\alpha < 1,$$

and θ_i and $\overline{y}_i$ are calculated assuming income stratification with $y_1 = y_{\text{med}}$ (recall equation [5]). Given that equation (A6) is satisfied and setting $p_1 = c$, equilibrium (with differentiated schools) is unique. Two of many sufficient conditions for satisfaction of equation (A6) are (a) c sufficiently low; or (b) $\alpha <$ y_{med}/y_{q3}.

PROOF. To show existence, we must show equations (15)–(17) have a solution (t_1, t_2, p_1, p_2) with $p_i \geq c$, $i = 1, 2$, and consistent with the residential preferences of proposition 6. Clearance of housing markets will be implied. We show equation (A6) implies an equilibrium exists with $p_1 = c$. Set $p_1 = c$, substitute for p_1 in equation (15), and substitute equations (15) and (16) into equation (17):

$$(A7) \quad H(p_2) = \left\{ y_{\text{med}} - c\left[1 + \alpha\left(1 - \frac{y_{\text{med}}}{y_{q1}} \right) \right] \right\} \left(1 - \frac{c}{y_{q1}} \right)^\alpha \Omega;$$

$$\text{where } H(p_2) \equiv \left\{ y_{\text{med}} - p_2\left[1 + \alpha\left(1 - \frac{y_{\text{med}}}{y_{q3}} \right) \right] \right\} \left(1 - \frac{p_2}{y_{q3}} \right)^\alpha.$$

Using $y_{q3} > y_{\text{med}}$, observe that $H'(p_2) < 0$ for p_2 such that $H(p_2) > 0$, and $H(p_2) \downarrow 0$ as p_2 rises. Note that the left-hand side of the inequality in condition (A6) is $H(c)$. The right-hand side of the inequality (A6) is positive since it has the same sign as the utility of median-income households when $p_1 = c$. It follows that, given equation (A6), a *unique p_2* satisfying equation (A7) exists. Note, too, that this $p_2 > c$. Hence, one can find a solution to equations (15)–(17) with $p_i \geq c$, $i = 1, 2$.

To show existence, it remains to be confirmed that the residential choices associated with the presumed allocation are actually optimal. This requires that Δ (defined in the proof of proposition 6) is increasing in y, or

$$(A8) \quad (1 - t_2)q_2 > (1 - t_1)q_1.$$

Rewrite the latter and substitute from equation (17):

$$(A9) \quad \frac{1 - t_2}{1 - t_1} > \frac{q_1}{q_2} = \frac{y_{\text{med}}(1 - t_2) - p_2}{y_{\text{med}}(1 - t_1) - p_1} \rightarrow p_2(1 - t_1) > p_1(1 - t_2).$$

Substitute from equations (15) and (16) and again rewrite the condition:

(A10)
$$p_2\left(1 + \alpha\frac{p_1}{y_{q1}}\right) > p_1\left(1 + \alpha\frac{p_2}{y_{q3}}\right).$$

Since $y_{q3} > y_{q1}$, $p_2 \geq p_1$ is sufficient for satisfaction of equation (A10). We have shown p_2 exceeds $p_1 = c$, completing the proof of existence.

We have already shown uniqueness given $p_1 = c$. Sufficiency of condition (a) for equation (A6) uses $\Omega < 1$. The left-hand side of the inequality (A6) converges to y_{med} as $c \downarrow 0$, and the right-hand side converges to Ωy_{med}. To show condition (b), let $g(y)$ denote the expression on the left-hand side of the inequality (A6) where $y = y_{q3}$. With this notation, the inequality (A6) is $g(y_{q3}) > \Omega g(y_{q1})$. It follows that the inequality is satisfied if $g(y)$ is an increasing function over $y \in [y_{q1}, y_{q3}]$. After straightforward manipulation one obtains

$$g'(y) = \frac{\alpha c y}{y^2(y - c)}\left(1 - \frac{c}{y}\right)^\alpha\left[c\left(\frac{y_{med}}{y} - \alpha\right) + \alpha c\frac{y_{med}}{y}\right].$$

Condition (b) is sufficient for $g' > 0$ in this range, proving the result.

Since equation (A6) involves nine parameters (counting θ_1/θ_2 as one), it is not particularly intuitive. However, condition (A6) is easily satisfied, for example, as in the two sufficient conditions for its satisfaction. One can see by inspection that if the construction cost c of a house is sufficiently low equation (A6) will be satisfied. Roughly, the sufficient conditions (and other sufficient conditions) ensure that voting effects do not contradict the sorting implications of peer effects. For example, as c declines toward zero, $t_2 < t_1$ is implied (use equations [15] and [16] and that $p_1 = c$), and tax effects reinforce income sorting. Note also that as Ω declines, it is more likely that equation (A6) will be satisfied. Hence, high correlation of (y, b), implying relatively low θ_1/θ_2, favors existence of stratified equilibrium. Moreover, equation (A6) is not necessary for existence of equilibrium. Absent satisfaction of equation (A6), $p_1 > p_2$ in an equilibrium. It appears that this is possible (but we have not worked out any such examples). Such an equilibrium would have a much higher tax rate in neighborhood 2 than in neighborhood 1, reflecting a relatively high y_{q3}, and such that a lower housing price in neighborhood 2 is necessary to keep the median-income household indifferent to residence.

An Interjurisdictional Choice Policy

The model is the same as in section 7.4.3 of the text except for the school choice policy. Following residential choice, households commit to attend school in their own neighborhood or the other one. Every household then votes for the tax-expenditure pair with those committed to the same school, and with tax base consisting of that school's households. Hence, those that attend a school comprise a jurisdiction independent of their residences. We assume transportation costs are negligible (zero).

We show that equilibrium will probably be the same as when there is frictionless choice across two neighborhoods of one jurisdiction. Since school and thus jurisdictional membership is independent of the first-stage residential choice, housing prices must be the same in the two neighborhoods. Hence, $p_2 = p_1 = c$, as we have argued earlier that $p_1 = c$ is a sensible convention.

The difference in utility if school and jurisdiction 2 are selected from the utility if school and jurisdiction 1 are selected is given by

(A11) $\Delta \equiv b^\beta \{ [y(1 - t_2) - c]q_2 - [y(1 - t_1) - c]q_1 \}$

$= b^\beta \{ [(1 - t_2)q_2 - (1 - t_1)q_1]y - c(q_2 - q_1) \}.$

Assuming $q_2 \geq q_1$ with no loss in generality, we see using equation (A11) that equilibrium has either (a) $q_2 > q_1$; $t_2 > t_1$; and income stratification; (b) $q_2 = q_1$; $t_2 = t_1$; and all households indifferent to their school/jurisdictional choice. If $q_2 > q_1$, then income stratification is implied by the linearity of Δ in y. For this case, if not $t_2 > t_1$, then school/jurisdiction 2 would be preferred by all. We emphasize that the conditions in (a) are merely selected necessary conditions for a stratified equilibrium; they are not sufficient. If $q_2 = q_1$ and $t_2 \neq t_1$, then equation (A11) would imply that everyone prefers the school/jurisdiction with lower tax rate. (If everyone were in one school, then a rich type with a bright child would be better off attending his own school.)

For realistic parameterizations, stratified equilibrium will not exist. We show why with some intuitive arguments, in lieu of a (more lengthy) computational analysis. Assume that there is a stratified equilibrium. Then $q_2 > q_1$ because the rich school/jurisdiction has a better peer group and a wealthier tax base ($t_2 > t_1$ is a necessary condition, recall). Such an equilibrium would have an indifferent household (income) as well, for whom equation (A11) would vanish. However, it is very difficult to satisfy all these conditions. The reason is that the tax rate that will be selected in equilibrium by the rich will not typically be high enough to keep out the poorer types, and there is no longer a housing price differential that can serve as a deterrent.

To see this, first suppose that c is small. Then the equilibrium tax rates will hardly differ. Equation (9) in the text describes the tax rate in each jurisdiction if y_{p1} is replaced by the median income in the jurisdiction. As $c \to 0$, $t_1 \to t_2$ for any allocation, and no indifferent household can exist. An analogous argument precludes stratified equilibrium as $\alpha \to 0$.

Another way to see the difficulty in obtaining a stratified equilibrium is by a graphic analysis. Assume initially that $E[b|y]$ is invariant to y. We will show that it is quite difficult to obtain a stratified equilibrium and then show that $E[b|y]$ that increases in y makes it more difficult.

Assuming a stratified equilibrium, figure 7A.2 depicts in the (X, t) plane a "voting indifference curve" of the pivotal voter in the poor school/juris-

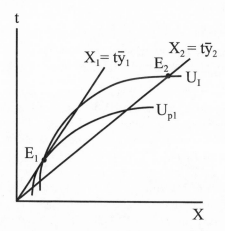

Fig. 7A.2   Illustration of analysis of interjurisdictional choice policy

diction (U_{p1}), an indifference curve of the type indifferent between schools (U_I), and the budget constraints of the two schools/jurisdictions. (The indifference curves are those discussed in and preceding lemma 1.) E_1 shows the equilibrium expenditure per student and tax rate in school/jurisdiction 1. The indifferent household has indifference curve through E_1 that is steeper than is the pivotal voter's because the former type has higher income (see lemma 1). (Note that in the extreme of $c = 0$, the indifference mappings of all types would be the same, again precluding equilibrium, as we will see momentarily.) Equilibrium in school/jurisdiction 2 would have to be at point E_2 so that "type I" is indifferent. Hence, the indifference curve of the pivotal voter in school/jurisdiction 2 (i.e., the median-income type there) would need to be tangent to $X_2 = t\bar{y}_2$ at E_2. This indicates that preferences for X need to rise precipitously with income to obtain such an equilibrium. If, for example, α is small, then this will not occur.

If we now let $E[b|y]$ increase with y, then the difficulty is exacerbated. The preference mappings are unchanged (due to the Cobb-Douglas specification), but the values of utility are higher in jurisdiction 2 than in jurisdiction 1. Utility at E_2 in school 2 is then higher than utility at E_1 in school 1 for type I. This implies that the equilibrium point in jurisdiction 2 is higher up $X_2 = t_2\bar{y}_2$ than E_2.

Given that equilibrium of type (a) above does not exist, then equilibrium is of type (b). In such an equilibrium, everyone is indifferent to residential and school/jurisdictional choice. Hence, assume types randomize over their choices, all with the same probabilities. This implies schools and jurisdictions that are homogeneous: That is, each school's distribution of types is the same as the population distribution. The outcome is the same as with frictionless choice and one jurisdiction.

Proof of Proposition 9

Proposition 9 is essentially an application of results in Epple and Romano (1998, 1999). Here we sketch proofs for the reader's convenience.

A. This is the "strict hierarchy result" in the papers just cited, developed assuming fixed expenditures across schools in Epple and Romano (1998) and extended to variation in expenditure in Epple and Romano (1999). The proof proceeds as follows. Assume $q_1 = q_2$ and show a Pareto improvement is feasible. First show that $q_1 = q_2$ implies $X_1 = X_2$ and $\theta_1 = \theta_2$ using quasi-concavity of $q(X, \theta)$. If, say, $\theta_2 > \theta_1$, then $X_2 < X_1$ and q_θ/q_x is higher in school 1 than in school 2. Using proposition 8 and the definition of SMC_i, it is implied that there is an ability threshold B, such that all types with $b >$ ($<$) B would choose to attend school 1(2). This contradicts $\theta_2 > \theta_1$.

Having established that $q_1 = q_2$ implies $X_1 = X_2$ and $\theta_1 = \theta_2$, we can regard the schools as having homogeneous student bodies (with respect to both b and y). Then it is shown that one can engender a Pareto improvement by having the schools exchange students in a particular way that leads one school to be of higher quality, with more able and also richer students, and the opposite for the other school. The Pareto improvement does not require changes in X_1 or X_2. Mathematically, this is somewhat involved, since it relies on second-order effects (as first-order effects vanish), so we refer the reader to the proof of proposition 1 in Epple and Romano (1998). The intuition is, however, not too complicated: Those in the improved school are obviously better off. Those in the school that has deteriorated are better off because the contribution to costs of the departed students is relatively low due to their high abilities and thus low SMC, and the reduced quality is of relatively low "cost" because the student body becomes relatively poor and cares less about quality.

B. Given $q_2 > q_1$, income stratification follows by equation (1) and because prices depend only on student ability (see equation [19] in the text). That is, for any given ability, if there is a household indifferent to the schools when $r_i = SMC_i$, $i, = 1, 2$, then all types having higher (lower) income strictly prefer school 2 (1). (If there is no indifferent type, then all types with that ability attend one of the two schools.)

The indifferent set in equation (22) is found simply by equating utilities given $r_i = SMC_i$ and using the definition of η_i.

C. Equation (23) is found from equation (20) and the analogue for X_2, again using $r_i = SMC_i$, $i = 1, 2$. Specifically, for $i = 1$,

$$(A12) \quad \frac{\partial U^1(b, y)/\partial X}{\partial U^1(b, y)/\partial y} = \frac{\alpha}{X_1}(y - c - r_1)$$

$$= \frac{\alpha}{X_1}\left[y - c - X_1 - \frac{q_\theta}{q_x}(\theta_1 - b)\right]$$

$$= \frac{\alpha}{X_1} \left[y - c - X_1 - \frac{\gamma X_1}{\alpha \theta_1}(\theta_1 - b) \right]$$

$$= \frac{\alpha}{X_1}(y - c) - \alpha - \frac{\gamma}{\theta_1}(\theta_1 - b),$$

the second-to-last equality using

(A13) $$\frac{q_\theta}{q_x} = \frac{\gamma X}{\alpha \theta}.$$

Then substitute equation (A12) into equation (20) and rearrange, while noting that the density of types in school 1 is given by $Af/\iint Afdbdy$. X_2 is found analogously.

The result in equation (24) is found by substituting equation (23) into equation (A13).

D, E. These are efficiently proved together. Note from equation (22) that the boundary locus in the (b, y) plane is linear (see figure 7.6 for an example), so that, given we have established income stratification, ability stratification corresponds to a downward-sloping boundary locus. Suppose this locus is not downward sloping. Then, for $E[b|y]$ constant in y, $\theta_2 \leq \theta_1$. Hence, $q_2 > q_1$ implies $X_2 > X_1$. This implies $\eta_2 > \eta_1$, which by equation (22) implies a downward-sloping boundary locus—a contradiction.

Hence, the boundary locus *is* downward sloping, obviously also implying $\theta_2 > \theta_1$.

F. $\eta_i q_i = \gamma/\alpha\, X_i^{1+\alpha}\theta_i^{\gamma-1}$. By part E of this proposition and equation (22), $\eta_2 q_2 > \eta_1 q_1$. Using part D of this proposition, then, $X_2 > X_1$ whenever $\gamma < 1$.

References

Arnott, Richard, and John Rowse. 1987. Peer group effects and educational attainment. *Journal of Public Economics* 32 (3): 287–305.

Barrow, Lisa. 1999. School choice through relocation: Evidence from the Washington, D.C., area. Federal Reserve Bank of Chicago Working Paper 99-7. Chicago: Federal Reserve Bank of Chicago, March.

Benabou, Roland. 1993. Workings of a city: Location, education, and production. *Quarterly Journal of Economics* 108 (3): 619–52.

———. 1996. Equity and efficiency in human capital investment: The local connection. *Review of Economic Studies* 63:237–64.

———. 2000. Unequal societies: Income distribution and the social contract. *American Economic Review* 90 (March): 96–129.

Betts, Julian. 1996. Is there a link between school inputs and earnings? Fresh scrutiny of an old literature. In *Does money matter? The effect of school resources on student achievement and adult success,* ed. Gary Burtless, 141–91. Washington, D.C.: Brookings Institution.

Black, Sandra E. 1999. Do better schools matter? Parental valuation of elementary education. *Quarterly Journal of Economics* 114 (2): 577–600.
Brueckner, Jan K. 2000. A Tiebout/tax-competition model. *Journal of Public Economics* 77 (August): 285–306.
Caucutt, Elizabeth M. 2002. Educational vouchers when there are peer group effects: Size matters. *International Economic Review* 43 (February): 195–222.
Cullen, Julie B., Brian A. Jacob, and Steven D. Levitt. 2000. The impact of school choice on student outcomes: An analysis of the Chicago public schools. NBER Working Paper no. 7888. Cambridge, Mass.: National Bureau of Economic Research, September.
de Bartolome, Charles A. M. 1990. Equilibrium and inefficiency in a community model with peer group effects. *Journal of Political Economy* 98 (1): 110–33.
———. 1997. What determines state aid to school districts. *Journal of Policy Analysis and Management* 16:32–47.
Durlauf, Steven N. 1996. A theory of persistent income inequality. *Journal of Economic Growth* 1 (March): 75–93.
Eden, Ben. 1992. How to subsidize education: An analysis of voucher systems. University of Iowa, Department of Economics. Working Paper.
Ellickson, Bryan. 1971. Jurisdictional fragmentation and residential choice. *American Economic Review Papers and Proceedings* 61 (May): 334–39.
Epple, Dennis, David Figlio, and Richard Romano. Forthcoming. Competition between private and public schools: Testing stratification and pricing predictions. *Journal of Public Economics.*
Epple, Dennis, Radu Filimon, and Thomas Romer. 1984. Equilibrium among local jurisdictions: Toward an integrated treatment of voting and residential choice. *Journal of Public Economics* 24 (August): 281–308.
Epple, Dennis, Elizabeth Newlon, and Richard Romano. 2002. Ability tracking, school competition, and the distribution of educational benefits. *Journal of Public Economics* 83 (January): 1–48.
Epple, Dennis, and Richard Romano. 1995. Public school choice and finance policies, neighborhood formation, and the distribution of educational benefits. University of Florida, Department of Economics Working Paper. July 1995.
———. 1996. Ends against the middle: Determining public service provision when there are private alternatives. *Journal of Public Economics* 62:297–325.
———. 1998. Competition between private and public schools, vouchers and peer-group effects. *American Economic Review* 88 (1): 33–62.
———. 1999. Educational vouchers and cream skimming. University of Florida, Department of Economics. Working Paper.
———. 2000. On Pareto efficient pricing and peer groups in schools. University of Florida, Department of Economics Working Paper, June.
Epple, Dennis, and Thomas Romer. 1991. Mobility and redistribution. *Journal of Political Economy* 99 (4): 828–58.
Evans, William N., Wallace E. Oates, and Robert M. Schwab. 1992. Measuring peer group effects: A study of teenage behavior. *Journal of Political Economy* 100:966–91.
Fernández, Raquel. 1997. Odd versus even: Comparative statics in multicommunity models. *Journal of Public Economics* 65 (2): 789–812.
Fernández, Raquel, and Richard Rogerson. 1996. Income distribution, communities, and the quality of public education. *Quarterly Journal of Economics* 111 (1): 135–64.
———. 1997a. Education finance reform: A dynamic perspective. *Journal of Policy Analysis and Management* 16 (1): 67–84.

————. 1997b. Keeping people out: Income distribution, zoning, and quality of public education. *International Economic Review* 38 (1): 23–42.

————. 1998. Public education and income distribution: A dynamic quantitative evaluation of education finance reform. *American Economic Review* 88 (4): 813–33.

Friedman, Milton. 1962. *Capitalism and freedom.* Chicago: University of Chicago Press.

Gans, J. S., and M. Smart. 1996. Majority voting with single-crossing preferences. *Journal of Public Economics* 59:219–37.

Glaeser, Edward, Matthew Kahn, and Jordon Rappoport. 2000. Why do the poor live in cities? NBER Working Paper no. 7636. Cambridge, Mass.: National Bureau of Economic Research, April.

Glomm, Gerhard, and B. Ravikumar. 1992. Public versus private investment in human capital: Endogenous growth and income inequality. *Journal of Political Economy* 100:813–34.

Gold, Steven D., David M. Smith, and Stephen B. Lawton, eds. 1995. *Public school finance programs of the United States and Canada 1993–94.* Albany, N.Y.: American Education Finance Association and Center for the Study of the States, Nelson A. Rockefeller Institute of Government, State University of New York.

Goodspeed, Timothy. 1989. A re-examination of the use of ability to pay taxes by local governments. *Journal of Public Economics* 38 (April): 319–42.

Hanushek, Eric. 1986. The economics of schooling: Production and efficiency in public schools. *Journal of Economic Literature* 24 (3): 1141–77.

————. 1997. Assessing the effects of school resources on student performance: An update. *Educational Evaluation and Policy Analysis* 19 (Summer): 141–64.

Henderson, Vernon, Peter Mieszkowski, and Yvon Sauvageau. 1978. Peer group effects in educational production functions. *Journal of Public Economics* 10 (1): 97–106.

Hoxby, Caroline Minter. 1995. Is there an equity-efficiency trade-off in school finance? Tiebout and a theory of the local goods producer. NBER Working Paper no. 5265. Cambridge, Mass.: National Bureau of Economic Research, September.

————. 2000a. Does competition among public schools benefit students and taxpayers? Evidence from natural variation in school districting. *American Economic Review* 90 (5): 1209–38.

————. 2000b. Peer effects in the classroom: Learning from gender and race variation. NBER Working Paper no. 7867. Cambridge, Mass.: National Bureau of Economic Research, August.

Inman, Robert P. 1978. Optimal fiscal reform of metropolitan schools: Some simulation results. *American Economic Review* 68 (1): 107–22.

Manski, Charles F. 1992. Educational choice (vouchers) and social mobility. *Economics of Education Review* 11 (4): 351–69.

McMillan, Robert. 1999. Heterogeneity, competition, and public school productivity. Stanford University, Department of Economics. Working Paper, May.

————. 2000. Parental pressure and private school competition: An empirical analysis of the determinants of public school quality. University of Toronto, Department of Economics. Mimeograph.

Moreland, Richard L., and John M. Levine. 1992. The composition of small groups. In *Advance in group processes,* vol. 9, eds. B. Markovsky, C. Ridgeway, and H. Walker, 237–80. Greenwich, Conn.: JAI Press.

Murray, Sheila E., William N. Evans, and Robert M. Schwab. 1998. Education finance reform and the distribution of education resources. *American Economic Review* 88 (4): 789–812.

Neal, Derek A., and William R. Johnson. 1996. The role of premarket factors in black-white wage differences. *Journal of Political Economy* 104 (5): 869–95.

Nechyba, Thomas. 1999. School finance induced migration patterns: The case of private school vouchers. *Journal of Public Economic Theory* 1 (1): 5–50.

———. 2000. Mobility, targeting, and private-school vouchers. *American Economic Review* 90 (1): 130–46.

Rees, Nina Shokraii. 2000. *School choice 2000: What's happening in the states.* Washington, D.C.: The Heritage Foundation.

Roberts, K. W. S. 1977. Voting over income tax schedules. *Journal of Public Economics* 8:329–40.

Rothschild, Michael, and Lawrence J. White. 1995. The analytics of the pricing of higher education and other services in which the customers are inputs. *Journal of Political Economy* 103 (3): 573–623.

Sacerdote, Bruce. 2000. Peer effects with random assignment: Results for Dartmouth roommates. NBER Working Paper no. 7469. Cambridge, Mass.: National Bureau of Economic Research. January.

Silva, Fabio, and Jon Sonstelie. 1995. Did Serrano cause a decline in school spending? *National Tax Journal* 48 (2): 199–215.

Solon, Gary. 1992. Intergenerational income mobility in the United States. *American Economic Review* 82 (3): 393–409.

Summers, Anita, and Barbara L. Wolfe. 1977. Do schools make a difference? *American Economic Review* 67 (4): 639–52.

Tiebout, C. 1956. A pure theory of local expenditures. *Journal of Political Economy* 65:416–24.

Toma, Eugenia. 1996. Public funding and private schooling across countries. *Journal of Law and Economics* 39 (1): 121–48.

U.S. Department of Education, National Center for Education Statistics. 1994. *Common core of data.* Washington, D.C.: U.S. Department of Education, National Center for Education Statistics.

———. 1996. Public school choice programs, 1993–94: Availability and student participation. Washington, D.C.: U.S. Department of Education, National Center for Education Statistics.

Westhoff, F. 1977. Existence of equilibria in economies with a local public good. *Journal of Economic Theory* 14:84–112.

Zimmer, Ron W., and Eugenia Toma. 1999. Peer effects in private and public schools across countries. *Journal of Policy Analysis and Management* 19:75–92.

Zimmerman, David J. 1992. Regression toward mediocrity in economic stature. *American Economic Review* 82 (3): 409–29.

School Choice and School Productivity
Could School Choice Be a Tide that Lifts All Boats?

Caroline M. Hoxby

A productive school produces high achievement in its pupils for each dollar it spends. Formally, a school's productivity is defined as achievement per dollar spent, controlling for incoming achievement differences of its students. In this chapter, I comprehensively review how school choice might affect productivity. I begin by describing the importance of school productivity, then explain the economic logic that suggests that choice will affect productivity, and finish by presenting much of the available evidence on school choice and school productivity. Readers are likely to be most intrigued by the final section of the paper, in which I examine the achievement and productivity effects of three important recent choice reforms: vouchers in Milwaukee, charter schools in Michigan, and charter schools in Arizona. However, readers are much less likely to find the evidence to be a "black box" if they read the earlier sections of the paper, which set up the relationship between choice, school conduct, student achievement, and productivity. I encourage impatient readers who jump to the final section to return to the earlier sections for answers to the questions that will naturally arise once they have seen the evidence.

8.1 Why the Productivity Consequences of School Choice Matter A Lot

Although a great deal of research has dealt indirectly with school productivity (most famously, the "does money matter?" debate), productivity has been neglected by research on school choice. School choice research has concentrated on *allocation* questions, which include the following: Who ex-

Caroline M. Hoxby is professor of economics at Harvard University and a research associate of the National Bureau of Economic Research.

ercises school choice? Who chooses which school? How does choice change the allocation of resources? How does reallocation of students change peer effects? The allocation questions are largely questions of redistribution. Although it is theoretically possible that school choice could improve achievement for *all* students through reallocation, such an outcome would require that, for *every* student, the benefits of going to a school that was a better match exceed the costs imposed upon him or her by school choice. The costs might include a worse peer group or a decline in resources.[1]

In general, then, allocation-oriented research presents a view of school choice that is rife with tensions about redistribution (which students gain, and which students lose?). One way to relieve these tensions is to devise allocation-related remedies, such as controls on how resources and peers shift when choice is introduced (see, e.g. Hoxby 2001). However, when advocates of school choice argue that every child would benefit from school choice, they are usually relying on the idea that school *productivity* would increase sufficiently to swamp any negative allocation effects that some students might experience. The basic logic is that choice would give schools greater incentives to be productive because less productive schools would lose students to more productive schools. That is, if a school could raise a student's achievement while spending the same amount as the current school, it would be expected to draw the student away from his or her current school. This process would shrink the less productive and expand the more productive school, until one of two things happened: the more productive replaced the less productive school or the less productive school raised its productivity and was thereby able to maintain its population of students. (This is the broad idea: later I discuss specific mechanisms through which choice might raise productivity.) In other words, a general increase in school productivity could be a rising tide that lifted all boats, and the gains and losses from reallocation might be nothing more than crests and valleys on the surface of the much higher water level.

Thus, the first reason that the productivity consequences of school choice matter is that they potentially determine whether choice will benefit all children. For the rising tide scenario to be a realistic probability and not just a possibility, however, one must ask what productivity schools could reasonably be expected to achieve. That is, what is the range of productivity over which choice *could* cause productivity to vary? Recent history suggests that school productivity could be much higher than it is now—60 to 70 percent

---

1. Strictly speaking, what is required is that (a) the current distribution of peers or teaching methods is inoptimal and (b) that school choice would cause people to redistribute themselves in such a way that a Pareto improvement in the distribution of peers or teaching methods would occur. It is reasonable to think that families might redistribute themselves so as to achieve better alignment between teaching methods and their children's learning styles. It is less reasonable to think that families, acting independently, could implement a Pareto improvement in peer effects.

higher. Consider the simplest productivity calculation, achievement per dollar. Such a calculation (which I later describe in detail) suggests that average public school productivity was about 65 percent higher in 1970–71 than in 1998–99. This means that, if choice were simply to restore school productivity to its 1970–71 level, then the *average* student in the United States would be scoring at an advanced level where fewer than 10 percent of students now score. This improvement in achievement would be so large that it would overwhelm any worst-case scenario suggested by allocation research on school choice.

8.1.1   How Much Higher Could School Productivity Plausibly Be?

How does one make such a calculation? We have one measure of student achievement in the United States that reflects the achievement of the entire population of students, is nationally representative, and is designed for comparison over a long period of time and across schools: the National Assessment of Educational Progress (NAEP). Other measures of achievement tend to fail at least one, usually a few, of these requirements.[2] If one simply calculates NAEP points per thousand real dollars spent per pupil, one generates the results shown in table 8.1.[3] (All money amounts in this chapter are adjusted into 1999 dollars using the Consumer Price Index, unless otherwise indicated.) They show that, between the 1970–71 and 1998–99 school years, productivity fell by between 54.9 percent (based on math tests for nine-year-olds) and 73.4 percent (based on reading tests for seventeen-year-olds). The bottom section of table 8.1 shows actual NAEP scores in its upper row and, in its lower row, what NAEP scores would be if schools returned to 1970–71 productivity (1972–73 productivity, in the case of math). For all of the tests, the average American student would have a score that fewer than 10 percent of American students currently attain. In fact, the *average* seventeen-year-old would have a score that fewer than 5 percent of American seventeen-year-olds currently attain. The mean American student would be classified by the NAEP as an advanced student.

One might wonder whether demographic changes in the United States account for the fall in school productivity, as measured by the simple calculation described above. Perhaps schools were not losing productivity; perhaps they were simply working with students from worse family backgrounds. There is no definitive way to address this issue, but a standard approach is to do the following:

---

2. The high school dropout rate, for instance, only reflects variation in the outcomes of low-achieving students. Students' self-selecting into the tests generates incurable biases when the Scholastic Aptitude Test (SAT) or ACT (formerly known as the American College Testing Program) is used for comparisons over time or across schools. The SAT and ACT also only reflect variation in the outcomes of high-achieving students. High school grades have been shown to be relative measures that cannot be compared successfully across schools.

3. The source for the table is U.S. Department of Education (2000).

Table 8.1   School Productivity in the United States, 1971–99

	Productivity[a] Based on the Test of:					
	Reading (9-year-olds)	Math (9-year-olds)	Reading (13-year-olds)	Math (13-year-olds)	Reading (17-year-olds)	Math (17-year-olds)
School year						
1970–71	46.0		56.6		63.3	
1972–73		45.5		55.3		63.2
1974–75	41.7		50.8		56.7	
1977–78		41.3		49.7		56.5
1979–80	41.3		49.6		54.8	
1981–82		40.8		50.1		55.7
1983–84	36.4		44.4		49.9	
1985–86		34.8		42.2		47.4
1987–88	30.5		37.1		41.8	
1989–90	28.9	31.8	35.5	37.3	40.1	42.2
1991–92	29.0	31.7	35.8	37.7	40.0	42.3
1993–94	28.7	31.4	35.1	37.2	39.2	41.6
1995–96	28.1	30.6	34.3	36.3	38.0	40.6
1998–99	26.8	29.4	32.8	35.0	36.5	39.0
Productivity decrease (%) since earliest year shown						
No adjustments	71.5	54.9	72.5	58.1	73.4	62.0
Adjusted for demographics	74.3	58.2	75.6	62.3	78.0	65.1
Adjusted for wages of females with advanced degrees	55.9	39.1	56.8	42.1	57.6	45.5
Actual mean NAEP score (1998–99)	212	232	259	276	288	308
Predicted NAEP score at productivity of earliest year shown (1998–99)	363	359	447	437	500	499

Source: U.S. Department of Education *Digest of Education Statistics 1999* (2000) and U.S. Department of Education *National Assessment of Educational Progress 1999 Long-Term Trend Summary Data Tables* (2000).

[a]NAEP points per thousand dollars of per-pupil spending.

- regress 1998–99 achievement on the characteristics of students who took the test in that year and thereby determine the effect of each characteristic (African American, Hispanic, single-parent family, family income, and so on);
- predict what achievement would have been in 1998–99 if the student population were the same as the 1970–71 student population—that is, substitute 1970–71 characteristics into the prediction equation with 1998–99 coefficients; and
- use predicted achievement to determine what 1998–99 productivity would have been if the student population had remained what it was in 1970–71.[4]

If one uses this method to hold student characteristics constant, then one finds that the decline in productivity from 1970 to 1999 is very slightly *larger* than the unadjusted estimates would suggest. See the row of table 8.1 in which productivity decrease is adjusted for demographics. For instance, consider the measured decrease in productivity based on the mathematics scores of seventeen-year-olds. It is a 62.0 percent decrease if student characteristics are not held constant, but it is a 65.1 percent decrease if student characteristics are held constant.[5] The decline in productivity is greater when one holds student characteristics constant mainly because a smaller share of students had high school graduate or college graduate parents in 1971–72 than in 1998–99. Such students tend to score better on the NAEP exam than students whose parents are high school dropouts. In addition, there were smaller shares of students in 1971–72 whose families had the incomes typical of families today. The shares of students who are African American and Hispanic have risen since 1971–72, and these students do tend to score worse on NAEP exam than non-Hispanic white students. However, the effect of changing racial composition is overwhelmed by the effect of changes in parents' education and income. Other changes in the composition of the student population, such as area of the country, have little effect on the adjustment.

If demographic changes do not account for the fall in school productivity, perhaps changes in career opportunities for women do. That is, over the

---

4. The calculation is

$$\rho = \frac{X_{1972\text{--}72}\,\hat{\alpha}_{1998\text{--}99}}{pps_{1998\text{--}99}},$$

where ρ is productivity, X_{1973} is the vector of characteristics of the 1971–72 student population, pps_{1998} is per-pupil spending in 1998–99, and $\hat{\alpha}$ is the vector of estimated coefficients from the regression

$$NAEP_{1998\text{--}99} = X_{1998\text{--}99}\,\alpha_{1998\text{--}99} + \varepsilon.$$

$NAEP_{1998}$ is a 1998–99 NAEP score (in reading, math, or science) and X_{1998} is the vector of characteristics of the 1998–99 student population.

5. The source of data for the calculations described in U.S. Department of Education (1999).

1970–99 period, it may have cost schools an increasing amount to hire a female with a given level of skills because non-teaching opportunities for women were opening up. One can examine this hypothesis by inflating nominal spending using a wage index for females rather the CPI. In order to give this hypothesis as much explanatory power as possible, I used the wage index for females in the college-educated occupation that experienced the most wage growth: professional specialty occupations (lawyers, physicians, etc.).[6] Use of this index exaggerates the degree to which females' wages account for the measured decline in productivity for two reasons. First, women in professional specialty occupations have always had higher-quality educations and higher ability than the average American school teacher, and highly skilled and able workers have experienced rapid earnings growth relative to all other workers (including less skilled college graduates) since 1970. Second, teachers are not the only input that schools require. They also need office equipment, buildings, less skilled service workers (custodians, bus drivers, food preparers), and other inputs; the prices of such inputs have not risen nearly as fast as the wages of female professional specialty workers. As long as we recognize that inflating by female professional specialty workers' wages is likely to give us a smaller decrease in productivity than has really occurred, the calculation is informative. The row in table 8.1 in which productivity increase is adjusted to the wages of females with advanced degrees shows that the wage-adjusted decrease in productivity ranges from 39.1 to 57.6 percent, whereas the CPI-based decrease in productivity ranges from 54.9 to 73.4 percent. In other words, although the wage-adjusted productivity losses *are* smaller, they are still very substantial.

The facts suggest that school conduct, not changing student characteristics or female career opportunities, is the main source of the decline in productivity. Consequently, policies that improve school conduct could potentially generate very large increases in productivity.[7] Of course, it is not

6. Earnings of full-time, full-year females working in professional specialty occupations are taken from U.S. Department of Commerce (1976, 1983, 1995, 1999). The index is for women in a constant age range. However, experience is not held constant. Because women have been gaining more experience for every year they age (they have spent less time out of the labor force for family reasons), using an index that holds experience (not age) constant would produce results that look more like the results using the CPI. This is yet another reason why the productivity loss shown in the row of table 8.1 that is adjusted for wages of females with advanced degrees is understated.

7. One could criticize the constant-student productivity by saying that some student characteristics mean different things in 1998 from 1971. For instance, coming from a single-parent family is more common in 1998 than in 1971, and thus it may be a different experience now from what it was in 1971. On the whole, however, such criticisms work in the wrong direction. Most of the student characteristics that are more common now than in the past are also less stigmatized—being a member of minority or being from a single-parent family, from the South or Southwest, and so on. The decline in productivity would be larger if one were to take account of the fact that having a single-parent household, say, is not as bad for achievement as it was in 1971.

enough to point out that school productivity could plausibly be much higher than it is. One must investigate whether choice actually induces schools to raise productivity. Such investigations—both how one conducts them and what they show—are the main content of this paper. Before I take up such matters, however, one more vital point about school productivity must be made.

8.1.2   How School Productivity Affects American Industry and Growth

For as long as we have been able measure the factor content of American net exports and the sources of American economic growth, they have been intensive in human capital. This was observed early on by Leontief (1956) and confirmed by a series of other researchers (Keesing 1966; Krueger 1968; Jorgenson 1984; and Jorgenson and Fraumeni 1989, 1992). In other words, the United States has a comparative advantage in producing goods and services that make intensive use of educated labor. This comparative advantage has existed because America has always had a relative abundance of educated labor. That is, the United States has always been able to produce education in its population relatively cheaply. America's "new economy" products (microprocessors, software, knowledge services) are some of the most human capital–intensive products in the world. However, we know from basic trade theory that the human capital–intensive economy is built on a foundation of American ability to produce education in its population relatively cheaply. Although it true that America can import some human capital (for instance, software engineers), imported human capital *cannot* be a source of comparative advantage in the middle to long run.[8] Thus, if Americans wish to continue enjoying a growing economy that is centered around human capital–intensive products, they cannot be indifferent about rapidly falling productivity in their schools. A school sector with falling productivity translates into America's having relatively costly human capital, which translates into a loss of comparative advantage in human capital–intensive goods.

In short, the effect of choice on school productivity is not interesting simply because it could overwhelm the allocation effects of choice on achievement; it is interesting because it also has broad implications for the macroeconomy, for trade, and for Americans' jobs.

8.2   How Productivity Fits into the School Choice Literature

The productivity implications of choice have been sadly neglected by the literature on school choice. This neglect has nothing to do with the impor-

8. Other countries can import human capital too, so imported human capital cannot be cheap relative to its cost in the rest of the world. Moreover, under a logical extension of current trends, countries that are currently net exporters of human capital would become the world's net exporters of human capital–intensive products.

tance of productivity (which is great, as has been discussed) and has everything to do with the roots of the theoretical literature. Models of school choice have grown out of models of local public goods provision, which have traditionally focused exclusively on allocation problems, such as who gets what local public good and how one person's local public good choice affects other people. This focus has been inherited by the school choice literature, and although allocation-focused models of choice are instructive, the intellectual history of the literature should not dictate neglect of productivity. Indeed, it is worth while to take a step back to look at some related research that demonstrates how important productivity effects can be when competition is introduced into a market.

Health care is an obvious and recent example. Legislation passed in the late 1980s and early 1990s allowed managed care organizations to compete.[9] The competition has affected the allocation of health care, but a wealth of research also documents the dramatic effects of competition on the productivity, which far exceeded what supporters of managed care had hoped. From 1990 to 2000, health care costs grew just one-half as quickly as in the previous decade, but key health indicators (such as life span) grew just as rapidly in the 1990s as in the 1980s. These facts suggest that productivity surged in the more competitive environment,[10] in part because competition induced providers to adopt efficiency-enhancing technology (such as computers that reduce paperwork) and to discourage conduct that created rents (such as doctors' referring patients to their friends without regard to cost). It should be noted that market competition was associated with productivity gains in nonprofit and public hospitals, as well as private hospitals.

Trucking and parcel services are other examples. Many researchers have documented how, following deregulation in the 1970s, competition in trucking grew dramatically. The result was a sharp increase in productivity, as documented by Rose (1987), Michel and Shaked (1987), Traynor and McCarthy (1991), and others. For the same money, a trucking customer could obtain faster, more specialized service after competition than before. In parcel services, the introduction of competition improved productivity not only because the private firms (United Parcel Services, Federal Express, DHL Worldwide Express, etc.) had higher productivity and productivity growth than the U.S. Postal Service did. The competition also induced the U.S. Postal Service to raise substantially its own productivity. Many commentators had doubted whether the U.S. Postal Service could rise to the occasion and compete, but it has maintained a large market share in parcel de-

9. Managed care organizations include health maintenance organizations, primary provider networks, and certain other physician and hospital networks.
10. See *Economic Report of the President* (2000). The literature on the productivity effects of managed care is voluminous, but Cutler and Sheiner (1998) may serve as a good introduction to it.

livery—largely by introducing services (like express mail and priority parcel post) that are competitive on price and quality with services offered by the private firms.

In fact, it is somewhat odd that school productivity should be so neglected in the school choice literature, because—although productivity was also neglected in the local public goods literature—there is increasing interest among economists in the productivity of not-for-profit, semipublic, and regulated enterprises. Economists are increasingly interested in giving market-like incentives to such enterprises in order to keep workers from rent-seeking despite the fact that they lack conventional profit-maximizing incentives. For instance, yardstick competition among not-for-profit providers of social services (awarding contracts to training programs on the basis of their performance relative to other sites) is increasingly used as a method of inducing productivity gains.

Finally, it is worth noting that one type of school-related research does implicitly contain substantial evidence on productivity, although productivity is rarely mentioned and productivity calculations are never made. I refer to research that compares students' outcomes in public and private schools and that attempts to eliminate selection bias. (Selection bias is the potential bias caused by the fact that students who self-select into private schools might be unobservably different from students who remain in public schools.) The body of research on this topic is well established and even includes some recent research comparing students who are assigned *by lottery* a private school voucher or no voucher (so that they remain in the public schools). Peterson et al. (chap. 4 in this volume) illustrate the best strain of such research. The consensus in public versus private achievement research appears to be that private schools produce statistically significantly better achievement, at least among minority children and children from lower- to lower-middle-income households.

This body of research could be reformulated as a comparison of public and private school productivity, because there is always an attempt to compare achievement and hold constant the quality of student inputs. Unfortunately, other inputs, especially spending, are *not* constant between private and public schools, and this body of research is often silent about this fact (and almost never controls for it). In particular, the typical private school in the United States spends only about 60 percent as much per pupil as the typical public school, but private school spending is also much more variable than is public school spending, so that minimum private school spending is lower than minimum public school spending and maximum private school spending is higher than maximum public school spending. Thus, even if researchers were to find that public and private schools produced identical achievement, it would probably be true that private schools were considerably more productive (because they spend less on average). However, if one is to get an accurate comparison of public and private school productivity, one really ought to make a productivity calculation for each school (thereby taking account of differences in the distribution of spending) and compare these calculations for students with the same backgrounds.

8.3   Why Should Choice Affect School Productivity?

Why, logically, should choice be expected to affect productivity? That is, what mechanism guarantees that low-productivity producers will be driven out by high-productivity producers? Ultimately, this is a question about (a) what schooling producers maximize and (b) what the production function for schooling is like. In fact, there are several answers to this question, and the answer is different for different types of schooling producers: for-profit firms (like Edison Schools), not-for-profit private schools, charter schools, and regular public schools. In this section, I describe the mechanism by which choice might affect productivity for each of these types of schools. Across all the cases, I do maintain one assumption: For any given cost to them, parents will choose the school that produces the schooling that they value most. For convenience, I will hereafter call what parents value in schools "school quality," but I do not assert that parents' notion of school quality necessarily matches that of the reader. In other work (Hoxby 1999a) I have presented empirical evidence that suggests that parents tend to prefer schools that have better academic achievement, emphasize academic standards, and promote a relatively structured (disciplined) school atmosphere.

8.3.1   A For-Profit School Producer That Takes Up Charter School Contracts

Let us start with a very straightforward case: a for-profit firm that opens a charter school. Such a case is fairly typical of Edison Schools and might become a common model if charter school programs were more widely enacted. The fee that the school could charge would be set by law, and parents would not be able to "top up" the fee. Also assume that the school must accept charter school applicants at random (a typical charter school restriction) and is risk neutral. In other words, a plan to include or exclude students cannot be part of the school's profit maximization strategy.

Then, the school would solve a problem such as

(1) $$\max_{q,l,k} \pi = px(q) - c(q, l, w, k, r)x(q).$$

This problem simply says that the school maximizes the difference between revenues (the fixed fee p times the number of students who enroll x) and costs (per-pupil costs c times the number of students who enroll x). The school chooses the quality q that it offers, the staff or labor l that it hires, and the other inputs k that it employs (textbooks, equipment, and so on). The school accepts the going wage rate for staff w and the going price for other school inputs r. Per-pupil costs c are assumed to be increasing in quality, staff hired, and other inputs purchased. I have assumed that per-pupil costs are the same regardless of the school's scale. This is a good starting assumption, but it is probably not true. I relax it below.

Given that we have said that parents choose the school that offers the highest quality for a given price, it is clear that enrollment x is increasing in quality q. Specifically, the school enrolls all of the public school students in an area if it offers quality that is higher than that of any other area charter school or regular public school (which would be equally free to parents). That is,

$$(2) \qquad x(q_{j*}) = \sum_{t=1}^{N} 1 \text{ if } q_{j*} > q_{j \neq j*} \text{ for all } j,$$

$$x(q_{j*}) = 0 \text{ if } q_{j*} < q_{j \neq j*} \text{ for any } j.$$

Assume that the school shares equally in enrollment if it offers exactly the same quality as another school.

In these circumstances, the best that the school can do is maximize quality subject to the constraint that its per-pupil cost must not exceed the charter school fee. Put another way, the school *must* maximize its productivity for a given cost, or another school will enroll all of the students in the area. Unproductive schools will be driven from the market. Note that the firm earns just enough profit on each student to repay its shareholders a market rate of return for the use of their capital, so the best it can do is maximize the number of students on whom it earns this slim profit. It does this by offering the highest possible quality that the charter school fee can sustain.

Managers of for-profit schooling firms believe that there are economies of scale in schooling because a firm can pay lower prices for its inputs if it pools purchasing, curricular research and development, and information processing across multiple schools.[11] If there are economies of scale, then large firms may be able to earn economic profits (profits that exceed the profits necessary to pay the cost of capital) in local markets where they compete with other schools that, for one reason or another, remain too small to take advantage of economies of scale.

8.3.2   A For-Profit School That Takes Up Vouchers

The case of a for-profit school producer that takes voucher students is quite similar to the case just examined, except that parents are assumed to be allowed to top up a voucher with extra tuition payments from their own funds. Otherwise, assume that the case is the same: The school must accept voucher applicants on a random basis conditional upon the applicants'

---

11. Pooling may occur even if the schools are in different areas and offer somewhat different levels of quality.

being willing to pay the school's fees with a combination of the voucher and extra tuition payments. Because the school can now set its fees, its problem is slightly more complicated:

(3) $\max_{p,q,l,k} \pi = px(p, q) - c(x, q, l, w, k, r)x(p, q).$

That is, when a school sets its fees, it takes into account that a higher fee means, on the one hand, greater revenue per student who enrolls but, on the other hand, lower enrollment (because a higher fee discourages enrollment for any given level of quality offered by the school). It can easily be seen that, for any given fee p, the school must maximize the quality it produces subject to the constraint that costs are less than or equal to p. In other words, the school must still maximize productivity if it is not to lose all its enrollment to another school that offers higher quality for the same price.

Note that, in the equation above, I have allowed for economies of scale. Thus, when a school considers aiming for a "better" but smaller niche of parents, who are willing to be charged higher fees for better quality, it must take into account the loss of economies of scale (and the consequent increase in its costs).

8.3.3   A Nonprofit School That Takes Up Charter School Contracts

The for-profit case is a nice place to begin because the firm's incentives to maximize productivity are obvious. The vast majority of school producers that take up charter school contracts or voucher students are, however, not-for-profits. At first glance, it might seem difficult to say what not-for-profits maximize, but in fact relatively simple modifications of the for-profit case capture not-for-profit behavior. The key difference between a nonprofit and a for-profit organization is the distribution of surplus.[12] A for-profit school distributes profits to its owners (private owners or shareholders). Thus, in the problem above, it was reasonable to assume straightforward profit maximization because owners benefit directly from profits. If a not-for-profit school has surplus (a difference between revenues and costs), it cannot pay them in a straightforward way to anyone. It can, however, use surplus in a variety of ways that make surplus a valuable thing to have. Surplus can be used to make working conditions pleasant for the school's staff (staff lunches, smaller classes, more classroom supplies, and so on) even if these conditions do not contribute to productivity. Surplus also allows a school to pursue social goals that its staff value: experiments with teaching methods, development of new curricula, a diverse student body, the exposing of students to nature. There are a few things to note about such distributions of surplus. First, they are nearly always inefficient compared to distribution

12. This point has been discussed by numerous researchers. See Glaeser and Shleifer (forthcoming) for a recent model of nonprofit entrepreneurs and for a review of the literature.

of cash (which is fungible). That is, some of the surplus is lost in the process of being transformed into goods or services that the staff values. As a result, the school staff faces weaker incentives than they would face if they could be given cash incentives. Second, although it is relatively simple to distribute a nonprofit school's surplus to its staff in the forms mentioned, it is difficult to distribute it (legally) to a single owner or even a concentrated subset of the staff. Thus, a school has less incentive to expand simply to increase the absolute size of the surplus: The surplus will increase as it expands, but so will the number of staff over whom the surplus must be divided. This is unlike the for-profit situation where owners have an incentive to expand their schooling production so long as they can earn some positive surplus on each additional enrollee.

One can incorporate these features of the distribution of surplus into a nonprofit charter school's maximization problem:

$$(4) \qquad \max_{q,l,k} \frac{(\alpha \cdot \pi)}{l} = \frac{\alpha \cdot [px(q) - c(q,l,w,k,r)x(q)]}{l}$$

where enrollment is given by

$$(5) \qquad x(q_{j*}) = \sum_{i=1}^{N} 1 \text{ if } q_{j*} \text{ for all } j,$$

$$x(q_{j*}) = 0 \text{ if } q_{j*} < q_{j \neq j*} \text{ for any } j,$$

just as before.

This problem simply says that a staff member at a nonprofit charter school wants the school to maximize $(\alpha\pi)/l$, where π is total surplus (what the for-profit school would call profit), α is a factor that is less than 1 (the share of surplus that remains after it has been transformed into goods for the staff), and l is the number of staff. Under this maximization problem, the school's incentives to expand enrollment are weaker (than those of a for-profit school), but its incentives to maximize productivity are strong. The school will still be driven out by competitors if it does not produce the maximum quality q attainable given the constraint that its costs must not exceed the fixed charter school fee.

Two comments about the nonprofit school's maximization problem are in order. First, if there are economies of scale, the school will have stronger incentives to expand enrollment than suggested just above. Second, one's measure of the productivity of a nonprofit school may slightly understate its true productivity if the school earns surplus and buys staff rewards with it that appear to be inputs (although they really make no contribution to outcomes that parents value). The understatement will be slight because competition among nonprofit schools will drive the surplus toward zero (even as each seeks to maximize its surplus).

8.3.4   A Nonprofit School That Takes Up Vouchers

The case of a nonprofit school that takes voucher students is just like the case of a for-profit school that takes voucher students except that its surplus can be distributed only in the indirect way described above. That is, the voucher school's maximization problem is

$$(6) \quad \max_{p,q,l,k} \frac{(\alpha \cdot \pi)}{l} = \frac{\alpha \cdot [px(q) - c(x, q, l, w, k, r)x(p, q)]}{l}$$

The nonprofit voucher school must maximize productivity if it is not to lose its enrollment to a similar school that offers higher quality for the same fee p. The only complication is that the school needs to choose its fee and quality simultaneously, and the only caveat is that the school has weaker incentives to expand enrollment than a for-profit voucher school.

8.3.5   A Summary for Fee-Based Schools (For-Profit and Nonprofit)

In all of the cases above, the school's revenues are derived from student fees. It is this fee basis that is crucial because it means that parents' choices determine whether a school is viable or not. If a school's students are enticed away by a competing school that charges the same fees, the school naturally has to increase its productivity (either by raising its quality for the given fee or lowering the fee it charges for its quality). As shown, the for-profit or nonprofit basis of the school is somewhat less crucial. A for-profit schooling firm will have stronger incentives to enter new markets and gain new enrollment, but both nonprofits and for-profits have incentives to maximize productivity.

People often wonder whether there will be an elastic supply of charter or voucher schools. This is an important question, especially for nonprofits, which do not have clear incentives to expand when they hope to earn only a slim surplus on additional students. If there are economies of scale, then the charter school fee or voucher that makes a school viable with a small number of students should guarantee that it is more than viable with higher enrollment. Thus, economies of scale suggest that both for-profits and nonprofits should have elastic supply once they are in business. On the other hand, there are some factors that might function like *diseconomies* of scale. For instance, a charismatic principal might become uninspiring if he or she managed a large school and therefore had little direct contact with students.

Buildings are often discussed as a possible factor that would limit the elasticity of supply of charter or voucher schools. This, however, would seem to be a short-run phenomenon that mainly plagues the start-up of new charter or voucher programs. The total number of students to be taught does not increase simply because a new school has entered, so the introduction of charter or voucher school competition does not require much of a net increase in school building. As enrollment shifts from less productive

to more productive schools, buildings should be sold by the shrinking or exiting schools and purchased by the expanding or entering schools. In fact,
there *is* an active market for school buildings and similar institutional buildings. If small fractions of school buildings could be sold easily, competition
would require *no* net increase in school buildings. Schools are, however,
somewhat indivisible: Although parts of school buildings are often sold or
leased to separate schools, only certain fractions of a building will generally
make a viable school. (For instance, most schools require an entrance area,
a set of bathrooms, and so on.) Realistically, then, competition requires a
small increase in the total stock of school buildings, simply to allow more
flexibility as parents' ability to choose makes enrollment more variable.

In any case, it is clear that some factors (economies of scale) suggest that
school supply will be very elastic, whereas other factors (which function like
diseconomies of scale) suggest that school supply will be less elastic. The
elastic response of charter and voucher schools is, thus, an empirical question and will depend on features of the reform, such as funds for the refur-
bishment of buildings.

8.3.6   Competition and the Productivity of Regular Public Schools

Does competition give *regular* public schools incentives to be productive?
We have seen that fee-based schools face straightforward incentives, but
what about regular public schools that are funded mainly by taxes?

If a regular public school faces competition from a charter or voucher
school, and the charter school fee or voucher comes directly from its budget, then the regular public school *is* fee-based at the margin and will have
marginal incentives to be productive. Whether these marginal incentives
work well or not depends on the size of the fee or voucher. Some vouchers
or fees are so small relative to regular per-pupil spending that they give
public schools perverse incentives to drive students away. That is, a voucher
or charter school fee that is small relative to per-pupil spending (or that is
not financed from the public school's revenues) *raises* per-pupil spending
nonnegligibly for each student who is driven away from the public schools.
Public school staff may be able to enjoy greater surplus if they drive students
away than if they try to attract them. Such perverse scenarios can be easily
avoided by setting a sufficiently high voucher or charter school fee.

What if, however, a regular public school does not face competition from
a charter or voucher school? If it is not fee-based at the margin, does it have
any incentives to be productive? The answer is yes if the public school is financed by local property taxes and faces a high degree of traditional choice
among public school districts.

Traditional choice among public school districts is what occurs when
parents choose a school district by choosing a residence. This traditional
form of choice is by far the most pervasive and important form of choice in
American elementary and secondary schooling today. In order that this

form of choice give schools incentives to be productive, it is essential that parents choose among *districts* that are fiscally independent. The mechanism that I am about to describe does not work with *intra*district choice.

Conventionally, public school districts in the United States have revenues that depend largely on local property taxes. If parents in a metropolitan area can choose among a large number of districts, they will tend to favor districts that produce higher achievement for a given local property tax liability or, equivalently, have lower local tax liability for a given level of achievement. That is, parents will tend to favor districts with high productivity. If a school district's productivity falls, it will be avoided by parents who happen to be moving. The resulting decrease in the demand for its houses will drive down the district's property prices. The falling property tax base will, in turn, drive down the school's budget, which depends on property tax revenues. The administrator will be encouraged to raise productivity, either by maintaining achievement in the face of a falling budget or by raising achievement sufficiently to make the district attractive to home buyers again.

Notice that, although only a fraction of households are moving at any given time, their observations of achievement and tax liabilities are "universalized" through the housing market so that *every* family's house price changes in such a way as to give schools incentives to be productive. Notice also that this productivity-inducing mechanism is sustainable over the long term because it depends on decentralized choices.[13] This is in contrast to centralized reward systems—for example, financial or other merit awards for successful school districts that are distributed by the state. Centralized rewards tend to be unsustainable because state governments cannot, ex post, credibly adhere to systems that reduce the amount of money going to failing school districts.

8.4   Finding Evidence on How Choice Affects School Productivity

In the next two sections of this paper, I show evidence on how choice affects school productivity. The next section focuses on traditional forms of choice (parents choosing among independent school districts and parents choosing private schools). Section 8.6 focuses on recent choice reforms: vouchers and charter schools. There are, however, some problems that arise in any analysis of how choice affects productivity, and the purpose of *this* section is to explain them.

8.4.1   The Endogenous Availability of Choice Options

One problem that plagues analysis is the fact that choice options do not arise randomly, but are frequently a response to school conduct. In partic-

---

13. The mechanism described is the subject of Hoxby (1999b), where it is described in much more detail.

ular, when people are dissatisfied with a particular school's conduct, they try to create alternative schools for themselves or maintain their access to existing alternative schools.

It is easy to see this phenomenon with respect to the creation (or maintenance) of private schools, charter schools, and voucher programs. In an area where the public schools are bad, parents are frustrated and are willing to make some effort or devote some money to obtaining alternative schooling. A collapse in the quality of local public schools (as sometimes occurs when an administrator leaves or school finance laws change) tends to send families scurrying toward local private schools. The result is an area in which private schooling is common because the public schools are bad. A recent illustration of this phenomenon is the substantial increase in private schooling that followed California's school finance equalization (Downes and Schoeman 1998).

Recent voucher and charter initiatives also illustrate this phenomenon. It is no accident that Washington, D.C. has both a voucher program and a rapidly growing population of charter schools. The Washington, D.C. district has historically had low productivity: Its per-pupil spending is in the 99th (highest) percentile for the United States, yet its average student scores between the 10th and 20th percentiles on the NAEP. Reports of malfeasance in the D.C. public schools, including the theft of school supplies and payrolls padded with nonworkers, are common.[14]

Although the mechanism is less obvious, choice options existing *because* the public schools are bad is a problem that also plagues traditional choice among public school districts. It turns out that voters resist district consolidation in areas where one or more districts (usually the largest central city district) has bad productivity. In areas where all the districts have good productivity, voters elect to consolidate them in order to enjoy economies of scale. In districts with bad productivity, subareas are keen to secede and form another district, whereas, in districts with good productivity, no such secessions occur. The end result of such phenomena is that areas with many districts often contain one or more districts with bad productivity.

Endogenous school choice in areas with bad public schools generates bias if a researcher naively estimates the effect of choice on productivity. Because schools with poor productivity induce the creation of choice, it can appear as though choice causes low productivity (instead of the other way around). Researchers can avoid this bias only by (a) comparing the same school district before and after a choice reform if panel data are available or (b) finding a source of variation in the availability of choice that is *not* correlated with the underlying causes of bad school productivity. The first so-

14. The sources are U.S. Department of Education, *Digest of Education Statistics* (2000) and U.S. Department of Education, *National Assessment of Educational Progress Long-Term Trend Summary Data Tables* (2000).

lution typically generates differences-in-differences strategies, in which schools that are "treated" with choice reforms are compared, before and after the reform, to similar control schools (which did not experience the reform). The second solution typically generates instrumental variables strategies, two of which are illustrated in section 8.5.

8.4.2 Unobserved Differences in Student Inputs That Appear to Be Differences in Productivity

Some families provide many learning opportunities and resources for their children at home; other families provide few. Children also differ in motivation and innate ability. When measuring a school's productivity, one should fully account for differences in student inputs so that one avoids describing a mediocre school as highly productive simply because it has such good student inputs that achievement is high even if it adds very little learning (beyond what its students learn at home and pick up for themselves). It is not possible, however, to measure all student inputs. In particular, motivation and innate ability are usually not observed and cannot be controlled for.

For finding the effect of choice on productivity, there are three ways that researchers can deal with this problem. Suppose a researcher wants to compare productivity across schools that face strong choice-based incentives (such as voucher or charter schools) and schools that face weak choice-based incentives (such as a large public school district that dominates a metropolitan area). Then, the researcher must ensure that a random mechanism (such as a lottery) that is *not* correlated with unobserved motivation or ability assigns students to schools. If such a mechanism is at work, schools will have an equal allocation of unobserved motivation or ability, and the difference in achievement per dollar spent will accurately reflect true differences in productivity. This approach is illustrated by Peterson et al. (chap. 4 in this volume).

An alternative is for a researcher to compare the achievement of *all* students from an environment in which there is little or no choice to that of *all* students from an environment in which there is a lot of choice. As long as the students cannot choose the environment to which they belong, this method generates good estimates. One example is comparing all students in a metropolitan area with little choice to all students in a metropolitan area with a great deal of choice. (Families are assumed to move among metropolitan areas for reasons *other* than the availability of choice.)

A final alternative is for a researcher to examine the achievement of students who are unlikely to benefit from choice unless it benefits *all* students. An example will illustrate this method. Suppose that a researcher wishes to compare school productivity before and after a private school becomes available, and the researcher sees that the private school draws students who were previously high achievers in the public schools. The researcher can compare measured productivity at the public schools before and after the private school's introduction, knowing that public schools' measured productivity is likely to rise only if the availability of private school choice benefits *all* students—that is, if the researcher may be reasonably confident that a measured increase in public school productivity is not generated by unobserved motivation and ability rising at the public school.

8.4.3   Measuring Productivity

Productivity is achievement per dollar spent in a school, and measuring productivity raises a few measurement issues, mostly related to measuring achievement. It goes almost without saying that one should avoid using measures of achievement, such as grades, that have different meanings in different schools and times. One should also avoid using scores on standardized tests that are taken by only a small, self-selected share of students, such as the Scholastic Aptitude Test (SAT1) or American College Test (ACT). Use of such tests generates self-selection bias that is impossible to solve without the use of other standardized tests that are given to the entire population of students. If one has such a populationwide standardized test, however, one should use it instead of the SAT1 or ACT.

Supposing that one has a standardized test administered to the entire population of students, there remains the question of whether to measure productivity with reading scores, math scores, science scores, elementary school scores, secondary scores, and so on. These are all valid measures of productivity, and the researcher is best off presenting several (especially math and reading). It is perfectly normal to find that a school has better productivity in some subjects or grades than in others. One may use scale scores, national percentile scores, or any other score designed by the testmaker to be comparable across schools and time.[15]

Measuring per-pupil spending presents few problems as long as the same definition is used for all schools. One may use either current spending or (preferably) total spending with smoothed capital expenditures.

8.5   The Effect of Traditional Forms of School Choice on Productivity

Parents' ability to choose among public school districts (through residential decisions) and to choose private schools are such established features of American education that they are taken for granted. Through these mechanisms, American parents have traditionally exercised some choice

---

15. Wages and income later in life are additional measures of achievement that are useful complements to measures based on standardized tests. They are useful because they are meaningful to people in a concrete way and because they are measured in dollars, as is the denominator of productivity. There are, however, several problems with using wages and income to measure achievement, including a paucity of data linked to schools, questionable validity for women, and the impossibility of analyzing a reform until at least twenty years after its occurrence. I do not present wage-based measures of productivity here, but see Hoxby (2000b) for some wage-based estimates.

over their children's schooling. These traditional forms of choice are useful for predicting the effects of choice on productivity, especially because the availability of traditional choice mechanisms varies greatly across metropolitan areas in the United States. Some metropolitan areas contain many independent school districts and a large number of affordable private schools. Other metropolitan areas are completely monopolized by one school district or have almost no private schooling.

In previous work, I have drawn upon traditional forms of choice to generate evidence about how choice affects productivity. I review this evidence here. In addition, I explain how traditional forms of choice generate important evidence on productivity that is otherwise unobtainable and illustrate empirical strategies for determining the effects of traditional forms of choice. For detail on the empirical work described here, see Hoxby (2000a, b). Rather than providing such detail here, I reserve space for evidence on the productivity effects of recent choice reforms (section 8.6).

8.5.1   Traditional Interdistrict Choice

The first traditional form of choice occurs when parents choose among independent public school districts by choosing a residence. The degree to which parents can exercise this form of choice depends on the number, size, and housing patterns of districts in the area of the parents' jobs. There are some metropolitan areas in the United States that have many small school districts with reasonably comparable characteristics. Boston, for instance, has seventy school districts within a thirty-minute commute of the downtown area and many more in the metropolitan area. Miami, on the other hand, has only one school district (Dade County), which covers the entire metropolitan area. Most metropolitan areas are, of course, somewhere between these two extremes. A typical metropolitan area has an amount of choice that corresponds to having four equal-sized school districts (or a greater number of unequally sized districts).

People with jobs in rural areas typically have only one or two school districts among which to choose. To avoid a much-choice/little-choice comparison that mainly reflects urban-rural differences in school productivity, it is useful to focus on metropolitan areas when analyzing traditional interdistrict choice.

It is essential that parents choose among districts that are fiscally and legally independent if this traditional form of choice is to be useful guide to the productivity effects of choice. This is because the mechanism previously described, by which parents' housing choices translate into incentives for a school to be productive, does not operate if, say, a district relies entirely on state revenue or is otherwise held harmless from repercussions associated with an inability to attract parents. *Intra*district choice among schools does not provide useful evidence about productivity effects because the schools in a district are fiscally dependent on one another, by definition.

How does one measure the degree of traditional interdistrict choice in a metropolitan area? A particularly good index of interdistrict choice is the probability that, in a random encounter, two students in the metropolitan area would be enrolled in different school districts. If there were only one district, as in Miami, this probability would be equal to zero. If there were many districts, as in Boston, this probability would be very close to one (greater than 0.95). We can calculate this choice index, C_m, using the following equation:

$$(7) \qquad C_m = 1 - \sum_{j=1}^{J} s_{jm}^2,$$

where s_{jm}^2 is the square of district j's share of enrollment in metropolitan area m. Table 8.2 lists the names and choice indexes of metropolitan areas

Table 8.2

Metropolitan Areas with the Most Choice among Public School Districts		Metropolitan Areas with Very Little Choice among Public School Districts	
Metropolitan Area	Choice Index	Metropolitan Area	Choice Index
Albany, N.Y.	0.97	Honolulu, Hawaii	0
Bergen-Pasaic, N.J.	0.97	Miami, Fla.	0
Boston, Mass.	0.97	Las Vegas, Nev.	0
Pittsburgh, Pa.	0.96	Fort Lauderdale, Fla.	0
Riverside-San Bernardino, Calif.	0.96	Daytona Beach, Fla.	0
		Fort Myers, Fla.	0
Monmouth-Ocean, N.J.	0.96	Albuquerque, N.Mex.	0
Minneapolis, Minn.	0.96	Hagerstown, Md.	0
Atlantic City, N.J.	0.95	Jacksonville, N.C.	0
San Francisco, Calif.	0.95	Sarasota, Fla.	0
St. Louis, Mo.	0.95	Odessa, Tex.	0
Binghamton, N.Y.	0.94	Cheyenne, Wyo.	0
York, Pa.	0.94	Lakeland/Winter Haven, Fla.	0
Scranton, Pa.	0.94		
Johnstown, Pa.	0.94	Reno, Nev.	0
San Jose, Calif.	0.94	Boca Raton, Fla.	0
Dayton, Ohio	0.94	Wilmington, N.C.	0
Allentown, Pa.	0.94	Ocala, Fla.	0
Anaheim-Santa Ana, Calif.	0.94	Melbourne/Palm Bay, Fla.	0
Seattle, Wash.	0.94	Panama City, Fla.	0
Rochester, N.Y.	0.94	Bradenton, Fla.	0
Phoenix, Ariz.	0.94	Portland, Oreg.	0.07
Youngstown, Ohio	0.94	Midland, Tex.	0.11

Source: U.S. Department of Education (1994b).

Notes: Hawaii is one school district, so the school district is larger than the metropolitan area of Honolulu. California has school districts that have almost no fiscal independence, so it is somewhat deceptive to describe metropolitan areas like Riverside-San Bernardino, San Francisco, San Jose, and Anaheim-Santa Ana as having significant choice among school districts.

in the United States that have very high or low degrees of interdistrict choice. It is interesting to note that metropolitan areas as disparate as Saint Louis and Seattle have comparably high degrees of interdistrict choice. Metropolitan areas as disparate as Las Vegas and Wilmington have zero interdistrict choice.

8.5.2   Traditional Choice of Private Schools

The second way in which parents have traditionally been able to exercise choice in the United States is by enrolling their children in private schools. Traditionally, private school tuition in America is not subsidized by public funds (as it is in Canada and many European countries), so parents can only afford private school if they can pay tuition and also pay taxes to support local public schools. Partly as a result, private schools enroll only 12 percent of American students.

In the United States, 85 percent of private school students attend a school with religious affiliation, but such schools include a variety of Christian and non-Christian schools and have tuition that ranges from a token amount to over $10,000. The remaining 15 percent of private school students attend schools with no religious affiliation; these include most of the independent, college-preparatory schools that charge tuition of $5,000 or more. The modal private school student in the United States attends a Catholic school that charges between $1,200 and $2,700.

A key feature of American private schools is that they typically subsidize tuition with revenues from donations or an endowment (or implicit revenues from an in-kind endowment such as buildings and land). The share of schooling cost that is covered by subsidies is larger in schools that serve low-income students, but even relatively expensive private schools charge subsidized tuition. For instance, Catholic elementary schools, on average, cover 50 percent of their costs with nontuition revenues.

The number of private school places (of a given quality) that are available at a given tuition varies greatly among metropolitan area in the United States.[16] For instance, in some metropolitan areas, 15 percent of the elementary student population is enrolled in private schools where tuition is about two-thirds of the schools' per-pupil expenditure. (Typical amounts would be tuition of $1,800 and expenditure of about $2,700). In other metropolitan areas, fewer than 1 percent of the elementary school population is enrolled in such schools, although places might be available in schools where tuition is higher because there are no tuition subsidies. In short, the

16. The quality of a private school can be measured in various ways, the simplest of which is merely the amount of money the private school spends on educating a student. Because private schools face strong incentives to be productive, their costs are a good guide to their quality. Private school expenditure sometimes understates the true cost of educating a private school student because, especially in schools with religious affiliation, labor is donated by volunteers and church buildings are used for educational purposes.

supply of private schooling varies among metropolitan areas, and, thus, so does the degree to which parents have choice between public and private schools.

It is reasonable to use the actual share of students who attend private school in a metropolitan area as a measure of private school availability *if* the measure is properly instrumented. The instruments must be variables that cause the nontuition revenue of private schools to vary but are otherwise unrelated to local public school achievement. That is, one wants to use only the variation in private school availability that is generated by factors that affect the *supply* of private schooling, not by factors that affect the *demand* for private schooling (such as the local public schools being bad). I describe the best available instruments below.

8.5.3 Why Evidence from the Traditional Forms of Choice is Necessary

Evidence from the traditional forms of choice is necessary because it can reveal the long-term, general equilibrium effects of choice. Evidence based on recent reforms cannot.

In the short term, administrators who are attempting to raise their school's productivity to respond to competition have only certain options. They can induce their staff to work harder; they can get rid of unproductive staff and programs; they can allocate resources away from non-achievement-oriented activities (building self-esteem) and toward achievement-oriented ones (math, reading, and so on). In the slightly longer term, they can renegotiate the teacher contract to make the school more efficient. If administrators actually pursue all of these options, they may be able to raise productivity substantially.

Nevertheless, choice can affect productivity through a variety of long-term, general equilibrium mechanisms that are not immediately available to an administrator. The financial pressures of choice may bid up the wages of teachers whose teaching raises achievement and attracts parents. Choice may thus draw people into teaching (or keep people in teaching) who would otherwise pursue other careers. Indeed, there is evidence that choice changes the entire structure of rewards in teaching and could thereby transform the profession. (It appears that schools under pressure from choice reward teachers more on the basis of merit and allow administrators more discretion in rewarding good teachers.)[17] The need to attract parents may force schools to issue more information about their achievement and may thus gradually make parents into better "consumers." Because parents' decisions are more meaningful when schools are financed by fees they control, choice may make schools more receptive to parent participation. The need to produce results that are competitive with those of other schools may force schools to recognize and abandon pedagogical techniques and curric-

17. See Hoxby (2002b) for more on this point.

ula that are unsuccessful in practice although philosophically appealing. Finally, in the long term, choice can affect the size and very existence of schools. Choice makes districts' enrollment expand and contract; it makes private schools enter and exit. In the short term, we mainly observe how the existing stock of schools changes its behavior.

Both traditional forms of choice potentially create the long-term, general equilibrium effects that interest us.

8.5.4   The Effect of Traditional Interdistrict Choice on School Productivity

We have a good measure of the degree of interdistrict choice in a metropolitan area: C_m, defined above. We are concerned, however, that the interdistrict choice available is endogenous to the conduct of local public schools; in particular, districts consolidate with productive districts but secede from unproductive districts. To obtain unbiased estimates, we need geographic or historical factors that increase a metropolitan area's tendency to contain many independent districts but that have no direct effect on contemporary public school conduct. As explained in Hoxby (2000b), streams and rivers provide good instruments because, early in American history, they were natural barriers that influenced the drawing of district boundaries. They increased students' travel time to school, causing school districts to be drawn smaller initially.[18] They probably have no direct effect on how schools conduct themselves now.

Formally, the set of instruments for C_m is a vector of variables that measure the number of larger and smaller streams in a metropolitan area. I estimate the effects of interdistrict choice using regressions in which the dependent variable is either achievement (the numerator of productivity) or per-pupil spending (the denominator of productivity).[19] The key independent variable is the choice index (instrumented). The key variation in the regression is at the metropolitan area level, but I am able to control for a wide range of background variables that might also influence schools or students. For instance, I control for the effect of household income, parents' educational attainment, family size, single-parent households, race, region, metropolitan area size, and the local population's income, racial composition, poverty, educational attainment, and urbanness. Because I have good measures of racial, ethnic, and income segregation by school and school

18. This typically took place about the time of Anglo-American settlement, which varies with the area of the country. Many of the original petitions for district boundaries cite streams as a reason for not extending the district lines further. Streams are by far the most common natural boundary for school districts. Note, however, that many of the streams that are preserved in boundaries are small and have never had industrial importance. Today, many of the boundary streams are of negligible importance in travel.

19. Per-pupil spending is the denominator in the measure of productivity. Because I compare productivity across metropolitan areas with widely varying costs of living, I adjust per-pupil spending using the Bureau of Labor Statistics metropolitan cost-of-living indexes.

Table 8.3   Effect of Traditional Interdistrict Choice on Productivity of Public Schools

	8th-Grade Reading Score	10th-Grade Math Score	12th-Grade Reading Score
Effect on Achievement (numerator of productivity)			
An increase of 1 in the index of interdistrict choice	3.818**	3.061**	5.770**
(no choice to maximum choice)	(1.591)	(1.494)	(2.208)
Effect on Per-Pupil Spending (denominator of productivity)			
An increase of 1 in the index of interdistrict choice	−7.63%**		
(no choice to maximum choice)	(3.41)		

Sources: The main source for this table is Hoxby (2000b). Observations are metropolitan area students from the National Education Longitudinal Study. The number of observations in each column are 10,790 (from 211 metropolitan areas), 7,776 (from 211 metropolitan areas), and 6,119 (from 209 metropolitan areas). The number of observations varies due to the availability of the dependent variable. Other data sources are the U.S. Department of Education (1993, 1994b), U.S. Department of Commerce (1994), and U.S. Geological Survey (1994).

Notes: Test scores are measured in national percentile points. Per-pupil spending is measured in natural log points so that the effect of choice is recorded in percentage terms. The coefficients shown come from instrumental variables estimation of regressions in which the dependent variable is one of the achievement measures shown or per-pupil spending. The independent variables in the regression include the index of choice (instrumented by a vector of streams variables; see text), several family background variables (household income, gender, race, parents' education), several neighborhood variables (mean household income in district, income inequality in district, racial composition of district, racial and ethnic homogeneity of district, educational attainment of adults in district), and several characteristics of the metropolitan area (population, land area, mean household income, income inequality, racial composition, racial homogeneity, ethnic homogeneity, educational attainment of adults, homogeneity of educational attainment, region of the country). The regressions are weighted by school enrollment. Standard errors are in parentheses and use formulas (Moulton 1986) for data grouped by districts and metropolitan areas.

**Statistically significantly different from zero at the 95 percent level of confidence.

district, I can even control for segregation that may be affected by interdistrict choice.

The principal results of these regressions are shown in table 8.3, which displays only the coefficients of interest, not the coefficients on control variables. The estimates show that interdistrict choice has a positive, statistically significant effect on productivity.[20] We can see this by looking at the two components of productivity: achievement (the numerator of productivity), which is shown in the top panel of the table; and per-pupil spending (the denominator of productivity), which is shown in the bottom panel.

The top panel shows that a metropolitan area with maximum interdistrict choice (index approximately equal to 1) has eighth-grade reading scores that are 3.8 national percentile points higher, tenth-grade math scores that are 3.1 national percentile points higher, and twelfth-grade reading scores that are 5.8 national percentile points higher. All of these effects

20. I consistently use the words "statistically significant" to mean "statistically significantly different from zero (for a two-sided test) with at least 90 percent confidence."

are statistically significant with at least 95 percent confidence. The bottom panel of table 8.3 shows that this better achievement is attained with *lower* per-pupil spending. Per-pupil spending is 7.6 percent lower in metropolitan areas where interdistrict choice is at its maximum level (choice index equal to 1), as opposed to its minimum level (choice index equal to 0). The combination of the top and bottom panels is striking: Schools can simultaneously have significantly higher achievement and significantly lower spending only if their productivity is substantially higher.

8.5.5   The Effect of Traditional Private School Choice on School Productivity

Recall that availability of private schooling varies among metropolitan areas in the United States. To estimate the effects of varying private school competition for public schools, we need factors that affect the supply of private schooling but have no direct effect on achievement. Such factors include historical differences in metropolitan areas' religious composition because religious groups left endowments that today generate differences in the amount of nontuition revenue enjoyed by private schools. A private school presented by history with a generous endowment can provide a given quality of schooling at a lower tuition (and can thus be more competitive with public schools) than a private school with little or no endowment.

Formally, the set of instruments for the share of enrollment in private schools is a vector of variables that measure the population densities of nine major religious denominations in 1950. As long as I control for *current* religious composition of metropolitan areas (which might affect the demand for private schooling), these historical religious population densities should mainly affect the supply of schooling and should have little or no direct effect on the achievement of public school students.[21] I estimate the effects of private school choice using regressions in which the dependent variable is either achievement (the numerator of productivity) or per-pupil spending (the denominator of productivity). The key independent variable is the percentage of metropolitan-area students in private schools (instrumented). I control for the same background variables that I used for interdistrict choice (see above).

The key estimates from these regressions are shown in table 8.4, which displays only the coefficients of interest, not the coefficients on control variables. The table shows that private school choice has a positive, statistically significant effect on *public* schools' productivity. For instance, compare two metropolitan areas, one with a moderately high degree of private school supply (about 17 percent of students in private schools) and the other with a moderately low degree of private school supply (about 7 percent of students in private schools). The difference between moderately high and low

21. See Hoxby (2000a) for further comment on this point.

Table 8.4   Effect of Traditional Private School Choice on Productivity of Public Schools

	8th-Grade Reading Score	8th-Grade Math Score	12th-Grade Reading Score	12th-Grade Math Score
Effect on Achievement (numerator of productivity)				
An increase of 1 in the index of interdistrict choice	0.271**	0.249**	0.342**	0.371**
(no choice to maximum choice)	(0.090)	(0.090)	(0.172)	(0.171)
Effect on Per-Pupil Spending (denominator of productivity)				
An increase of 1 in the index of interdistrict choice		0.85%		
(no choice to maximum choice)		(0.68)		

Sources: The main source for this table is Hoxby (2000a). Observations are metropolitan area students from the National Education Longitudinal Study. Other data sources are U.S. Department of Education (1993, 1994b) and U.S. Department of Commerce (1994).

Notes: Test scores are measured in national percentile points. The coefficients shown come from instrumental variables estimation of regressions in which the dependent variable is one of the achievement measures shown. The independent variables in the regression include the percentage of metropolitan area students enrolled in private schools (instrumented by a vector of religious composition variables from 1950; see text), several family background variables (household income, gender, race, parents' education), several neighborhood variables (mean household income in district, income inequality in district, racial composition of district, racial and ethnic homogeneity of district, educational attainment of adults in district), and several characteristics of the metropolitan area (population, land area, mean household income, income inequality, racial composition, racial homogeneity, ethnic homogeneity, educational attainment of adults, homogeneity of educational attainment, region of the country). The regressions are weighted by school enrollment. Standard errors are in parentheses and use formulas (Moulton 1986) for data grouped by districts and metropolitan areas.

**Statistically significantly different from zero at the 95 percent level of confidence.

private school choice is, thus, a 10 percentage point difference in the share of students in private schools. This means that we can interpret the coefficient shown in the top panel of table 8.4 as follows. A *public* school in the metropolitan area with moderately high private school choice (as opposed to moderately low private school choice) has eighth-grade reading scores that are 2.7 national percentile points higher, eighth-grade math scores that are 2.5 national percentile points higher, twelfth-grade reading scores that are 3.4 national percentile points higher, and twelfth-grade math scores that are 3.7 national percentile points higher.

Of course, in order to see whether these effects on achievement are generated by higher productivity or just higher spending, we need to examine the effect of private school choice on per-pupil spending in the public schools. This result is shown in the bottom panel of table 8.4. Compared to public schools in metropolitan areas with moderately low private school choice, public schools in areas with moderately high private school choice have per-pupil spending that is 0.53 percent (approximately half of 1 percent) higher. Not only is this change very small, but it is not statistically significantly different from zero. In other words, traditional private school choice has no effect on public school spending. This is probably because of offsetting effects. Increased availability of private school choice draws some students away from the public schools, raising per-pupil spending through the reduction in the number of pupils served but lowering per-pupil spending through the reduction in voters who will support higher public school spending.

In summary, the effect of private school choice on productivity is substantial and occurs purely through an effect on achievement: Per-pupil spending in the public schools does not change, but their achievement is higher.

8.5.6   Discussion of the Effects of Traditional Forms of School Choice

Are the effects of traditional choice on productivity large or small? One way to answer this question is to ask how much higher American school productivity would be if every school were to experience a high level of interdistrict choice and private school choice, as opposed to zero interdistrict choice and moderately low private school choice. There would be a 28 percent improvement in American school productivity, based on the estimates described above. 28 percent is close to half of the decline in American school productivity since 1970.

One should keep in mind, however, that both traditional forms of choice provide rather weak incentives compared to choice reforms like vouchers and charter schools. Moreover, many poor families cannot exercise either of the traditional forms of choice: A family can only choose among districts if it can afford to live in a variety of areas, and it can only exercise traditional private school choice if it can pay tuition. Thus, even if every metropolitan area in the United States had the maximum degree of the traditional forms of choice, poor families would probably be left with relatively unproductive schools.

8.6   The Effect of Recent Choice Reforms on School Productivity

As mentioned above, recent choice reforms can only partially answer our questions about how competition affects productivity. The recent vintage of most reforms means that we are unlikely to witness major changes in the supply of schools. Also, short-term reactions to choice can differ from long-term reactions. For instance, consider a regular public school that has had low productivity for years and that has become the target of voucher or charter school competition. Under pressure, the school might make dramatic productivity gains in the short run. The principal might quickly eliminate unsuccessful instructional programs or personnel and reallocate resources toward core instructional programs in reading, language, math, history, and science. The rate of productivity increase might, however, slow after the first few years as good policy changes become less obvious. On the other hand, even a school that is raising its productivity might appear to have productivity losses in the short run if it faces adjustment costs when it makes changes. For instance, a school that puts an academic monitoring system in place may face short-run costs for computers and training.

Can we learn much, then, from recent choice reforms? The answer is yes if we follow a few principles. First, although it is interesting to examine the productivity of the choice schools themselves (as Peterson et al. implicitly do in chap. 4 in this volume), it is even more important to study the productivity reactions of regular public schools that are newly facing competition. This is because the productivity reactions of regular public schools are in much more doubt than the productivity of choice schools. An unproductive choice school is unlikely to enter and even less likely to survive, but critics of school choice doubt whether regular public schools even have the knowledge or tools to raise their productivity. Second, we should focus on the productivity reactions of regular public schools that face nonnegligible incentives due to a choice reform. This immediately limits our investigation to a few choice reforms that meet the following requirements: (a) There is a realistic possibility that at least 5 percent of regular public enrollment could go to choice schools; (b) the regular public schools lose at least some money (not necessarily the entire per-pupil cost) when a student goes to a choice school, and (c) the reform has been in place for a few years. Three reforms that satisfy these basic requirements are school vouchers in Milwaukee, charter schools in Michigan, and charter schools in Arizona. I describe each of these reforms below in the course of examining the reaction to it. Apart from these three reforms, most choice reforms fail to meet at least one of these requirements. In fact, choice reforms are typically characterized by constraints on enrollment (for instance, no more than 1 percent of local students can attend choice schools) or perverse financial incentives (for instance, the local district loses no money when it loses a student to a choice school).[22]

8.6.1 The Effect of Vouchers on Achievement in Milwaukee Public Schools

Vouchers for poor students in Milwaukee were enacted in 1990 and were first used in the 1990–91 school year. Currently, a family is eligible for a voucher if its income is at or below 175 percent of the federal poverty level (at or below $17,463 for a family of four).[23] For the 1999–2000 school year, the voucher amount was $5,106 per student or the private school's cost per

---

22. See Rees (2000) for a thorough review of current school choice reforms. In most cases where I have not used materials directly obtained from the relevant state's department of education, I have relied upon Rees for a description of reforms.

23. As a rule, any child who is eligible for free or reduced-price lunch is also eligible for a voucher. The actual cutoff for reduced-price lunch is 185 percent of the federal poverty level, but the difference between 175 percent (the cutoff for the vouchers) and 185 percent is not rigorously enforced (and would be difficult to enforce).

student, whichever was less. For every student who leaves the Milwaukee public schools with a voucher, the Milwaukee public schools lose state aid equal to half the voucher amount (up to $2,553 per voucher student in 1999–2000). Milwaukee's per-pupil spending in 1999–2000 was $8,752 per pupil, so the district was losing 29 percent of the per-pupil revenue associated with a voucher student. Currently, the vouchers may be used at secular and nonsecular private schools.[24]

The voucher program had a difficult start. Although approximately 67,000 students were initially eligible for vouchers, participation was initially limited to only 1 percent of Milwaukee enrollment. In 1993, the limit was raised to 1.5 percent and, in 1998, to 15 percent of enrollment. The 1998 changes followed a prolonged legal dispute in which most voucher students had to use privately donated, not publicly funded, vouchers. For instance, in 1997–98, only 1,500 students (about 1.4 percent of Milwaukee students) were able to use publicly funded vouchers. Also, until 1998, the future of the program was very much in doubt.[25] Overall, although the voucher program began in 1990 and might have been expected to have had a small impact on the Milwaukee public schools beginning with the 1990–91 school year, the program generated very little potential competition until the 1998–99 school year. However, because the program was already somewhat established and familiar to Milwaukee residents by 1998, one would expect a quicker response to the program than for a completely new program. In short, it is plausible to look for a productivity impact, if any, over the few most recent school years. The 1996–97 school year effectively predates serious competition.

Not all schools in Milwaukee experienced the same increase in competition as the result of the voucher program. The greater a school's share of poor children, the greater the potential competition, because the greater was the potential loss of students (after 1998). Some Milwaukee schools had as few as 25 percent of their students eligible for vouchers, whereas other Milwaukee schools had as many as 96 percent eligible. Also, because private elementary schools cost significantly less than private high schools, more than 90 percent of vouchers were used by students in grades one through seven in 1999–2000. Thus, only elementary schools in Milwaukee faced significant potential competition.

These facts about the voucher program suggest that the following type of evaluation is most appropriate for examining the productivity response of

24. The information on the Milwaukee program and Wisconsin schools is obtained from several publications of the Wisconsin Department of Public Instruction (2000a–e).

25. The future of the program is still somewhat in doubt, for two reasons. First, state supreme courts' opinions conflict on the question of whether it is constitutional to have vouchers that can be used at schools with religious affiliation. Therefore, it is likely that the U.S. Supreme Court will eventually rule on such vouchers. Second, the Wisconsin legislature has threatened to fund the vouchers at such a low level that they are unusable.

Milwaukee public schools. First, one should focus on the productivity of Milwaukee schools in grades one through seven. Second, schools' productivity should be compared from 1996–97 (before significant competition) to 1999–2000 (after significant competition). Third, schools in Milwaukee can be separated into those that were "more treated" by competition because a large number of students were eligible and those that were "less treated." More-treated schools are likely to have responded more strongly to the program. We can think of the less-treated schools in Milwaukee as a partial control group, but *all* schools in Milwaukee were eligible for nonnegligible treatment. Therefore, it is desirable to have a control group of schools from Wisconsin that were truly unaffected by the voucher program. It turns out that it is not easy to find such schools in Wisconsin because Milwaukee's schools are much poorer and have much larger shares of black and Hispanic students than most other schools in the state. I chose the most similar schools available for the evaluation, but it is likely that the results will understate the productivity effects of school competition. We expect understatement because schools that have fewer poor and minority students typically enjoy greater productivity and higher productivity *growth* than schools with more poor and minority students. Thus, the control schools, which are richer than the treated schools, would probably have higher productivity growth (all else being equal) than the treated group of schools. Also, the less-treated schools in Milwaukee would probably have higher productivity growth (all else being equal) than the more-treated schools.[26]

Because my evaluation compares *treated and control* schools *before and after* 1998, it is what is sometimes called a difference-in-differences evaluation. It has a fairly obvious analog in scientific experiments.

Table 8.5 shows some demographic indicators for the three groups of elementary schools: most treated (Milwaukee schools where at least two-thirds of students were eligible for vouchers), somewhat treated (Milwaukee schools where less than two-thirds of students were eligible for vouchers), and untreated comparison schools. Note that 30 percent was the minimum share of students eligible for vouchers among the somewhat treated Milwaukee elementary schools. There are thirty-two most-treated and sixty-six somewhat-treated elementary schools. All of the Milwaukee elementary schools have enrollment of about seventy-one to seventy-two students in a grade.

In the most-treated schools, an average of 81.3 percent of students were

26. It is fairly obvious that better-off schools will have better productivity if one does not control for demographic differences among students. It is less obvious that better-off schools will also have better productivity growth, but in fact they do. For instance, prior to 1996, Wisconsin elementary students took statewide tests in reading (only). In the prevoucher period, productivity growth was negative (based on these reading tests) in the schools that were later to become most-treated and somewhat treated. In contrast, productivity growth (based on reading tests) was positive in the schools that form the untreated comparison group.

Table 8.5   Demographics of Wisconsin's Most-Treated, Somewhat Treated, and
                   Untreated Comparison Schools

	% of Students Eligible for Free/ Reduced-Price Lunch	% of Students Who Are Black	% of Students Who Are Hispanic
Most-treated schools	81.3	65.4	2.9
Somewhat treated schools	44.5	49.1	13.7
Untreated comparison schools	30.4	30.3	3.0

Sources: Wisconsin Department of Public Instruction (2000a–e) and U.S. Department of Education (1994b).

Notes: "Most-treated" schools were Milwaukee elementary schools where at least two-thirds of students are eligible for free or reduced price lunches (and thus eligible for vouchers). There are thirty-two most-treated elementary schools, each of which has an average fourth grade enrollment of seventy-two students. "Somewhat treated" schools were Milwaukee elementary schools where fewer than two-thirds of students are eligible for free or reduced price lunch (and thus eligible for vouchers). In all of these schools, at least 30 percent of students are eligible for free lunch. There are sixty-six somewhat treated elementary schools, each of which has an average fourth-grade enrollment of seventy-one students. The untreated comparison schools are all the Wisconsin elementary schools that (a) are urban, (b) have at least 25 percent of their students eligible for free lunch, and (c) have at least 15 percent of their students being black. There are twelve untreated comparison elementary schools, each of which has an average fourth-grade enrollment of fifty-one students.

eligible for free or reduced-price lunches (and thus eligible for vouchers), 65.4 percent of students were black, and 2.9 percent of students were Hispanic. In the somewhat treated schools, an average of 44.5 percent of students were eligible for vouchers, 49.1 percent of students were black, and 13.7 percent of students were Hispanic.[27]

I included a Wisconsin elementary in the untreated comparison group if it (a) was not in Milwaukee, (b) was urban, (c) had at least 25 percent of its students eligible for free or reduced-price lunch, and (d) had black students composing at least 15 percent of its students. There were only twelve schools in Wisconsin that met these criteria. It was not possible to choose a group of untreated schools that were more closely matched to Milwaukee schools. In the untreated comparison schools, average enrollment in a grade was fifty-one students, 30.4 percent of students were eligible for free or reduced-price lunch (and, thus, would have been eligible for vouchers had they lived in Milwaukee), 30.3 percent of the students were black, and 3.0 percent of students were Hispanic.

Students in Wisconsin take statewide examinations in grades four, eight, and ten. Because I am necessarily focusing on the productivity reactions of elementary schools, I measure productivity by dividing a school's fourth-

27. Note that all of these demographic numbers reflect what the schools looked like in 1990, before the voucher program was enacted. This is the correct method for choosing treated and control schools. One does not want to measure the extent of treatment using measures of student composition that potentially reflect how students reacted to the voucher program.

Table 8.6   **Productivity Time Trends in Wisconsin Most-Treated, Somewhat Treated, and Untreated Comparison Schools, from Regressions with School Fixed Effects**

Annual Change in Productivity by School Type	Productivity Calculation is Based on Exam in:				
	Math	Science	Social Studies	Language	Reading
Most-treated schools	0.732[a]	0.889[ac]	0.475[bc]	0.248[ad]	−0.035[bd]
	(0.071)	(0.072)	(0.070)	(0.066)	(0.066)
Somewhat treated schools	0.527	0.729[a]	0.327	0.123[b]	−0.141
	(0.056)	(0.057)	(0.055)	(0.052)	(0.052)
Untreated comparison schools	0.342	0.255	0.188	−0.081	−0.235
	(0.172)	(0.176)	(0.170)	(0.160)	(0.162)

Sources: Wisconsin Department of Public Instruction (2000a–e) and U.S. Department of Education (1994b).

Notes: Productivity is measured in national percentile points per thousand dollars of per-pupil spending, where per-pupil spending is measured in 1999 dollars. The deflator used is the Consumer Price Index. Each regression includes a fixed effect for each school, a time trend for most-treated schools, a time trend for somewhat treated schools, and a time trend for untreated comparison schools. The observations are school-level averages based on fourth-graders' scores, and the regressions are therefore weighted by the schools' fourth-grade enrollment.

[a]Time trend is statistically significantly different from the time trend for untreated comparison schools at the 95 percent level of confidence.

[b]Time trend is statistically significantly different from the time trend for untreated comparison schools at the 85 to 95 percent level of confidence.

[c]Time trend is statistically significantly different from the time trend for somewhat treated schools at the 95 percent level of confidence.

[d]Time trend is statistically significantly different from the time trend for somewhat treated schools at the 85 to 95 percent level of confidence.

grade score (expressed in national percentile points) by its per-pupil spending in thousands of real (1999) dollars. Achievement is measured on five tests: mathematics, science, social studies, language, and reading. It is worth noting that, during the period in question, Wisconsin enacted a controversial new reading curriculum that emphasized whole-language methods, as opposed to phonics.

Table 8.6 shows productivity growth rates in most-treated, somewhat treated, and untreated comparison schools in Wisconsin between 1996–97 and 1999–2000. The statistics in the table are based on regressions in which the dependent variable is productivity and the independent variables are an indicator for each school, a time trend for most treated schools, and time trend for somewhat treated schools, and a time trend for untreated comparison schools. This regression incorporates the best differences-in-differences method, given the application, because it allows each school to have its own starting point for productivity. Intuitively, the regression is based on the idea that productivity growth rates might look like the following figure.

Figure 8.1 shows what productivity might look like in three schools, one

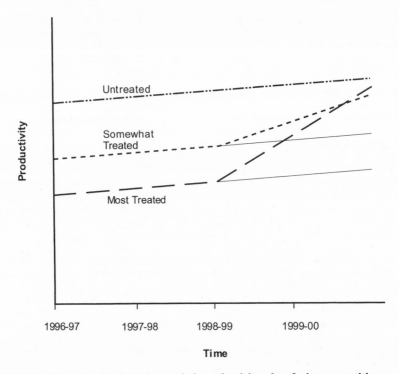

Fig. 8.1   How schools might change their productivity when facing competition

of which is most treated, one of which is somewhat treated, and one of which is untreated. It would be fairly typical to find that the most-treated schools had the lowest initial productivity if we did not correct for differences in student demographics, for the simple reason that poorer students tend to have lower achievement and the most-treated schools have more poor students. Thus, the figure shows the most-treated school having the lowest initial productivity, somewhat treated schools having medium initial productivity, and untreated schools having the highest initial productivity. If competition has little or no effect on productivity, then the time trends for productivity might all be stable, as indicated by the solid lines. On the other hand, if competition makes schools raise their productivity, then the time trends might look the dashed lines, in which the most-treated schools raise their productivity the most, somewhat treated schools raise their productivity somewhat, and untreated schools raise their productivity the least (or perhaps not at all).[28]

28. Actually, we expect the untreated schools to have higher *initial* productivity growth because richer schools tend to have better productivity growth, all else being equal. This tendency (richer schools, higher productivity growth) will make the difference-in-difference estimates understate the effect of competition on productivity.

Formally, the regression equation can be written as follows:

$$(8) \quad \frac{\text{Ach}_{it}}{\text{PPExp}_{it}} = \alpha_1 I_1 + \ldots + \alpha_N I_N + \beta^{\text{most treated}} I_i^{\text{most treated}} \text{time}_t$$

$$+ \beta^{\text{somewhat treated}} I_t^{\text{somewhat treated}} \text{time}_t + \beta^{\text{untreated}} I_i^{\text{untreated}} \text{time}_t + \varepsilon_{it},$$

where Ach_{it} is a national percentile rank score for students at school i in year t, PPExp_{it} is the per-pupil expenditure at school i in year t, I_1 through I_N are indicator variables for schools, α_1 through α_N are initial productivity levels at individual schools, $I^{\text{most treated}}$ is an indicator variable for the school being most treated, $I^{\text{somewhat treated}}$ is an indicator variable for the school being somewhat treated, $I^{\text{untreated}}$ is an indicator variable for the school being untreated, and time$_t$ is the school year. The coefficients $\beta^{\text{most treated}}$, $\beta^{\text{somewhat treated}}$, and $\beta^{\text{untreated}}$ pick up the different productivity growth rates for most-treated, somewhat treated, and untreated schools, respectively.

The left-hand column of table 8.6 shows that, based on mathematics achievement, productivity grew annually by about 0.7 national percentile points per thousand dollars between 1996–97 and 1999–2000 in the most-treated schools. It grew more slowly in somewhat treated schools (about 0.5 national percentile points per thousand dollars) and yet more slowly in untreated schools (about 0.3 national percentile points per thousand dollars). Productivity growth based on science, social studies, and language (grammar) is shown in the next three columns, all of which show patterns that are similar to the mathematics-based pattern. In all these columns, productivity growth in the most-treated schools is statistically significantly different from that in the untreated schools, with a 95 percent confidence level. Reading-based measures of productivity are falling in all the schools over the period in question, perhaps because of whole language methods. However, reading-based productivity is falling least quickly in schools that were most treated to voucher school competition.

Table 8.7 shows statistics that are very similar to those in table 8.6. They are easier to interpret for those unfamiliar with regression analysis, but they are less ideal because each school does not have its own initial level of productivity. For instance, examine the top panel, which shows productivity calculations based on the mathematics exam. In 1996–97, the most-treated schools earned 4.18 national percentile points for every thousand dollars of per-pupil spending. In the same year, the somewhat treated and untreated schools earned 4.08 and 5.65 national percentile points (respectively) for every thousand dollars. Over the next few years, however, productivity growth was the highest in the most-treated schools, second highest in the somewhat treated schools, and lowest in the untreated schools (see right-hand column). In fact, by 1999–2000, productivity in the most-treated schools was closer to that of the untreated schools than it was to that of the somewhat treated schools! The productivity growth rates shown in table 8.7

Table 8.7   **Productivity in Wisconsin's Most-Treated, Somewhat Treated, and Untreated Comparison Schools**

	1996–1997	1999–2000	Annual Change
Productivity calculation is based on math exam			
Most-treated schools	4.18	6.09	0.64
Somewhat treated schools	4.08	5.50	0.47
Untreated comparison schools	5.65	6.65	0.33
Productivity calculation is based on science exam			
Most-treated schools	3.87	6.04	0.72
Somewhat treated schools	3.91	5.67	0.59
Untreated comparison schools	6.33	6.92	0.20
Productivity calculation is based on social studies exam			
Most-treated schools	5.05	6.19	0.41
Somewhat treated schools	5.26	5.80	0.18
Untreated comparison schools	6.90	7.21	0.10
Productivity calculation is based on language exam			
Most-treated schools	5.07	5.64	0.19
Somewhat treated schools	5.07	5.28	0.07
Untreated comparison schools	6.04	5.85	–0.06
Productivity calculation is based on reading exam			
Most-treated schools	5.35	5.31	–0.01
Somewhat treated schools	5.46	4.98	–0.16
Untreated comparison schools	6.68	6.04	–0.21

Sources: Wisconsin Department of Public Instruction (2000a–e) and U.S. Department of Education (1994b).

Notes: Productivity is measured in national percentile points per thousand dollars of per-pupil spending, where per-pupil spending is measured in 1999 dollars. The deflator used is the Consumer Price Index. Statistics are based on weighted averages over schools in the relevant group, where each school is weighted by its enrollment.

are dramatic for the most-treated schools. The basic pattern (highest productivity growth in the most-treated schools) is repeated in the other panels of the table, for the science, social studies, language, and reading examinations.

Tables 8.8 and 8.9 are very much like tables 8.6 and 8.7, except that they show achievement growth instead of productivity growth. That is, they leave out the changes in productivity that come about as a result of changes in per-pupil spending. An examination of them shows that achievement growth displays patterns like that of productivity growth, which suggests that the improvements in productivity in the most-treated and somewhat treated schools occurred because achievement was rising in those schools, not because achievement was holding steady while per-pupil spending fell. (Indeed, use of the vouchers causes per-pupil spending to rise in the Milwaukee public schools, so if achievement were to hold steady, productivity would fall if schools did not respond to competition by raising it.)

Look, for example, at table 8.8. It shows that math scores rose by about 7

Table 8.8   **Achievement Growth in Wisconsin's Most-Treated, Somewhat Treated, and Untreated Comparison Schools, from Regressions with School Fixed Effects**

Annual Change in Test Scores by School Type	Math	Science	Social Studies	Language	Reading
Most-treated schools	7.06[ac]	8.39[ac]	4.97[bc]	2.98[ad]	0.57[bd]
	(0.61)	(0.62)	(0.59)	(0.56)	(0.57)
Somewhat treated schools	5.27	6.99[a]	3.68	1.88[b]	−0.37
	(0.48)	(0.49)	(0.46)	(0.44)	(0.45)
Untreated comparison schools	3.71	2.96	2.40	−0.10	−1.42
	(1.48)	(1.50)	(1.43)	(1.37)	(1.38)

Sources: Wisconsin Department of Public Instruction (2000a–e) and U.S. Department of Education (1994b).

Notes: Test scores are measured in national percentile points. Each regression includes a fixed effect for each school, a time trend for most-treated schools, a time trend for somewhat treated schools, and a time trend for untreated comparison schools. The observations are school-level averages for fourth-graders, and the regressions are therefore weighted by the schools' fourth-grade enrollment.

[a]Time trend is statistically significantly different from the time trend for untreated comparison schools at the 95 percent level of confidence.

[b]Time trend is statistically significantly different from the time trend for untreated comparison schools at the 85 to 95 percent level of confidence.

[c]Time trend is statistically significantly different from the time trend for somewhat treated schools at the 95 percent level of confidence.

[d]Time trend is statistically significantly different from the time trend for somewhat treated schools at the 85 to 95 percent level of confidence.

percentile points per year in the most-treated schools, by about 5 percentile points per year in somewhat treated schools, and by about 4 percentile points in untreated schools. Alternatively, examine table 8.9. It shows that social studies scores in the most-treated schools rose by 4.2 percentile points per year, whereas social studies scores in untreated schools rose by only 1.5 percentile points per year.

Overall, an evaluation of Milwaukee suggests that public schools have a strong, positive productivity response to competition from vouchers. The schools that faced the most potential competition from vouchers had the best productivity response. In fact, the schools that were most treated to competition had dramatic productivity improvements. On the one hand, such bursts of productivity growth may slow down after a few more years of competition. On the other hand, the productivity effects of competition may be understated because the control group of schools was a slightly unfair comparison group, with fewer poor and minority students.

8.6.2 The Effect of Charter Schools on Achievement in Michigan Public Schools

In 1994, Michigan enacted a charter school law as part of a series of changes in its method of financing schools. Michigan charter schools receive a per-pupil fee that is essentially the same as the state's foundation level of per-pupil spending (the state's minimum level of per-pupil spending, given

Table 8.9   Fourth-Grade Test Scores in Wisconsin's Most-Treated, Somewhat Treated, and Untreated Comparison Schools

	1996–97	1999–2000	Annual Change
Math			
Most-treated schools	34.5	53.3	6.3
Somewhat treated schools	33.7	48.2	4.8
Untreated comparison schools	50.0	60.6	3.5
Science			
Most-treated schools	31.9	52.8	7.0
Somewhat treated schools	32.3	49.7	5.8
Untreated comparison schools	56.0	62.9	2.3
Social studies			
Most-treated schools	41.6	54.2	4.2
Somewhat treated schools	43.4	50.7	2.4
Untreated comparison schools	61.0	65.6	1.5
Language			
Most-treated schools	41.8	49.4	2.5
Somewhat treated schools	41.8	46.2	1.5
Untreated comparison schools	53.4	53.2	−0.1
Reading			
Most-treated schools	44.2	46.5	0.8
Somewhat treated schools	45.1	43.6	−0.5
Untreated comparison schools	59.0	55.0	−1.3

Sources: Wisconsin Department of Public Instruction (2000a–e) and U.S. Department of Education (1994b).

Notes: Test scores are measured in national percentile points. Statistics are based on weighted averages over schools in the relevant group, where each school is weighted by its enrollment.

the characteristics of the school's student population). For instance, in 1999–2000, the average charter school student in Michigan had $6,600 spent on his education, whereas the average regular public school student had about $7,440 spent on his education. Detroit public schools spent $8,325 per pupil, and the average charter school student in Detroit had about $6,590 spent on his education. A district that loses a student to a charter school loses approximately the foundation level of per-pupil revenue. Charter competition tends to be most substantial in the elementary grades because the charter fees more adequately cover costs for the lower grades. By the 1999–2000 school year, approximately 3.5 percent of all nonprivate elementary students in Michigan were enrolled in charter schools. The corresponding number for secondary students was 0.7 percent. Charter schools can receive their charters from statewide organizations, such as universities, so they can compete with local public schools, unlike charter schools in many other states that have their charters granted and renewed by their local district.[29]

29. The information on Michigan charter schools and all the data on Michigan schools are taken from publications of the Michigan Department of Education (2000a–d).

A difference-in-differences strategy, analogous to the strategy used on Milwaukee, is appropriate for evaluating the effect of charter school competition on Michigan public schools. There are two additional issues, however, that did not arise with Milwaukee. First, it was easy to define ex ante the treatment and control schools in Wisconsin: No school outside of Milwaukee received any voucher treatment, and the scale of treatment within Milwaukee schools varied with students' poverty, a variable that we observe. In Michigan, "treatment" and "control" and "before" and "after" must be defined on a district-by-district basis, so that a district is being "treated" and is in the "after" period once it is forced to recognize that it is losing a critical share of students to charter schools. Of course, we do not know what this critical share might be, but it is useful to know that the mean year-to-year change in a Michigan school's enrollment *prior to 1994* was 5.1 percent. Therefore, a small drawing-away of enrollment by a local charter school would be hard to differentiate from normal year-to-year variation in enrollment. However, a persistent drawing-away of enrollment of more than 5 percent, say, would be likely to be noticed and attributed to charter schools. I initially looked for a critical level of 6 percent, and, because it worked well, I kept it. A critical level of 7 or 8 percent works very similarly.[30]

The left-hand side of table 8.10 lists the Michigan districts in which charter schools account for at least 6 percent of total enrollment inside the district's boundaries.[31] There are 597 districts in Michigan and only 34 listed in the table, so a nonnegligible charter school presence is still the exception and not the rule. Michigan's large city districts are well represented among the districts that face charter school competition: Detroit, Lansing, and Kalamazoo all have at least 6 percent of enrollment in charter schools.

Second, the Michigan districts that had to face competition from charter schools were not selected randomly or according to a simple rule. Instead, charter schools probably formed as a response to local circumstances. In some cases, charter schools may have formed where parents were unusually active and concerned about education (good circumstances for public school productivity and achievement). In other cases, charter schools may have formed where parents and teachers were frustrated because the district

30. Results for a critical level of 7 or 8 percent are available from the author. If one chooses a critical level much higher than 8 percent, the results depend unduly on just a few districts, simply because only a few districts ever face more than an 8 percent drawing-away of their students. Descriptive statistics for the Michigan data set are also available from the author.

31. Note that the charter schools' share of local enrollment is based, in table 8.10, on the assumption that students attend charter schools in the district in which they reside. Because students who are in particularly unappealing districts are disproportionately likely to attend a charter school outside their district if they do attend a charter school, the statistics on which the table is based slightly understate the enrollment losses of bad districts. It is possible to construct estimates of the share of a district's students who attend charter schools, but such estimates are somewhat noisy and (in any case) generate results that are qualitatively similar to the results shown in tables 8.11 and 8.12. The alternative set of results may be found in the working paper version of this paper, available from the author.

Table 8.10 **Michigan School Districts and Arizona Municipalities Where at Least 6 Percent of Enrollment Entered Charter Schools**

Michigan School Districts		Arizona Municipalities	
Alba	Inkster-Edison	Benson	Keams Canyon
Bark River-Harris	Jackson[b]	Bisbee	Kingman[b]
Big Rapids	Kalamazoo[a]	Camp Verde	Mayer
Boyne Falls	Kenowa Hills	Cave Creek	Page
Buena Vista	Kentwood[b]	Chinle	Phoenix[a]
Caledonia	Lansing[a]	Chino Valley	Pima
Charlevoix	Mount Pleasant	Clarkdale	Prescott
Coldwater	Oak Park	Concho	Queen Creek
Detroit[a]	Onekama	Coolidge	Safford
Elk Rapids	Pentwater	Cottonwood	Saint Johns
Flat Rock	Petoskey	Enrenberg	Scottsdale[a]
Forest Hills[b]	Sault Sainte Marie	Flagstaff[b]	Sedona
Godwin Heights	Southfield[b]	Fountain Hills	Show Low
Grand Blanc[b]	Wane-Westland[a]	Gilbert[b]	Sierra Vista
Hartland	Westwood	Globe	Tempe[a]
Hillsdale	Wyoming[b] Avondale[b]	Golden Valley	Tuba City
Holland[b]		Green Valley	Vail
Huron		Higley	Winslow

Sources: Michigan Department of Education (2000a–d) and Arizona Department of Education (2000a–d).

Notes: The share of students who live in a district and attend charter schools is difficult to calculate because students can attend charter schools located outside of their districts (Michigan) or municipality (Arizona). These statistics are calculated under the assumption that students attend a charter school located in their district (Michigan) or municipality (Arizona).

[a]Very large city district (enrollment in one grade typically exceeds 1,000).

[b]Large city district (enrollment in one grade is typically between 500 and 1,000).

was run poorly (bad circumstances for public school productivity and achievement). Thus, it is important that the difference-in-differences strategy look *within* a school—that is, how a *given* school changes when it is faced with new competition. I present differences-in-differences results that control for school fixed effects, which pick up all the unobserved characteristics of a school that are stable over the several-year period that I analyze.

The difference-in-differences strategy might not be convincing, however, if the districts that were eventually forced to complete with charter schools had preexisting productivity *trends* that were different from other public schools in Michigan. Different preexisting trends would not be unlikely because charter schools chose where to locate: A charter school would expect to find little demand for its services in a district that was improving rapidly on its own. In cases where different trends are possible, a more sophisticated, detrended differences-in-differences strategy is appropriate. Therefore, I also present estimates of how schools' productivity *trends* changed when they began to face charter competition.

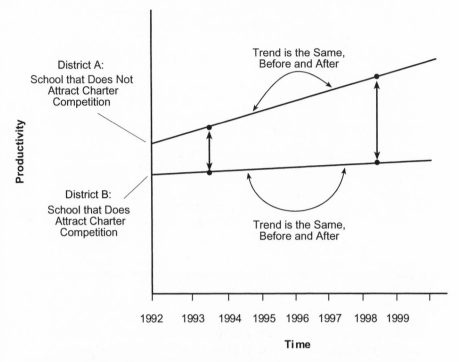

Fig. 8.2   The fact that there is no reaction to competition can be discerned, even with different preexisting trends

Figures 8.2 through 8.4 illustrate why a detrended differences-in-differences strategy can be a useful complement to a typical differences-in-differences strategy. In figure 8.2, the top line represents the productivity of district A, which initially enjoys strong positive productivity growth. The bottom line represents the productivity of district B, which initially has very low productivity growth. Suppose that charter schools are deterred from entering district A because it is already improving rapidly and parents are pleased with the current course of events. Suppose that charter schools do enter district B, however, and are able to claim a critical share of local parents (who were not pleased with the course that the public school was on) by 1996. Finally, suppose that the district B does not respond to the charter school competition: It remains on its initial path after 1996. A simple differences-in-differences strategy would compare the change in district A's *level* of productivity to the change in district B's *level* of productivity. (Notice the indications on the figure of possible "before" and "after" points that could be used for comparison). In such a comparison, charter school competition would seem to have a negative effect (although it truly has no effect), simply because charter schools enter where districts' productivity trends are already worse. On the other hand, if we compared the change in district A's

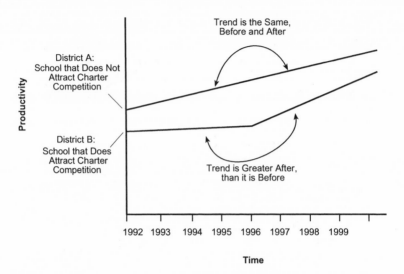

Fig. 8.3   A positive reaction to competition can be discerned, even with different preexisting trends

trend in productivity to the change in district B's *trend* in productivity, we would correctly see that district B did not respond to competition.

Figures 8.3 and 8.4 illustrate situations in which district B responds positively when it begins to face charter school competition (figure 8.3) and responds negatively when it begins to face competition (figure 8.4). Observe that the difference between district A's change in trend and district B's change in trend is an accurate indicator of the response to charter school competition. In short, the advantage of detrended difference-in-differences is that it generates consistent estimates even when schools that eventually face charter competition have different preexisting trends from schools that never face competition. The disadvantage of detrended difference-in-differences is that it demands a lot of information from the data because each school's preexisting *trend* in achievement (not just its level of achievement) must be identified. Because it is so demanding statistically, detrended difference-in-differences will not generate statistically significant estimates of effects that are small. Thus, we can foresee that the estimated effects for higher grades (which are likely to be small because charter competition affected them relatively little) are likely to be hard to identify using detrended difference-in-differences.

To summarize, it is important that difference-in-differences strategies control for *each* school's initial conditions (levels or trends). We need to control for schools' unobservable characteristics, especially characteristics that might attract charter competition. Difference-in-differences strategies also control for what was happening to Michigan schools in general over

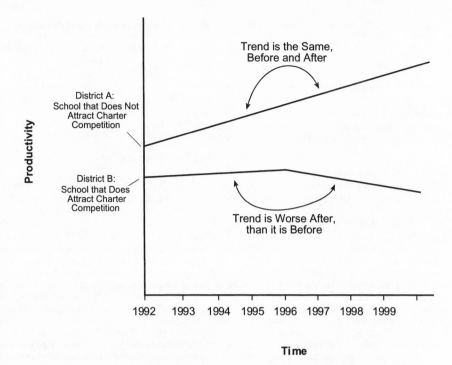

Fig. 8.4   A negative reaction to competition can be discerned, even with different preexisting trends

the period. This is important as well because Michigan enacted a major school finance reform in 1994 that affected all schools in the state. The strategies will identify changes that occurred in schools facing competition, *above and beyond* whatever occurred in other schools in the state (which were presumably responding to the finance reform).

I use regression to carry out both the simple difference-in-differences analysis and the detrended difference-in-differences analysis. The top panel of table 8.11 presents the estimated effect of charter school competition on productivity, using the simple differences-in-differences analysis. The bottom panel presents the estimated effect on productivity, using the detrended analysis. Formally, the regression used in the top panel is

$$(9) \qquad \frac{\text{Ach}_{ijt}}{\text{PPExp}_{ijt}} = I_{ij}^{\text{school}} \delta^{\text{school fixed effects}} + I_t^{\text{year}} \delta^{\text{year fixed effects}}$$
$$+ \; \delta^{\text{critical charter competition}} I_{jt}^{\text{charter} \geq 6\%} + \varepsilon_{jt} + \varepsilon_{ijt}$$

where Ach_{it} is the scale score for school i in district j in year t, PPExp_{it} is the per-pupil expenditure for the same school, $\mathbf{I}^{\text{school}}$ is a vector of school indi-

Table 8.11   **Effects of Charter School Competition on Michigan Public Schools' Productivity**

	4th-Grade Reading Exam	4th-Grade Math Exam	7th-Grade Reading Exam	7th-Grade Math Exam
Dependent Variable (productivity based on exam)				
Difference-in-differences (levels)				
Change in productivity level after district	1.60**	1.37**	1.87**	1.53**
is faced with charter school competition	(0.45)	(0.39)	(0.86)	(0.73)
Dependent Variable (change in productivity based on exam)				
Detrended difference-in-differences				
Change in productivity trend after district	0.31*	0.27*	0.15	0.06
is faced with charter school competition	(0.17)	(0.14)	(0.46)	(0.54)

Source: Michigan Department of Education (2000a–d).

Notes: Standard errors in parentheses. Regressions include school fixed effects and year fixed effects. Charter schools represent at least 6 percent of enrollment in district. The table is based on regressions of school-level data from 1992–93 to 1999–2000. In the top panel, the dependent variable is a school's productivity—specifically, a school's scale scores divided by its per-pupil spending in thousands of 1999 dollars. In the bottom panel, the dependent variable is the trend (annual change) in a school's productivity (or this year's productivity minus last year's). The regression includes school indicator variables to pick up characteristics of schools that are constant over the period (location, neighborhood, organization) and year indicator variables that allow for statewide changes from year to year in the test itself or in the pressure to perform on the test. The inflator for per-pupil spending is the Consumer Price Index. The numerator for productivity is the school's scale score on the Michigan Assessment of Educational Progress (MEAP) tests, which are administered to fourth- and seventh-graders. See the text for details on the tests.
**Change in productivity is statistically significantly different from zero with 95 percent confidence.
*Change in productivity is statistically significantly different from zero with 90 percent confidence.

cator variables, $\delta^{\text{school fixed effects}}$ is the vector of school fixed effects, I^{year} is a vector of year indicator variables, δ^{year} is the vector of year fixed effects, $I^{\text{charter}\geq 6\%}$ is an indicator variable for the district's having at least 6 percent of enrollment in charter schools, and $\delta^{\text{critical charter competition}}$ picks up the effect of facing a critical level of charter competition. Note that the year fixed effects pick up changes over time in the test or in the pressure to perform well on the test. The school fixed effects pick up unobserved characteristics of each school that are stable.

The regression used in the bottom panel of table 8.11 is identical, except for the dependent variable, which is the *difference* between this year's and last year's productivity:

$$(10) \quad \frac{\text{ACH}_{ijt}}{\text{PPExp}_{ijt}} - \frac{\text{Ach}_{ij,t-1}}{\text{PPExp}_{ij,t-1}} = I_{ij}^{\text{school}}\delta^{\text{school fixed effects}} + I_t^{\text{year}}\delta^{\text{year fixed effects}}$$
$$+ \delta^{\text{critical charter competition}}I_{jt}^{\text{charter}\geq 6\%} + \varepsilon_{jt} + \varepsilon_{ijt}$$

The estimates in the top panel of table 8.11 indicate that Michigan public schools raised their productivity in response to competition from charter schools. Productivity rose by 1.60 (scale points per thousand dollars spent)

Table 8.12   Effects of Charter School Competition on Michigan Public Schools' Achievement

	4th-Grade Reading Exam	4th-Grade Math Exam	7th-Grade Reading Exam	7th-Grade Math Exam
Dependent Variable (productivity based on exam)				
Difference-in-differences (levels)				
Change in achievement level after district	1.21**	1.11*	1.37**	0.96*
is faced with charter school competition	(0.65)	(0.62)	(0.60)	(0.48)
Dependent Variable (change in achievement based on exam)				
Detrended difference-in-differences				
Change in achievement trend after district	2.40*	2.50**	0.25	0.77
is faced with charter school competition	(1.37)	(1.04)	(0.58)	(0.69)

Source: Michigan Department of Education (2000a–d).

Notes: Standard errors in parentheses. Regressions include school fixed effects and year fixed effects. Charter schools represent at least 6 percent of enrollment in district. The table is based on regressions of school-level data from 1992–93 to 1999–2000. In the top panel, the dependent variable is a school's achievement—specifically, a school's scale scores on the Michigan Assessment of Educational Progress (MEAP) tests, which are administered to fourth- and seventh-graders. In the bottom panel, the dependent variable is the trend (annual change) in a school's scale scores (this year's achievement minus last year's). The regression includes school indicator variables to pick up characteristics of schools that are constant over the period (location, neighborhood, organization) and year indicator variables that allow for statewide changes from year to year in the test itself or in the pressure to perform on the test. From 1992 to 2000, the means and standard deviation of schools' average scores (weighted by the number of test-takers) were mean of 611, standard deviation of 19 on fourth-grade reading; mean of 528, standard deviation of 16 on fourth-grade math; mean of 600, standard deviation of 17 on fourth-grade reading; mean of 521, standard deviation of 14 on fourth-grade math.

**Change in achievement is statistically significantly different from zero with 95 percent confidence.

*Change in achievement is statistically significantly different from zero with 90 percent confidence.

based on the fourth-grade reading exam, by 1.37 based on the fourth-grade mathematics exam, by 1.87 based on the seventh-grade reading exam, and by 1.53 based on the seventh-grade mathematics exam. All of these estimates are statistically significantly different from zero with a high level of confidence.

Moreover, the bottom panel of table 8.11 shows that charter school competition made Michigan public schools improve their productivity *relative to their own initial trends.* Productivity trends based on fourth-grade tests improve to a degree that is statistically significant. Not surprisingly, given the greater impact of charter competition on lower grades, the seventh-grade results are statistically insignificant.

It is difficult to interpret productivity improvements until we know whether they arise as a result of improvement in achievement or a fall in per-pupil spending, or both phenomena occurring simultaneously. Therefore, table 8.12 examines the effects of charter competition on achievement. Its structure is identical to that of table 8.11, except that it shows results for achievement instead of productivity. That is, it leaves out the changes in productivity that come about as a result of changes in per-pupil spending. Table 8.12 shows that the effect of charter school competition on achievement looks much like the effect on productivity, which suggests that Michigan's regular public schools raised their productivity mainly by raising their achievement for a given level of per-pupil spending, rather than by maintaining a steady level of achievement and cutting their per-pupil spending. For instance, the top panel of table 8.12 shows that fourth-grade reading and mathematics scores were, respectively, 1.21 and 1.11 scale points higher in schools that faced charter competition *after* they began to face competition. Seventh-grade reading and mathematics scores were, respectively, 1.37 and 0.96 scale points higher. Recall that these improvements in scores are not only relative to the schools' own initial performance (the first difference), but also relative to the gains made over the same by schools that did not face charter competition (the difference-in-differences).

The bottom panel of table 8.12, which shows detrended difference-in-differences results, shows how the schools facing charter competition accomplished these achievement gains. For instance, examine the fourth-grade reading and mathematics coefficients, which are statistically significant. (The seventh-grade detrended difference-in-differences coefficients are, as in table 8.11, statistically insignificant.) Schools that faced charter competition raised their annual improvement in achievement by 2.40 scale points a year in fourth-grade reading and 2.50 scale points in mathematics. Recall that this is a change relative to their previous rate of change in achievement, which was actually about 0.4 scale points *lower* on average than that of schools that were never faced with charter competition. In fact, the results give us a picture much like that shown in figure 8.4: The achievement trend of schools that eventually face charter competition is initially lower than that of other schools, but, once charter competition commences, schools that face competition have a higher rate of growth.

The change in achievement for schools subjected to charter competition is statistically significant and positive, but it is not unrealistically large, particularly when one considers that such schools were making up for years of slower achievement growth. Even with mathematics and reading achievement growth that is about 2.5 scale points per year better than that of other schools, a district like Detroit would take approximately two decades to catch up with the achievement of one of its affluent suburbs, like Grosse Point. (Of course, it is possible that, as Detroit caught up, a suburb like Grosse Point would feel competitive pressure to increase its own rate of achievement growth. This would lengthen the catch-up period but further raise Michigan students' scores.)

Overall, the picture that one draws from Michigan is the following. Public schools that were subjected to charter competition raised their productivity and achievement in response, not only exceeding their own previous performance but also improving relative to other Michigan schools not subjected to charter competition. The improvements in productivity and achievement appear to occur once charter competition reaches a critical level that coincides with the enrollment at which charter schools' taking students would be easily discernible (not to be confused with regular fluctuations in enrollment). The increase in productivity and achievement is larger and more precisely estimated in fourth grade, probably because elementary schools faced more competition from charter schools than middle schools did.

8.6.3   The Effect of Charter Schools on Achievement in Arizona Public Schools

Like Michigan, Arizona enacted a charter school law in 1994. Arizona's charter school law is widely regarded as the most favorable to charter schools in the United States, as it allows charter schools to have considerable fiscal and legal autonomy. There are also few constraints on the growth of charter schools in Arizona. As a result, 5.3 percent of Arizona's nonprivate enrollment was in charter schools in 1999–2000. This percentage is the highest of any American state.

In Arizona, state-sponsored charter schools get a fee equal to the state's share of revenue (45 percent of total revenue for a regular public school). District-sponsored charter schools get a fee equal to local per-pupil revenue but are less able to compete with the regular public schools because they must seek renewal of their charters from the very districts with which they compete.

My evaluation of Arizona follows the same strategy as I employ for Michigan, so I will merely highlight a few differences between the Michigan and Arizona situations here. In Arizona, a municipality may contain multiple districts: for instance, a few elementary districts, a middle school district, and a high school district. A local charter school may therefore be competing with multiple districts. Therefore, I associate regular public schools and charter schools with a municipality, not a district. All Arizona fourth- and seventh-graders were required to take the Iowa Test of Basic Skills (ITBS) through 1995–96 and have been required to take the Stanford 9 test since then. The shift in the test does not pose problems for the analysis because both tests offer national percentile rank scores (which have a 0.97 correlation at the school level). Moreover, all of the schools switched tests in the same year, so it is simple to establish each school's prereform trend and postreform trend allowing for a statewide shift in the intercept.[32] I use national percentile rank scores at the school level for the school years from 1992–93 to 1999–2000. I again use 6 percent of enrollment as the critical level at which charter schools are held to be a nonnegligible competitive

32. More precisely, a separate statewide shift is estimated for each percentile rank. The information on Arizona charter schools and all the data on Arizona schools are taken from publications of the Arizona Department of Education (2000a–d).

threat. I use the same critical level as I use for Michigan in order that the two states' results be as comparable as possible. However, a variety of critical levels between 6 percent and 11 percent produce similar results for Arizona.[33]

The right-hand panel of table 8.10 lists the Arizona municipalities that had at least 6 percent of local enrollment in charter schools. Municipalities of all sizes are represented. The list includes some of Arizona's largest cities (Phoenix, Tempe, Scottsdale), some medium-sized cities (Avondale, Flagstaff, Gilbert, Kingman), and thirty smaller municipalities.

As in Michigan, it is important that the Arizona difference-in-differences strategies control for each school's initial conditions. We need to control for schools' unobservable characteristics, particularly because some of those characteristics may actually attract charter competition. Also, it is important that the difference-in-differences strategy generate estimates that control for what was happening to Arizona schools in general over the period. Although Arizona did not experience a major school finance reform, it did have a very activist state department of education that enacted numerous programs (including a school report card program so that parents would be better informed about performance).

Table 8.13 has the same structure as table 8.11: The effect of charter competition on productivity is estimated using difference-in-differences in the top panel and using detrended difference-in-differences in the bottom panel. The equations estimated are (9) and (10), shown above.

The estimates in the top panel of table 8.13 suggest that Arizona public schools raised their productivity in response to competition from charter schools. Productivity rose by 0.55 (national percentile points per thousand dollars spent) based on the fourth-grade reading exam, by 0.70 based on the fourth-grade mathematics exam, by 0.38 based on the seventh-grade reading exam, and by 0.53 based on the seventh-grade mathematics exam. All of these estimates are statistically significantly different from zero with a high level of confidence.

The bottom panel of table 8.13 shows that charter school competition made Arizona public schools improve their productivity *relative to their own initial trends.* Productivity trends based on fourth-grade tests improve to a degree that is statistically significant. The seventh-grade results are statistically insignificant, but this is not surprisingly because charter competition had a greater impact on lower grades.

As noted previously, interpreting productivity gains is hard until we look at one of the components of productivity separately. Table 8.14 shows the effect of charter competition on achievement—that is, it leaves out the changes in productivity that come about as a result of changes in per-pupil

---

33. These results and descriptive statistics for the Arizona data set are available from the author. Choosing a level much higher than 11 percent makes the results depend unduly on just a few districts, simply because only a few districts ever face more than an 11 percent drawing away of their students.

Table 8.13   **Effects of Charter School Competition on Arizona Public Schools' Productivity**

	4th-Grade Reading Exam	4th-Grade Math Exam	7th-Grade Reading Exam	7th-Grade Math Exam
Dependent Variable (productivity based on exam)				
Difference-in-differences (levels)				
Change in productivity level after district	0.55**	0.70**	0.38*	0.53**
is faced with charter school competition	(0.16)	(0.19)	(0.21)	(0.17)
Dependent Variable (change in productivity based on exam)				
Detrended difference-in-differences				
Change in productivity trend after district	0.31*	0.28**	0.33	0.35
is faced with charter school competition	(0.17)	(0.13)	(0.22)	(0.26)

Source: Arizona Department of Education (2000a–d).

Notes: Standard errors in parentheses. Regressions include school fixed effects and year fixed effects. Charter schools represent at least 6 percent of enrollment in district. The table is based on regressions of school-level data from 1992–93 to 1999–2000. In the top panel, the dependent variable is a school's productivity—specifically, a school's national percentile rank (NPR) score divided by its per-pupil spending in thousands of 1999 dollars. In the bottom panel, the dependent variable is the trend (annual change) in a school's productivity (this year's productivity minus last year's). The regression includes school indicator variables to pick up characteristics of schools that are constant over the period (location, neighborhood, organization) and year indicator variables that allow for statewide changes from year to year in the test itself or in the pressure to perform on the test. The inflator for per-pupil spending is the Consumer Price Index. The numerator for productivity is the school's national percentile rank on a nationally normed standardized test (the Iowa Test of Basic Skills or the Stanford 9). See the text for details on the tests.
**Change in productivity is statistically significantly different from zero with 95 percent confidence.
*Change in productivity is statistically significantly different from zero with 90 percent confidence.

spending. The table has the same structure as the previous two tables. It shows that the effect of charter school competition on achievement looks much like the effect on productivity, which suggests that Arizona's regular public schools raised their productivity mainly by raising their achievement for a given level of per-pupil spending, rather than by maintaining a steady level of achievement and cutting their per-pupil spending. The top panel of table 8.14 shows that fourth-grade reading and mathematics scores were, respectively, 2.31 and 2.68 national percentile points higher in schools that faced charter competition *after* they began to face competition. Seventh-grade mathematics scores were 1.59 national percentile points higher. (The estimate for seventh-grade reading is statistically insignificant.) These are important gains, especially when one recalls that these gains are relative not only to the schools' own initial performance (the first difference), but also to the gains made over the same period by schools that did not face charter competition (the difference-in-differences).

The bottom panel of table 8.14 shows the detrended difference-in-differences results, which suggest that schools facing charter competition raised achievement relative to their own previous trends. Such schools

Table 8.14   **Effects of Charter School Competition on Arizona Public Schools' Achievement**

	4th-Grade Reading Exam	4th-Grade Math Exam	7th-Grade Reading Exam	7th-Grade Math Exam
Dependent Variable (achievement based on exam)				
Difference-in-differences (levels)				
Change in achievement level after district	2.31**	2.68**	1.11	1.59*
is faced with charter school competition	(0.69)	(0.79)	(0.95)	(0.89)
Dependent Variable (change in achievement based on exam)				
Detrended difference-in-differences				
Change in achievement trend after district	1.40*	1.39*	1.48	1.29
is faced with charter school competition	(0.79)	(0.81)	(1.13)	(1.10)

Source: Arizona Department of Education (2000a–d).

Notes: Standard errors in parentheses. Regressions include school fixed effects and year fixed effects. Charter schools represent at least 6 percent of enrollment in district. The table is based on regressions of school level data from 1992–93 to 1999–2000. In the top panel, the dependent variable is a school's achievement—specifically, a school's national percentile rank (NPR) score on a nationally normed standardized test (the Iowa Test of Basic Skills or the Stanford 9). See the text for details on the tests. In the bottom panel, the dependent variable is the trend (annual change) in a school's achievement (this year's achievement minus last year's). The regression includes school indicator variables to pick up characteristics of schools that are constant over the period (location, neighborhood, organization) and year indicator variables that allow for statewide changes from year to year in the test itself or in the pressure to perform on the test.

**Change in achievement is statistically significantly different from zero with 95 percent confidence.
*Change in achievement is statistically significantly different from zero with 90 percent confidence.

raised their annual improvement in achievement by 1.40 national percentile points a year in fourth-grade reading and 1.39 national percentile points in mathematics. Recall that this is a change relative to their previous rate of change in achievement, which was actually about 0.6 national percentile points *lower* on average than that of schools that were never faced with charter competition. Again, the results give us a picture much like that shown in figure 8.4: Schools that eventually face charter competition start with lower rate of growth in achievement but begin to catch up with higher growth rates once charter competition commences.

The improvements in achievement among schools subjected to charter competition are significant, but not unrealistically large. Even if its scores rise about 1.4 national percentile points more each year than do the scores of schools that do not attract competition, the typical Phoenix area school that is now competing with charter schools will take ten years to catch up with top-performing Phoenix area schools.

Overall, the evaluation of Arizona suggests conclusions that are broadly similar to those one draws from the Michigan evaluation. Charter competition focused on public schools that initially had below-average achievement and productivity growth, but charter competition induced public schools to improve their productivity and achievement. The improvements are relative to the schools' own past performance and also relative to gains made, over the same period, by schools that were not subjected to charter competition.

8.6.4   Discussion of the Effects of Recent School Choice Reform

Are the productivity effects of the Milwaukee vouchers, Michigan charter schools, and Arizona charter schools sufficient to make us think that choice could remedy the American school productivity problem? All three forms of choice did boost productivity. If all schools in the United States were to enjoy productivity growth rates like those in Milwaukee's most-treated schools, American schools could return to their 1970–71 productivity levels in under a decade. Of course, we should be cautious about extrapolating from the short voucher and charter school experiences described in this section. On the one hand, the bursts of productivity growth seen in Milwaukee may settle down to a lower level of growth. On the other hand, many of the long-term, general equilibrium effects of choice are not yet in operation.

In order to get a sense of the magnitude of the productivity effects, without having to extrapolate so much, consider the following alternative question. Is it likely that the productivity effects of Milwaukee's voucher program (the "rising tide") are likely to overwhelm the allocation effects for students who experience the worst possible allocation changes in Milwaukee? We can get a sense of the students who are available in Milwaukee to be reallocated if we examine the very high scoring (top decile) and very low scoring (bottom decile) elementary schools in the city. Such schools score about 32 national percentile points apart on the math exam. Thus, a Milwaukee student's worst-case scenario would be to experience a fall of about 32 national percentile points in his or her peer group. Moreover, let us make the extreme assumption that the student is *very* strongly influenced by his or her peers so that the student's scores fall by 32 points. This scenario is truly pessimistic! It is not strictly impossible, but it is so pessimistic that it is barely plausible. Nevertheless, if the student enjoys the achievement growth rates that Milwaukee students in the most-treated schools are enjoying now, he or she will "grow out of" the bad allocation effects within 4.5 years. That is, the student will be better off for having experienced vouchers within five years of the voucher program's affecting his or her schooling.

Many commentators on school choice are obsessed with the possibility that choice schools will "cream-skim" from the public schools. Thus, it seems odd even to raise the possibility of reverse cream-skimming. Nevertheless, given that public school students are positively affected by choice, one might worry that the effects are due to reverse cream-skimming. It is, however, easy to show that the effects of choice on public school students cannot be largely the result of reverse cream-skimming: There are simply too few students changing schools to affect average test scores to the degree they were actually affected. For instance, between 1996–97 and 1999–2000, the Milwaukee public schools lost no more than 498 fourth-graders to voucher schools. (The actual number is smaller because 498 is the total increase in vouchers for fourth-graders, and some of the vouchers went to students who had previously been attending private schools, not the Milwaukee public schools). Witte, Sterr, and Thorn (1995) inform us that disappointed voucher applicants (applicants who lost the lottery and therefore remained in the Milwaukee public schools) scored 5.6 points lower in reading and 10.2 points lower in math than the average Milwaukee student. They also show that voucher applicants performed at about the same level as other low-income Milwaukee students who were eligible for the vouchers. If we assume that the departing voucher students were like the disappointed applicants, then their departure would raise fourth-grade scores in Milwaukee public schools by at most 0.4 points in reading and 0.8 points in math between 1996–97 and 1999–2000. These gains would imply an annual improvement of 0.14 points in reading and 0.26 points in math. Compare such improvements to 1.3 points in reading and 1.8 points in math, which are the actual annual gains of Milwaukee public school students, above and beyond the gains recorded by the control students in non-Milwaukee schools. (The just-quoted numbers can be derived from table 8.9, once you know that there were 2,376 students in schools facing more competition and 4,554 in schools facing less competition.) In short, the change in Milwaukee scores that could plausibly be caused by reverse cream-skimming is an order of magnitude too small to account for the actual change in Milwaukee scores.

For Michigan and Arizona, there are no scores available for disappointed charter applicants, but I have compared the demographics of charter school students and regular public school students in these states elsewhere (Hoxby 2000a). For instance, in Michigan's ten largest districts, some charter schools enroll a higher share of black students, some charter schools enroll a smaller share of black students, and some charter schools enroll a virtually identical share of black students as the regular public schools do. In the ten next largest districts, there is a similar lack of pattern. In Arizona, charter schools' shares of Hispanic students typically differ by only few percent from those of their municipalities. Moreover, there is no consistent pattern to the differences that do exist. In short, demographic data suggest that cream-skimming and reverse cream-skimming are not important phenomena in Michigan and Arizona.

8.7 Conclusions

In this paper, I have presented evidence that suggests that we should care deeply about the productivity effects of school choice, not only because they potentially relieve tensions generated by the allocation effects of choice but also because American schools are in a productivity crisis. Policies that boost American schools' productivity are sorely needed, if only to return the schools to their 1970 productivity levels.

I have also explained how schools that face choice-driven incentives can be induced to raise their productivity. I presented models of for-profit choice schools, nonprofit choice schools, and even regular public schools that just face interdistrict choice.

In section 8.5 of the paper, I show evidence that traditional forms of choice raise school productivity. I present results for traditional forms of choice because they can have long-term, general equilibrium effects of productivity, such as may arise when schools enter or exit or when a different reward system draws better individuals into teaching. If all schools in the United States experienced high levels of the traditional forms of choice, school productivity might be as much as 28 percent higher than it is today.

In section 8.6 of the paper, I present evidence on three recent choice reforms: vouchers in Milwaukee, charter schools in Michigan, and charter schools in Arizona. In each case, I find that regular public schools boosted their productivity when exposed to competition. In fact, the regular public schools responded to competitive threats that were surprisingly small. In each case, the regular public schools increased productivity by raising achievement, not by lowering spending while maintaining achievement. This achievement-oriented response may, of course, be related to the nature of the actual reforms. One can summarize the productivity effects of a reform like Milwaukee's voucher program by noting that a student would have better achievement in five years under the voucher program *even* if his peer group plunged by the maximum amount possible in Milwaukee and his achievement fell one-for-one with that of his peer group.

Of course, one must be cautious about extrapolating unduly from recent reforms or traditional forms of school of choice that only partially mimic choice reforms. Nevertheless, it seems safe to conclude that analyses that ignore the productivity effects of choice are likely to be misleading. Improvements in productivity may be *the* key effects of choice.

References

Arizona Department of Education. 2000a. *Arizona educational directory.* Phoenix, Ariz.: Arizona Department of Education. Electronic files.

———. 2000b. *Arizona pupil achievement testing, statewide report.* 1988–95 editions. Phoenix, Ariz.: Arizona Department of Education.

———. 2000c. *Average daily membership and average daily attendance reports,* 1988–2000 editions. Phoenix, Ariz.: Arizona Department of Education.

———. 2000d. *School report card program,* 1996–2000 editions. Phoenix, Ariz.: Arizona Department of Education. Electronic PDF files and spreadsheet files.

Cutler, David M., and Louise Sheiner. 1998. Managed care and the growth of medical expenditures. In *Frontiers in health policy research,* vol. 1, ed. Alan M. Garber, 77–115. Cambridge: MIT Press.

Downes, Thomas, and David Schoeman. 1998. School finance reform and private school enrollment: Evidence from California. *Journal of Urban Economics* 43: 418–43.

Economic report of the President. 2000. Washington, D.C.: United States Government Printing Office.

Glaeser, Edward, and Andrei Shleifer. Forthcoming. Not-for-profit entrepreneurs. *Journal of Public Economics.*

Hoxby, Caroline M. 1999a. The effects of school choice on curriculum and atmosphere. In *Earning and learning: How schools matter,* ed. Susan Mayer and Paul Peterson, 281–316. Washington, D.C.: Brookings Institution.

———. 1999b. The productivity of schools and other local public goods producers. *Journal of Public Economics* 74 (1): 1–30.

———. 2000a. Do private schools provide competition for public schools? NBER Working Paper no. 4978 (revised). Cambridge, Mass.: National Bureau of Economic Research, August.

———. 2000b. Does competition among public schools benefit students and taxpayers? *American Economic Review* 90 (5): 1209–38.

———. 2001. Ideal vouchers. Harvard University, Department of Economics. Manuscript, January.

———. 2002a. How school choice affects public school students' achievement. In *Choice with equity,* ed. Paul Hill, 141–78. Stanford: Hoover Institution Press.

———. 2002b. Would school choice change the teaching profession? *Journal of Human Resources* 37 (4): 846–91.

Jorgenson, Dale W. 1984. The contribution of education to U.S. economic growth, 1948–73. In *Education and economic productivity*, ed. Edwin Dean, 95–162. Cambridge, Mass.: Harper and Row, Ballinger.

Jorgenson, Dale W., and Barbara M. Fraumeni. 1989. The accumulation of human and nonhuman capital, 1948–84. In *The measurement of saving, investment, and wealth,* ed. Robert E. Lipsey and Helen Stone Tice, 227–82. Chicago: University of Chicago Press.

———. 1992. Investment in education and U.S. economic growth. *Scandinavian Journal of Economics* 94 (supplement): S51–S70.

Keesing, Donald B. 1966. Labor skills and comparative advantage in international economics: Progress and transfer of technical knowledge. *American Economic Review* 56 (March): 249–58.

Krueger, Anne O. 1968. Factor endowments and per capita income differences among countries. *Economic Journal* 78 (September): 641–59.

Leontief, Wassily. 1956. Factor proportions and the structure of American trade: Further theoretical and empirical analysis. *Review of Economics and Statistics* 38 (November): 386–407.

Michel, Allen, and Israel Shaked. 1987. Trucking deregulation and motor-carrier performance: The shareholders' perspective. *Financial Review* 22 (2): 295–311.

Michigan Department of Education. 2000a. *Directory of Michigan public school academies.* Lansing, Mich.: Michigan Department of Education.

———. 2000b. *K-12 database.* Lansing, Mich.: Michigan Department of Education. Electronic file.

———. 2000c. *Michigan educational assessment program and high school test results.* Lansing, Mich.: Michigan Department of Education. Electronic file.

———. 2000d. *School code master.* Lansing, Mich.: Michigan Department of Education. Electronic file.

Moulton, Brent R. 1986. Random group effects and the precision of regression estimates. *Journal of Econometrics* 32 (3): 385–97.

Rees, Nina Shokraii. 2000. *School choice 2000: What's happening in the states.* Washington, D.C.: Heritage Foundation.

Rose, Nancy L. 1987. Labor rent sharing and regulation: Evidence from the trucking industry. *Journal of Political Economy* 95 (6): 1146–78.

Traynor, Thomas L., and Patrick S. McCarthy. 1991. Trucking deregulation and highway safety: The effect of the 1980 Motor Carrier Act. *Journal of Regulatory Economics* 3 (4): 339–48.

U.S. Department of Commerce, Bureau of the Census. 1976. *Statistical abstract of the United States.* Washington, D.C.: Government Printing Office.

———. 1983. *Statistical abstract of the United States.* Washington, D.C.: Government Printing Office.

———. 1994. *County and city data book.* 1993 edition. Washington, D.C.: Bureau of the Census. Electronic file.

———. 1995. *Statistical abstract of the United States.* Washington, D.C.: Government Printing Office.

———. 1999. *Statistical abstract of the United States.* Washington, D.C.: Government Printing Office.

U.S. Department of Education, National Center for Education Statistics. 1980–2000. *Digest of education statistics.* 1979–99 annual editions. Washington, D.C.: U.S. Government Printing Office.

———. 1993. *Common core of data.* 1990 edition. Washington, D.C.: National Center for Education Statistics. Computer file.

———. 1994a. *National education longitudinal study, 1988: Third follow-up.* Washington, D.C.: National Center for Education Statistics. Restricted access computer file.

———. 1994b. *School district data book: 1990 census school district special tabulation.* Washington, D.C.: National Center for Education Statistics. Computer file.

———. 1995. *Common core of data: School years 1987–88 through 1992–93.* Washington, D.C.: National Center for Education Statistics. Computer file.

———. 1999. *National assessment of educational progress restricted use database.* 1990–99 editions. Washington, D.C.: National Center for Education Statistics. Electronic files.

———. 2000. *National assessment of educational progress 1999 long-term trend summary data tables.* Washington, D.C.: National Center for Education Statistics. Electronic files.

U.S. Geological Survey. 1994. *Geographic names information system.* Washington, D.C.: U.S. Geological Survey. Electronic file.

Wisconsin Department of Public Instruction. 2000a. *Knowledge and concepts examinations: Test results.* Madison, Wis.: Wisconsin Department of Public Instruction. Electronic file.

———. 2000b. *Milwaukee parental school choice program: Facts and figures.* Madison, Wis.: Wisconsin Department of Public Instruction.

———. 2000c. *Reading comprehension test results.* Madison, Wis.: Wisconsin Department of Public Instruction. Electronic file.

———. 2000d. *School finance data.* Madison, Wis.: Wisconsin Department of Public Instruction. Electronic file.

———. 2000e. *School performance report.* Madison, Wis.: Wisconsin Department of Public Instruction. Electronic file.

Witte, John F., Troy D. Sterr, and Christopher A. Thorn. 1995. Fifth-year report: Milwaukee parental choice program. Madison, Wis.: Department of Political Science and the Robert La Follette Institute of Public Affairs.

Contributors

David E. Campbell
Center for the Study of Democratic
    Politics
Woodrow Wilson School
Princeton University
Princeton, NJ 08544

Julie Berry Cullen
Department of Economics
University of Michigan
Ann Arbor, MI 48109-1220

Dennis Epple
Graduate School of Industrial
    Administration
Carnegie Mellon University
Posner Hall, Room 233C
Pittsburgh, PA 15213

Raquel Fernández
Department of Economics
New York University
269 Mercer Street
New York, NY 10003

David N. Figlio
Department of Economics
University of Florida
Gainesville, FL 32611-7140

Eric A. Hanushek
Hoover Institution
Stanford University
Stanford, CA 94305-6010

William G. Howell
Department of Political Science
416 North Hall
University of Wisconsin
1050 Bascom Mall
Madison, WI 53706

Caroline M. Hoxby
Department of Economics
Harvard University
Cambridge, MA 02138

Thomas J. Nechyba
Department of Economics
Duke University
Durham, NC 27708

Marianne E. Page
Department of Economics
One Shields Avenue
University of California, Davis
Davis, CA 95616-8578

Paul E. Peterson
John F. Kennedy School of
   Government
Harvard University
Taubman 306
79 JFK Street
Cambridge, MA 02138

Steven G. Rivkin
Department of Economics
Amherst College
PO Box 5000
Amherst, MA 01002-5000

Richard Rogerson
Department of Economics
College of Business
Arizona State University
Tempe, AZ 85287

Richard Romano
Economics Department
Warrington College of Business
University of Florida
PO Box 117140
Gainesville, FL 32611-7140

Patrick J. Wolf
Georgetown Public Policy Institute
3600 N Street NW
Suite 200
Washington, DC 20007

Author Index

Subject Index

Accountability systems, school, 50; and Florida voucher program, 51–53, 57–63; voucher programs and, 64–65

Achievement: effect of charter schools on, in Arizona public schools, 333–37; effect of charter schools on, in Michigan public schools, 323–33; effect of Milwaukee voucher program on, 315–23

Alum Rock choice program, 1–2, 2n3, 107

American College Test (ACT), 289n2, 305

Arizona public schools, effect of charter schools on achievement in, 333–37

Catholic schools, 24–25, 24n2. *See also* Private schools

Charter schools, 19; cream-skimming and, 94; effect of, on achievement in Arizona public schools, 333–37; effect of, on achievement in Michigan public schools, 323–33; for-profit schools, 296–97; nonprofit schools, 298–99; for special needs students, 93–98. *See also* Neighborhood schools; Private schools; Public schools

Chicago, open enrollment systems for special needs students in, 90–93

Class size, productivity and, 6

Cleveland Scholarship Program, 100

Climate, school, private schools vs. public schools and, 128–29

Coleman Report, 6, 6n4

Competition: health care industry and, 294; importance of threat of, 11–12; parcel services industry and, 294; of regular public schools, 301–2; school quality and, 30–37; school quality in absence of, 170–74; sources of, 24; teacher quality and, 37–45; trucking industry and, 294

Cream-skimming, 6; charter schools and, 94

Disabled students. *See* Special needs students

Economic growth, school productivity and, 293

Economists: advantages of, and study of school choice, 3–4; interest in school choice and, 1–2; tools of, and school choice, 3

Education for all Handicapped Children Act (EHA), 68

Educators: labor markets for, and school choice, 7–8; quality of, 26–28; quality of, and competition, 37–45; school choice and labor markets for, 7–8; turnover and, 39

Efficiency, school, 30–31

Empirical analysis, nonexperimental, for collecting evidence on school choice, 8–9

Epple-Platt-Sieg (EPS) approach, 180–83

349